Classic
Holiday Cooking

HC5008

TABLE OF CONTENTS

HC5008

FAVORITE RECIPES
FROM MY COOKBOOK

Recipe Name	Page Number

HOLIDAY MENUS

Early Morning Starters

Marinated Fruit

Easy Baked French Toast

Company Breakfast Casserole

Brown Sugar Streusel Coffee Cake

Orange-Marmalade Muffins

Swiss Mocha

Orange Juice Delight

MARINATED FRUIT

1 (20 oz.) can
  unsweetened
  pineapple chunks
2 green apples,
  peeled and
  sliced
1 banana, sliced
1 large orange,
  peeled and
  sectioned
Several strawberries
5 to 6 fresh mint
  leaves, diced
2 Tbsp. honey
4 oz. orange juice

Drain pineapple; reserve juice. Mix with orange juice, honey, and mint. Pour over fruit and chill. Serve in glass bowls and garnish with whole fresh mint leaves.

Variation: Fresh fruit in season (melon, peaches, kiwi, blueberries, etc.) may be added or substituted.

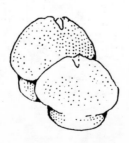

EASY BAKED FRENCH TOAST

⅓ c. butter or
  margarine (at
  room temperature)
6 large eggs
1½ c. milk
1½ Tbsp.
  confectioners
  sugar
1 tsp. vanilla extract
½ tsp. ground
  cinnamon
½ thick slices firm
  white bread
Confectioners sugar
  for dusting

Adjust oven racks so that one is in lowest position and the other is in the middle. Heat oven to 425°F. Using about 2 tablespoons of the butter, grease 2 jelly-roll pans.

Lightly beat eggs with a fork in a medium-size bowl. Stir in milk, confectioners sugar, vanilla, and cinnamon until blended. Dip bread, 1 slice at a time, in egg mixture, turning bread to coat well on both sides. Place 6 slices in each prepared jelly-roll pan. Cut remaining butter in tiny pieces and scatter over bread.

Place 1 pan on each oven rack. Bake 15 minutes, switching positions of pans once, until bread is golden brown. Remove to serving platter. Dust with confectioners sugar.

COMPANY BREAKFAST CASSEROLE

1 lb. sausage, bacon
  or ham
8 oz. Cheddar or
  Swiss cheese
2 c. milk
6 eggs, beaten
12 slices bread,
  crusts trimmed
Butter

Butter bread on both sides. Grease a 9x13 inch cake pan. Line bottom and sides with slices of bread; use ½ slices for the sides. Sprinkle grated cheese over bread. Pour eggs and milk over slices of bread. Top with crumbled meat. *Refrigerate overnight.* Bake at 350° for 45 to 60 minutes. Serves 6 to 8.

BROWN SUGAR STREUSEL COFFEE CAKE

Cake:
½ c. butter
1¼ c. sugar
3 eggs
2 c. flour
½ tsp. baking powder
1 tsp. soda
½ tsp. salt
1 tsp. vanilla
½ pt. sour cream

Streusel:
1 c. brown sugar
1 tsp. cinnamon
4 Tbsp. butter,
  melted
4 heaping Tbsp. flour
1 c. nuts, chopped

Cake: Cream butter and sugar. Add eggs and beat well. Sift together flour, baking powder, soda, and salt. Add dry ingredients alternately with sour cream. Stir in vanilla.

Streusel: Combine ingredients and pour half of mixture into a well greased Bundt pan. Add cake batter and top with the remainder of the Streusel. Bake at 300° for 50 minutes.

ORANGE-MARMALADE MUFFINS

2 c. all-purpose flour
1 c. sugar
¾ tsp. baking powder
2 beaten eggs
1 c. dairy sour cream
¼ c. orange
  marmalade
1 Tbsp. butter,
  melted
1½ tsp. vanilla

Grease muffin cups or line with paper bake cups. Stir together flour, sugar, and baking powder. Make a well in the center. Combine eggs, sour cream, marmalade, butter, and vanilla. Add sour cream mixture all at once to flour mixture. Stir till moistened. Fill the muffin cups ⅔ full. Bake them in a 400° oven 20 to 25 minutes. Makes 12 muffins.

SWISS MOCHA

2 c. Swiss Miss cocoa
2 c. Cremora
¾ c. instant coffee
½ c. sugar

Combine ingredients. Store in airtight container. To use, add 2 heaping teaspoons in cup of boiling water.

ORANGE JUICE DELIGHT

1 (6 oz.) can frozen
  orange juice
1 c. water
1 c. milk
1 tsp. vanilla
¼ c. sugar
9 to 10 ice cubes

Put everything in blender and mix well.

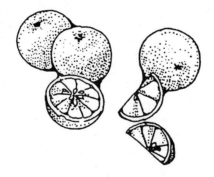

Holiday Breakfast or Brunch

Gala Fresh Fruit Bowl

Christmas Quiche

French Breakfast Puffs

Raspberry Cream Cheese Coffee Cake

Holiday Spiced Tea

Coffee

GALA FRESH FRUIT BOWL

6 medium oranges
¼ c. sifted powdered
  sugar
1 pt. fresh or frozen
  strawberries,
  halved
2 kiwi fruit, peeled
  and sliced ¼ inch thick
⅓ c. coconut

Peel and section the 6 oranges over a large glass serving bowl to catch the juices. Add the sifted powdered sugar to orange sections and juice in the serving bowl; toss to coat. Gently stir in the halved strawberries and sliced kiwi fruit. Cover and chill the mixture till serving time.

Before serving the fruit, sprinkle the coconut over top of the mixture.

CHRISTMAS QUICHE

Pastry crust for 9 inch
  quiche pan
1½ c. half & half
4 eggs
1 c. (4 oz.) Swiss
  cheese, shredded
1 Tbsp. flour
¼ c. sliced green
  onion
1 tsp. dried parsley
Pinch of nutmeg
Salt and pepper to
  taste
5 slices cooked bacon
5 links cooked pork
  sausages

Toss shredded cheese with flour. Add onion, parsley, nutmeg, salt, and pepper; sprinkle on base of pastry shell. Whisk eggs with half & half; pour over cheese mixture. Bake 35 minutes at 375°. Place bacon and sausage on top. Bake an additional 10 minutes.

FRENCH BREAKFAST PUFFS

⅓ c. Crisco or butter
½ c. sugar
1 egg
1½ c. flour, sifted
1½ tsp. baking
  powder
½ tsp. salt
¼ tsp. nutmeg
½ c. milk
⅓ c. butter, melted
½ c. sugar
1 tsp. cinnamon

Heat oven to 350°. Grease muffin pans. (Makes 2 dozen small or 2 dozen medium size puffs.) Mix the shortening and sugar until light and fluffy; add egg. Sift together flour, baking powder, salt, and nutmeg. Add to creamed mixture alternately with milk. Fill muffin cups ⅔ full. Bake for 20 minutes, or until golden brown. Remove from oven. Roll immediately in melted butter, then in mixture of cinnamon and sugar. Serve hot.

RASPBERRY CREAM CHEESE COFFEE CAKE

1 (3 oz.) pkg. cream
  cheese
¼ c. butter
2 c. biscuit mix
¼ c. milk
½ c. raspberry
  preserves

Glaze:
1 c. powdered sugar
1 to 2 Tbsp. milk
½ tsp. vanilla

Cut cream cheese and butter into biscuit mix. Stir in ¼ cup milk. On floured board, knead 8 to 10 strokes. On waxed paper, roll dough into a 12x8 inch rectangle. Invert onto a greased baking sheet. Remove paper. Spread preserves down center of dough. Make 2½ inch long cuts at 1 inch intervals on long sides. Fold strips over filling. Bake at 375° for 15 to 20 minutes or till brown. Cool 5 minutes. Pour glaze over. Serve warm.

HOLIDAY SPICED TEA

2 (26 oz.) jars instant
  orange
  breakfast drink
1 (3 oz.) jar instant tea
2 (8½ oz.) pkg. red
  hot candies
1 (6 oz.) pkg.
  sweetened
  lemon drink
1 c. sugar
2 tsp. ground
  cinnamon
2 tsp. ground nutmeg
2 tsp. ground cloves
2 tsp. ground allspice

Mix all ingredients in a large bowl. Store in airtight container.

Can be fixed in 1 pint jars with pretty ribbon for gifts. To serve, place 1 tablespoon dry mix in large cup. Add boiling water.

Rise and Shine

Hot Fruit Compote
Rise and Shine Cheesy Egg Bake
Sausage and Hash Brown Breakfast
Big Banana Muffins
Hot Apple Cranberry Wassail
Coffee

HOT FRUIT COMPOTE

8 soft coconut
    macaroons
1 (16½ oz.) can
    pitted dark
    sweet cherries,
    drained
1 (16 oz.) can sliced
    peaches,
    drained
1 (15¼ oz.) can
    pineapple
    chunks, drained
1 (17 oz.) can apricot
    halves, drained
1 (16 oz.) can pear
    halves, drained
1 (21 oz.) can cherry
    pie filling
½ c. pineapple juice

Crumble macaroons in a shallow pan. Bake at 400° for 3 to 4 minutes or until lightly toasted, stirring constantly; cool. Sprinkle ½ of macaroons in a 2½ quart casserole. Layer remaining ingredients in order given. Sprinkle on remaining macaroons. Cover and refrigerate for 8 hours or overnight.

Remove from refrigerator; let stand for 30 minutes. Bake, uncovered, at 350° for 35 to 40 minutes or until bubbly. Serves 8 to 10.

RISE AND SHINE CHEESY EGG BAKE

2 cans cream of
  chicken soup
1 c. milk
4 tsp. instant minced
  onions
1 tsp. mustard
2 c. shredded Swiss
  cheese
12 eggs
12 (½ inch) slices
  buttered
  French bread

Combine soup, milk, onion, and mustard. Cook, stirring until smooth. Stir in cheese. Pour 1 cup of sauce in 8x12 inch baking dish sprayed with Pam. Break eggs in dish. Spoon in rest of sauce around eggs. Stand bread around edge of dish. Bake for 20 minutes at 350°.

SAUSAGE AND HASH BROWN BREAKFAST

¼ lb. smoked
  sausage, cut
  into ½ inch slices
⅓ c. oil
4 c. frozen Southern
  style hash
  browns
¼ c. green pepper
3 slices Velveeta
  cheese

Cook sausage in large skillet. Remove from skillet. Add oil; heat over medium heat. Add potatoes and peppers. Cover and cook for 8 to 10 minutes. Stir in sausage. Remove from heat. Top with cheese.

BIG BANANA MUFFINS

2 c. all-purpose flour
1½ c. whole-wheat
  flour
1¼ c. packed dark
  brown sugar
4 tsp. baking powder
1 tsp. salt
¾ c. milk
½ c. salad oil
3 large eggs
1½ c. walnuts,
  chopped
4 ripe small bananas,
  mashed

Preheat oven to 400°F. Grease twelve 3 x 1½ inch muffin-pan cups. In large bowl, mix first 5 ingredients. In small bowl, beat milk, salad oil, and eggs until blended; stir into flour mixture just until flour is moistened (batter will be lumpy). Reserve ¼ cup walnuts for garnish. Fold bananas and remaining walnuts into batter.

Spoon batter into muffin-pan cups; top with reserved walnuts. Bake muffins 25 to 30 minutes until golden and toothpick inserted in center comes out clean (muffins will rise very high). Immediately remove muffins from pan; serve warm, or cool on wire rack. Reheat if desired. Makes 12 muffins.

HOT APPLE CRANBERRY WASSAIL

1 gal. apple cider
1 qt. cranberry juice
3 cinnamon sticks
3 Tbsp. whole cloves
1 c. sugar
Dash of ginger

Mix in large container; bring to a boil and serve.

Autumn Morning Get-together

Fresh Fruit

Fresh Fruit Dip

Apple Pancakes

Sugar-Plum Bacon

Sour Cream Scrambled Eggs

Quick Eggnog

Percolator Punch

Coffee

FRESH FRUIT DIP

1 small pkg. vanilla
  instant pudding
1½ c. cold milk
1 (16 oz.) sour cream
2 Tbsp. orange juice
  concentrate

Beat pudding and cold milk together well. Add sour cream and orange juice concentrate. Beat until well blended. Refrigerate and serve with fresh fruit.

APPLE PANCAKES

1 c. milk
2 eggs
1 Tbsp. sugar
1 Tbsp. salad oil
1 c. unbleached flour
2 tsp. baking powder
¼ tsp. cinnamon
1 apple, cut in eighths

Put all ingredients, except apple, into blender. Cover and process at low until blended. Stop and add apples, cover, and process at high only until apples are finely grated. Pour into a hot well-greased griddle. Yield: 10 to 12 pancakes.

SUGAR-PLUM BACON

½ lb. sliced bacon
½ c. packed brown
    sugar
1 tsp. ground
    cinnamon

Let bacon come to room temperature. Cut each slice in half crosswise. Combine sugar and cinnamon. Coat each bacon slice with the brown-sugar mixture. Twist and place in a shallow baking pan. Bake in a 350° oven for 15 to 20 minutes or till bacon is crisp and sugar is bubbly. (Watch bacon closely; sugar burns easily.)

Place the cooked bacon slices on foil to cool. Serve at room temperature. Makes 8 servings.

SOUR CREAM SCRAMBLED EGGS

4 slices bacon, cut
    into small
    pieces
4 eggs
2 Tbsp. commercial
    sour cream
2 Tbsp. process
    American
    cheese spread
¼ tsp. seasoned salt
Dash of pepper

Fry bacon in a large skillet; drain off all but 3 tablespoons drippings. Combine remaining ingredients in container of electric blender; process on low speed until light and fluffy. Pour into skillet with bacon and hot drippings. Cook over low heat, stirring gently, until done. Serve immediately. Yield: About 2 servings.

QUICK EGGNOG

2 qt. (8 c.)
    commercial
    eggnog
3 Tbsp. plus 1 tsp.
    rum flavoring
    (optional)
6 egg whites (room
    temperature)
Nutmeg for top
    (freshly grated
    if possible)

Pour eggnog into a large bowl; add rum flavoring. Whip egg whites until stiff, but not dry. Fold into eggnog mixture. Refrigerate until ready to serve. Lightly sprinkle nutmeg on top of each serving.

PERCOLATOR PUNCH

2¼ c. pineapple juice
1¾ c. water
2 c. cranberry juice
1 tsp. whole cloves
½ tsp. whole allspice
3 sticks cinnamon,
  broken
¼ tsp. salt
½ c. brown sugar

Mix juices and water; place in percolator. Put remaining ingredients into the percolator basket. Perk as you would coffee and serve.

Traditional Thanksgiving

Relish Tray
Vegetable Dip
Creamy Fruit Salad
Cranberry Mold Salad
Roast Turkey and Stuffing
Giblet Gravy
Sweet Potato Casserole with Marshmallows
Green Bean Casserole
Carrot Pineapple Cake
Pumpkin Pie

VEGETABLE DIP

⅔ c. commercial sour
  cream
⅔ c. mayonnaise
1 Tbsp. dried dill
  weed
1 Tbsp. finely
  chopped
  parsley
1 Tbsp. instant
  minced onion
¼ tsp. dry mustard

Combine all ingredients; mix well and chill.
Serve as a dip for assorted fresh vegetables.

CREAM FRUIT SALAD

1 large can fruit
  cocktail
1 (6 oz.) bar cream
  cheese
2 bananas, sliced
1 apple, sliced in
  small pieces
1 c. small
  marshmallows
1 c. pecans

Combine cream cheese with the syrup from
fruit cocktail until mixture is creamy. Add
fruit cocktail, bananas, apple, marshmallows, and pecans. Other fruits may be
added. Chill before serving. Serves 8 to 10.

CRANBERRY MOLD SALAD

1 (16 oz.) can whole
   cranberry
   sauce
1 large pkg.
   strawberry Jell-O
1½ c. hot water
1 (4½ oz.) jar
   applesauce
1 pt. sour cream
1 c. miniature
   marshmallows

Mix together the cranberry sauce, Jell-O, water, and applesauce. Pour into mold and chill. Mix together the sour cream and marshmallows that have been melted. Pour into the middle or onto the mold.

ROAST TURKEY

To thaw: Place turkey in original bag on tray in refrigerator. Allow 2 days for 8 to 11 pound bird, 2 to 3 days for 11 to 14 pound bird, 3 to 4 days for 14 to 24 pound bird. Refreezing is not recommended.

To prepare: Free legs and tail from tucked position; remove neck from body cavity and giblets from neck cavity. Rinse and drain turkey. If desired, stuff neck and body cavities lightly, allowing ¾ cup stuffing per pound weight of uncooked turkey. Return tail and legs to tucked position. Skewer neck skin to back. Insert meat thermometer into center of thigh, next to body but not touching bone. Place turkey, breast side up, on rack in shallow open pan. Do not add water or cover. Use the following baking times (approximate roasting times). For an 8 to 12 pound turkey, bake for 3½ to 4 hours. For a 12 to 16 pound turkey, bake 4 to 4½ hours. For a 16 to 20 pound turkey, bake 4½ to 5 hours. For a 20 to 24 pound turkey, bake 5 to 6 hours. Bake in a 325° oven.

APPROXIMATE ROASTING TIME

Weight

8 to 12 lb	3½ to 4 hours
12 to 16 lb	4 to 4½ hours
16 to 20 lb	4½ to 5 hours
20 to 24 lb	5 to 6 hours

Brush skin with melted butter to prevent drying. Baste frequently during roasting unless using a prebasted turkey. When light golden brown, shield breast and neck with lightweight aluminum foil to prevent overbrowning. During last hour of cooking, check for doneness.

To test for doneness: Before removing from oven, check to be sure meat thermometer is in original position. Thigh temperature should be 180° to 185°. Protect fingers with paper. Press thigh and drumstick. Meat should feel soft. Prick skin at thigh. Juices should no longer be pink.

STUFFING

8 c. soft bread
  crumbs
½ c. butter
1 large onion, grated
1½ tsp. salt
¼ tsp. pepper
Sage or poultry
  seasoning to
  taste

Tear or grate bread. (If using crusts, cut into fine shreds.) Mix together crumbs, soft butter, onion, salt, and pepper. Add desired seasonings. Toss together lightly. Makes 9 cups.

Note: A 1 pound loaf of bread makes about 10 cups of bread crumbs.

GIBLET GRAVY

Giblets and neck from
  turkey
⅓ c. all-purpose flour
1 tsp. salt

In 3 quart saucepan, place giblets and neck with enough water to cover. Heat on high until water boils. Reduce heat to low; cover and simmer 1 hour or until giblets are tender. Drain, reserving broth. Pull meat from neck and discard bones; chop meat and giblets. Refrigerate.

To make gravy, pour drippings from roasting turkey into 4 cup measure. Let drippings stand a few seconds until fat separates. Skim ⅓ cup fat from drippings and put into 2 quart saucepan; skim and discard remaining fat. Add reserved giblet broth to roasting pan; stir until brown bits are loosened. Pour into 4 cup measure and add enough water to make 4 cups of liquid.

Into fat over medium heat, stir in flour and salt. Gradually stir in meat juice mixture; cook and stir until mixture thickens slightly and is smooth. Stir in reserved giblets and neck meat; heat through. Pour gravy into gravy boat. Serve.

SWEET POTATO CASSEROLE WITH MARSHMALLOWS

8 medium size sweet
  potatoes
1 c. milk
1 tsp. vanilla
3 Tbsp. sugar
½ stick butter or
  margarine
¼ tsp. cinnamon
A few dashes of
  nutmeg
2 Tbsp. orange juice
Mini marshmallows

Bake sweet potatoes in a 350° oven or boil in a saucepan, covered with water, until tender. Peel hot potatoes and put through a ricer until mashed, or mash with a potato masher. To potatoes, add cinnamon, nutmeg, and orange juice; stir. Scald milk; add vanilla, sugar, and butter. Add milk mixture to potatoes and stir well.

Spread half the potatoes in a casserole dish; cover with a layer of marshmallows and finish with the rest of the potatoes. Bake at 350° until very hot (about 20 to 25 minutes). Add a top layer of marshmallows; return to oven until lightly browned. Serves 8 to 10.

GREEN BEAN CASSEROLE

2 Tbsp. butter,
  melted
2 Tbsp. flour
1 tsp. salt
1 tsp. sugar
¼ tsp. pepper
1 small onion, grated
1 c. sour cream
2 pkg. frozen French
  style green
  beans
½ lb. Swiss cheese,
  shredded
1 c. corn flakes,
  crushed

Cook and drain green beans. Mix first 7 ingredients in a bowl. Layer half the beans, sour cream mixture, and cheese in a 1½ quart casserole. Repeat layers. Top with corn flake crumbs. Bake at 400° for 20 minutes. Serves 6.

CARROT PINEAPPLE CAKE

3 eggs
2 c. sugar
1 c. oil
1 (8 oz.) can crushed
pineapple and
juice
2 c. grated carrots
1 tsp. vanilla
2 c. flour
2 tsp. baking powder
1 tsp. soda
¾ tsp. salt
2 tsp. cinnamon
1 tsp. allspice
1 c. chopped nuts

Cream Cheese
Frosting:
8 oz. cream cheese
1 stick butter
1 lb. powdered sugar
1 tsp. vanilla

Beat together eggs, sugar, oil, pineapple juice, carrots, and vanilla. Sift together flour, baking powder, soda, salt, cinnamon, and allspice. Combine flour mixture with pineapple mixture and add nuts. Bake at 325° for 45 to 50 minutes in a greased and floured pan.

Cream Cheese Frosting: Blend. Spread on cooled cake.

PUMPKIN PIE

Pie crust
1 tsp. flour
2 eggs, slightly
beaten
1 (16 oz.) can solid
pack pumpkin
¾ c. sugar
½ tsp. salt
1 tsp. ground
cinnamon
½ tsp. ground ginger
¼ tsp. ground cloves
1 (12 oz.) can
evaporated
milk

Heat oven to 425°F. Prepare pie crust. Flute edge to stand ½ inch above rim. Mix filling ingredients in order given. Pour into pie crust-lined pan. Bake at 425°F. for 15 minutes. Reduce heat to 350°F.; continue baking 35 to 45 minutes or until knife inserted near center of pie comes out clean. (If necessary, cover edge of crust with a strip of aluminum foil to prevent excessive browning.) Cool completely. Garnish, if desired, with whipped topping.

Holiday Open House

Pineapple-Cheese Ball
Cocktail Meat Balls
Ham Roll-Ups
Cheese Straws
Fresh Vegetable Pizza
Toasted Butter Pecans
Candied Popcorn
Mincemeat Ball Cookies
Black Walnut Fudge
Wassail

PINEAPPLE-CHEESE BALL

2 (8 oz.) pkg. cream
  cheese,
  softened
2 Tbsp. chopped bell
  pepper
2 Tbsp. finely
  chopped onion
¼ c. drained crushed
  pineapple
2 tsp. seasoned salt
1½ c. chopped
  pecans

Beat cream cheese with a fork until smooth. Add other ingredients, saving ¾ cup pecans for later use. Form into a ball and refrigerate until firm. Roll in ¾ cup pecans until well covered. Serve at room temperature with crackers.

COCKTAIL MEAT BALLS

2 lb. ground round
1 pkg. Lipton onion
   soup
1 egg
1 tsp. Worcestershire
   sauce
½ c. bread crumbs

Sauce:
1 (7 oz.) jar grape jelly
1 bottle chili sauce
2 tsp. lemon juice
½ c. water

Mix together and form into balls (makes 60). Put in refrigerator for at least ½ hour.

Sauce: Mix and simmer for ½ hour; add meat balls and cook for ½ hour slowly.

Meat is not cooked when added to sauce. If made a day ahead of time and warmed up, the flavor is much better.

HAM ROLL-UPS

6 slices boiled ham
1 (8 oz.) pkg. cream
   cheese (room
   temperature)
6 small green onions,
   cut the length of
   ham
Crackers

On each slice of ham, spread cream cheese. Place green onions, 1 on each slice. Roll up and add extra cream cheese on each end. Chill for 1 hour. Slice and place on tray with crackers.

Norma Brooks

CHEESE STRAWS

14 oz. pkg. frozen
   puff pastry,
   thawed
1 egg, beaten
¼ c. grated Romano
   cheese

Preheat oven to 450°F. Roll pastry to a thickness of ¼ inch on a lightly floured surface. Brush with beaten egg and sprinkle with cheese. Cut the pastry crosswise into strips ½ inch wide. Cut to desired lengths.

Twist strips several times and place on an ungreased baking sheet, pressing down the ends to prevent the pastry from unrolling. Bake in oven 8 to 10 minutes or until golden.

FRESH VEGETABLE PIZZA

2 pkg. crescent rolls
8 oz. cream cheese
1 c. cottage cheese
¾ c. mayonnaise
1 pkg. dry Ranch
   dressing
½ green pepper
1 c. broccoli
1 c. cauliflower
¼ c. black olives
1 large seeded
   tomato
½ c. green onion
½ c. carrots

Press crescent rolls into bottom of jelly roll pan that has been sprayed with oil. Bake at 400° for 10 minutes; cool. Mix cream cheese, cottage cheese, mayonnaise, and Ranch dressing. Spread over rolls. Finely chop all other ingredients. Mix and put on top of other ingredients. Cut into small bars.

TOASTED BUTTER PECANS

1 lb. pecan halves (4
   c.)
1 Tbsp. seasoned salt
½ stick margarine

In a 1½ quart casserole, place pecan halves. Sprinkle with seasoned salt. Cut margarine into small pats and place evenly over the top. Microwave on HIGH 5 to 6 minutes. Mix well. Serve warm or cold.

CANDIED POPCORN

4 qt. popped corn
1 c. brown sugar,
   packed
½ c. oleo
½ c. Karo syrup
Dash of salt
½ tsp. vanilla
½ tsp. soda
Peanuts (if desired)

Spread popped corn in shallow roasting pan, with peanuts if desired. Combine brown sugar, oleo, syrup, and salt in saucepan; stir constantly over medium heat until it boils. Let cook 5 minutes over slightly lower heat. Remove from heat and stir in vanilla and soda. Pour over popcorn; mix well. Bake 1 hour at 250°, stirring once or twice while cooking. Let cool and break into small pieces.

MINCEMEAT BALL COOKIES

1 c. butter
¼ c. sugar
2 egg yolks
2⅔ c. flour
Mincemeat

Cream butter and sugar. Add egg yolks and beat until fluffy. Add flour and mix well. Shape into small balls and place on greased cookie sheets. Press thumb in center of each cookie and fill center with mincemeat. Bake at 350°F. about 10 to 12 minutes.

BLACK WALNUT FUDGE

3 c. sugar
¼ tsp. cream of tartar
¼ tsp. salt
1 c. milk
2 Tbsp. oleo
1 tsp. black walnut
   extract
½ c. chopped nuts

Cook sugar, cream of tartar, salt, and milk to soft ball stage, stirring frequently. Wipe down sides of pan to remove crystals. Remove from heat; add butter. Cool, without stirring, until lukewarm. Add extract and nuts; beat until creamy. Pour into greased square pan; cut in squares. Makes 1½ pounds.

WASSAIL

1 c. fresh lemon juice
2 c. fresh orange juice
   or frozen
   orange juice
   properly
   diluted
2 c. unsweetened
   pineapple juice
2 qt. (8 c.) apple cider
1 tsp. whole cloves
1 stick cinnamon
¼ c. sugar

Tie cloves and cinnamon in a piece of cheesecloth or a clean, thin handkerchief. If not a available, put in pot as is and strain when finished cooking.

In a large pan, pour lemon juice, orange juice, pineapple juice, and apple cider. Add cloves and cinnamon. Bring to a simmering boil over medium heat. Cover pan, reduce heat, and simmer on low for 1 hour. Add sugar, stirring until dissolved. Remove from heat. Serve warm in heated bowl surrounded by holly or Christmas greenery. Serves 16.

Christmas Eve Gathering

Hearty Steak Soup
Onion Corn Bread
Assorted Cheese and Crackers
Red and White Layered Christmas Salad
Assorted Christmas Cookies
Gingerbread
Spiced Apple Cider

HEARTY STEAK SOUP

2 to 2½ lb. round
  steak, trimmed and
  cubed
Oleo
1 stick butter or oleo
1 c. flour
8 c. water
1 c. carrots, diced
1 c. celery, diced
1 onion, diced
4 beef bouillon cubes
1 Tbsp. Accent
3 Tbsp. Kitchen
  Bouquet
2 c. frozen mixed
  vegetables
1 (No. 303) can
  tomatoes,
  drained
Salt and pepper

Brown round steak in a little oleo. Melt butter or oleo in large pan. Add flour and mix well. Gradually add water and mix well. Add the following: Round steak, carrots, celery, onion, beef bouillon cubes, Accent, Kitchen Bouquet, frozen mixed vegetables, tomatoes, salt, and pepper. Cook over low heat for a long time, 6 to 8 hours. The longer the better.

ONION CORN BREAD

¼ c. margarine
1½ c. chopped onion
¼ tsp. salt
1 c. shredded sharp
  cheese
1 pkg. Jiffy corn
  muffin mix
1 egg
½ c. milk
8 oz. sour cream
1 c. cream style corn

In medium skillet, on medium heat, saute onion in margarine until tender (about 10 minutes). Cool slightly and add sour cream, salt, and half the cheese. Set aside. Combine mix, egg, milk, and corn. Stir until smooth. Spread batter in 8 or 9 inch pan. Spoon onion mix evenly and gently on top of batter. Sprinkle remaining cheese on top. Bake for 30 to 35 minutes in a 400° oven. Let set for 5 to 10 minutes before slicing in squares.

RED AND WHITE LAYERED CHRISTMAS SALAD

Red layer:
1 (3 oz.) pkg. cherry
  gelatin
8 oz. can jellied
  cranberry
  sauce
1 c. hot water

White layer:
1 (3 oz.) pkg. lemon
  gelatin
1 c. hot water
1 (3 oz.) pkg. cream
  cheese
⅓ c. mayonnaise
1 small can crushed
  pineapple,
  drained
1 pkg. whipped
  topping
2 c. small
  marshmallows
¼ c. chopped nuts

For red layer, dissolve cherry gelatin in cup of very hot water. Stir until dissolved. Add cranberry sauce and stir till smooth. Pour into 7x11 inch pan. Chill until firm.

For white layer, dissolve lemon gelatin in very hot water in a large bowl. In small bowl, combine the softened cream cheese with mayonnaise and stir till very smooth. Add this to gelatin mixture. Stir in drained pineapple. Fold in whipped topping and marshmallows. Spoon this over the red layer. Sprinkle with nuts. Chill until firm. Serves 12.

CHRISTMAS HOLIDAY COOKIES

1 c. butter or oleo,
   softened
1¾ c. sugar
2 oz. melted
   chocolate
1 tsp. vanilla
¼ tsp. salt
2 eggs
2½ c. all-purpose
   flour
6 oz. semi-sweet
   chocolate morsels
6 oz. peanut butter
   morsels

Preheat oven to 375°. Beat butter and sugar well. Add melted chocolate, vanilla, and salt. Mix well. Beat in eggs. Gradually add flour, mixing until well combined. Chill dough for 30 minutes. Press dough through a cookie gun onto ungreased cookie sheet. Place a chocolate or peanut butter morsel in the center of each cookie. Bake for 8 to 10 minutes. Cool cookies for 1 minute. Remove from cookie sheets to cool completely on wire racks.

WALNUT OAT CRISPS

1¼ c. walnuts
1 c. brown sugar,
   packed
1½ tsp. grated
   orange peel
⅔ c. whole wheat
   flour
½ tsp. soda
1⅓ c. uncooked
   quick cooking
   oats
½ c. butter
1 egg
½ tsp. salt
¼ tsp. cinnamon

Chop walnuts; set aside. Cream butter, sugar, eggs, and orange peel. Stir whole wheat flour, salt, soda, and cinnamon together; blend into creamed mixture. Stir in oats and ⅓ cup walnuts. Shape into 1 inch balls and place on lightly greased baking sheets. Flatten with bottom of glass dipped in sugar; sprinkle with remaining ½ cup walnuts. Bake at 350° for about 10 minutes. Cool slightly, then remove to wire rack to cool completely before storing. Makes about 5 dozen 2 inch round crisps.

HOLIDAY FRUIT COOKIES

1 c. shortening
2 c. brown sugar
2 eggs
½ c. sour milk or
  cream
2 c. maraschino
  cherries, cut up
3½ c. flour
1 tsp. baking soda
½ tsp. salt
1½ c. pecans
2 c. chopped dates

Cream shortening and sugar. Beat in eggs. Stir in sour milk. Sift flour, soda, and salt. Add to creamed mixture. Add cherries, dates, and pecans. Chill for 1 hour. Drop by teaspoons on greased baking sheet. Bake at 350° for 15 minutes.

May garnish with half the cherries and nuts.

GINGERBREAD

3 eggs
1 c. sugar
1 c. molasses
1 tsp. cloves
1 tsp. cinnamon
1 Tbsp. ginger
1 c. chopped pecans
1 c. oil
2 c. flour
1 tsp. soda
⅛ c. hot water
1 c. hot water

Place all ingredients, except flour, soda, and water, in large bowl and beat well. Dissolve soda in ⅛ cup hot water. Add to beaten mixture. Sift in flour; beat well. Add 1 cup boiling water, then beat lightly and quickly. Pour into rectangular pan and bake 45 minutes in moderate oven.

The batter will seem incredibly thin. Do not make the mistake of adding more flour. This bakes into the most delicate and delicious Gingerbread ever. Serve hot in squares. May be topped with whipped cream or other toppings like lemon custard sauce.

SPICED APPLE CIDER

1 pt. cranberry juice
2 qt. apple juice
¾ c. sugar
2 sticks cinnamon
1 tsp. allspice
1 small orange
Whole cloves

Mix together in crock pot; cover. Turn on HIGH for 1 hour, then on LOW for 4 to 8 hours. Makes 12 cups.

Christmas Day Buffet

Cheese-Nut Ball

Relish Tray

Clove-Studded Black Forest Ham

Holiday Confetti Salad

Waldorf Deluxe Salad

Cranapple Salad

Green Beans with Mushrooms and Almonds

Maple-Baked Acorn Squash

Christmas Fruitcake

Classic Walnut Pie

CHEESE-NUT BALL

¼ lb. Blue cheese
3 oz. cream cheese
¼ lb. Cheddar
  cheese,
  softened
1 small onion, grated
1 tsp. Worcestershire
  sauce
¼ lb. coarsely
  chopped
  pecans

Mix all ingredients, except nuts, with electric mixer until well blended. Add half the pecans. Form into large ball; wrap in waxed paper. Refrigerate overnight. Remove cheese ball from refrigerator 1 hour before serving. Roll in remaining nuts. If necessary, add more nuts to completely cover ball. Serve with crackers surrounding the ball. Yield: 1½ cups.

CLOVE-STUDDED BLACK FOREST HAM

5 lb. smoked Black
   Forest ham
20 cloves
½ c. apricot
   preserves
½ c. white grape jelly
   or apple jelly
1 Tbsp. Dijon
   mustard
1½ c. brown sugar
¼ tsp. ground
   cinnamon
¼ tsp. allspice

Preheat oven to 325°F. Cut ⅛ inch deep crisscross lines in the ham. Stud each diamond with 1 clove.

In a saucepan, heat the preserves, jelly, mustard, sugar, cinnamon, and allspice. Boil down into a glaze. Bake the ham in oven for 2¼ hours. Brush with glaze every 5 minutes during the final ½ hour; serve.

HOLIDAY CONFETTI SALAD

6 oz. pkg. lime gelatin
2 c. boiling water
1 c. crushed
   pineapple
6 oz. cream cheese,
   softened
1 c. diced celery
½ c. chopped nuts
½ c. maraschino
   cherries, diced
1 c. whipping cream

Dissolve gelatin in boiling water. Chill until it begins to thicken. Whip pineapple and cheese together until smooth and add, with diced celery, nuts, and cherries, to gelatin mixture. Whip cream and fold into gelatin mixture. Serves 8 to 12.

WALDORF DELUXE SALAD

3 large apples
¾ c. cubed Muenster
 (or Cheddar)
 cheese
½ c. chopped dates
¼ c. toasted nuts (or
 more)
1 stalk chopped
 celery

Dressing:
Juice from ½ lemon
½ c. mayonnaise
¾ c. orange juice
½ tsp. fresh orange
 rind (optional)
Honey to taste
 (optional)

Cut apples into chunks.

Dressing: Mix the ingredients with a whisk in a small bowl.

In a serving bowl, mix together other ingredients. Add dressing and chill.

CRANAPPLE SALAD

2 c. fresh cranberries
¾ c. sugar
3 c. miniature
 marshmallows
2 c. diced apples
 (Delicious)
½ c. broken walnuts
1 c. cream, whipped
½ c. seedless green
 grapes
 (optional)
¼ tsp. salt

Grind cranberries in blender. Mix with sugar and marshmallows; store overnight in refrigerator. Add apples, walnuts, cream, grapes, and salt.

GREEN BEANS WITH MUSHROOMS AND ALMONDS

**2 (10 oz.) pkg. French
style green
beans
2 (4 oz.) cans sliced
mushrooms,
drained
⅛ tsp. pepper
½ c. toasted, slivered
almonds
½ c. boiling water
¼ tsp. salt
2 Tbsp. chopped
parsley
¾ tsp. salt
¼ c. butter or
margarine**

Add beans to boiling, salted water; cook for 15 minutes or until just tender. Add remaining ingredients to beans. Stir gently until thoroughly combined. Keep warm over very low heat. Serves 8.

MAPLE-BAKED ACORN SQUASH

**6 large acorn or other
winter squash
Salt to taste
⅓ c. butter
½ c. maple syrup**

Preheat oven to 325°. Cut squash in halves lengthwise and seed. Sprinkle cut sides with salt and arrange, cut sides down, in a baking dish. Bake until shells can easily be pierced with a sharp knife, 45 to 60 minutes. Run fork over cut sides of squash, then spread with butter and drizzle with maple syrup. Bake 3 minutes longer. Makes 12 servings.

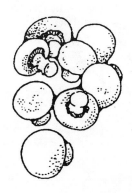

CHRISTMAS FRUITCAKE

1 c. butter
1 c. sugar
5 eggs
2 tsp. vanilla extract
1 tsp. almond extract
2 c. all-purpose flour
2 tsp. baking powder
¼ c. concentrated
   orange juice
1 Tbsp. lemon juice
1 c. flour (all-
   purpose)
7 c. pecans
1 lb. candied cherries
1 lb. candied
   pineapple,
   chopped
¼ lb. candied lemon
   peel
¼ lb. candied orange
   peel
1 (15 oz.) pkg. golden
   raisins

Cream butter and eggs till light and fluffy. Add eggs, one at a time, beating well. Add extract and mix. Add flour and baking powder alternately with the juice.

Mix fruit and nuts with the remaining 1 cup flour. Stir this mixture into batter. Use a greased and waxed paper lined 10 inch tube pan. Bake at 250° for 3 hours or till done. Cool for about 15 minutes before removing. Chill and let set for about 1 week before eating for best flavor. Freezes well.

CLASSIC WALNUT PIE

3 eggs, lightly beaten
1 c. sugar
2 Tbsp. all-purpose
   flour
1 c. light or dark corn
   syrup
2 Tbsp. butter,
   melted
1 tsp. vanilla
1 (9 inch) unbaked
   pastry pie shell
1½ c. large pieces
   walnuts

Heat oven to 400°F. Combine eggs, sugar, flour, corn syrup, butter, and vanilla; blend well. Pour into unbaked pie shell; arrange walnuts on top. Bake in lower third of oven at 400°F. for 15 minutes. Reduce oven temperature to 350°F.; bake an additional 35 to 45 minutes or until center appears set. Cool completely.

Yuletide Feast

Cranberry Salad

Roast Goose

Orange Marmalade Dressing

Broccoli Bake

Orange-Pecan Stuffed Yams

Smoky Peas and Potatoes

Refrigerator Rolls

Christmas Coconut Cake

Old-Fashioned Mince Pie

CRANBERRY SALAD

1 large pkg.
  raspberry jello
2 c. hot water
1 pinch of salt
1 (20 oz.) can crushed
  pineapple
1 c. chopped pecans
1 (16 oz.) can whole
  cranberry sauce
Juice of 1 lemon
3 c. miniature
  marshmallows

Dissolve jello in hot water. Add cranberry sauce; mix well. Add salt, lemon juice, pineapple, and nuts. Mix well. Put marshmallows on top. Congeal. Serves 12 to 15.

ROAST GOOSE

1 goose (about 10
  lb.), thawed
1 Tbsp. salt
½ tsp. pepper
1 tsp. seasoned salt
½ tsp. garlic powder
1 tsp. poultry
  seasoning
½ tsp. ground ginger
4 to 5 dashes of
  cayenne pepper

Heat oven to 350°. Remove giblets and neck from goose cavity. Rinse goose and pat dry. Remove any large pockets of fat inside cavity. Prick with fork over the entire surface of the goose, pricking every inch. Combine all ingredients, except goose, in a small bowl. Rub this seasoning mixture thoroughly inside and outside the goose. Place goose on a rack in a roasting pan. Roast goose, uncovered, for 3 hours. Drain drippings as they accumulate. During the last 30 minutes, raise temperature so that the outside skin will crisp.

Do not try to stuff a goose. The fat given off during cooking will end up in the stuffing. Do not baste. It will keep the skin from being crisp. A 10 pound goose will serve 6 to 8 people.

ORANGE MARMALADE DRESSING

1 large pkg.
  Pepperidge
  Farm corn bread
  dressing
2 cans chicken broth
1 can sliced water
  chestnuts
1 jar orange
  marmalade
1 can sliced
  mushrooms
2 large onions, diced
3 eggs

Mix all ingredients and put in greased pan. Bake at 375° for 45 minutes.

BROCCOLI BAKE

2 pkg. frozen
  broccoli,
  thawed
1 can cream of
  chicken soup
½ c. Cheez Whiz
2 Tbsp. butter
¾ c. milk
1 c. Minute rice
Onions (optional)

Place broccoli in baking dish. Heat together in pan the soup, cheese, milk, and butter. Stir in uncooked rice; pour over broccoli. Bake at 350° for 30 to 35 minutes.

This is good also with 1 package broccoli and 1 package cauliflower.

ORANGE-PECAN STUFFED YAMS

4 medium yams
1 Tbsp. grated
  orange peel
½ tsp. nutmeg
1 Tbsp. sour cream
½ tsp. salt
¼ c. chopped pecans
8 pecan halves
8 orange sections

Pierce yams with a fork and bake in oven at 400°F. for 15 minutes, then reduce heat to 375°F. and continue baking for 45 minutes. Cut yams in halves and scoop out flesh, leaving ¼ inch shells. Mash yams with sour cream, orange peel, salt, and nutmeg. Fold in pecans. Fill yam shells. Top each with an orange section and pecan half. Return to oven and bake 10 minutes longer. Serves 8.

SMOKY PEAS AND POTATOES

1½ lb. small potatoes
1 pkg. frozen peas
2 Tbsp. flour
2 Tbsp. butter
1⅔ c. milk
1 (6 oz.) roll smoked
  process cheese
4 slices bacon,
  cooked crisp
  and crumbled

Scrub potatoes; cook in boiling, salted water just until done, 15 to 20 minutes. Drain. Cook peas. In small saucepan, melt butter. Stir in flour; add milk all at once. Cook and stir over low heat until mixture thickens and bubbles. Cut cheese in small pieces; add to sauce. Cook and stir until cheese melts. Add half of crumbled bacon.

Combine hot potatoes and peas in serving dish. Cover with cheese sauce. Sprinkle remaining bacon. Serve immediately.

REFRIGERATOR ROLLS

1 pkg. yeast
½ c. sugar
1 tsp. salt
1 egg
7 c. flour
3 Tbsp. shortening, melted
2 c. lukewarm water

Put yeast into large mixing bowl. Add sugar, salt, and water. Add well beaten egg. Sift flour once before measuring. Add half of flour and beat well. Add melted shortening and mix in remainder of flour. Let rise to double its bulk. Punch down, cover tightly, and place in refrigerator.

About 1 hour before baking, remove desired amount of dough. Shape into small rolls and place on greased pan. Bake in hot oven (425°F.) for 20 to 25 minutes.

CHRISTMAS COCONUT CAKE

1 c. butter
2 c. sugar
7 eggs
2¾ c. all-purpose flour
1 tsp. baking powder
1 tsp. baking soda
Dash of salt
1 c. buttermilk
2 Tbsp. vegetable oil
1 tsp. vanilla extract
1 tsp. coconut extract

Frosting:
1 c. milk
¼ c. all-purpose flour
½ c. butter, softened
½ c. shortening
1 c. sugar
1 tsp. vanilla extract
1 tsp. coconut extract
1 c. flaked coconut

Cream butter; gradually add sugar. Add eggs, 1 at a time. Combine flour, baking powder, soda, and salt. Add to creamed mixture alternately with buttermilk and oil, beginning and ending with flour mixture. Stir in flavorings. Bake at 350° for 20 to 25 minutes in three 9 inch pans.

Frosting: Combine milk and flour in saucepan and cook until mixture thickens. Let cool. Mix with other ingredients. Sprinkle top and sides with another cup of coconut. Cover and chill before serving.

OLD-FASHIONED MINCE PIE

**Pastry for 9 inch two-
  crust pie
1 (28 oz.) jar
  prepared
  mincemeat
1½ c. diced, pared
  tart apples**

Heat oven to 425°. Prepare pastry. Mix mincemeat and apples. Turn into pastry-lined pie pan. Cover with top crust which has slits cut in it; seal and flute. Cover edge with 2 to 3 inch strip of aluminum foil to prevent excessive browning. Remove foil last 15 minutes of baking. Bake 40 to 45 minutes. Serve warm. Makes one 9 inch pie.

Carolers Treats

Apple Eggnog
Hot Spiced Tea
Holiday Fruit Drops
Almond Christmas Cookies
Minty Fudge Brownies
Santa's White Fudge
Date Balls

APPLE EGGNOG

4 eggs, separated
2 Tbsp. sugar
2 c. vanilla ice cream
2 c. apple juice
Nutmeg

In large bowl, beat egg yolks until thick. Add sugar, ice cream, and apple juice; mix until blended. Beat egg whites until stiff peaks form; fold into apple juice mixture. Pour into glasses; sprinkle with nutmeg. Makes 7 (1 cup) servings.

HOT SPICED TEA

6 tsp. tea
2 c. boiling water
1 (6 oz.) frozen lemon juice
1 (6 oz.) frozen orange juice
1¼ c. sugar
2 qt. water
1 stick cinnamon
5 whole cloves

Pour water over tea and let cool. Strain and add rest of ingredients. Simmer mixture for 20 minutes; remove. Add cinnamon and cloves.

HOLIDAY FRUIT DROPS

1 c. shortening
2 c. brown sugar,
　packed
2 eggs
½ c. buttermilk
3½ c. flour (self-
　rising)
1½ c. pecans, broken
2 c. candied cherries
2 c. chopped dates

Preheat oven to 350°. Mix shortening, sugar, and eggs well. Stir in milk. Blend in flour; stir. Add pecans, cherries, and dates; drop rounded teaspoons of dough about 2 inches apart on lightly greased baking sheet. Place a pecan half on each cookie. Bake for 8 to 10 minutes until no imprint remains when touched lightly. Makes 8 dozen cookies.

ALMOND CHRISTMAS COOKIE

1 lb. butter, softened
1 c. powdered sugar
2 tsp. vanilla
½ lb. ground
　almonds
4 c. flour

Mix together. Bake for 10 minutes at 350°. Roll in powdered sugar while warm.

MINTY FUDGE BROWNIES

1¼ c. all-purpose
　flour
½ tsp. baking soda
½ tsp. salt
1 c. sugar
½ c. butter
3 Tbsp. water
1 (10 oz.) pkg. (1½ c.)
　mint chocolate
　morsels
1½ tsp. vanilla
　extract
3 eggs
1 c. chopped nuts
Walnuts halves
　(optional)

Preheat oven to 325°F. In small bowl, combine flour, baking soda, and salt; set aside. In medium saucepan, combine sugar, butter, and water; bring just to boil. Remove from heat. Add mint chocolate morsels and vanilla extract; stir until morsels are melted and mixture is smooth. Transfer to large bowl.

Add eggs, one at a time, beating well after each addition. Gradually blend in flour mixture. Stir in nuts. Spread into greased 13x9 inch baking pan. Bake at 325°F. for 30 to 35 minutes. Cool completely on wire rack; cut into 1½ inch squares. Garnish with halves if desired. Makes 4 dozen 1½ inch brownies.

SANTA'S WHITE FUDGE

2 c. sugar
½ c. sour cream
⅓ c. white Karo syrup
2 Tbsp. margarine
¼ tsp. salt
2 tsp. vanilla
¼ c. candied
  cherries,
  chopped
1 c. pecans, chopped

In large heavy skillet, mix first 5 ingredients; cook to soft ball stage or 236°. Remove from heat; let stand 15 minutes. Add vanilla and beat; add cherries and nuts. Pour into buttered 8x8 inch pan.

DATE BALLS

1 c. sugar
1 c. chopped nuts
  (pecans or
  walnuts)
1 stick margarine
1 egg, beaten
1 (8 oz.) pkg.
  chopped
  sugar rolled dates
1 tsp. vanilla
Rice Krispies
Confectioners sugar
Coconut

Mix first 6 ingredients together. Put in boiler; cook for 5 or 6 minutes. Remove from heat. Add 2 cups Rice Krispies. Shape into balls and roll in confectioners sugar or coconut.

APPETIZERS, BEVERAGES

FESTIVE HAM BALLS

3 lb. ham, ground
2 eggs
1 small onion,
    chopped fine
1 tsp. dry mustard
2 c. crushed cereal
    (corn flakes or
    bran flakes)
1 small can
    evaporated
    milk
2 cans cherry pie
    filling

Combine ham with other ingredients, except pie filling. Knead thoroughly until all ingredients are combined. Make into meatballs and bake in oven for 20 minutes at 350°. Transfer to glass baking dish. Cover with cherry pie filling and bake 20 minutes more. Serve with rice or as an appetizer or party dish.

HAM-IT-UP CRESCENT SNACKS

1 (8 oz.) can crescent
    dinner rolls
4 thin slices (4x7
    inches) ham
4 tsp. pure prepared
    mustard
4 oz. (1 c.) shredded
    Swiss or
    Cheddar cheese
2 Tbsp. sesame seed

Heat oven to 375°. Unroll dough into 4 long rectangles. Firmly press perforations to seal. Place one slice ham on each rectangle. Spread ham slices with mustard; sprinkle with cheese. Starting with shortest side, roll up each rectangle and press edges to seal. Coat rolls with sesame seed. Cut each of the 4 rolls into 5 slices, forming 20 slices in all. Place each slice, cut side down, on ungreased cookie sheet. Bake for 15 to 20 minutes or until golden brown. Immediately remove from cookie sheet. Serve warm. Makes 20 appetizers.

SAUSAGE WRAPS

2 (8 oz.) cans crescent
    dinner rolls
48 fully cooked small
    smoked
    sausage links

Heat oven to 375°. Separate dough into 8 triangles. Cut each triangle lengthwise into thirds. Place sausages on shortest side of each triangle. Roll up from shortest side to opposite point. Bake on ungreased cookie sheet for 12 to 15 minutes or until golden brown. Serve warm. Makes 48 snacks.

WATER CHESTNUT AND BACON APPETIZERS

2 cans whole peeled
  water chestnuts
2 lb. bacon (thick
  slice)
Toothpicks
1 c. ketchup
1 c. brown sugar

Wrap each chestnut with ½ slice bacon; secure with toothpicks. Bake in oven at 350° till bacon is crisp. (You will need to drain the pan once.)

In the meantime, mix ketchup and brown sugar. Cook until clear and bubbly - do not burn. Spoon over cooled chestnuts. Warm up before serving.

PARTY PIZZA

1 lb. hamburger
1 lb. Rice's hot pork
  sausage
8 oz. Cheez Whiz
1 (10 oz.) can Ragu
  Pizza Quick
  sauce
2 party rye breads
  (Pepperidge Farm)
2 Tbsp. minced onion
Green pepper
  (optional)
Mozzarella cheese

Brown hamburger, sausage, onion, and green pepper; drain. Add Cheez Whiz. Mix and refrigerate. Spread pizza sauce on rye bread, then meat mixture. Top with Mozzarella cheese. Spray cookie sheets with Pam. Bake 15 minutes at 375°. *Delicious!*

MINI CRAB PIZZAS

1 (7 oz.) can crab,
  drained well
  (soak in ice water)
1 stick butter
1 jar Old English
  cheese
1½ tsp. mayonnaise
½ tsp. garlic salt
6 English muffins,
  split

Combine crab, butter, cheese, mayonnaise, and garlic salt until a smooth spread. Spread on muffin halves. Cut into quarters, wrap, and freeze. Will freeze up to 7 days. Remove from freezer, place on cookie sheet, and broil until brown.

SAVORY POTATO SKINS

4 Idaho potatoes,
  baked
3 Tbsp. butter,
  melted
Salt
Garlic powder
Paprika

Cut potatoes in halves lengthwise. Scoop out the insides and serve as mashed potatoes, leaving ¼ inch of potato to the shell. Cut shells in halves lengthwise. On baking sheet, brush skins with butter; sprinkle lightly with salt, garlic powder, and paprika. Broil until golden brown, about 5 minutes. Makes 16 potato skin snacks.

CHEESY ARTICHOKE APPETIZERS

2 (8 oz.) cans crescent
  dinner rolls
¾ c. (3 oz.) shredded
  Mozzarella
  cheese
¾ c. grated
  Parmesan
  cheese
½ c. mayonnaise
14 oz. can artichoke
  hearts, drained and
  chopped
4 oz. can chopped
  green chilies

Unroll dough into rectangles; press onto bottom and sides of 15x10x1 inch jelly roll pan to form crust. Bake at 375° for 10 minutes. Combine remaining ingredients; mix well. Spread over crust. Bake at 375° for 15 minutes or until cheese is melted. Let stand for 5 minutes before serving. Makes approximately 3 dozen.

MINI QUICHE

1 small ctn. whipping
  cream
Pinch of salt and
  pepper
Flaky biscuits
Shredded cheese
  (Swiss, sharp,
  Mozzarella)
1 egg
Pinch of sugar
Pinch of nutmeg
Crumbled bacon
Chopped green
  onions

Beat egg and stir in whipping cream, salt, pepper, sugar, and nutmeg. Spray Pam in muffin cups. Using flaky biscuits, separate each biscuit into 3 to 4 layers. Lay 1 in the bottom; arrange the others along the sides. Pop in oven for 5 minutes. Remove and punch the bottom down lightly with a spoon. Put in the bottom of each one a little crumbled bacon, cheese, and chopped onions. Pour some of the cream-egg mixture in and bake at 350° for about 15 to 20 minutes. Top with paprika.

CHILI CHEESE LOG

1 pkg. chili seasoning
2 pkg. (8 oz.) cream
   cheese
3 Tbsp. salsa

Beat chili seasoning, cream cheese, and salsa. Shape and top with chopped nuts and shredded Monterey Jack cheese. Chill until firm. Decorate as desired. Serve with assorted crackers and vegetables.

PINEAPPLE CHRISTMAS TREE CHEESE BALL

1 (8 oz.) pkg. cream
   cheese
¾ c. crumbled Blue
   cheese (about 4
   oz.)
1 c. shredded
   Cheddar
   cheese (about 8
   oz.)
¼ c. minced onion
1 Tbsp.
   Worcestershire
   sauce
Chopped pecans
1 fresh pineapple

Let cheese stand at room temperature in small mixing bowl until soft. Add onion and Worcestershire sauce. Blend on low speed until mixed. Beat on medium speed until fluffy, scraping bowl often. Cover and chill for at least 8 hours.

Pat cheese mixture onto pineapple, letting green top of pineapple show through top of cheese ball. Pat pecans onto cheese and serve with crackers.

ORANGE BREAKFAST NOG

2 small bananas
1½ c. buttermilk
3 eggs
⅓ c. frozen orange
   juice
   concentrate
2 Tbsp. brown sugar
½ tsp. vanilla
4 large ice cubes

Cut bananas in 1 inch slices. Freeze for several hours. In blender, combine milk, eggs, orange juice, brown sugar, and vanilla. Add half of frozen banana pieces. Cover and blend well. Add remaining banana slices; blend till smooth. Add ice; blend till frothy. Makes 3 servings.

CHRISTMAS PUNCH

2 pt. cranberry juice
2 (1 qt.) cans
  pineapple juice
1 c. lemon juice
3 c. sugar
3 c. water (or more if
  you wish)
2 qt. ginger ale
Red food coloring
  (optional)

Mix together all ingredients, except ginger ale. Just before serving, add ginger ale. Punch has a perky tart flavor.

PEACH NECTAR PUNCH

1 (6 oz.) can frozen
  orange juice
  concentrate
1 qt. peach nectar
1 qt. ginger ale
1 qt. frozen peach
  slices
1 small jar cherries

Combine all ingredients in punch bowl; stir. Float frozen peaches and cherries in bowl. Makes 17 (4 ounce) servings.

MULLED CIDER

2 qt. apple cider
2 cinnamon sticks
8 whole cloves
2 Tbsp. granulated
  sugar
Several small red
  apples, studded
  with cloves
Cinnamon stick
  stirrers

Simmer apple cider, 2 cinnamon sticks, whole cloves, and granulated sugar for 30 minutes. Discard cinnamon sticks and cloves, then pour into a heatproof serving bowl. Add several small apples studded with cloves (they'll float). Serve hot cider in mugs with cinnamon stick stirrers. Serves 8.

CRANBERRY SUNRISE

For each serving:
1 tsp. frozen
  cranberry-
  juice-cocktail
  concentrate
Orange juice

Put cranberry-juice-cocktail concentrate in a goblet or glass. Fill with orange juice. For festive stirrers, slip cranberries onto bamboo sticks.

BANANA "DAIQUIRI"

1 cut up banana
2 Tbsp. frozen
   pineapple-juice
   concentrate
1 tsp. fresh lemon or
   lime juice
1 c. crushed ice

Whirl banana, frozen pineapple-juice concentrate, and fresh lemon or lime juice in a blender. Add crushed ice, a little at a time. Blend until mixture is thick and smooth. Serve immediately. Serves 2.

HAWAIIAN HOLIDAY

1½ c. chilled
   pineapple juice
1 (8¼ oz.) can
   crushed
   pineapple
¼ c. canned cream of
   coconut

Mix pineapple juice, pineapple, and cream of coconut. Serve over ice cubes in tall glasses. Serves 4.

SOUPS, SALADS, VEGETABLES

OYSTER STEW

1 pt. oysters
1 c. canned milk
2 c. whole milk
1 stick butter
1 tsp. Worcestershire
   sauce
⅛ tsp. cayenne
   pepper
⅛ tsp. black pepper
Salt to taste

Heat oysters over medium heat until the edges curl. Add the 3 cups of milk, butter, Worcestershire sauce, peppers, and salt to taste. Heat slowly until hot, but do not let mixture boil. Pour in bowls and sprinkle with paprika. Serve with catsup and oyster crackers.

VEGETABLE-CHEESE CHOWDER

2 c. chopped
   potatoes
1 c. shredded carrots
1 c. chopped celery
1 c. chopped onion
4 Tbsp. butter
4 c. chicken broth
   (canned is fine)
2 c. milk
½ c. flour
3 c. shredded
   Cheddar
   cheese
2 c. sharp process
   cheese
Salt and pepper to
   taste

In a large soup kettle, saute vegetables in butter for about 5 minutes. Stir in chicken broth. Simmer for 30 minutes. Vegetables should be fork tender. Blend flour with milk and add to kettle. When broth has thickened, lower heat and stir in cheeses. Do not allow to boil. Serve hot in bowls sprinkled with parsley and grated carrots.

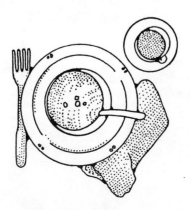

FIRESIDE CHEESE SOUP

½ c. finely chopped
  carrot
¼ c. finely chopped
  celery
¼ c. finely chopped
  onion
2 c. milk
1½ c. shredded sharp
  American
  cheese
2 Tbsp. butter
¼ c. flour
1½ c. chicken broth
  or 2 chicken
  bouillon cubes,
  dissolved in 1½
  c. boiling water
Dash of paprika

In saucepan, melt butter; cook vegetables, covered, until tender on low heat. Add the flour, then the milk, broth, and paprika. Cook and stir until thick. Stir in the cheese until melted. *Do not boil!* Makes 4 to 5 servings.

BAKED POTATO SOUP

4 large potatoes
4 Tbsp. oil
1½ c. flour
1½ qt. milk
Salt and pepper
4 green onions,
  chopped
1 c. sour cream
2 c. crisp bacon,
  crumbled
5 oz. Cheddar, grated

Bake potatoes until tender (350°). Melt butter in saucepan. Slowly blend in flour with whisk until thoroughly blended. Gradually add milk to butter/flour mixture, whisking constantly. Whisk in salt and pepper. Simmer over low heat, stirring constantly.

Cut potatoes in halves, scoop out, and set aside. When milk mixture is very hot, whisk in potatoes. Add green onions. Whisk well and add sour cream and crumbled bacon. Heat thoroughly. Add cheese a little at a time, until all is melted in. Garnish with chives, grated cheese, and bacon crumbles.

TURKEY-ALMOND SALAD

2 c. cubed, cooked
    turkey
1 c. chopped red
    grapes, seeded
⅓ c. diced celery
½ c. almonds,
    toasted
Salad dressing

Combine turkey, grapes, celery, and almonds. Add enough salad dressing to moisten. Serve on lettuce. Serves 6 to 8.

CRANBERRY SALAD WITH CHEESE

1 qt. cranberries,
    ground
2 c. sugar
1 c. celery, chopped
1 c. nuts, chopped
1 c. grapes, seeded
    and chopped
1 c. American
    cheese,
    chopped
6 marshmallows, cut
    fine
½ pt. cream,
    whipped

Grind cranberries; add sugar and let set overnight. Drain off excess juice. Add other ingredients and refrigerate a few hours before serving.

CALICO SALAD

1 can green beans
1 can wax beans
1 can kidney beans
1 c. green peppers,
    chopped
1 red onion, sliced
¾ c. sugar
⅔ c. vinegar
⅓ c. salad oil
1 tsp. pepper
1 tsp. salt

Wash kidney beans and drain all the beans. Add onion. Combine sugar, vinegar, oil, salt, and pepper. Pour over ingredients and marinate overnight.

LAYERED LETTUCE SALAD

½ medium head
  iceberg lettuce
½ c. chopped celery
1 green pepper,
  chopped
1 pkg. frozen green
  peas
½ medium red onion
1 c. mayonnaise
¼ c. salad oil
2 Tbsp. sugar
¼ c. Parmesan
  cheese
1 c. grated Cheddar
  cheese
8 slices bacon (crisp)
Croutons

Layer a 9x13 inch casserole dish first with lettuce, then continue layering with celery, green pepper, uncooked peas, and onion. Mix together mayonnaise, oil, sugar, and Parmesan cheese. Gently sprinkle over layered vegetables. Top with cheese and crumbled bacon. Cover and refrigerate 24 hours. Serve untossed. Garnish with croutons.

MARINATED VEGETABLE SALAD

1 head cauliflower
1 head broccoli
1 pkg. cherry
  tomatoes
1 lb. fresh
  mushrooms
1 large bottle Italian
  dressing

Cut cauliflower and broccoli into flowerets. Stem mushrooms. Add tomatoes. Mix together and add dressing. Cover and refrigerate. Let marinate for 7 hours or overnight.

GREEN BEAN SALAD

2 cans (French style)
  green beans
2 large tomatoes
1 large cucumber
4 green onions
Red wine vinegar
Vegetable oil
Salt
Pepper

Drain cans of beans. In a large bowl, add green beans, cut tomatoes, sliced cucumber, diced green onions, oil, vinegar, and spices to taste; chill. Serve cold.

PASTA SALAD

Dressing:
1 pt. Hellmann's
mayonnaise
1 can Eagle Brand
milk
¾ c. vinegar
1 c. sugar

Additional
Ingredients:
3 carrots, grated
Small green pepper,
chopped
Small red onion,
chopped fine
16 oz. rotini noodles

Dressing: Mix together mayonnaise and milk. Slowly add vinegar and sugar. Mix until sugar is dissolved.

Cook noodles according to package directions and drain well; cool. Add carrots, pepper, and onion. Add dressing and mix well. Chill overnight. Keeps in refrigerator for 2 weeks.

CONGEALED PINEAPPLE-CHEESE SALAD

1 (No. 2) can crushed
pineapple
2 Tbsp. gelatin
2 lemons
1 c. sugar
2 tsp. grated lemon
rind
1 c. chopped pecans
1 c. grated cheese
2 Tbsp. mayonnaise
1 c. evaporated milk,
whipped

Let gelatin set in ½ cup cold water for 10 minutes. Heat pineapple, lemon juice and rind, and sugar. Add gelatin. Place in refrigerator until cool or beginning to set; add remaining ingredients and chill until firm.

CHRISTMAS EVE SALAD

10 to 12 c. fresh
  fruits, sliced
  and peeled (if
  needed)*

Dressing:
1 c. mayonnaise
1 tsp. grated lime
  peel
¼ c. honey
3 Tbsp. lime juice

Garnish:
½ c. pomegranate
  seeds
½ c. peanuts

Arrange the fresh fruit slices on a large platter. Garnish with about ½ cup each pomegranate seeds and peanuts if desired. Serve with dressing to spoon over.

Dressing: Stir mayonnaise, lime peel, honey, and lime juice together. Cover and chill if made ahead.

To keep some of the fruits from darkening, brush with lime or orange juice.

* Suggestions: Oranges, pineapple, apples, bananas, papaya, and jicama.

LIME GELATIN SALAD

1 large pkg. cream
  cheese
5 Tbsp. mayonnaise
½ pt. whipping
  cream,
  whipped
1 can crushed
  pineapple,
  drained
½ lb. small
  marshmallows
2 small pkg. lime
  gelatin

Mix first 5 ingredients and spread in bottom of dish. Dissolve gelatin as directed on package and cool. When gelatin is cold, pour over mixture and chill until set.

ORANGE SHERBET SALAD

1 (15¼ oz.) can
  crushed
  pineapple
1 (10½ oz.) can
  mandarin
  oranges
1 (6 oz.) pkg. orange
  Jell-O
2 c. boiling water
2 Tbsp. lemon juice
1 pt. orange sherbet
½ c. sugar
1 env. unflavored
  gelatin
1 beaten egg
1 c. whipping cream
Additional mandarin
  oranges for
  garnish (optional)

Drain fruits, reserving 1 cup combined syrup for topping. Dissolve orange gelatin in boiling water. Add lemon juice. Add sherbet by spoonfuls, stirring until melted. Chill until partially set. Fold in drained fruits. Turn into a 9x13x2 inch baking dish. Chill until almost firm.

Meanwhile, in small saucepan, combine sugar and unflavored gelatin. Add reserved syrups and egg; cook and stir until thickened and bubbly. Cool thoroughly but do not allow to set. Whip cream; fold in cooked mixture. Spread over partially set gelatin. Chill until firm. Cut in squares to serve. Garnish top of each square with drained mandarin slice if desired.

COMPANY POTATOES

2 lb. frozen hash
  browns
¼ c. melted oleo
1 tsp. salt
¼ tsp. pepper
2 c. sour cream
½ c. chopped onion
2 c. shredded
  Cheddar
  cheese
1 can cream of
  chicken soup

Topping:
2 c. crushed corn
  flakes
¼ c. melted oleo

Thaw potatoes and combine with remaining ingredients. Put in flat glass baking dish (9x12 inches). Top with corn flake mixture. Bake at 350° for 45 minutes.

Topping: Mix corn flakes with melted oleo.

MALLOW-WHIPPED SWEET POTATOES

1½ c. miniature
   marshmallows
2 (17 oz.) cans sweet
   potatoes,
   drained and
   mashed
¼ c. melted
   margarine
¼ c. orange juice
½ tsp. cinnamon

Reserve ½ cup marshmallows. Combine remaining ingredients; mix lightly. Spoon into 1 quart casserole. Bake at 350° for 20 minutes. Sprinkle with reserved marshmallows. Broil until lightly browned. Serves 6.

CHEDDAR SCALLOPED POTATOES

3½ lb. baking
   potatoes (about
   7 large), peeled and
   sliced ⅛ inch
   thick (10 c.)
4 oz. Cheddar
   cheese,
   shredded (1 c.)
½ c. sliced scallions
1 tsp. salt
½ tsp. pepper
2 Tbsp. all-purpose
   flour
3 c. milk

Heat oven to 350°. Grease a shallow 3 quart baking dish. Layer half the potatoes over bottom of prepared dish. Sprinkle with half the cheese, scallions, salt, and pepper. Cover with remaining potatoes. Put flour into a small bowl. Whisk in milk until blended. Pour evenly over potatoes. Sprinkle with remaining cheese, scallions, salt, and pepper.

Bake, uncovered, 1 hour to 1 hour and 10 minutes until potatoes are very tender and top is lightly browned.

SWISS CORN BAKE

3 c. fresh corn, cut
   from cob, or 2
   (9 oz.) pkg. frozen
   corn, or 1 (16
   oz.) can corn
1 (15½ oz.) can
   evaporated
   milk
1 egg, beaten
2 Tbsp. chopped
   onion
½ tsp. salt
Dash of pepper
1 c. Swiss cheese,
   shredded
½ c. soft bread
   crumbs
1 Tbsp. melted butter

Heat oven to 350°. Cook fresh corn in 1 cup boiling water (salted) for 2 to 3 minutes or until tender or cook frozen corn according to package directions; drain well. Combine corn, milk, egg, onion, salt, pepper, and ¾ cup of the cheese. Mix and pour in greased baking dish. Toss bread crumbs with butter and ¼ cup cheese. Sprinkle over corn mixture. Bake for 25 to 30 minutes. Serves 6.

BROCCOLI CASSEROLE

2 pkg. frozen
   chopped
   broccoli
1 can cream of
   mushroom soup
1 c. mayonnaise
2 eggs, beaten
1 c. medium sharp
   cheese, grated
Salt and pepper to
   taste
Crushed cracker
   crumbs

Cook broccoli according to directions on package and drain. Mix soup, mayonnaise, and eggs. Add cheese, salt, and pepper. Carefully fold in broccoli. Top with crushed cracker crumbs. Bake at 350° until brown.

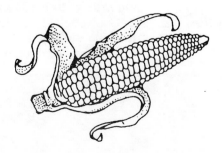

GREEN BEANS WITH SHALLOT BUTTER

½ c. butter or
  margarine
1 Tbsp. olive oil
⅔ c. thinly sliced
  shallots or
  white part of
  scallions
½ tsp. salt
½ tsp. pepper
3 lb. fresh green
  beans, ends
  trimmed
⅓ c. chopped fresh
  parsley

Melt ¼ cup butter with the oil in a small skillet. Add shallots and cook 7 to 9 minutes over low heat, stirring occasionally, until very tender. Stir in remaining butter, the salt, and pepper. Remove from heat.

Cook green beans, uncovered, in a large pot of water 5 to 7 minutes until crisp-tender. Drain well. Add shallot butter and parsley. Toss to mix and coat.

PEAS AND RICE

½ c. raw regular rice
2 Tbsp. butter or
  margarine
1 c. frozen peas
⅛ tsp. rubbed sage
1 can Campbell's
  chicken broth
2 Tbsp. diced
  pimiento

In saucepan, brown rice with sage in butter. Add broth. Bring to boil; reduce heat. Cover; simmer 15 minutes. Add peas. Simmer 10 minutes more or until done. Stir occasionally. Stir in pimiento. Makes about 3 cups.

SQUASH-CARROT CASSEROLE

5 c. sliced squash or
  zucchini
½ c. chopped onion
1 (10 oz.) can
  condensed
  cream of chicken
  soup
1 c. shredded carrots
1 c. sour cream
2 c. herb seasoned
  stuffing mix
½ c. margarine,
  melted

In a Dutch oven, cook squash and onion, uncovered, in boiling, salted water for 5 minutes; drain. Stir together the cream of chicken soup, carrot, and sour cream. Fold in drained vegetables. Stir together stuffing mix and margarine. Sprinkle ⅔ of the stuffing mixture into a 12x7x2 inch baking dish. Spoon vegetable mixture atop. Sprinkle remaining stuffing mixture around edges of dish. Bake, uncovered, about 30 to 35 minutes at 350°.

MAIN DISHES

BARBEQUE BRISKET

1 brisket
Liquid smoke
Celery salt
Nutmeg
Paprika
Garlic salt
Meat tenderizer

Barbeque Sauce:
1 gal. ketchup
½ c. liquid smoke
½ c. Worcestershire
　sauce
1½ lb. brown sugar
Dash of garlic powder

Sprinkle meat liberally with liquid smoke, celery salt, nutmeg, paprika, garlic salt, and meat tenderizer. Wrap meat in foil and leave in refrigerator for 8 hours or overnight. Cook in foil in oven for 3½ hours at 300°; cool. Drain juice and fat. Slice, cover with barbeque sauce, and cover with foil. Return to oven for 1 hour at 300°.

Barbeque Sauce: Combine all ingredients and let simmer on stove for 15 minutes or until sugar dissolves.

CRANBERRY MEATBALLS

1 lb. ground beef
½ c. tomato juice
2 slices white bread,
　crumbled
1 tsp. salt
⅛ tsp. pepper
1 Tbsp.
　Worcestershire
　sauce
1 Tbsp. minced
　parsley
1 egg, slightly beaten
1 (1 lb.) can cranberry
　sauce (whole or
　jellied)
1 Tbsp. lemon juice
⅓ c. brown sugar

Combine meat, tomato juice, and bread. Mix well. Add salt, pepper, Worcestershire, parsley, and egg. Roll into meatballs and brown in small amount of margarine. Beat cranberry sauce with lemon juice and brown sugar. Pour over meatballs and simmer ½ hour. Serves 4.

This recipe can also be made into a meat loaf; pour sauce over and bake at 350°F. for 1 hour.

FRENCH-STYLE BEEF ROAST

3 lb. boneless chuck
　or rolled rump
　roast
1 tsp. salt
1 tsp. dried thyme
　leaves
6 whole cloves
5 peppercorns
1 bay leaf
1 large clove garlic,
　cut into fourths
4 c. water
4 medium carrots, cut
　into fourths
2 medium onions, cut
　into fourths
2 turnips, cut into
　fourths
2 celery stalks, cut
　into fourths

Place roast, salt, thyme, cloves, pepper-corns, bay leaf, and garlic in Dutch oven; add water. Heat to boiling point; reduce heat. Cover and simmer for 2½ hours.

Add remaining ingredients. Cover and simmer until beef and vegetables are tender, about 30 minutes. Remove beef and vegetables; cut beef into ¼ inch slices. Strain broth; serve with beef and vegetables.

PRIME RIB

Roast

Bring roast to room temperature. Preheat oven to 400°. Rub roast lightly with flour. Season with salt and a generous amount of freshly ground pepper. Place roast on rack in uncovered shallow roasting pan and place in preheated oven. When cooking time is finished, turn off oven at least 2 hours and not more than 4 hours, depending on size of roast.

Cooking time: For 2 rib or 4 to 4½ pounds, 20 to 25 minutes. For 3 rib or 8 to 9 pounds, 40 to 45 minutes at 400°. For 4 big or 11 to 12 pounds, 55 to 60 minutes.

Slow roasting method: Preheat oven to 200°. (It is not safe to cook meat at a lower temperature.) Roast 6 hours for a 4 to 6 pound roast with or without ribs. During the last 30 minutes of cooking, turn oven to 325° to brown surface.

FESTIVE GLAZED HAM

1 (5 lb.) ham

Festive Glaze:
½ c. firmly packed
brown sugar
1 Tbsp. cornstarch
¼ tsp. ground cloves
Dash of ground
ginger
½ c. ReaLemon
reconstituted
lemon juice

Place ham in a shallow baking dish with SilverStone or Teflon surface; heat according to label instructions.

Festive Glaze: In a small saucepan, combine brown sugar, cornstarch, cloves, and ginger; add ReaLemon. Heat, stirring constantly, until thickened. Spoon glaze over ham during last 30 minutes of heating time.

PORK MEDALLIONS WITH PEAR-CRANBERRY SAUCE

1 Tbsp. vegetable oil
1 large onion, finely
chopped
4 firm pears, peeled,
cored, and
finely diced
½ c. fresh orange
juice (2
oranges)
¼ c. cranberries
¼ tsp. ground
cinnamon
¼ tsp. ground ginger
1 lb. pork tenderloin,
trimmed of fat and
membrane and cut
into 1 inch thick slices
Salt and freshly
ground black pepper
to taste

In a medium saucepan, heat 1½ teaspoons oil over medium heat and saute onions until softened, about 4 minutes. Add pears, orange juice, cranberries, cinnamon, and ginger; simmer, stirring frequently, for 3 to 5 minutes, or until the cranberries just start to burst. Remove from the heat.

Meanwhile, season pork with salt and pepper. In a nonstick skillet, heat the remaining 1½ teaspoons oil over medium-high heat until hot but not smoking. Add pork and cook until browned, about 2 minutes per side. Add the pear-cranberry mixture to the skillet and cook for another 2 to 2½ minutes, or until the center of the pork has just a trace of pink. Remove the pork and keep warm. Boil the sauce for 5 minutes, or until slightly thickened. Season with salt and pepper. Place the pork on plates with the pear-cranberry sauce on top. Serves 4.

ROAST PORK LOIN

1 (4 to 5 lb.) pork loin
  roast
3 cloves garlic,
  crushed
3 Tbsp. olive oil
2 tsp. chopped fresh
  thyme
2 tsp. chopped fresh
  rosemary
½ tsp. salt
¼ tsp. pepper

Trim excess fat. Place on a rack in a roasting pan. Rub garlic over roast. Brush with olive oil and sprinkle with herbs. Cover roast and refrigerate for at least 2 hours. Sprinkle roast with salt and pepper. Bake at 500° for 15 minutes. Reduce heat to 325° and bake for 1 hour and 20 minutes.

APRICOT STUFFED CHOPS

6 to 8 double rib
  chops
¼ c. fine dry bread
  crumbs
Parsley (optional)
Dash of ground sage
1 Tbsp. bottled steak
  sauce
Salt and pepper for
  chops
1 (12 oz.) can
  Mexicorn
¼ c. chopped onion
½ tsp. thyme
1 (30 oz.) can whole
  apricots
1½ tsp. salt
1 tsp. whole cloves

Cut pocket in each chop, cutting from fat side almost to bone edge. Season with salt and pepper. Combine corn, crumbs, onion, ½ teaspoon salt, thyme, and sage. Spoon stuffing lightly into chop pockets. Arrange chops in single layer in 13x9x2 inch pan. Cover tightly with foil. Bake at 350° for 30 minutes.

Drain apricots and pour juice in bowl; stir in steak sauce and remaining 1 teaspoon salt. Boil, uncovered, until reduced to ½ cup. Stud apricots with cloves. Uncover chops; do not turn. Bake 45 minutes longer. Add apricots to baking dish. Brush chops and apricots with apricot glaze. Bake, uncovered, 25 additional minutes. Garnish with parsley if desired.

PARSLEY

MARVELOUS CHICKEN

Chicken breasts and
   thighs (about 3
   lb.)
Cooking oil
Salt
Pepper
Juice of a lemon
¾ c. water
3 cloves garlic
8 to 10 green onions,
   chopped
5 Tbsp. capers
1 Tbsp. thyme
Freshly sliced
   mushrooms
Sliced Provolone
   cheese
Paprika

In skillet, brown chicken on all sides in small amount of cooking oil. Salt and pepper to taste. Arrange chicken pieces in large baking dish (9x13 inches). Remove fat from skillet previously used; add lemon juice and water. Let simmer a few minutes, then add garlic, green onions, and capers. Let simmer 5 minutes longer. Pour mixture over chicken. Sprinkle with thyme. Cover and bake at 400° for 20 to 25 minutes. Remove lid; spread mushrooms over chicken, then cover entire surface with Provolone cheese. Sprinkle with paprika and return to 375° oven for 6 to 7 minutes, until cheese is melted.

ROSEMARY ROAST CHICKEN

2¼ lb. fryer chicken
1 Tbsp. melted butter
¼ tsp. salt
Pinch of pepper
Pinch of paprika
1 Tbsp. rosemary

Preheat oven to 325°F. Stuff chicken if you choose. Use your favorite stuffing. Place chicken in a roasting pan. Brush with melted butter. Sprinkle with seasonings. Roast in oven for 60 minutes. Serves 4.

If you use a stuffing, a little longer cooking time may be required.

CHICKEN CORDON BLEU

8 skinned, boned
   chicken breasts
¼ lb. shaved, baked
   ham (slices)
¼ lb. Swiss cheese
   (slices)

Sauce:
2 cans condensed
   cream of chicken soup
1 c. mayonnaise
1 tsp. lemon juice
½ tsp. curry powder

Sauce: Combine.

Pound breasts between sheets of wax paper. Put ham and cheese on breast and roll up. Secure with toothpick. Put in baking dish on top of thin layer of sauce. Pour remaining sauce on top. Bake at 350° for 1 hour and 15 minutes.

CHICKEN AND BROCCOLI CASSEROLE

1 whole small
  chicken
2 cans cream of
  mushroom
  soup
2 pkg. frozen
  broccoli,
  chopped
1 pkg. Cheddar
  cheese
1 c. bread crumbs or
  Durkee onions

Boil chicken for 1 hour. Cook broccoli according to package directions. Debone and chop chicken; place in casserole dish. Cover with broccoli, then soup, then shredded cheese. Cover with bread crumbs. Cook for 15 minutes at 350° until cheese melts.

CHICKEN KIEV

4 chicken breasts
  (skinless and
  boneless)
½ lb. butter
1 Tbsp. chives
1 Tbsp. lemon juice
Chicken gravy
½ c. Parmesan
  cheese
½ c. fine Italian bread
  crumbs

Tenderize both sides of chicken breasts; salt and pepper breasts. Combine ¼ pound butter and 1 tablespoon chives; make a ball of butter and chives; place in center of each breast. Fold sides of breast and pin with toothpick. Combine ¼ pound melted butter and 1 tablespoon lemon juice in bowl. Dip chicken breasts in butter and lemon juice. Dunk chicken in gravy.

Combine Parmesan cheese and bread crumbs in bowl. Dunk chicken in cheese and crumbs. Bake in baking pan for 25 to 30 minutes at 425°. Baste halfway through.

GLAZED CORNISH HENS

4 Cornish hens
½ c. white grape juice
½ c. grape juice
  concentrate,
  thawed
2 Tbsp. lemon juice
1 Tbsp. grated lemon
  peel
2 tsp. salt
¼ tsp. pepper
2 Tbsp. melted butter

Wash hens; pat dry. Salt and pepper cavities. In large bowl, combine grape juice, lemon juice and peel, salt, and pepper. Add melted butter. One at a time, bathe hens in marinade and set on platter. Cover and chill for 1 hour.

Heat oven to 350°. Drain hens, reserving marinade. Bake for 30 minutes; baste with marinade, then baste every 15 minutes for 30 more minutes.

TURKEY-CRANBERRY SQUARES

2 Tbsp. butter
½ c. sugar
1 tsp. grated orange
  peel
2 c. fresh cranberries
5 c. ground turkey,
  cooked
1 c. turkey stock
1 c. milk
1 tsp. salt
¼ tsp. pepper
2 Tbsp. finely
  chopped onion
2 c. soft bread
  crumbs or
  leftover stuffing
2 eggs, slightly
  beaten

Melt butter in an 8 inch baking pan. Blend in sugar and orange peel. Cover with cranberries. Combine remaining ingredients, mixing thoroughly. Pack firmly over cranberries. Bake at 400° for 45 minutes. Turn out upside-down onto serving platter. Cut into squares and serve hot. Serves 8.

TURKEY CASSEROLE

1 (10½ oz.) can
  cream of
  mushroom soup
½ c. milk
1 (8 oz.) pkg. wide
  noodles,
  cooked and
  drained
1½ c. diced, cooked
  turkey
10 pimento stuffed
  olives, sliced
⅛ tsp. salt
Paprika

Preheat oven to 375°. Heat milk and soup in saucepan over low heat for 5 minutes. Arrange half the noodles in a greased 2½ quart casserole. Add half the turkey, half the olives, and half the salt. Top with half the soup mixture. Repeat layers, ending with soup. Sprinkle with paprika. Bake for 25 minutes at 375°.

FESTIVE LAMB-CHOPS

Olive or salad oil
1 large onion, diced
1 large tomato, diced
1 Tbsp. white wine
   vinegar
¾ tsp. sugar
Salt
1 Tbsp. chopped
   parsley
8 lamb rib chops
   (about 2 lb.)
1 bunch broccoli
1 small garlic clove,
   minced
½ tsp. dried
   rosemary
   leaves, crushed
⅛ tsp. pepper
Parsley sprigs for
   garnish

In 2 quart saucepan over medium heat, in 1 tablespoon hot olive or salad oil, cook onion until very tender and golden, stirring occasionally. Stir in tomato, white wine, vinegar, sugar, and ¼ teaspoon salt; over high heat, heat to boiling. Reduce heat to low, cover, and simmer 5 minutes. Uncover and cook 5 minutes longer, stirring frequently. Stir in chopped parsley; keep relish warm.

Preheat broiler if manufacturer directs. Trim excess fat from lamb chops and steam broccoli. In 1 quart saucepan over medium heat, in 2 tablespoons hot olive or salad oil, cook garlic, dried rosemary, pepper, and ¾ teaspoon salt until garlic begins to brown; remove saucepan from heat.

Place lamb on rack in broiling pan; brush tops of chops with half of garlic mixture. With pan at closest position to source of heat, broil chops 8 to 10 minutes for medium-rare or until of desired doneness, turning chops once and brushing with remaining garlic mixture. Remove chops to warm platter. Serve with tomato relish and broccoli. Garnish with parsley. Serves 4.

ROAST LEG OF LAMB

1 (5 lb.) leg of lamb
1 tsp. salt
1 tsp. freshly ground
   pepper
1 Tbsp. oregano
1 clove garlic, halved
¼ c. butter
Juice of 1 large lemon
2 small onions,
   chopped
3 or 4 sprigs parsley
2 or 3 mushrooms,
   washed and
   chopped
1 c. water

Preheat oven to 500°. Place lamb, skin side up, on a rack in an open roasting pan. Rub the meat with salt, pepper, oregano, and garlic. Melt the butter, add the lemon juice, and pour over the meat. Add onions, parsley, mushrooms, and ½ cup water to the pan. Place in oven and roast 20 minutes. Add remaining water, lower temperature to 350° and cook to desired degree of doneness. Baste occasionally. Serve with pan juices and rice pilaf. Best when served rare; allow 12 to 15 minutes per pound for rare.

HOLIDAY DRESSING

1 lb. sausage (sage,
  mild or hot)
2½ c. (8 oz. bag) corn
  bread stuffing
  or crumbled corn
  bread
2½ c. (8 oz. bag) herb
  seasoned
  stuffing or bread
  crumbs
2 cans (14½ oz. size)
  chicken or
  turkey broth
1 large onion,
  chopped
2 stalks celery,
  chopped
½ c. butter or
  margarine,
  melted
1 tsp. salt
¼ tsp. black pepper

Brown sausage; drain. Cook onion and celery in butter or margarine until tender. Mix stuffing, poultry seasoning, salt, and black pepper. Stir in broth, celery, onion, butter, and sausage. Mix well. Stuff 14 to 20 pound turkey lightly. Do not overstuff. Dressing may be baked separately in an uncovered dish for 30 to 35 minutes at 350°.

CRANBERRY-HAZELNUT STUFFING

½ c. dried
   cranberries or
   raisins
¼ c. orange juice
1¼ c. chopped celery
1¼ c. chopped onion
¼ c. margarine or
   butter
1 tsp. poultry
   seasoning
1 (8 oz.) pkg. herb-
   seasoned
   stuffing mix (2 c.)
2 c. peeled, chopped
   apples (2 apples)
½ lb. bulk pork
   sausage,
   cooked and well
   drained
1 c. cooked wild rice
½ c. chopped
   hazelnuts or
   slivered almonds
½ c. snipped parsley
¾ to 1 c. chicken
   broth
Salt and pepper to
   taste

In a small saucepan, bring cranberries or raisins and orange juice to boiling. Remove from heat and set aside.

In a large skillet, cook celery and onion in hot margarine or butter till tender. Stir in poultry seasoning; set aside. In a large bowl, combine stuffing mix, apple, cooked sausage, wild rice, hazelnuts or almonds, and parsley. Stir in the cranberry mixture and celery-and-onion mixture. Drizzle with enough chicken broth to moisten, tossing lightly. Season with salt and pepper. Use to stuff one 8 to 10 pound turkey, or, bake, covered, in an ungreased 3 quart casserole in a 325° oven for 40 to 60 minutes or till heated through.

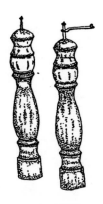

DESSERTS

CHRISTMAS RAINBOW CAKE

1 pkg. SuperMoist
  white cake mix
1 pkg. cherry jello
1 pkg. lime jello
2 c. boiling water
Fluffy white frosting
  mix
½ c. flaked coconut

Prepare cake according to directions. Bake in 9x13 inch pan as directed. Mix gelatin in 2 separate cups with 1 cup boiling water each. With a fork, poke holes in cake. With a tablespoon, spoon gelatin liquid in alternating diagonal bands 3 inches wide across entire cake. When completely cool, frost with fluffy frosting and top with coconut. Store in refrigerator.

OATMEAL SPICE CAKE

1¼ c. boiling water
1 c. oatmeal (quick
  uncooked)
½ c. butter, softened
1 c. granulated sugar
1 c. brown sugar,
  finely packed
1 tsp. vanilla
1½ c. sifted flour
¼ tsp. nutmeg
2 eggs
1 tsp. soda
½ tsp. salt
¾ tsp. cinnamon

Topping:
¼ c. melted butter
½ c. brown sugar
3 Tbsp. evaporated
  milk or half & half
¾ c. shredded
  coconut
⅓ c. chopped nuts

Pour boiling water over oatmeal; cover and let stand 20 minutes. Cream butter and sugar together. Blend in vanilla and eggs. Add oats mixture; mix well. Sift together dry ingredients. Add to creamed mixture. Mix well. Pour batter into well greased 9 inch square pan. Bake at 350° for 50 to 55 minutes.

Topping: Combine; spread on cake. Broil until frosting becomes bubbly. *Watch closely!*

PUMPKIN-SPICE PULL-APART CAKE

1 (16 oz.) pkg. hot-
roll mix
⅓ c. dried currants
¼ tsp. ground ginger
¼ tsp. ground
nutmeg
¼ tsp. ground
allspice
Sugar
Ground cinnamon
½ c. canned solid
pack pumpkin
(not pumpkin pie
mix)
1 large egg
Margarine or butter
½ c. packed light
brown sugar

Grease well 10 inch Bundt pan. In large bowl, mix flour mixture and yeast in foil packet from package of hot-roll mix with currants, ginger, nutmeg, allspice, 2 tablespoons sugar, and 1 teaspoon cinnamon. Stir in pumpkin, egg, 2 tablespoons softened margarine or butter (¼ stick), and ¾ cup *hot water* (120°F. to 130°F.) to form a soft dough. On floured surface, knead dough until smooth and elastic, about 5 minutes. Cover dough with large bowl; let rest 5 minutes.

Meanwhile, in small bowl, mix brown sugar, ⅓ cup sugar, and ½ teaspoon cinnamon. In 1 quart saucepan over low heat, heat 4 tablespoons margarine or butter (½ stick) until melted.

Cut dough in half and cut each half into 16 pieces. Shape each piece of dough into a smooth ball. Dip balls in melted margarine, then roll in cinnamon-sugar mixture; place in pan. Cover; let rise in warm place (80°F. to 85°F.) until doubled, about 30 minutes.

Preheat oven to 375°F. Bake coffee cake 25 to 30 minutes until browned and cake sounds hollow when lightly tapped with fingers. Immediately invert coffee cake onto plate. Serve warm, or cool cake on wire rack to serve later; reheat if desired.

VIENNESE TORTE

1 white cake mix
3½ oz. instant
  chocolate
  pudding
4 eggs
1 c. soft type oleo
¾ c. cold water
14 oz. chocolate
  frosting mix
¼ c. milk
1 c. heavy cream,
  whipped
1 c. chopped nuts

Combine cake mix, pudding mix, eggs, ⅔ cup oleo, and water in mixing bowl. Beat on medium for 3 minutes. Line two 10½ x 15 inch jelly roll pans with oiled waxed paper. Divide batter into pans. Spread flat. Bake at 350° for 15 minutes. Cool 5 minutes. Turn out on towels to cool thoroughly. Take frosting mix, milk, and ⅓ cup oleo. Beat until smooth. Cut each cake lengthwise into 3 strips. Assemble 6 strips with frosting between and on top. Frost sides and whipped cream; sprinkle with nuts.

GERMAN CHOCOLATE CAKE

1 (4 oz.) pkg.
  German's sweet
  chocolate
½ c. boiling water
1 c. butter
2 c. sugar
4 eggs, separated
1 tsp. vanilla
2 c. flour
1 tsp. baking soda
½ tsp. salt
1 c. buttermilk

Coconut Pecan
  Frosting:
1½ c. evaporated
  milk
1½ c. sugar
4 egg yolks
¾ c. butter
1½ tsp. vanilla
2 c. coconut
1½ c. chopped
  pecans

Melt chocolate in water and cool. Beat butter and sugar. Beat in egg yolks. Stir in vanilla and chocolate. Mix flour, baking soda, and salt. Beat into chocolate mixture alternately with buttermilk. Beat egg whites until stiff; fold into batter. Pour into 3 (9 inch) layer pans (grease and flour). Bake at 350° for 30 minutes or until done. Cool for 15 minutes.

Coconut Pecan Frosting: In a saucepan, slightly beat yolks. Add remaining ingredients. Cook and stir over medium heat until thickened. Stir in coconut and pecans. Cool until thick enough to spread.

POPPY SEED CAKE

3 c. flour
2¼ c. sugar
3 eggs
1½ tsp. baking
   powder
1½ tsp. salt
2 Tbsp. poppy seeds
1½ c. milk
1⅛ c. vegetable oil
1½ tsp. vanilla
1½ tsp. almond
   extract
1½ tsp. imitation
   butter flavoring

Orange Glaze:
¾ c. sugar
¼ c. orange juice
½ tsp. vanilla
½ tsp. almond
   flavoring
½ tsp. imitation
   butter flavoring

Combine all ingredients in large bowl. Beat for 2 minutes. Pour into 2 greased 8x4 inch loaf pans. Bake at 350° for 1 hour or until pick is clean. Prick loaves with a fork while hot and in pan. Spoon glaze over top. Allow to cool in pans.

Orange Glaze: Combine glaze ingredients in saucepan and beat until sugar dissolves.

RED VELVET CAKE

½ c. shortening
1½ c. sugar
2 eggs
2 Tbsp. cocoa
2 oz. red food
   coloring which has
   been mixed with
   cocoa
1 c. buttermilk, mixed
   with 1 tsp.
   vanilla
2½ c. flour, sifted
   with 1 tsp. salt
1 tsp. soda
1 tsp. vinegar

Icing:
5 Tbsp. flour
1 c. milk
1 c. sugar
1 c. butter
1 tsp. vanilla

Cream shortening and sugar. Add eggs. Add and beat well the cocoa, and red food coloring mixed with cocoa. Add alternately the buttermilk mixed with vanilla and flour sifted with salt. Beat well 4 to 5 minutes. Mix together soda and vinegar. Add to cake mixture and beat well. Bake in two 9 inch pans for 35 minutes at 350°.

Icing: Cook until thick and let cool the flour and milk. Cream sugar, butter, and vanilla. Add to cooled milk/flour mixture and beat well. Store in refrigerator.

PUNCH BOWL CAKE

1 box yellow cake mix
   (2 layers),
   prepared
1 large box instant
   vanilla
   pudding, prepared
2 cans cherry pie
   filling
1 small can mandarin
   oranges, drained
2 cans crushed
   pineapple,
   drained
7 oz. pkg. coconut
2 (12 oz.) ctn. Cool
   Whip, divided
½ or 1 c. chopped
   pecans

Put some Cool Whip in bottom of punch bowl. Place 1 cake layer on top of Cool Whip, then pour ½ of vanilla pudding mix on top of cake layer. Layer remaining ingredients, ½ at a time. Layer twice, ending with cherries on top.

GUMDROP CAKE

1 c. butter
1 c. sugar
2 eggs
1 c. applesauce
1 c. chopped nuts
1 lb. raisins, boiled
    for 5 minutes
    and cooled
3 c. flour
1 Tbsp. cinnamon
1 Tbsp. nutmeg
2 tsp. baking powder
1 tsp. salt
¼ tsp. baking soda
1 lb. gumdrops, cut
    and floured (no
    licorice)

Cream butter and sugar. Add beaten eggs. Sift dry ingredients and add. Add applesauce, raisins, nuts, and gumdrops. Line a tube pan with greased brown paper. Bake at 325° for 1½ hours. Remove from oven; leave in pan for 10 minutes. Place on plate; remove paper after 5 minutes.

BLACK WALNUT POUND CAKE

3 c. sugar
1 c. shortening
½ c. butter
6 eggs
3 c. plain flour
⅔ c. self-rising flour
1 c. sweet milk
1 tsp. vanilla
    flavoring
1 tsp. black walnut
    flavoring
1 c. black walnuts,
    chopped fine

Glaze:
1 c. sugar
½ c. buttermilk
¼ c. butter
½ tsp. soda
2 tsp. white corn
    syrup
1 c. black walnuts,
    chopped

Beat shortening, butter, and sugar until well blended. Add eggs, one at a time, beating well after each addition. Add flours and milk alternately. Add nuts and flavorings. Bake in large tube pan at 300° for 1½ hours.

Glaze: Cook first 5 ingredients for 5 minutes. Add walnuts. Glaze cooled cake.

APPLE BUTTER POUND CAKE

1½ c. sugar
½ c. margarine,
  softened
1 (8 oz.) cream
  cheese,
  softened
2 eggs
2 c. flour
1 c. corn meal
2 tsp. baking powder
· 1 tsp. cinnamon
¼ tsp. salt (optional)
1 c. spiced apple
  butter
1 tsp. vanilla
1 c. chopped pecans
1 c. powdered sugar
4 to 5 tsp. milk
1½ tsp. corn syrup
½ tsp. vanilla

Heat oven to 350°. Grease 10 inch tube pan or 12 cup Bundt pan. In large bowl, beat sugar, margarine, and cream cheese until light and fluffy. Add eggs, one at a time. Mix well. Add combined flour, corn meal, baking powder, cinnamon, and salt alternately with combined apple butter and vanilla. Mix at low speed until well blended. Stir in pecans. Spread evenly to edges of pan. Bake 60 to 70 minutes until wooden pick comes out clean. Cool 10 minutes in pan. Remove to wire rack. Cool completely. Combine powdered sugar, milk, corn syrup, and vanilla; drizzle over cake. Store, tightly covered. Serves 16.

CHRISTMAS COOKIES

1½ c. flour
½ c. soft butter or
  margarine
¾ c. sifted powdered
  sugar
1 egg yolk
½ tsp. salt
1 tsp. vanilla

Mix together egg yolk, butter, and powdered sugar until creamy. Add salt and vanilla. Add flour, ½ cup at a time, and mix well. Dough will be quite stiff. If necessary, add a small amount of milk. Roll out on floured surface. Cut with cookie cutters. Bake at 350° for 8 to 10 minutes until slightly browned; frost.

WALNUT TASSIES

8 oz. cream cheese
1 c. butter
2 c. flour

Filling:
3 eggs
1½ c. brown sugar
2 c. chopped walnuts
3 Tbsp. melted butter
2 tsp. vanilla

Cream together softened butter and cream cheese. Add flour and mix well. Press mixture into miniature cupcake tins.

Filling: Mix ingredients together. Put filling into centers of cupcakes. Bake 25 to 40 minutes at 350°. Roll in confectioners sugar.

THUMBPRINT COOKIES

¼ c. packed light or
  dark brown
  sugar
¼ c. regular stick
  margarine
  (not spread) or
  butter (at room
  temperature)
¼ c. solid vegetable
  shortening (at
  room temperature)
½ tsp. vanilla extract
1 egg, yolk and white
  separated
1 c. all-purpose flour
¼ tsp. salt
1 c. finely chopped
  nuts
¼ c. 1 or more flavor
  jelly

Heat oven to 350°F. Have cookie sheet(s) ready. In a large bowl, beat sugar, margarine, shortening, vanilla, and egg yolk with a wooden spoon or electric mixer until blended and smooth. Add flour and salt. Stir until dough holds together. Refrigerate dough, if needed, until firm enough to handle. Shape into 1 inch balls.

In a small bowl, beat egg white slightly with a fork. Dip balls into egg white, then roll in nuts. Place about 1 inch apart on ungreased cookie sheet. Press thumb deeply in center of each. Bake about 10 minutes or until light brown. Remove to wire rack to cool. Spoon jelly into thumbprints.

SANTA'S WHISKERS

1 c. margarine
1 c. sugar
2 Tbsp. milk
1 tsp. vanilla
2½ c. flour
¾ c. red and green
  candied
  cherries
½ c. chopped pecans
¾ c. coconut

Cream margarine and sugar. Add remaining ingredients, except coconut. Roll dough into a log shape and roll in coconut until it's well covered. Slice ½ inch thick and bake on a greased cookie sheet for 10 minutes at 375°.

CHURCH WINDOW COOKIES

1 stick oleo
1 c. nuts
Coconut
1 large bag semi-
  sweet chocolate chips
1 small bag colored
  small
  marshmallows

Melt 1 stick oleo and chocolate chips; cool. Add 1 cup chopped nuts and 1 bag small colored marshmallows. Mix and form 2 logs. Roll in coconut over wax paper. Cool; slice in thin slices.

CINNAMON RAISIN OAT TRIANGLES

2 c. rolled oats
1 c. all-purpose flour
¾ c. packed brown
   sugar
1 tsp. cinnamon
½ tsp. baking soda
¾ c. butter, melted
1 c. raisins
¼ c. apple jelly
Cinnamon Icing

Cinnamon Icing:
½ c. powdered sugar
¼ tsp. cinnamon
2 tsp. milk

Combine oats, flour, brown sugar, cinnamon, and soda; mix well. Stir in butter until evenly mixed. Remove 1 cup crumb mixture; set aside. Pat remaining mixture into greased 9 inch square pan. Combine raisins and jelly; toss with reserved crumb mixture. Sprinkle over layer in pan. Bake at 350° for 30 minutes or until edges are golden brown. While warm, cut into nine 3 inch squares. Cut each square diagonally to make triangles. Cool in pan. Drizzle with Cinnamon Icing. Makes 18 cookies.

Cinnamon Icing: Blend powdered sugar with cinnamon and milk to make a thin icing.

LEMON LOVE NOTES

½ c. butter
1 c. flour
¼ c. powdered sugar
2 Tbsp. lemon juice
Grated rind of 1
   lemon
2 beaten eggs
1 c. sugar
½ tsp. baking powder

Frosting:
¾ c. powdered sugar
1 tsp. vanilla
1 Tbsp. butter
1½ tsp. milk

Mix butter, flour, and powdered sugar. Pat into 9 inch square pan and bake in a 350° oven 15 minutes; cool. Blend lemon juice, grated rind of lemon, beaten eggs, sugar, and baking powder. Pour on baked crust and return to oven for 25 minutes longer; cool.

Frosting: Mix together; frost. Cut into bars.

HOLIDAY RICE KRISPY BARS

¼ c. butter or
   margarine
½ lb. marshmallows
½ tsp. vanilla
½ c. chopped
   candied
   cherries
½ c. chopped pecans
1 (5½ oz.) pkg. crisp
   rice cereal

Heat butter and marshmallows over hot water till thick and syrupy. Beat in vanilla. Add cherries and pecans. Place cereal in large pan. Pour marshmallow mixture over. Mix gently. Press into 9x9x1 inch pan. Press extra candied cherries and pecans on top if desired. (Wetting hands with cold water makes handling sticky stuff easier.)

PUMPKIN BARS

4 eggs
2 c. sugar
1 c. oil
15 oz. can (2 c.)
  pumpkin
2 c. flour
2 tsp. baking powder
1 tsp. soda
¾ tsp. salt
2 tsp. cinnamon
1 c. raisins or
  chopped nuts

Frosting:
3 oz. pkg. cream
  cheese, softened
⅓ c. margarine or
  butter, softened
1 Tbsp. milk
1 tsp. vanilla
2 c. powdered sugar

Heat oven to 350°F. Grease (not oil) 15x10 inch jelly roll pan. In large bowl, beat eggs until foamy. Add sugar, oil, and pumpkin; beat 2 minutes at medium speed. Add flour, baking powder, soda, salt, and cinnamon; beat 1 minute at low speed. Stir in raisins. Pour into prepared pan. Bake at 350°F. for 25 to 30 minutes or until toothpick inserted in center comes out clean; cool.

In small bowl, beat cream cheese, margarine, milk, and vanilla until fluffy. Add powdered sugar; blend until smooth. Spread frosting over cooled bars. Cut into bars.

CHEWY WALNUT SQUARES

6 Tbsp. margarine or
  butter (¾ stick)
6 oz. white chocolate
⅔ c. sugar
1 tsp. vanilla extract
¼ tsp. salt
2 large eggs
1 c. all-purpose flour
1 (8 oz.) can walnuts,
  coarsely chopped

Preheat oven to 325°F. Grease and flour 9 inch square baking pan. In heavy 2 quart saucepan over very low heat, heat margarine or butter and white chocolate until melted and smooth, stirring frequently. Remove saucepan from heat. With spoon, beat in sugar, vanilla extract, salt, and eggs until blended. Stir in flour and half of chopped walnuts. Evenly spread batter in pan. Sprinkle top of mixture with remaining walnuts. Bake 30 to 35 minutes until golden and toothpick inserted in center comes out clean. Cool in pan on wire rack.

When cold, cut walnut mixture into 4 strips, then cut each strip crosswise into 4 pieces. Store in tightly covered container.

BUTTER PECAN TURTLES

Crust:
2 c. all-purpose flour
1 c. brown sugar
½ c. butter
1 c. pecan halves

Caramel layer:
⅔ c. butter
1 c. chocolate chips
½ c. brown sugar

Crust: Combine all and mix at medium speed for 2 to 3 minutes or until particles are fine. Pat firmly into a 9x13 inch pan. Sprinkle with 1 cup pecan halves.

Caramel layer: Cook butter and sugar in a heavy saucepan over medium heat, stirring constantly, until entire surface begins to boil. Boil for ½ to 1 minute. Pour over crust. Bake for 18 to 22 minutes or until caramel layer is bubbly and crust is a light golden brown. Remove from oven and top with chocolate chips. Allow to melt slightly. Swirl some chips; leave some whole for marbled effect.

CHRISTMAS PECANS

1 lb. pecans
2 egg whites, beaten
  stiff
1 c. sugar
¼ tsp. salt
2 Tbsp. cinnamon

Mix pecans and egg whites, then mix with dry ingredients. Spread in pan. Bake for 20 minutes at 350°. Break apart and store in airtight container.

CHRISTMAS CANDY

1 (6 oz.) pkg.
  chocolate chips
2 Tbsp. milk
½ tsp. almond
  flavoring
1 (6 to 8 oz.) jar
  maraschino cherries,
  drained and diced

In top of double boiler over hot water, melt chocolate chips. Stir in milk to make thick, not runny, sauce. Add almond flavoring and diced cherries. Drop by teaspoons into aluminum foil cups or on wax paper. Cool until set.

MOUNDS BALLS

1 lb. coconut
¼ lb. butter, melted
2 lb. powdered sugar
1 c. nuts (walnuts preferred)
1 can sweetened milk (Eagle Brand)
12 oz. bag chocolate chips
1 brick paraffin

Mix together coconut, butter, powdered sugar, nuts, and milk. Shape into balls. Refrigerate overnight. Melt chocolate with paraffin in double boiler. With toothpick, dip each refrigerated ball.

CHOCOLATE DIPPED PEANUT BUTTER BALLS

1 stick margarine
2 c. chunky peanut butter
1 tsp. vanilla
1 lb. powdered sugar
3 c. Rice Krispies

Chocolate Dip:
2 oz. paraffin wax
12 oz pkg. chocolate chips

Melt margarine and while hot, stir in peanut butter. Mix well and add vanilla, powdered sugar, and Rice Krispies. Work in with hands until it will form balls. Dip in chocolate.

Chocolate Dip: Melt together in double boiler; keep warm. Use toothpick to dip balls in chocolate. Cool on waxed paper. Can shape like eggs for Easter.

CHRISTMAS WREATHS

1 stick margarine or butter
40 large marshmallows
4 c. corn flakes
1 tsp. vanilla
1 to 2 tsp. green food coloring
Red hot candies

Melt and cook 1 minute the margarine and marshmallows. Remove from heat and add corn flakes, vanilla, and food coloring. Work with when warm enough to handle and very sticky. Drop large spoonfuls onto wax paper. Flatten center and work into shape with buttered fingers. Kids love to help with this. Use red hots for the berries. Let set several hours or overnight.

CHRISTMAS TREES

5 Tbsp. margarine
1 c. sugar
2 eggs, beaten
1½ c. chopped dates
1 tsp. vanilla
3 c. Rice Krispies

Combine the margarine, sugar, eggs, dates, and vanilla; cook over medium heat for about 10 minutes. Stir often to keep from burning. Put the mixture in a large bowl with the Rice Krispies. Mix well. Cool so the mixture can be easily handled. Shape into 1½ to 2 inch cones. Roll in green sugar. Place close together on a cookie sheet and sprinkle with powdered sugar to look like snow.

BUTTERSCOTCH FUDGE

1 c. sugar
1 stick butter
¾ tsp. salt
1 (7½ oz.) jar
marshmallow
creme
1 (5⅓ oz.) can
evaporated
milk
1 (12 oz.) bag
butterscotch
chips
½ tsp. vanilla
½ c. chopped pecans

Combine sugar, butter, salt, marshmallow creme, and milk in a heavy saucepan. Cook to rolling boil over medium low heat. Continue to boil for 5 full minutes, stirring frequently. Remove from heat and add butterscotch chips, vanilla, and pecans. Stir until chips are melted. pour into well-buttered 9x9 inch square pan. Cool and cut into squares.

PEANUT BRITTLE

1½ c. sugar
⅔ c. water
½ c. white corn syrup
1½ c. blanched raw
peanuts
½ tsp. salt
2 Tbsp. butter
1 tsp. vanilla
½ tsp. soda

In a 2 quart saucepan, combine sugar, water, and syrup. Cook to soft ball stage (238°). Stir only until sugar dissolves. Add raw peanuts and salt; cook to hard crack stage (290°). Remove from heat. Add butter, vanilla, and soda. Stir until bubbling stops. Pour on buttered baking sheet. Spread thinly and let cool. Break into pieces.

CHOCOLATE PEANUT CLUSTERS

1 small pkg.
  chocolate
  pudding powder
1 c. sugar
½ c. canned milk
1 Tbsp. butter
1 c. salted peanuts

Mix in a 1½ quart saucepan, pudding, sugar, milk, and butter. Cook to soft ball stage. Take off heat. Stir in peanuts all at once. Beat until candy starts to thicken. Drop from teaspoon onto waxed paper.

ALMOND TOFFEE

1 c. butter
1 c. sugar
3 Tbsp. water
1 Tbsp. light corn
  syrup
⅓ c. almonds
4 sq. chocolate
  (sweet or semi-
  sweet)

Melt butter; add sugar. Stir until sugar is dissolved. Pour in water and syrup. Stir constantly while cooking. Cook until hard stage (300°), remove from heat, and stir in nuts. Spread on greased pan, cool, then cover with half of the chocolate which has been melted. When chocolate is dry, turn candy over and cover other side with remaining chocolate. Break into desirable size pieces.

PECAN PRALINES

3 c. pecan halves
3 Tbsp. butter
1¼ c. light cream
  (half & half)
1¾ c. granulated
  sugar
1¾ c. light brown
  sugar, packed
Candy thermometer

Bring to boil in a heavy, large saucepan the sugars and cream. Stir! Bring to the soft ball stage (234°), while stirring only to withstand sticking. Take off burner and place butter on top *without stirring*. Cool to 150° and stir in pecan halves; beat till glossy and thickened. Drop onto waxed paper baking sheet by the tablespoon. Makes about 40.

You can add a few drops of *hot* water and beat if candy becomes stiff to drop easily. Cooling takes 20 to 30 minutes. Watch the thermometer.

DIVINE DIVINITY

2 c. granulated sugar
½ c. light corn syrup
⅓ c. water
⅛ tsp. salt
2 egg whites
1 tsp. vanilla
1½ c. coarsely
   chopped
   Diamond walnuts

In 2 quart glass measuring cup with handle, combine sugar, corn syrup, water, and salt. Microwave at HIGH 5 minutes. Stir well until sugar dissolves. Microwave at HIGH 5 to 6 minutes, or until mixture reaches 260°F. In large mixer bowl, beat egg white until stiff peaks form. While beating at low speed, slowly pour hot syrup into egg whites. Continue beating until mixture loses its gloss, about 10 to 12 minutes. Blend in vanilla; stir in walnuts and quickly press candy mixture into buttered 8 inch square pan. Let stand until firm, then cut into squares.

FUDGE

2 c. sugar
⅔ c. evaporated skim
   milk
12 large
   marshmallows
½ c. butter
Few grains of salt
1 (6 oz.) pkg. semi-
   sweet
   chocolate morsels
1 c. chopped nuts
1 tsp. vanilla extract

Combine first 5 ingredients in a large saucepan. Cook over medium heat until mixture comes to a boil, stirring constantly. Boil 5 minutes, stirring constantly. Remove from heat. Add chocolate morsels to marshmallow mixture, stirring until melted. Add nuts and vanilla, stirring well. Spread evenly in a buttered 8 inch square pan. Cut into 1 inch squares when cool.

CREAM CHEESECAKE

1 pkg. graham
   crackers
½ c. sugar
1 stick butter, melted
4 pkg. cream cheese
1⅓ c. sugar
6 whole eggs

Topping:
1 (12 oz.) ctn. sour
   cream
1 tsp. vanilla
3 Tbsp. sugar

Mix thoroughly the graham crackers, ½ cup sugar, and butter; press on sides and bottom of 10 inch spring form pan. In blender, combine cream cheese, 1⅓ cups sugar, and eggs. Pour into crust. Bake at 350° for 40 minutes. When center is set, remove from oven and cool 20 minutes.

Topping: Mix. Put on cake after cooled. Return to oven 10 to 15 minutes longer at 350°.

FABULOUS HOLIDAY DESSERT

½ c. butter or
margarine,
softened
¼ c. sugar
1 c. all-purpose flour
1 c. finely chopped
pecans
1 (8 oz.) pkg. cream
cheese,
softened
1 c. sugar
3½ c. (8 oz.) Cool
Whip non-dairy
whipped topping,
thawed
1 (4 serving size) pkg.
Jell-O vanilla
flavor instant
pudding and
pie filling
1 (4 serving size) pkg.
Jell-O
chocolate flavor
instant pudding and
pie filling
3 c. milk
½ c. crushed
chocolate
toffee candy

Beat butter and ¼ cup sugar in medium bowl of electric mixer at medium speed until light and fluffy. Mix in flour until well blended. Stir in pecans. Press mixture into bottom of greased 13x9 inch baking pan. Bake at 350° for 15 to 20 minutes or until lightly browned. Cool on rack.

Beat cream cheese with 1 cup sugar in large bowl until smooth. Fold in 1¾ cups of the whipped topping. Spread over cooled crust. Prepare vanilla and chocolate pudding mixes together as directed on package, using 3 cups milk. Let stand for 5 minutes. Spread over cream cheese layer. Chill several hours or overnight. Spread remaining whipped topping over pudding. Sprinkle with crushed candy. Cut into squares.

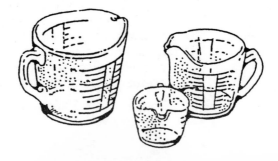

LIGHT HONEY-NUT STRUDEL

Honey
2 Tbsp. water
4 Tbsp. margarine
¾ tsp. ground
  cinnamon
½ tsp. vanilla extract
¼ tsp. allspice
12 sheets frozen
  (thawed) phyllo
⅓ c. walnuts, finely
  ground

Preheat oven to 300°F. Spray 15½ x 10½ inch jelly-roll pan with *vegetable cooking spray*; set aside. In 1 quart saucepan over low heat, heat 6 tablespoons honey, margarine, and 2 *tablespoons water* just until margarine melts. Stir in cinnamon, vanilla, and allspice; remove from heat, but keep warm. Cut two 25 inch lengths of waxed paper; overlap two long sides about ½ inch. Fasten with cellophane tape.

On waxed paper, place 1 sheet of phyllo; brush sparingly with honey mixture. Repeat to make 3 more layers. Sprinkle evenly with ⅓ of walnuts to within 1 inch of a narrow end. Using the waxed paper, lift phyllo from nut-covered narrow end; roll phyllo jelly-roll fashion. Place roll in pan, seam-side down. Brush lightly with honey mixture. With a sharp knife, cut roll into seven 1½ inch slices. Repeat process to make 2 more rolls. Bake 30 minutes or until golden brown. Cool about 30 minutes.

In 1 quart saucepan over low heat, heat 2 tablespoons honey and 1 tablespoon *water* until warm; brush over rolls. Serve warm or cold.

APPLE TORTE

Crust:
½ c. soft butter
⅓ c. sugar
¼ tsp. vanilla
1 c. flour

Cream Cheese
  Filling:
8 oz. cream cheese,
  softened
¼ c. sugar
1 egg
1 tsp. vanilla

Apple Topping:
4 c. peeled, sliced
  apples
⅓ c. sugar
½ tsp. cinnamon

Crust: Cream butter and sugar in small bowl. Stir in vanilla. Add flour and mix well. Spread on bottom and 2 inches up sides of a greased 9 inch springform pan.

Cream Cheese Filling: Combine cheese and sugar; add egg and vanilla, mixing well. Spread filling evenly over pastry.

Apple Topping: Place apples in large bowl. Sprinkle sugar and cinnamon on top and stir to coat. Spoon topping over filling. Add a few chopped walnuts. Bake at 450° for 10 minutes. Reduce to 400° for 25 minutes. Cool before removing from pan. Serve with whipped cream or ice cream.

BROKEN GLASS TARTS

1 (3 oz.) pkg. lime
  gelatin
1 (3 oz.) pkg. orange
  gelatin
1 (3 oz.) pkg. cherry
  gelatin
3 c. boiling water
2 c. cold water
1 c. pineapple juice
¼ c. sugar
1 (3 oz.) pkg. lemon
  gelatin
1½ c. graham
  cracker crumbs
⅓ c. melted butter
2 env. dry whipped
  topping mix, prepared
  as per pkg.
  directions

Prepare the 3 flavors of gelatin separately, using 1 cup boiling water and ½ cup cold water for each. Pour into three 8 inch square pans. Chill until very firm. Mix pineapple juice and sugar. Heat until sugar is dissolved. Remove from heat. Dissolve lemon gelatin in hot juice, then add ½ cup cold water. Chill until slightly thickened.

Meanwhile, mix crumbs and butter; press into bottom of a 9 inch springform pan. Cut the firm gelatins into ½ inch cubes. Prepare topping mix and blend with lemon gelatin. Fold in gelatin cubes. Pour into pan and chill at least 5 hours. Run knife between sides of pan and dessert; remove sides of pan.

THE SIMPLEST RICE PUDDING

1½ c. sugar
2 c. milk
1 tsp. vanilla
2 c. heavy cream
1½ c. rice (not
  converted)
1 c. raisins
2 tsp. cinnamon

Dissolve the sugar in the milk. Add the vanilla and cream; bring to a boil. Add the rice. Cook, covered, for about 40 minutes, over low heat. Stir in the raisins. Pour into a shallow pan. Sprinkle with cinnamon; chill.

RAISIN CUSTARD PUDDING

½ c. raisins
2 c. bread cubes
2 eggs
⅓ c. granulated sugar
⅛ tsp. salt
½ tsp. vanilla
2 c. scalded milk
⅓ c. graham cracker
  crumbs
3 Tbsp. brown sugar

Rinse and drain raisins. Put raisins and bread cubes in 8 inch round baking dish. Beat eggs lightly and stir in sugar, salt, vanilla, and milk. Pour over bread and raisins. Bake until set on top, then sprinkle with crumbs and brown sugar. Continue baking until custard is set. Top may be browned a minute or two under broiler. Serve warm or chilled, plain or with sauce. Bake 20 minutes; sprinkle with crumbs, then 10 to 15 minutes longer at a temperature of 350°.

INDEX OF RECIPES

MAIN DISHES

DESSERTS

PUZZLES

TO

Keep You Sharp

PUZZLES

TO

Keep You Sharp

BARNES
&NOBLE
BOOKS
NEW YORK

2 4 6 8 10 9 7 5 3 1

Published by Sterling Publishing Co., Inc.
387 Park Avenue South, New York, NY 10016
This book is comprised of material from the following Sterling titles:
Word Search Puzzles to Keep You Sharp © 2003 by Mark Danna
Super 30-Minute Crosswords © 2003 by Harvey Estes, Bob Klahn, Fred Piscop & Mel Rosen
Hard-to-Solve Word Puzzles © 2000 by Henry Hook
Cryptograms to Keep You Sharp © 2002 by Dell Magazines,
a division of Crosstown Publications

© 2004 by Sterling Publishing Co., Inc.

Designed by StarGraphics Studio

Printed in China
All rights reserved

0-7607-5625-2

Table of Contents

Word-Search Puzzles

Rarin' To Go

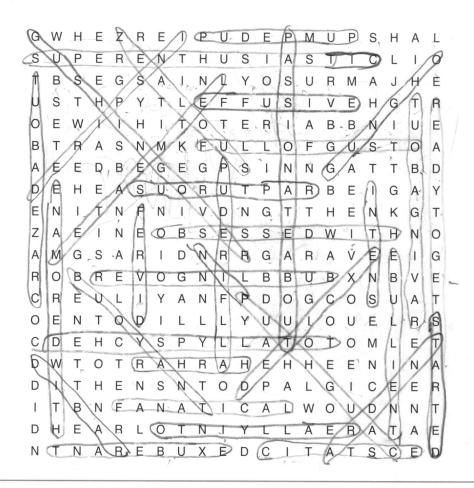

```
G W H E Z R E I P U D E P M U P S H A L
S U P E R E N T H U S I A S T I C L I O
T B S E G S A I N L Y O S U R M A J H E
U S T H P Y T L E F F U S I V E H G T R
O E W I I H I T O T E R I A B B N I U E
B T R A S N M K F U L L O F G U S T O A
A E D B E G E G P S I N N G A T T B D Y
D E H E A S U O R U T P A R B E I G A Y
E N I T N N N I V D N G T T H E N K G T
Z A E I N E O B S E S S E D W I T H N O
A M G S A R I D N R R G A R A V E E I G
R O B R E V O G N I L B B U B X N B V E
C R E U L I Y A N F P D O G C O S U A T
O E N T O D I L L L Y U U L O U E L R S
C D E H C Y S P Y L L A T O T O M L E T
D W T O T R A H R A H E H H E E N I N A
D I T H E N S N T O D P A L G I C E E R
I T B N F A N A T I C A L W O U D N N T
D H E A R L O T N J Y L L A E R A T A E
N T N A R E B U X E D C I T A T S C E D
```

ALL FIRED UP
ARDENT
BUBBLING OVER
BUOYANT
CAUGHT UP IN
CRAZED ABOUT
EBULLIENT
ECSTATIC
EFFUSIVE
ENAMORED WITH
EXCITED

EXUBERANT
FANATICAL
FERVID
FULL OF GUSTO
GUNG-HO
GUSHING OVER
INSPIRED
INTENSE
"LET ME AT 'EM!"
OBSESSED WITH
PASSIONATE ABOUT

PUMPED UP
RABID
RAH-RAH
RAPTUROUS
RAVING ABOUT
READY TO GET
STARTED
REALLY INTO
SUPER-ENTHUSIASTIC
TOTALLY PSYCHED
ZEALOUS

Answer on page 248

So How Sharp Are You?

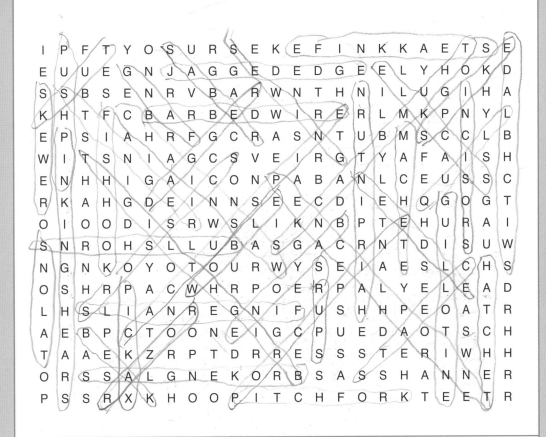

```
I P F T Y O S U R S E K E F I N K K A E T S E
E U U E G N J A G G E D E D G E E L Y H O K D
S S B S E N R V B A R W N T H N I L U G I H A
K H T F C B A R B E D W I R E R L M K P N Y L
E P S I A H R F G C R A S N T U B M S C C L B
W I T S N I A G C S V E I R G T Y A F A I S H
E N H H I G A I C O N P A B A N L C E U S S C
R K A H G D E I N N S E E C D I E H Q G O G T
O I O O D I S R W S L I K N B P T E H U R A I
S N R O H S L L U B A S G A C R N T D I S U W
N G N K O Y O T O U R W Y S E I A E S L C H S
O S H R P A C W H R P O E R P A L Y E L E A D
L H S L I A N R E G N I F U S H H P E O A T R
A E B P C T O O N E I G C P U E D A O T S C H
T A A E K Z R P T D R R E S S T E R I W H H
O R S S A L G N E K O R B S A S S H A N N E R
P S S R X K H O O P I T C H F O R K T E E T R
```

BARBED WIRE
BAYONET
BEAK
BRIGHT LIGHT
BROKEN GLASS
BULL'S HORNS
CACTUS SPINE
CHAIN SAW
CLEATS
DAGGER
ELBOW
FANG
FINGERNAILS
FISHHOOK

GUILLOTINE
HAIRPIN TURN
HATCHET
INCISORS
JAGGED EDGE
MACHETE
PENCIL POINT
PICKAX
PINKING SHEARS
PITCHFORK
PORCUPINE
QUILL
PUSHPIN
RAZOR

SABER
SCISSORS
SEWING
NEEDLE
SICKLE
SKEWER
SPIKE
SPURS
STEAK KNIFE
STINGER
SWITCHBLADE
TALONS
THUMBTACKS
TUSK

Answer on page 248

Shaped like a galloping horse, the grid below contains references to horse racing.

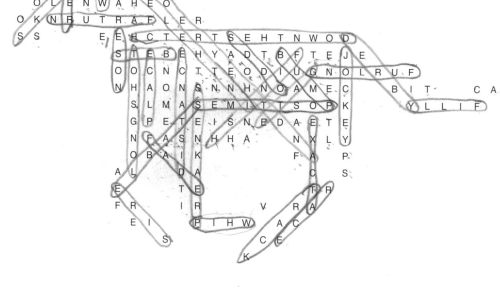

~~"AND THEY'RE OFF!"~~	~~FILLY~~	~~POST TIMES~~
~~BETS~~	~~FINISH~~	~~PREAKNESS~~
~~BUMP~~	~~FURLONG~~	~~RACE~~
~~DERBY~~	~~GATE~~	~~REINS~~
~~DISTANCE~~	~~IN THE LEAD~~	~~SHOW~~
~~"DOWN THE STRETCH!"~~	~~JOCKEY~~	~~SILKS~~
~~EXACTA~~	~~LONG SHOT~~	~~SIRE~~
~~FADE~~	~~NOSE~~	~~STABLE~~
~~FAR TURN~~	~~ODDS~~	~~TRACK~~
~~FAVORITE~~	~~PLACE~~	~~WHIP~~

Answer on page 249

Gossip Columns

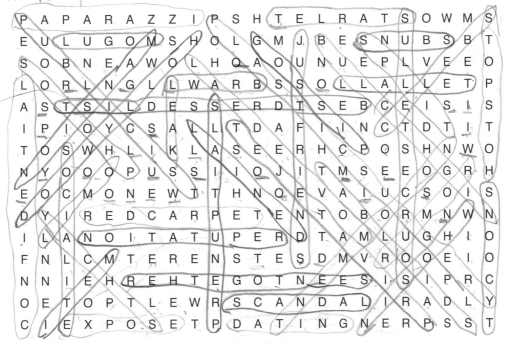

SHOW ME SOMEONE WHO NEVER GOSSIPS AND I'LL
SHOW YOU SOMEONE WHO IS ON T. INTERESTED
IN PEOPLE — WALTERS

P A P A R A Z Z I P S H T E L R A T S O W M S
E U L U G O M S H O L G M J B E S N U B S B T
S O B N E A W O L H Q A O U N U E P L V E E O
L O R L N G L L W A R B S S O L L A L L E T P
A S T S I L D E S S E R D T S E B C E I S I S
I P I O Y C S A L L T D A F I N C T D T I T
T O S W H L I K L A S E E R H C P Q S H N W O
N Y O O O P U S S I I O J I T M S E E O G R H
E O C M O N E W T T H N O E V A I U C S O I S
D Y I R E D C A R P E T E N T O B O R M N W N
I L A N O I T A T U P E R D T A M L U G H I O
F N L C M T E R E N S T E S D M V R O O E I O
N N I E H R E H T E G O T N E E S I S I P R C
O E T O P T L E W R S C A N D A L I R A D L Y
C I E X P O S E T P D A T I N G N E R P S S T

BEST DRESSED	LIMO	RUMOR
LIST	MANSION	SCANDAL
BRAWL	MOGUL	SEEN TOGETHER
CELEBS	MOVIE DEAL	SNUBS
CONFIDENTIAL	NIGHTCLUB	SOCIALITE
DATING	"NO COMMENT"	"SOURCES TELL
DENIAL	PAPARAZZI	US ..."
EXPOSÉ	PHOTOS	SPLIT
GOSSIP	PLASTIC SURGERY	STARLET
HOLLYWOOD	PRENUPTIALS	TABLOIDS
HOT SPOTS	PRIVATE JET	TELL-ALL
ITEM	PUBLICIST	TYCOONS
"JUST FRIENDS"	RED CARPET	WHO'S IN
LEAK	REPUTATION	YACHTS

Answer on page 249

It's In The Cards

Shaped like a spade in a deck of cards, the grid below contains references to cards and card games.

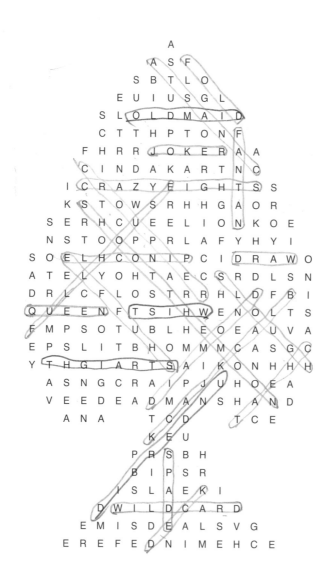

- BLACKJACK
- CANASTA
- CASINO
- CHEAT
- CHEMIN DE FER
- CLUBS
- CRAZY EIGHTS
- CRIBBAGE
- CROUPIER
- DEAD MAN'S HAND
- DECK
- DIAMOND
- DRAW
- DUPLICATE BRIDGE
- EUCHRE
- FAN-TAN
- FOLD
- FULL HOUSE
- GO FISH
- HEARTS
- HOYLE
- JOKER
- MISDEALS
- NO TRUMP
- OLD MAID
- PINOCHLE
- QUEEN
- RAISE
- ROYAL FLUSH
- SHOOT THE MOON
- SHUFFLE
- SLOUGH
- SOLITAIRE
- SPADE
- STRAIGHT
- STUD POKER
- TRICKS
- UNDERBID
- WHIST
- WILD CARD

Answer on page 250

Bad Ideas For Movie Sequels

This grid contains titles of movie sequels that—thank goodness!—were never made. It's up to you to determine what those titles are. To do so, use the list of clues below, which give hints to the titles of the original movies. (To help, we've put these originals in alphabetical order: ignore the "The" at the start of any titles.) If you want the word list, you'll find it on page 68.

```
H T N E E T R U O F E H T Y A D I R F O U R T H M A N A S M
N H D B E S U R S T N E M D N A M M O C N E V E L E E E E A
N I N E A N D T H R E E Q U A R T E R S W E E K S Y V V L G
O R U L M E I G H T Y E A R I T C H T I S S X T W E O L D N
F T L A E W O V E G R S R H E N I N Y T R O F I N T T E N I
S E V E N D A Y S E I G H T N I G H T S H E C T S U U W A F
P E C S T N E M E L E H T X I S K O H F O S H N E O S T C I
E N T H F O U R C O I N K S I N T H I E O S F O U N T S N C
T A N T T W O E Y E D J A C K S T A R I E U N S N E O N E E
S N T H R E E F O R T H E R O A D W D N W H R I T M E A E N
Y G A G N D T H E E I G H T D L W A S R F S A A N E D E T T
T R S I X E A S Y P I E C E S A C E T R O U N D M N T C N E
R Y H E V E F O S E C A F R U O F O R E W O R L D I I O E I
O M N E I S E I B A B O W T D N A N E M R U O F G N G H V G
F E T C B E N O D N A N O I L L I M E N O Y O N E D A O E H
Y N S F I V E W E D D I N G S A N D T W O F U N E R A L S T
```

1988 John Cusack; baseball
1997 Bruce Willis; sci-fi
1970 Jack Nicholson
1982 Nick Nolte, Eddie Murphy
1933 Ruby Keeler; backstage musical
1994 Hugh Grant, Andie MacDowell
1980 First of a horror series
1960 Yul Brynner, Steve McQueen; western
1986 Mickey Rourke, Kim Basinger
1980 Jane Fonda, Lily Tomlin, Dolly Parton

1960 (original) Frank Sinatra, Dean Martin
1961 Marlon Brando; western
1940 Victor Mature; cavemen (1966 remake with Raquel Welch)
1957 Director: Ingmar Bergman
1955 Marilyn Monroe, Tom Ewell
1998 Harrison Ford, Anne Heche
1984 Molly Ringwald
1999 Bruce Willis, Haley Joel Osment
1956 Charlton Heston; Bible epic

1949 Orson Welles; espionage
1935 Director: Alfred Hitchcock
1986 Steve Martin, Chevy Chase, Martin Short
1957 Joanne Woodward, Joanne Woodward, Joanne Woodward
1987 Tom Selleck, Steve Guttenberg, Ted Danson
1957 Henry Fonda, Lee J. Cobb
1949 Gregory Peck, Dean Jagger; WWII flyers
1967 Audrey Hepburn, Albert Finney

Answer on page 250

Give Me A Break!

The mug-shaped grid below contains words and phrases associated with coffee.

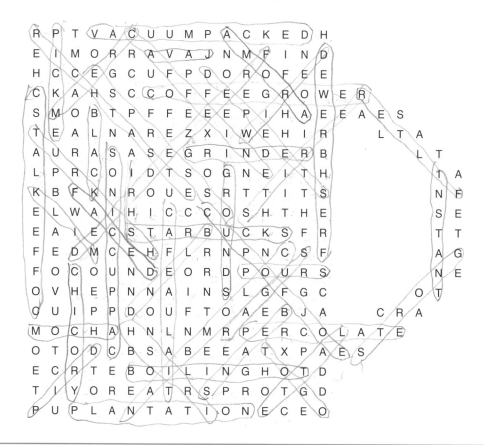

AROMA	DECAF	PERCOLATE
BEANS	DRIP	PICK-ME-UP
BLACK	ESPRESSO	PLANTATION
BLEND	FILTER	POURS
BOILING HOT	FREEZE-DRIED	RICH TASTE
CAFÉ AU LAIT	FRESH-BREWED	STARBUCKS
CAFFEINE	GRINDER	STEEPED
CAPPUCCINOS	GROUNDS	STIRRER
CHICORY	INSTANT	STRONG
COFFEE GROWER	IRISH	SUGAR
COFFEE KLATSCH	JAVA	TO-GO
COLOMBIAN	LATTE	TURKISH
CREAM	MILK	VACUUM-PACKED
CUP OF JOE	MOCHA	WIRED

Answer on page 251

Car Pool

In the car-shaped grid below, every item in the word list contains the letters CAR in consecutive order. When these letters appear in the grid, they have been replaced by a [CAR]. So take [CAR]E when solving.

```
            D [CAR] R E T S A M D I
        [CAR] S A S Y D K E [CAR] D [CAR] A
        A D O S F O E T A N O B [CAR] I B
      [CAR] I F [CAR] E R E R E I E N E U D P G
    T A C Y D E [CAR] S E [CAR] I D E M T H R A N [CAR]
    O F W [CAR] A O F Y S Y M T E I E A N B E D I N
  O L E N N U T L A P [CAR] Y I O U P X [CAR] N M R T B A E P L
  T O T M Q A T W E E V Y J O [CAR] U [CAR] O A R A H O T T E L [CAR] S
[CAR] [CAR] R S A T A I H R E S [CAR] G O T Y T I E S S U R M P [CAR] A S
  H N E E S [CAR] N T A E S P A I O R D E E D N I [CAR] A G U A C [CAR]
V C H I L I C O N [CAR] N E H E O [CAR] D I N A L N B [CAR] A R Y O C I D
  T I M V P P O N E D S L N T H R E E [CAR] D M O N T E R I D V
        A P [CAR] R I                     I X B V E
          L A E                     [CAR] E [CAR]
          M                               D
```

APOTHECARY	CARESS	MASCARA
APPLECART	CARIBOU	MASTERCARD
BETA-CAROTENE	CARNIVAL	MEDICARE
BICARBONATE OF SODA	CARPAL TUNNEL	NICARAGUA
BOX CAR	CARPE DIEM	PLACARD
CAPTAIN PICARD	CARRY-ON BAG	SCAREDY-CAT
CARAFE	CARTOON	SCARLETT O'HARA
CARAMEL	CARTWHEEL	SCARVES
CARAWAY SEEDS	CHILI CON CARNE	SCORECARD
CARBON DIOXIDE	ESCARGOT	SHAG CARPET
CARBURETOR	I.D. CARD	SQUAD CAR
CARDINAL	JIM CARREY	THREE-CARD MONTE
CAREEN	MACARONI	VICARS
	MACAROON	

Answer on page 251

Let's Celebrate

The birthday-cake-shaped grid below contain causes for and means of celebration.

ANNIVERSARY
APRIL FOOLS' DAY
BAPTISM
BAR MITZVAH
BIRTHDAY
BRIDAL SHOWER
BRIS
CINCO DE MAYO
COMMUNION
COSTUME BALL
EASTER
EQUINOX

FIESTA
GALA
GRADUATION
HALLOWEEN
HOEDOWN
HOMECOMING
HOUSEWARMING
JUBILEE
KWANZA
LENT
LUAU
MARDI GRAS

MOTHER'S DAY
NEW JOB
OKTOBERFEST
OPENING NIGHT
PAGEANT
PARADE
PARTY
PAY RAISE
PROM
REUNION
SOIREE
WEDDING

Answer on page 252

White On Schedule

```
N W L I G H T N I N G Y R E N O I T A T S I M
R U T E H T N C O S R K L N N O Y W K I N A S
I T R N Y E H E O F E L L V A N I L L A R A W
A M A S H E D P O T A T O E S O A C I B I R E
H W E E E T P C A B T S T L E H T H L L E S A
S K B I L S O A G D W O G O C N E E O O N O T
N L R A E P S N R W H N N P N E E R R O U S S
O A A E S U O H E T I H W E H T S X I D I D O
S D L T O P U H O I T S M G U U E S S C T B C
R S O D G O R N B E E S T U N D E R W E A R K
E W P N R O C I N U S O R I R E Y E V L E E S
P R I Y T H R I V E H N F G Y N N U B L L A L
D P T R I C E U H O A O R N O K N I G H T D U
L T A L H L A C O R R E C T I O N F L U I D W
O H S N O W M A N M K Y I T M O B Y D I C K E
```

ALBINO	IVORY	POLAR BEAR
BIRCH	KLEENEX	RICE
BLOOD CELL	KNIGHT	SAILOR'S
BREAD	LIGHTNING	UNIFORM
BUNNY	LILY	SNOWMAN
CHALK	LINEN	SOUR CREAM
CHESSMEN	MARBLE	STATIONERY
CLOUD	MASHED POTATOES	SWAN
CORRECTION FLUID	MOBY DICK	SWEAT SOCKS
COTTON	NOISE	TEETH
ENVELOPE	NURSE'S SHOES	THE WHITE HOUSE
EYE PART	OLD PERSON'S HAIR	UNDERWEAR
GREAT WHITE	PEARL	UNICORN
SHARK	PING-PONG BALL	VANILLA

Answer on page 252

Start The Music

Shaped like a CD, the grid below contains a compilation of many kinds of music plus words relating to compact discs.

```
            M G M O T O W N
          B U S A I E C C I K S Y
        F L I O N A V U E L R K J N
      D O U W N G N A E E D C X E Z P
    E O I E N G S R R Z I O Y W W I Z R
    E N E S E K T P M G R N A Z E C P A
  Y I H E R C Y A E I K O G U R L O T G J
  R D C L A H M R T N R E N R U B D C T O
  T L E R A U G A U D H A T S E O C S I D
  N O T O Y T L P N     S T B O X U N M R
  U N P W P A E A R     Y I I S D S O E M
  O E I F U E B M E F Y L O U O T D M O N
  C D T D O G R C Y S L I N E R N O T E S
  G L I L I R I A A V V S E U I O A T I P
    O T B W O T L L N A T M F D T C L O
    G S O U L S Y P O S E N U T W O H S
      M P E A W P D O N N H S U T P O
        F E Y I S C T O I U I R I H
          O L N O A R N N P O H A
            G L R K E G R N
```

BEBOP	GANGSTA RAP	NEW AGE
BIG BAND	GOLDEN	OPERA
BLUES	OLDIE	PUNK ROCK
CALYPSO	GOSPEL	RAGTIME
CD BURNER	HEAVY METAL	RAVE
CD PLAYER	HIP-HOP	REGGAE
COUNTRY	INSPIRATIONAL	SALSA
DIGITAL AUDIO	INSTRUMENTAL	SHOW TUNES
DISCMAN	JAZZ	SOUL
DISCO	JEWEL BOX	SWING
EASY	KLEZMER	TECHNO
LISTENING	LINER NOTES	TOP FORTY
FUNK	MOOD	TRACKS
FUSION	MOTOWN	ZYDECO

Answer on page 253

Black Hole #1

In this puzzle, the letters in the center of the grid are missing. It's up to you to write them in by figuring out which words in the list are missing some of their letters in the grid. When you've completed the puzzle, the missing letters will spell out a quip about a certain activity. The uncircled letters will reveal two other quips—plus their authors—on the same theme. (Note: Many, but not all, of the words on the list also are also associated with the theme.)

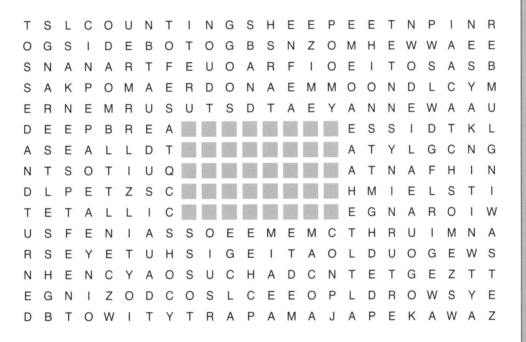

```
T S L C O U N T I N G S H E E P E E T N P I N R
O G S I D E B O T O G B S N Z O M H E W W A E E
S N A N A R T F E U O A R F I O E I T O S A S B
S A K P O M A E R D O N A E M M O O N D L C Y M
E R N E M R U S U T S D T A E Y A N N E W A A U
D E E P B R E A                 E S S I D T K L
A S E A L L D T                 A T Y L G C N G
N T S O T I U Q                 A T N A F H I N
D L P E T Z S C                 H M I E L S T I
T E T A L L I C                 E G N A R O I W
U S F E N I A S S O E E M E M C T H R U I M N A
R S E Y E T U H S I G E I T A O L D U O G E W S
N H E N C Y A O S U C H A D C N T E T G E Z T T
E G N I Z O D C O S L C E E O P L D R O W S Y E
D B T O W I T Y T R A P A M A J A P E K A W A Z
```

APNEA	FADERS	RESTLESS
AWAKE	FANTASIA	SAWING LUMBER
B AND B	FILE CLERK	SHUTEYE
CAMEO	GO TO BED	SIESTA
CATCH SOME Z'S	GUNMAN	SNOOZE
CATNAP	ITEMIZE	SNORE
CHEESE	JODIE FOSTER	SUTURE
COUNTING	LIE DOWN	THEME SONG
SHEEP	MOSQUITOS	TIC-TAC-TOE
DEEP BREATH	NIGHT	TIRED OUT
DISSECTS	ORANGE PEELS	TOSSED AND
DOZING	OSCILLATE	TURNED
DREAM	PAJAMA PARTY	TURN IN
DROWSY	REAL ESTATE	YAWN

Answer on page 253

It's A Shoe Thing

Shaped like a half-boot, the grid below contains words and phrases relating to footwear.

BLISTERS
BUNIONS
CLOG
CORNS
COWBOY BOOT
DOCKSIDER
FLATS
HEELS
INSOLE
JAZZ SHOE
LACES
LIFT

LOAFER
MOCCASINS
MULES
OXFORD
PATENT LEATHER
PLATFORM
PLIMSOLLS
POLISH
PUMPS
SABOT
SANDAL
SCUFF

SHINY
SHOEHORN
SLIP-ON
SLIPPER
SNAKESKIN
SNEAKERS
SPATS
SPIKE
STRAP
WEDGIE
WINGTIP
ZORI

Answer on page 254

Give It The Old College Try

The pennant-shaped grid below contains words and phrases about college.

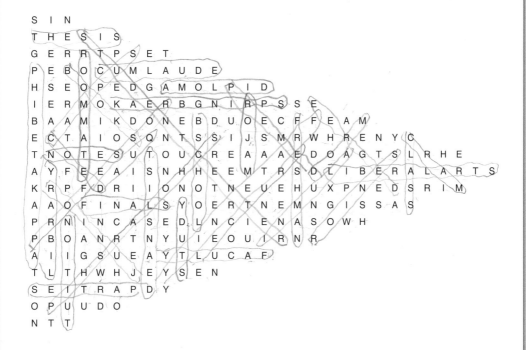

```
S I N
T H E S I S
G E R R T P S E T
P E B O C U M L A U D E
H S E O P E D G A M O L P I D
I E R M O K A E R B G N I R P S S E
B A A M I K D O N E B D U O E C F F E A M
E C T A I O S Q N T S S I J S M R W H R E N Y C
T N O T E S U T O U C R E A A A E D O A G T S L R H E
A Y F E E A I S N H H E E M T R S D L I B E R A L A R T S
K R P F D R I I O N O T N E U E H U X P N E D S R I M
A A O F I N A L S Y O E R T N E M N G I S S A S
P R N I N C A S E D L N C I E N A S O W H
P B O A N R T N Y U I E O U I R N R
A I I G S U E A Y T L U C A F
T L T H W H J E Y S E N
S E I T R A P D Y
O P U U D O
N T T
```

ALUMNI
ASSIGNMENT
BOOKS
B-SCHOOL
CAMPUS
CLASS
COED
CRAM
CUM LAUDE
DEAN'S LIST
DEGREE
DIPLOMA

DORM
FACULTY
FINALS
FRATERNITY
FRESHMAN
JUNIOR
LECTURE
LIBERAL ARTS
LIBRARY
MAJOR
NOTES
PARTIES

PHI BETA KAPPA
PREMED
PROFESSOR
QUAD
ROOMMATE
SCHOLARSHIP
SENIOR
SPRING BREAK
STUDENT CENTER
STUDY
THESIS
TUITION

Answer on page 254

Just Add Water

The hidden message explains the theme.

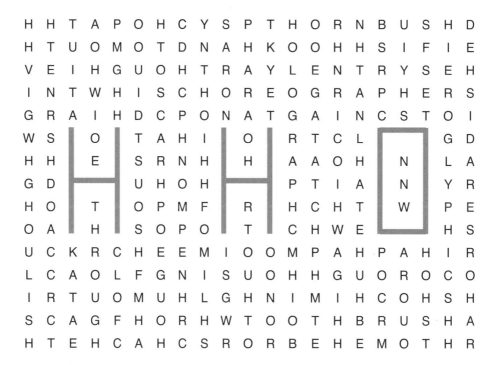

```
H H T A P O H C Y S P T H O R N B U S H D
H T U O M O T D N A H K O O H H S I F I E
V E I H G U O H T R A Y L E N T R Y S E H
I N T W H I S C H O R E O G R A P H E R S
G R A I H D C P O N A T G A I N C S T O I
W S   O   T A H I   O   R T C L       G D
H H   E   S R N H   H   A A O H   N   L A
G D   T   U H O H   T   P T I A   N   Y R
H O   T   O P M F   R   H C H T   W   P E
O A   H   S O P O   T   C H W E       H S
U C K R C H E E M I O O M P A H P A H I R
L C A O L F G N I S U O H H G U O R O C O
I R T U O M U H L G H N I M I H C O H S H
S C A G F H O R H W T O O T H B R U S H A
H T E H C A H C S R O R B E H E M O T H R
```

BEHEMOTH
CHOREOGRAPHERS
DISHCLOTH
FISHHOOK
FORTHWITH
GHOULISH
HAND-TO-MOUTH
HICCOUGH
HIEROGLYPHICS

HO CHI MINH
HOGWASH
HOLOGRAPH
HOOKAH
HOPSCOTCH
HORSERADISH
OOMPAH-PAH
PHARAOH
PHNOM PENH

PSYCHOPATH
RORSCHACH
ROUGHHOUSING
THORNBUSH
THOUGH
THROUGH
TOOTHBRUSH
UH-OH
WHOOSH

Answer on page 255

Smell It Like It Is

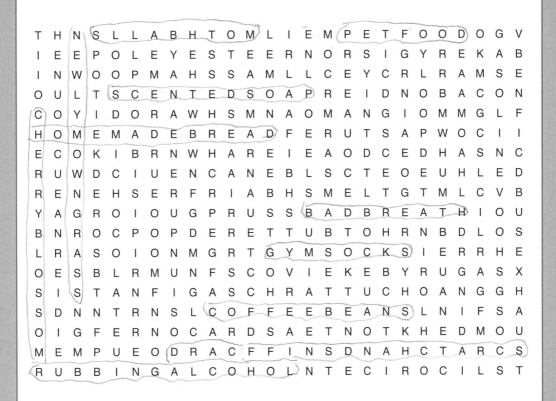

```
T H N S L L A B H T O M L I E M P E T F O O D O G V
I E E P O L E Y E S T E E R N O R S I G Y R E K A B
I N W O O P M A H S S A M L L C E Y C R L R A M S E
O U L T S C E N T E D S O A P R E I D N O B A C O N
C O Y I D O R A W H S M N A O M A N G I O M M G L F
H O M E M A D E B R E A D F E R U T S A P W O C I I
E C O K I B R N W H A R E I E A O D C E D H A S N C
R U W D C I U E N C A N E B L S C T E O E U H L E D
R E N E H S E R F R I A B H S M E L T G T M L C V B
Y A G R O I O U G P R U S S B A D B R E A T H I O U
B N R O C P O P D E R E T T U B T O H R N B D L O S
L R A S O I O N M G R T G Y M S O C K S I E R R H E
O E S B L R M U N F S C O V I E K E B Y R U G A S X
S I S T A N F I G A S C H R A T T U C H O A N G G H
S D N N T R N S L C O F F E E B E A N S L N I F S A
O I G F E R N O C A R D S A E T N O T K H E D M O U
M E M P U E O D R A C F F I N S D N A H C T A R C S
R U B B I N G A L C O H O L N T E C I R O C I L S T
```

AIR FRESHENER
BACON
BAD BREATH
BAKERY
BARN
BURNING RUBBER
BUS EXHAUST
CHERRY BLOSSOM
CHLORINATED POOL
CHOCOLATE
CIGAR
COFFEE BEANS
COW PASTURE
FISH MARKET
FRESH LAUNDRY

GARBAGE DUMP
GARLIC
GASOLINE
GYM SOCKS
HOMEMADE BREAD
HOT BUTTERED
  POPCORN
INCENSE
LEATHER
LEMON
LICORICE
LIMBURGER CHEESE
MINT
MOTHBALLS
NEWLY MOWN GRASS

ORANGE
PERFUME
PET FOOD
PINE FOREST
ROTTEN EGGS
RUBBING
  ALCOHOL
SALOON
SCENTED SOAP
SCRATCH-AND-SNIFF
  CARD
SEA AIR
SEWER
SHAMPOO
SKUNK

Answer on page 255

Tennis, Anyone?

Shaped like a tennis racket, the grid below contain words and phrases about tennis.

```
            K A D I N
          W I N N E R S
        N O A D H C T A M
      W W H H N O Y I Y C E
    T Y E L L A O U E U S K L
    D R O P S H O T B H O O E
U O F U C L K D G R L B R N T
F T O L O L C R G E S E T S O
O O O U P C A H S A M S S T N
W N T I A S B Y T K D H D T S
G A F T S E N A N E W E N N E
A N A M S E N I L R I E U V R
M I U N I S D S P L M L O C V
E A L E N I L E S A B L R Y E
  E T P G R T I N O L O G H
  N I O S M L R C E E O Y P
    R S H V U E Y E D M O
      U O O E A N S O I
        T O P S P I N
        E           T
        N R       N S
          O       E
          L C     T
          A H     J
          N A     U
          D M     D
          G P     G
          A I     E
          R O     O
          R N     T
          O H     I
          S N     G
```

ACES
AD IN
ALLEY
BACKHAND
BALL BOY
BASELINE
CHAMPION
CLAY
COURT
DEUCE
DINK
DOUBLES
DROP SHOT
FOOT FAULT
FOREHAND
GAME
GRASS
GROUND STROKE
LINESMAN
LOBS
LONG
LOVE
MATCH
NET JUDGE
ON SERVE
PASSING SHOT
POINT
RACKET
RETURN
ROLAND GARROS
SETS
SLICE
SMASH
TIE-BREAKER
TOPSPIN
TOURNAMENT
U.S. OPEN
VOLLEY
WIMBLEDON
WINNERS

Answer on page 256

What A Beast!

The grid below is filled with words and phrases that contain the names of animals. To determine those entries, fill in the blanks surrounding the listed animals by using the crossword-style clues next to them. When properly completed, the list will appear in alphabetical order. That list can be found in full on page 68.

```
T  V  H  E  J  E  D  S  E  S  W  R  A  T  H  S  H  A  R  E  S  I  R
E  I  T  O  E  A  L  E  A  V  E  I  T  T  O  B  E  A  V  E  R  T  C
A  D  K  T  E  M  Y  A  Y  E  S  R  O  H  W  A  S  E  S  D  Y  I  O
C  E  A  I  N  O  I  L  E  D  N  A  D  H  O  T  D  O  G  B  R  N  M
T  O  G  I  P  S  I  I  E  E  I  S  N  S  P  H  E  S  R  H  E  A  M
G  T  P  S  N  L  T  N  H  N  P  E  A  A  G  I  R  R  T  S  T  E  A
E  A  A  T  R  T  E  G  S  R  O  T  M  F  B  N  E  E  I  O  T  A  N
R  P  T  E  D  U  R  W  E  R  E  U  G  O  W  G  H  G  L  I  O  C  D
H  E  G  D  E  K  R  A  H  S  L  O  O  P  B  S  N  I  S  W  L  L  E
T  I  T  I  D  N  D  X  V  E  G  K  R  U  G  U  A  C  A  M  O  L  E
T  I  S  T  R  E  H  E  T  E  W  S  F  M  P  I  L  L  A  A  N  B  R
E  X  C  L  A  M  A  T  I  O  N  P  O  I  N  T  W  L  F  N  M  R  O
M  A  N  G  E  C  I  M  R  A  T  O  R  T  X  O  F  L  E  A  T  S  D
O  C  L  T  B  O  S  M  R  W  I  L  U  L  C  I  A  M  L  T  O  E  S
L  E  E  C  R  O  W  N  J  E  W  E  L  S  Y  L  F  F  I  T  S  R  R
```

MULE Talisman
BAT____ ____ Swimwear
BEAR___ Having chin hair
____WORM Bibliophage
_OWL__ Tenpins player
BULL__ Revolver ammo
_ANT__ Horse's gait
_____DEER Seize for military purposes
CROW_ _____ Royal British gems
_____LION Yellow weed
__CLAM____ _____ Punctuation mark
LAMB Served on fire

FOX ____ Ballroom dance
FROG___ Navy diver
GOAT__ Chin growth
_____MOLE Avocado dip
___-BEE_ Passé celebrity
___ DOG Frankfurter
___RAVEN___ Type of hospital hook-up
JAY ____ Late-night host
_____ __ __ BEAVER Old TV show
OTTER Keno's cousin
____ SHARK Hustler
___HORSE Carpenter's frame for cutting wood

_CAT___ Disperse
COW Show displeasure
SEAL___ ___ Material once used to secure envelopes
HARE Fair portions
__GN U_ Enroll
_PIG__ Faucet
_____-EAGLE Sprawled
____FLY Rigidly
TIGER ____ Orange flower
TOAD_____ Mushroom
_____APE Use a home camera
RAT Deep anger

Answer on page 256

Up In The Air

The blimp-shaped grip below contains items that are seen in the air or sky.

```
            W K C O C E L T T U H S
        A I R P L A N E N A M R E P U S K H E
      W F L Y I N G F I S H N R I T C U O R M E S   H D S
    T O O O P L N R E D I C T A I I R N S G R O C K E T R T E
  H E W B E A O U T H G I E L S S A T N A S H E W L R E A A I
N O O M N T N S E G E E M F S T I S H T G P A T I E D T G
S H U E I B L S E K A L F W O N S K I K E E L C I I R L O
H D S O A P B U B B L E S O D O D Y K T P F O O L S E I N
  F U L R A N E Y Y F M S R O R E W E I C P N G M T A S F
  L O C U S T E S N O O L L A B R I A T O H O J A V E L I N
    L T B E N B I P N T G R P I I E G E K H C R T I Y S C
      C O M O P S M L E H A T T R E L E Y U P S
        H C T I W G N I D I R M O O R B
            L R I N T H N
            B E F A I R G
```

AIRPLANE	FRISBEE	RAINBOW
BLIMP	GLIDERS	RAINDROPS
BROOM-RIDING WITCH	HELICOPTER	ROCKET
CANNONBALL	HONEYBEE	SANTA'S SLEIGH
CLOUDS	HOT-AIR BALLOONS	SEA GULL
CONFETTI	JAVELIN	SHUTTLECOCK
DRAGONFLY	KITE	SKYWRITING
DUMBO	LOCUST	SMOKE
EAGLE	MOON	SNOWFLAKES
FIREWORKS	MOTH	SOAP BUBBLES
FLARE	PEGASUS	STARS
FLYING FISH	PETER PAN	SUPERMAN

Answer on page 257

Think Big

```
S O I Y D F T H U N E A O C C A S I O N F G O
V M T N I A T N U O M M E R N M E N T O A I S
S I I B P I I G C I E A T N E M E V O R P M I
C L N L P V O U H T N Z G H W T O T G I I V E
I H E R E L T S E R W O M U S O B Y O P H U E
P C C R R L V E E O R N Y I Y A R T A H S L I
M T S O N G E Y S P O U D N L C O L I S E U M
Y E W A N N T P E I T E A L A I A S D A S B E
L R C A S T L E H T A I L O G C I G G C I E T
O T N O E P I D U A G I L H E T D U O T U A I
K S E N L C O N V E N T I O N C E N T E R P T
L A W A A A Y A E E E T Z V E S S E A R C R E
Y A N T H E H B M N I N D G K A E R B R A Y P
O S E U W H C E A V T E O G E F R R A E G L P
T B E D L A N O I T A N G D F O T O H S R D A
```

AMAZON
APPETITE
BAND
BREAK
CASTLE
CHEESE
CITY
COLISEUM
CONTINENT
CONVENTION
  CENTER
CRUISE SHIP
DEAL
DESERT

DIPPER
ELEPHANT
FEET
FOOTBALL
  LINEMEN
GODZILLA
GOLIATH
GRAND CANYON
HEART
IDEA
IMPROVEMENT
LEAGUES
MOUNTAIN
NAME

NATIONAL DEBT
OCCASION
OCEAN
OLYMPICS
PALACE
PLANS
PORTION
SHOT
SMILE
STRETCH LIMO
SUMO WRESTLER
UNIVERSE
WHALE
WORLD CUP

Answer on page 257

Gridlock And Key

In the lock-shaped grid below, every item in the word list contains either the letters LOCK or KEY in consecutive order. When these letters appear in the grid, they have been replaced by a 🔒 or 🔑 respectively. So that's the 🔑 to solving. Good 🔒!

```
              🔑  I    🔒
           P  I  R  G    🔑
        🔒  F  E  H  A  E  D
        S  M  W  A  T  L  R
     H  M  H              E  A  🔒
     A  I  R              🔒  O  M
  H  S  T                 B  E  🔑
  🔑  L  H              🔑  H  D
  E  S  O                 L  N  A
  R  🔑  A                 N  A  D
  S  P  A                 🔒  R  F
  O  A  I                 R  I  G
  🔑  N  D  C  U  C  K  O  O  C  🔒  R  D  E  A  B  O
  A  C  H  I  P  O  F  F  T  H  E  O  L  D  B  🔒  O
  U  L  🔒  L  D  M  I  D  D  🔑  A  D  I  N  C  🔑  S
  O  C  🔑  A  E  B  D  🔑  O  N  H  S  H  U  D  N  H
  🔒  C  L  A  C  I  G  O  L  O  I  B  C  O  R  T  E
  G  D  E  🔒  D  N  A  L  C  T  H  O  🔑  O  N  K  R
  R  T  E  K  🔒  A  O  🔑      E  P  I  H  S  O  C  🔒
  I  R  O  H  M  T  E  🔒      S  D  🔒  C  R  Y  W  H
  D  A  E  M  T  I  R  I      P  T  H  T  🔑  M  L  O
  🔒  E  R  R  O  O  M  I      E  C  S  A  🔑  🔑  E  L
  D  H  R  O  P  N  R  O      A  🔑  D  L  L  N  I  M
  E  Y  Y  A  W  🔒  🔑  T  O  K  R  D  U  I  L  P  E
  J  M  V  D  I  T  H  B  🔑  E  T  U  A  M  R  S  S
  J  O  H  N  M  A  Y  N  A  R  D  🔑  N  E  S  N  N
  O  T  C  U  W  T  T  D  O  R  U  B  E  P  H  E  A
  S  🔑  C  🔒  H  B  🔒  A  D  E  S  T  🔒  I  🔑  🔒  M
  O  V  E  I  E  S  U  O  M  🔑  C  I  M  E  E  G  B
```

A CHIP OFF THE OLD BLOCK
ALICIA KEYS
BIOLOGICAL CLOCK
BLOCKADE
BLOCKHEAD
COMBINATION LOCK
CUCKOO CLOCK
DOOHICKEY
DREADLOCKS
FIELD HOCKEY
GLOCKENSPIEL
GRIDLOCK
HAMMERLOCK
HAWKEYE
HEMLOCK
HOKEY-POKEY
JOCKEY
JOHN MAYNARD KEYNES
KEYBOARD
KEY GRIP
KEY LARGO
KEY LIME PIE
KEYNOTE SPEAKER
KEYSTROKE
KEY TO MY HEART
LANDLOCKED
LATCHKEY CHILD
LOCKER ROOM
LOCKHEED
LOCK HORNS
LOCKSMITH
MALARKEY
MICKEY MOUSE
MONKEY BARS
OKEY-DOKEY
SHERLOCK HOLMES
TURKEY TROT
UNDER LOCK AND KEY
VAPOR LOCK
WHISKEY

Answer on page 258

Don't Touch Me!

```
S I H W N L A C D L O C E H T N I T U O E A S
L L C I W O O P D O N T T O U C H M E R I F T
D U U T S N O D A N T D I S O L A T E D N L A
D N O H H E E D R L E N F I S T D E E D E N
E L T N A W L N I E T H W F W I T H L N E S D
T I F O S O E I S S P C O O A R A G S W P E O
C N O T T L E O C U N A S T E S N S E A E N F
E K T I N F A J R L O T E U W I E O C R N O F
N E U E R L D S E C S T N H S H T I L D D Y I
N D O S O N T I T E H A O S E E O G U H E B S
O R I O D C O D E R N N N N E R M C D T N F H
C T F D I S T I N C T U O W I M E T E I T F H
S E A W A Y F R O M I T A L L I R A D W C O H
I D E R E T S E U Q E S O T H T E C U T O F F
D D I S T A N T E N O L A E B O T T N A W I R
```

ALOOF
APART
AWAY FROM IT ALL
CUT OFF
DISCONNECTED
DISCRETE
DISJOINED
DISTANT
DISTINCT
"DON'T TOUCH ME!"

HERMIT
INDEPENDENT
ISOLATED
"I WANT TO BE ALONE"
LONE WOLF
OFF BY ONESELF
ON ONE'S OWN
OUT IN THE COLD
OUT OF TOUCH
RECLUSE

REMOTE
SECLUDED
SEQUESTERED
SHUT OFF
SINGLE
STANDOFFISH
UNATTACHED
UNLINKED
WITHDRAWN
WITH NO TIES

Answer on page 258

Hair Apparent

Shaped like a bouffant hairdo, the grid below contains references to hair and hairstyles.

```
                  H A I R D O
                O N T U C W E R C C
              I T N S C L A O K S E I O K
            B A R B E R S H O P A N A C L S
          G B U D A Y H E A H A I E I D A O R
          S B A D H A I R D A Y S L P L L A R
        M U L O N N N T D Y N H W T O S A O E S
        A P T W D G B E A E C O R N R O W S C S
      T R O S D H O S U V J C T L T I E N O E K G
      O C N R I U A T A S O D Y O B E G A P D O S
      P E Y O F E N W O L B D N I W D R S K I I F
      K L T F T O T                 R E G O N U W
      N O A R D N                   P H U G P T
      O N I E E O                   U C C H S P
      T A L N S R                   M O H A W K
        I A C G I                   P I X I E
      N T M H H O G                 A F T R E L H
    S D R A S T S N                 I F D L P E B H
    P E E U A W N I K               C B U I I N R T O
    P L R L D I A L A               O B R U N E T T E
      B A Y Y S R R G               M O E A E N E T
      T I N T L U O                 B E E H I V E
      M T O S C                     R R O W D
```

AUBURN
BAD HAIR DAY
BANGS
BARBER SHOP
BEEHIVE
BLEACHED
 BLONDE
BOUFFANT
BRAID
BRUNETTE
BRUSH
COIFFURE
COLORS
COMB
CONK

CORNROWS
COWLICK
CREW CUT
CURLING IRON
DREADLOCKS
DYE JOB
FRENCH TWIST
HAIRDO
HENNA
MARCEL
MOHAWK
PAGEBOY
PERMANENT
 WAVE
PIXIE

PLAIT
PONYTAIL
RECEDING
 HAIRLINE
SALON
SNARLS
STREAK
STYLED
TEASED
TINT
TOPKNOT
UPSWEEP
WASH-AND-DRY
WIDOW'S PEAK
WINDBLOWN

Answer on page 259

On A Roll

The grid below contains things that roll or can be rolled.

```
L R B E L L Y D A N C E R S B E L L Y N O C O
K I E N G L C O U D T T U O P N H O E A A N T
R B T D L H E O F U I T C U L A R W E I L I U
E O C O N U O U I L R C D N N L S O S T S C M
L A D N T U G U R N E Y E D O P A S D A E H B
L T P E I T H G I B S F M I A T O W W I S S L
O S E T R H E T A S H O P P I N G C A R T K E
R I D A L E R L E G W I E K E U T H E Y M A W
M N I L C A L Y S E E R S Y O T L L U P B T E
A A I P C A E L R T Y P I S T S C H A I R E E
E S R F S R R S O K I P P I I T J W U T S B D
T T L B U T K T A R E E W H E E L B A R R O W
S O P O L S R Y O L T A B O R C A N L V U A I
G R Y N G E A A L O N S G C H U K R C G E R H
I M R O C K S I N A N A V A L A N C H E L D L
```

ACROBAT
BELLY DANCER'S
  BELLY
BOATS IN A STORM
BOCCE BALL
CAISSON
CLAY
COINS
DICE
DOLLY
DOUGH
GOLF CART
GURNEY

HAND MOWER
HEADS
KAYAK
LUGGAGE
MARBLES
NEWSPAPER
PLATEN
PULL TOY
ROCKS IN AN
  AVALANCHE
ROLLAWAY BED
SHOPPING CART
SKATEBOARD

STEAMROLLER
STROLLER
STUNT PLANE
TANK
TEACART
THUNDER
TIRES
TUMBLEWEED
TYPIST'S
  CHAIR
WAVE
WHEELBARROW
YOUR EYES

Answer on page 259

What's On TV

Shaped like a TV set, the grid below contains references to television watching.

```
          C                           G
        O                           O
      U                           O
    C                         D
  H                     R
P                 E
  O             C
    T         E
      A     P
R E W A S T R O P E R T E K R A M K C O T S S
D I E C N G M H V T I E O L P G S T O A O M C
G N I K O O C O B O A K E C A B A P M E B R R
S F V S V O L R N M O C A N I W E M M L L L E
I R R I O U O O U E R R H O P R I M E T I M E
N D E E M A S T D R T E G A M A R D R S D S N
W S P E D T P I A O O R A D N N O E C S H S I
T E Y C R O V O O L A U T L I N N S I T C O M
M G A O N C I N P P K N N F I E E R A O N T W
U S P T I O S F H E H S I D E T I L L E T A S
T S A S H T H Y E T R V H G O N Y B S B V W L
E P U I N E T W O R K A N O G A S T U N E I N
E M A R G O R P E R U T A N W N A C V N K S L
```

ANTENNA	LIVE	RERUNS
BIOGRAPHY	MOVIES	SATELLITE DISH
BROADCAST	MUSIC VIDEO	SCI-FI
CABLE	MUTE	SCREEN
CARTOONS	NATURE	SITCOM
CHANNELS	PROGRAM	SOAP OPERA
COMMERCIALS	NETWORK	SPORTS
COOKING	NEWS	STOCK MARKET
COUCH POTATO	ON TAPE	REPORTS
DRAMA	PAY-PER-VIEW	TALK SHOW
GAME SHOW	PRIME TIME	TUNE IN
GOOD	REALITY TV	VOLUME
RECEPTION	REMOTE	WEATHER

Answer on page 260

Black Hole #2

In this puzzle, the letters in the center of the grid are missing. It's up to you to write them in by figuring out which words in the list are missing some of their letters in the grid. When you've completed the puzzle, the missing letters will spell out one quote while the uncircled letters, as usual, will reveal another quote plus the source and author of both quotes. (Note: A few of the items in the word list relate to the theme.)

```
L K H S U R B T N I A P E O X P P C
L A T N O Z I R O H E B I E E R R R
I N R E N A C E N I G R A N S O T H
E G D O R I A N G R A Y G C W O N A
P A M T M E E V R N T U E S K F R D
Y R R O N M E G E I I V F E N R S N
T O I O V T ▦ ▦ ▦ ▦ ▦ ▦ D O M E U A
P O H N I N ▦ ▦ ▦ ▦ ▦ ▦ D E I A R B
M C A R C H ▦ ▦ ▦ ▦ ▦ ▦ I I S D T S
J O U S T I ▦ ▦ ▦ ▦ ▦ ▦ L L E N T U
N U A K O E ▦ ▦ ▦ ▦ ▦ ▦ S F L R O H
O R M T R S ▦ ▦ ▦ ▦ ▦ ▦ B R E A K L
I T H E I S P G L T M L A Y L P G A
T A H D A Y W T B I E E N D U E R E
A T S E N R A E D E N I Z E N S M D
X E R R L E L A S F T A D O N B Y I
I A O S A L O M E S U A C A N R W N
F I L D Y N O I T A M A F E D E E A
```

"AN IDEAL HUSBAND"
ARCHERY
BACKRUB
CROW'S FEET
DEFAMATION
DENIZENS
DORIAN GRAY
EARNEST
EXCELLENT
FAR EAST
FIXATION
HERITAGE

HORIZONTAL
IMMORAL
INSIST
JOUSTING
KANGAROO COURT
MADE-UP
MODERN
MOMENTUM
"NO DICE!"
NONGREASY
OTHELLO
PAINTBRUSH

PENGUINS
PORTRAIT
POTBELLY
PRINCIPAL
PROOFREAD
"SALOME"
SCENARIO
STATION BREAK
TAG TEAM
TIME ZONE
VICTORIAN
VILLAGE

Answer on page 260

It's A Shore Thing

The seashell-shaped grid below contains references to a day at the beach.

```
                    B  W  F  H  S  H  E
                 P  U  B  L  I  C  B  E  A  C  H
              N  Y  R  A  O  O  C  N  A  U  A  U  S  W  E
           L  E  N  Y  A  S  T  A  O  B  B  M  S  S  A  B  H
        D  O  O  W  T  F  I  R  D  C  R  B  A  A  H  T  E  U  L
     L  S  W  A  O  N  T  H  I  E  L  R  A  U  N  D  E  R  T  O  W
     E  L  T  S  A  C  D  N  A  S  E  S  H  L  D  A  R  L  O  B  Y
     R  C  I  E  A  S  I  D  R  L  V  E  B  Y  A  O  W  L  L  U  G
     H  U  D  M  O  K  E  R  L  S  O  H  O  A  L  R  I  A  E  S  T
        S  E  H  I  A  W  A  T  C  H  T  H  E  S  U  N  S  E  T
           I  B  D  W  T  O  B  T  S  H  W  H  E  K  G  S  Y
              F  A  Y  S  B  R  R  L  P  A  E  E  S  S  G
                 R  R  A  F  T  J  E  R  V  T  E  A  G
                    A  A  R  S  E  K  E  E  H  L  U
                       T  U  L  T  R  E  Z  G  B
                          S  L  S  O  L  N  E
                             S  K  N  U  N
                                I  S  U
                                   D
```

BASK	FLOAT	SHOVEL
"BAYWATCH"	GULL	SLEEP
BIKINI	JET SKI	SNORKEL
BLANKET	LOW TIDE	STARFISH
BOATS	PUBLIC BEACH	SUNGLASSES
BUOY	RADIO	SURFBOARD
BURN	RAFT	SWIM
CABANA	SANDALS	UMBRELLA
CONCH	SANDCASTLE	UNDERTOW
CORAL	SEA BREEZE	WATCH THE SUNSET
DRIFTWOOD	SEASHELLS	WATER WINGS
DUNE BUGGY	"SHARK!"	WAVE

Answer on page 261

We're In The Money

Shaped like a dollar sign, the grid below contains references to money and finance.

```
        B S P       M I S
        V A E       U G E
        Y V N       N O X
    T T D P S E I S K C U B A G E M O N
  O M U N T U C N H G R S H T M U O S N E
  Y I T U E K R G E C O U N T E R F E I T
  D L B F E V O S K L A B P S S O T P M
  E L F L     L B E     I B T
  O I O R     T O L     R O O
  H O E G     R N S     U R C
  D N A R     C D E     L R K
  S A T O F S A F E D E P O S I T B O X
  H I G H F I N A N C E E W M Y L W L I T
  F R K N A B Y G G I P R I M E R A T E R
    E E J F R O Z E N A S S E T S L I U E
        U S E     O T A     L I R A
        S S P     N L O     E N M S
        P G U     A E A     T U S U
        A E R     L I S     P B T R
    D O L L A R L T P O C K E T M O N E Y
  E G N A H C E S O O L H C D A E I O N D
  E Q U I T Y A R T O N E U W H M G A V E
    T O B U B D U Y A M C B A S N Y G T
        I B O     K W U
        M L H     S A I
        E E L     N S G
```

BANKRUPT	LOAN	RIAL
BORROW	LOOSE CHANGE	RUBLE
"CAN YOU SPARE A	MEGABUCKS	RUPEE
DIME?"	MILLIONAIRE	SAFE-DEPOSIT
C-NOTE	MOOLA	BOX
COUNTERFEIT	NEST EGG	SAVINGS BOND
DEBT	NICKEL	SAWBUCK
DOLLAR	PAY STUB	SHEKEL
"E PLURIBUS UNUM"	PERSONAL	SOLVENT
EQUITY	CHECKS	STOCKS
EURO	PESO	T-BILL
FROZEN ASSETS	PIGGY BANK	TAXES
FUND	POCKET MONEY	TREASURY
GOLD	PRIME RATE	U.S. MINT
HIGH FINANCE	PURSE	WALLET
LIRA	RAND	WAMPUM

Answer on page 261

Cover Letter

```
Y S O F A N M A I L E S U I D
M I S S I V E N O N S V T N W
U N N O I T A D N E M M O C R
N C I T A B E B N E C A U L E
A E S D O T P I R C S T S O P
N R E T Y C S O U W E A N S I
S E T O N U O Y K N A H T I S
W L T W B T O P S A L Y Y N T
E Y S H O M C E Y T E L T G L
R H F O L L O W U P D I H B E
E Y N M G Y N O U N W W G E R
D R I I T E D B O R I E I S C
L E T T E R O F I N T E N T A
U N C M S E L T Y O H U R R C
M O V A S S E R D D A E E E E
A I G Y P S N O R T K C V G R
I T S C O S C M O I I M O A T
L A N O S R E P E P S T H R I
B T N N I M S L I N S R E D F
O S G C O T O E B S A P A S I
X Y F E I T N Z G U L E R E E
Y O U R S T R U L Y O A L D D
S I G N A T U R E R E D N E S
```

ADDRESS
BEST REGARDS
BUSINESS
CERTIFIED
COMMENDATION
CONDOLENCES
COPY
DATE
DEAR SIR
DOUBLE-SPACED
EPISTLE
FAN MAIL
FOLLOW-UP

FONDLY
IN A BOTTLE
IN CLOSING
LETTER OF
 INTENT
LOVE
MAILBOX
MEMO
MISSIVE
OVERNIGHT
PERSONAL
POSTSCRIPT
RECIPIENT

REPLY
SEALED WITH A
 KISS
SENDER
SIGNATURE
SINCERELY
STATIONERY
THANK-YOU NOTE
TO WHOM IT MAY
 CONCERN
UNANSWERED
WRITE SOON
YOURS TRULY

Answer on page 262

The house-shaped grid below contains the names of common around-the-house/ everyday activities. The hidden message contains two quotes: the first unattributed, the second by American journalist Don Marquis.

```
                    R R
                V N E E
              T V S S A R E G O T O O F F I C E R P
            H U H T T D N E I R F A H T I W H C N U L
          C D A     O N F F N D T E E F F O C K N I R D
        T D V E     O E T O U N M S L L I B Y A P P L M O
      A R E R O B W W W A S H D I S H E S H A R O T O N Y I
    W O H S A C T E G S T U C A N D F P U T O H D M F F O R T
    A O T S G H E D K P E L Z Z U P E V L O S A E N P L Y O A
    T A K E O U T T R A S H E M O H E V I R D N F T U I E N G
    E R T R       P M T A       D O A M O       Y A O C R
    R U R D       E O W T       K P R H O       D M L L G
    P C R T       R A S S       I T P M I       I P N O A
    L E T E       W I H N       D F O N U       T U D T D
    A I E G       S O T A       S H L E C U A R T K O H F
    N W A L W O M K E W E R C   S R O O D K C O L C P E I
    T N G U S T A K E N A P K   P W O I S T H A Y I E S S
    S E I R E C O R G Y U B T   E K A B E S W R V P D A Y
```

BAKE	GO TO OFFICE	SHOP
BUY GROCERIES	HAVE DINNER	SHOWER
COOK	IRON CLOTHES	SLEEP
DO LAUNDRY	LOCK DOORS	SOLVE PUZZLE
DRINK COFFEE	LUNCH WITH A	TAKE NAP
DRIVE HOME	FRIEND	TAKE OUT
DUST	MAKE BED	TRASH
EAT SNACK	MOW LAWN	TIDY UP
FEED KIDS	PAY BILLS	VACUUM
FLOSS	PHONE MOM	WALK DOG
GET CASH	PICK UP MAIL	WASH DISHES
GET DRESSED	READ NEWSPAPER	WATCH TV
GET UP	REST	WATER PLANTS
GO ONLINE	SHAVE	WORK

Answer on page 262

At The Pharmacy

```
V R X S S T A P U R Y S H G U O C N Y D S F O
A R F T Y H E L R A S T I N N S P O R D E Y E
P I L L B O T T L E S S I W O R D F H O N R R
O E C O U I T P G G S K G M N O S E S P R A Y
R E C T S M O N U A S C A U I O A P R P E S C
I P A I N R E L I E V E R S R T I C R H I P T
Z G M O I Z P D L O R N I I I D A N T A C I D
E A E N O R S O I C A R E N P C I P T R I S L
R U R L A E M D E C O N G E S T A N T M C P A
F Z A E O R M R I X I P I N A G I I N A E O X
N E F O R P U B I B A N D A G E S O G C B N A
R P I E D T A I Y D E M E R D L O C N I A G T
E A L G N I R O L O C R I A H N T S T S G E I
O D M E M A C O S M E T I C S N I M A T I V V
K S D I A P E R S L I O H T A B E A D R U G E
```

ANTACID	DRUGS	MOLESKIN
ASPIRIN	EARPLUGS	NOSE SPRAY
BANDAGES	EYE DROPS	OINTMENT
BATH OILS	FLU MEDICINE	PAIN RELIEVERS
CAMERA FILM	GAUZE PADS	PHARMACIST
CANDY	HAIR COLORING	PILL BOTTLES
COLD REMEDY	HEATING PAD	PRESCRIPTIONS
COSMETICS	IBUPROFEN	SOAP
COUGH SYRUP	ICE BAG	SPONGE
DECONGESTANT	LAXATIVE	TOYS
DENTURE CREAM	LOTION	VAPORIZER
DIAPERS	LOZENGES	VITAMINS

Answer on page 263

Wordy Gurdy

A Wordy Gurdy is a two-word rhyming phrase such as SMALL BALL or OCEAN MOTION. We've hidden 32 such rhymes in the grid, but first you'll have to discover them by using the clues below. The number after each definition gives the number of syllables in each word, and the rhymes are in alphabetical order. Should you need it, the complete list can be found on page 68.

```
J A G G E R S D A G G E R S M X A E K E M P Y
P L F E T P T E P R B E E T T A E R U O O R G
T E I R I V E D S E H C T E K S S E H C T E F
R M E N E Y L E R S E S O T O X Z R P E W N Y
Y G P R L E O A U I R J Y L A A N O Z D O E Q
I I D H F I T R N L A P P L W T I O S B U N
N E R E F E R E N C E P R E F E R E N C E C C
G A R A Y E A A A E E E E D E P C O I E R T L
S I W T H A N R G E T S D R S K W W N I T E A
P I N S G B T E N T E G D E A U T S O M A K W
Y E U U N B A S Y V E R Y A S R J E W L O I L
I R S I E O A C D A N E D Y N E L L A F L L A
N O I T A C I D N I N O I T A C I D N I V E W
G O U E C T O M A M A I T N A R E H E Y M E Y
C G R A Y D A Y R D I M S E O F E S O H C M E
```

1. Everyone collapses (1)
2. Lousy commercial (1)
3. Picked enemies (1)
4. Bear hand statute (1)
5. Loved hearing organ (1)
6. Looks at a reward (1)
7. Gets quick drawings (2)
8. Gratis hot beverage (1)
9. Obtain volleyball court separator (1)
10. Gloomy 24 hours (1)
11. Warm up connected hotel rooms (1)
12. Yours truly fibs (1)
13. Singer Mick's knives (2)
14. Retain an army car (1)
15. Cyclist Armstrong's waltzes (2)
16. Servant didn't go (1)
17. Unused billiard stick (1)
18. Zero winter flakes (1)
19. Atop "ugly duckling" (1)
20. Jury member dread (1)
21. Lovely urban center (2)
22. Hive leader's Levi's (1)
23. Scarce twosome (1)
24. One's choice of a dictionary, e.g. (3)
25. Whirl a needle's cousin (1)
26. Highest-ranking policeman, for short (1)
27. Attempting activity of agent 007 (2)
28. One who hurries a theater seater (2)
29. Sign that points to the clearing of one's name (4)
30. Band instrument made of candle material (1)
31. Banana-colored string instrument (2)
32. Animal house personnel (1)

Answer on page 263

Give Me A Ring

Shaped like an engagement ring, the grid below contains things with rings.

```
E O G H C T A M G N I X O B R T H H
N R A R C H E R Y T A R G E T K
C O L L A R P E O M I W L D I M
  O H L F O O A C D N E N N Y
  M O P T C P O E N C A G I R
    M I E L I E M A A E S B
    N S T L S P R A L I I T
      T R E E B M A G E F
      O I B M T N Y H I T
      A N O R O C H E L O C S
    M S S A                 O U I A
    L U H                   L S A
  C I C                     D E N
  R J R                     R C R
  L U I                     A E U
  O G C                     O O T
  O G F                     B D A
  L L O                     T O S
    E A L                 W R R
    R V E I             D D A F
      H A N D G R E N A D E D
      I N B U T H T A B N
        G R A I N G
```

ARCHERY TARGET
AUDI LOGO
BATHTUB
BELL
BINDER
BOXING MATCH
BRIDE
CHARM BRACELET
CIRCUS
COLLAR

CORONA
DARTBOARDS
EARS
FIANCÉE
FRODO
GROOM
GYMNAST
HALO
HAND GRENADE
JUGGLER

KING
MAGICIAN
NAVEL
OLYMPIC FLAG
OPERA HOUSE
PISTONS
POPE
SATURN
TELEPHONE
TREE

Answer on page 264

In The Papers

```
E D I T O R I A L S C N E A H
P O L P E O E N B O C N B E O
O N E P A S E H R R I I G P R
A D R T E N T R T L I A M H O
E S A P I R E R D A P D I O S
N M U L O C S A O T E D G M C
C F Y O T L E O N P R W U E O
L B R I H H I O N O E S T D P
A I O D L A R T S A A R S E E
S N E N N F A E I W L S D L R
S P A P D A U E R C E S A I E
I P T H E A T E R S S A S V S
F U A N R N I S E M T O E E T
I Z B R O O B L S E A N L R A
E Z L T H I O O Y W T B A Y U
D L O F E H T W O L E B S E R
S E I F A S E I I S E N A E A
K R D E L A D S D T E V V H N
O E S A T F T N P E A I A T T
O H M O H I U S A O E N V R S
B U S I N E S S D W R T B O T
A Y O G R P I S S O G T A N M
E T S T O C K Q U O T E S L S
```

ARTS	FASHION	POLITICS
BELOW THE FOLD	FRONT PAGE	PUZZLE
BOOKS	GOSSIP	REAL ESTATE
BRIDGE	HEADLINE	REPORTS
BUSINESS	HEALTH	RESTAURANTS
BYLINE	HOME	REVIEWS
CLASSIFIEDS	DELIVERY	SALES ADS
COLUMN	HOROSCOPE	SPORTS
COMICS	LATE EDITION	STOCK
CORRECTIONS	MOVIES	QUOTES
CRIME	NEWSSTAND	TABLOIDS
DAILY	OBITUARIES	THEATER
EDITORIALS	OP-ED	TRAVEL
EVENT LISTINGS	PERSONALS	WEATHER

Answer on page 264

Solar Eclipse

It's a bright idea to consider the title when searching the sun-shaped grid below.

```
                              E
                           W  N  H
         K                    E  I  S                          N
             C  T  E       N  T  H  T  H          E  M  Y
             B  E  A  M    O  A  S  E  O       N  D  S  I
             M  S  D  N  M  I  D  E  R  S  T  A  N  D  I  N  G
                T  E  H  L  E  E  S  U  E  T  S  T  D  B  N
                   G  F  L  O  W  E  R  H  E  D  E  A  U
                   D  B  R  N  T  O  G  T  R  O  K  Y  M
                N  R  U  B  E  I  O  I  B  O  F  E  N  S  G  I  A
          T  N  E  R  F  S  D  F  L  O  O  T  D  A  N  C  E  K  I  D
          C  L  H  S  I  T  P  A  S  U  E  H  N  T  Y  O  H  S  C  R  E  E  N
          U  T  E  A  O  V  A  L  L  E  Y  I  D  A  H  O  T  C  N  O  U
                Y  A  H  L  E  D  S  S  E  F  A  E  K  O  R  T  S
                   L  V  S  T  Y  H  I  F  T  S  P  L  R
                   A  S  R  P  D  G  A  O  F  S  O  E  A
                   R  R  E  O  E  M  L  R  E  H  T  A  B  M  I
             D  O  E  R  G  R  F  A  N  D  A  S  T  U  L  R  D
             A  T  C  L       I  S  L  I  U       N  W  O  D
             S  H  U       S  S  E  R  D       N  B  C
          L                 E  E  O                       K
                            S  C  S
                            K
```

ASUNDER	SUNDAY SCHOOL	SUNROOF
"GESUNDHEIT!"	SUN DECK	SUNSCREEN
HOT FUDGE SUNDAE	SUNDIAL	"SUNSET BOULEVARD"
MISUNDERSTANDING	SUNDOWN	SUNSHADE
RIDE OFF INTO THE	SUNDRESS	SUNSHINE
SUNSET	SUNFLOWER	SUN SPOT
SUNBAKED	SUNGLASSES	SUNSTROKE
SUNBATHER	SUNKEN TREASURE	SUNTAN LOTION
SUNBEAM	SUNLAMPS	SUN VALLEY, IDAHO
SUNBLOCK	SUNLIGHT	SUN YAT-SEN
SUNBURN	SUNNY SIDE OF THE	"THE SUN ALSO
SUNBURST	STREET	RISES"
SUNDANCE KID	SUN PORCH	TSUNAMI

Answer on page 265

Picture Perfect

```
S O M E P W Y T R E P O R P L A N O S R E P E
P I E D P I P E R O E E L A O L K E N O E W P
N P P S A K R W P R N E I L L I P P E P P E
P I E P L A T E E A M O B N L O O O R Y P R T
I P C D A S R A S P A H S T O L I P M L A P E
P A O P A P P R E P N P I P P S R P O E C L R
I R I L A L L T A A E Y P O R E E S P N S L P
C K E C A Y P R P P N A A T S T A Y T P Y I R
K P K N P E C U A U T P K S G E L C P O E M I
P L T T E E R S S P P U I P K E H H T O R N
O A A V L P O R K H R R Y P C I G O A P N D C
C C E P A T E N T P E N D I N G T L M I I H I
K E O E N P I N K I S R R P A N T O H E E T P
E S P E T E R P A N S P S G N O P G N I P R L
T P I A N O P L A Y E R E P O O P Y T R A P E
```

PAINT POT
PALM PILOT
PARCEL POST
PARK PLACE
PARTY POOPER
PATENT PENDING
PAY PHONE
PEACH PIT
PEA PLANT
PEDAL PUSHERS
PEER PRESSURE

PEN PAL
PEP PILL
PERMANENT PRESS
PERSONAL
 PROPERTY
PETER PAN
PETER PRINCIPLE
PET PEEVE
PIANO PLAYER
PICKPOCKET
PIED PIPER

PIE PLATE
PIKES PEAK
PING-PONG
PLAYPEN
POLO PONY
POMPOM
POP PSYCHOLOGY
POT PIE
POWER PACK
PRICKLY PEAR
PUSHPIN

Answer on page 265

Changing Direction

Shaped like a light bulb, the grid below contains things that change or are changed.

```
            S I F D L I K M
          S N E D N I M R U O Y S
        M A R A D D R E S S E S K O
        L S P E T P E I D E O P C L
    P E Y R O P U C L D U O J O B S
    N L T I S E A T S U L T I L E I
    H K A N E L Y I C H D L I N A B
    A L U C K N G O D E F E A T L E
    I E C E E H A N U I N L H U T H
    R N Y I G S S E L R Y I B C O A
    S S U N R C A T T T T T I S V
    T T N T H M E N U U H U D U E I
    Y D O O H R O B H G I E N A O O
    L B O A I O U T I C H F A E N R
    E L G T E N A L S N I A R T N D
    S Y R O T S I H F O E S R U O C
        P Y A S H O P O I U H M I H
          E D G E H T O T E I N A
            E S E H J O A Y O N
              D T T T B V C N
              H S L A O E E N
                Y A G Y L E
                F E O S E C
                  H N V R
                  M O O D
                  A S I M
                  C E C H
                  T R E A
                  N I S G
                    T E
```

ADDRESSES
ATTITUDE
BEHAVIOR
BOYS' VOICES
CHANNELS
CLOTHES
[THE] COURSE OF HISTORY
DIAPERS
DIET
DIRECTION
ELEVATION
FASHION
HAIRSTYLES
HEALTH
JOBS
LANES
LIGHT BULB
LOCKS
LUCK
MENU
MONEY
MOOD
MUSICAL KEYS
NEIGHBORHOOD
OIL FILTER
OPINIONS
PLACES
PLANS
PRINCE INTO A TOAD
ROUTINE
SCHEDULE
SCHOOLS
SEATS
SHEETS
SHOES
SPEEDS
TIRES
TRAINS
YOUR MIND
YOUR TUNE

Answer on page 266

Things You Make

The hidden message is made up of two quotes: the first is a New England saying; the second is from a speech by a U.S. diplomat.

```
F  U  S  F  E  Y  I  Y  T  U  P  D  F  W  C  E  S  A  P  E  A  C  E
I  R  U  I  A  E  W  A  V  E  S  T  I  G  O  O  D  S  A  L  A  R  Y
R  S  O  U  P  N  T  D  M  A  G  K  R  F  F  E  N  I  T  T  A  A  D
S  F  O  O  L  O  F  Y  O  U  R  S  E  L  F  O  E  T  F  R  W  N  E
T  O  O  R  A  M  E  M  A  D  A  N  O  W  E  E  I  D  A  A  I  T  S
M  H  M  L  Y  O  N  U  R  M  D  T  T  D  E  H  R  E  T  C  C  M  R
O  O  O  E  F  A  O  E  N  S  E  N  S  E  W  A  F  E  H  K  T  E  O
V  V  O  O  O  M  N  A  M  K  N  N  E  C  W  S  G  N  N  S  O  M  W
E  I  B  R  R  N  I  E  S  T  U  E  D  I  B  K  E  S  U  C  X  E  S
G  A  E  K  I  M  E  R  R  Y  T  E  N  S  C  I  S  D  O  E  E  S  R
N  N  L  D  O  T  L  H  T  S  R  G  U  I  T  H  G  I  L  F  S  U  E
L  L  I  H  E  L  O  M  A  F  O  T  U  O  N  I  A  T  N  U  O  M  T
L  U  E  V  A  L  H  H  L  P  F  Q  Y  N  M  A  K  E  I  T  A  E  T
I  N  V  Y  I  T  H  I  P  O  P  C  O  R  N  N  G  P  E  M  A  H  A
W  E  E  L  E  L  B  U  O  R  T  Y  O  U  R  B  E  D  P  M  E  S  M
```

AMENDS
A PLAY FOR
BELIEVE
[THE] BIG TIME
COFFEE
CONTACT
[A] DECISION
[A] DETOUR
[A] DIFFERENCE
DINNER
[A] DRAWING
ENDS MEET
[AN] EXCUSE
[A] FACE
[A] FIRE
[THE] FIRST MOVE

[A] FLIGHT
[A] FOOL OF
   YOURSELF
[A] FORTUNE
FRIENDS
[A] FUSS
[A] GOOD
   SALARY
[THE] GRADE
HASTE
[A] HOLE-IN-ONE
[A] LIVING
LOVE
MATTERS WORSE
MERRY
MONEY

[A] MOUNTAIN OUT OF
   A MOLEHILL
MY DAY
PEACE
PLANS
POPCORN
[A] QUICK GETAWAY
ROOM
SENSE
SOMEONE HAPPY
[THE] TEAM
TRACKS
TROUBLE
WAVES
[A] WILL
YOUR BED

Answer on page 266

Road Signs

Shaped like a stop sign, the grid below contains inscriptions on signs commonly seen on U.S. streets and highways.

```
          W H I Y L E Y D
        P N O P A S S I N G
        O C R I V W I N E G I G
      T S I A S C H O O L Z O N E
    S W A F S I G G N T D H A I T S
  A I I D F A L L I N G R O C K S T T
E N G Y E A A S R H D E T O U R S A F T
Y L N O S R A C T D T H E S A A M E E L
O C A A T T E W N E H W Y R E P P I L S
I L L O T Y A P O D E N N O W O M K E O
S T A B U A S G A I R P O R T N R I G N
E A H S S W E S N V W O H U L O D B R E
P D E R N O T H G I R O N I W R O U E D
O F A R T W H A F D X T A T L C B U M P
  H D I A T E U V E M D A E N L T B O
    N E X T E X I T O N E M I L E N
      U T L S T H I E S W P A S E
        A R L E O M A D C R E W
        W O N R U T U O N A
          W R O N G W A Y
```

AIRPORT	NEXT EXIT ONE MILE	SCHOOL ZONE
BUMP	NO PARKING	SIGNAL AHEAD
CARS ONLY	NO PASSING	SLIPPERY WHEN WET
DETOUR	NO RIGHT ON RED	SLOW
DIVIDED HIGHWAY	NO U-TURN	STEEP HILL
FALLING ROCKS	ONE-WAY	STOP
FUEL	PAY TOLL	TWO-WAY TRAFFIC
MEN AT WORK	PED XING	WRONG WAY
MERGE LEFT	REST AREA	YIELD

Answer on page 267

Black Hole #3

In this puzzle, the letters in the center of the grid are missing. It's up to you to write them in by figuring out which words in the list are missing some of their letters in the grid. When you've completed the puzzle, the missing letters will spell out a humorous question. (You may consider whether any of the items on the list answer it.) The uncircled letters, as usual, will reveal another quote that relates to the theme.

```
E I N T E L E V I S I O N R V E N T
Z I I R E N G I S P A P E X R A Y S
N S T E N G A M C U A H U O M R B S
O I H T N A T I O M S P N L E O F E
R W B S S C I T S A L P E T L E R R
B A R A P I I N W N S A T R T E N P
W D O O M A ░ ░ ░ ░ ░ L T Z A Y G
I T T T E R ░ ░ ░ ░ ░ E R I R A N
N I O L R I ░ ░ ░ ░ ░ K P A D S I
D L M S D T ░ ░ ░ ░ ░ H M E M E T
M A C H I N ░ ░ ░ ░ ░ I O R E N N
I O I B I R ░ ░ ░ ░ ░ O U T S A I
L A R H I N O A S L S A R Y O R L R
L U T C U S M T E D T S H O E E P P
S O C L L O E H E W S U I M M S R M
N A E T O E S S E O R R A N I S I A
L S L L Y O V U B R I C K S G N A E
E L E V A T O R S K E D S R E S A L
```

AIRPLANES
BATHS
BATTERY
BEER
BLESSINGS
BRICKS
BRONZE
CAMERA
CD-ROMS
CRUSADER
DISHWASHER
DOMES
ELECTRIC
  MOTOR

ELEVATORS
FIELDWORK
LASERS
LOOM
MACHINES
MAGNETS
MARIONETTE
NOTHING
PAPER
PASTE
PLASTICS
PRINTING
  PRESS
PULLEY

PYRAMIDS
READOUTS
SIRLOIN
SPUMANTE
TELEVISION
THAWS
THINKPAD
TOASTER
TWIST TIE
VELCRO
WALTZ
WHEEL
WINDMILLS
X-RAYS

Answer on page 267

Word-Search Puzzles 47

Holiday Highlights

Shaped like a Christmas tree, the grid below contains words and phrases associated with Christmas.

```
                        R
                     E     L  T
                  H     M  E  O  B
               S     W  M  G  N  H  O
            A     E  O  R  N  T  S  D  W
         D     E  C  O  R  A  T  I  O  N  S
               R     E  O  P  Y
            E     R  C  U  I     P  P
         D     W  K  C  S  A  R  I  G
      N     R  I  E  R  A  A  E  T  N  X
   O     R  N  A  M  E  N  T  S  R  M  G  A
D     S  G  G  I  F  C  I  N  E  Z  T  I  L  B
         E     N  S  I  N
      R     S  A  N  T  T  E
   U     E  N  D  R  L  S  I  X
      D     L  T  E  T  E  O  S  T  A  I
   O     L  A  E  W  A  B  R  Y  S  R  T  V
L     C  H  R  I  S  T  M  A  S  E  V  E  H  E
P  R  I  G  S  E  V  L  E  C  H  I  M  N  E  Y  H
H  G  I  E  L  S  T  S  I  C  A  N  D  Y  C  A  N  E  Z
                     E
                     D
                     E
```

ANGEL	DANCER	RUDOLPH
BLITZEN	DASHER	SANTA
BOWS	DECEMBER	SLEIGH
CANDY CANE	DECORATIONS	STOCKING
CAROL	DONDER	TINSEL
CHIMNEY	ELVES	TREE
CHRISTMAS EVE	ORNAMENTS	VIXEN
COMET	PRANCER	WRAPPING
CUPID	PRESENTS	WREATH
	REINDEER	

Answer on page 268

As Good As Cold

Shaped like an ice cube, the grid below contains things that are or may be cold.

```
        I G E W T S H O U L D E R
        T R U G O Y N E Z O R F A D
        R E R N U N G N G N Y M N O N
        J F E S S L S S F R E E Z E R I
        A R A E A Y N A S C C A R A T C W
        C I D C C O M H A Y N T S E R E V E
        K G I T S     P   T   L   H   B   R
        F E N E O     S N A E C O A T S E F A
        R R G N D P A R N T A C S I W R R F
        O A U L E     C C O U H K B W G G O F
        S T N E M T R A P A D E T A E H N U
        T O D H I     E V W E R R T U R A T S
        I R Y C W S K A T I N G R I N K T I
        C A V E     I N A T N E O R C D S O
          I I H A R D F A C T S O A M R N
          C L   I D T O M C E O L L A A
          L I Q U I D N I T R O G E N
          E L C I S P O P D S L I Y
```

ANTARCTICA
CAVE
DEEP SPACE
DOG'S NOSE
EVEREST
FREEZER
FRONT
FROZEN YOGURT
FUSION
GLACIER
HARD FACTS

ICEBERG
ICICLE
IGLOO
JACK FROST
LIQUID NITROGEN
MEAT LOCKER
OCEAN
POPSICLE
READING
REFRIGERATOR
SHOULDER

SIBERIA
SKATING RINK
SNOW
SWEAT
TRAIL
TUNDRA
UNHEATED
 APARTMENT
UNSYMPATHETIC MAN
WIND
WINTERS

Answer on page 268

The Play's The Thing

```
L A S R A E H E R S S E R D S E P L S W C A S T H
E N E Y R O U D O P I S P H C A L T I K E U S U H
E E N I T A M P O E N A L N E R A E T G H D E O Y
R T O H S I N R K P T Y A O N G Y U M U H I T Y S
A S T A E S D O O G E M Y T E B W T H E A T E R E
E I C N H K T E L U R N B N R C R S L I I I T G
P B A L C O N Y N O M E I N Y D I R E C T O R N T
S B E A R C A D F A I L L N U S G F K M B N I W G
E R B E O T E R H E S Y L T G H H E F R U A I O N
K C O T S R E M M U S I C A L N T K O O T T Y T O
A U U T S P D N R D I E D R D S U A T R X A S F N
H D W T C R H O P R O P S E A L D M U T Y O A O O
S E U C A A H U R E N S A Y I W I C B N G R B T C
Y D E M O C H E T O N Y A W A R D B L E C E N U M
Y I A R A N D R E W L L O Y D W E B B E R R E O N
```

ACT ONE	COSTUMES	ORCHESTRA
ACTORS	CUES	OUT-OF-TOWN
AD LIB	CURTAIN	TRYOUT
ANDREW LLOYD	DIRECTOR	PERFORMANCE
WEBBER	DRAMA	PLAYBILL
ASIDE	DRESS REHEARSAL	PLAYWRIGHT
AUDITION	FARCE	PROPS
BACKDROPS	GOOD SEATS	SCENERY
BALCONY	HOT TICKET	SHAKESPEARE
BOX OFFICE	INTERMISSION	STAGE
BROADWAY	LIGHTING	SUMMER STOCK
CAST	MATINEE	THEATER
CHORUS LINE	MUSICAL	TONY AWARD
COMEDY	OPENING NUMBER	UNDERSTUDY

Answer on page 269

You Wanna Pisa Me?

Shaped like the Leaning Tower of Pisa, the grid below contains references to Italy.

```
        N W H
      E I A A A T G
    N A N C T R E H
    I T A L I A N E
    E N M A I T O O
  O P U M Z O T A N
  H I O I Z R O T V
  S R F M I A R F Y
  E F I I P S I A
  U O V C U E A S
A A R E H E A I H
F L O R E N C E I
Y A O T L E S L O
A C I D A A K E N
T S V E N I C E A
I A G M G O S B
V L A E E P G I
D E R M I L A N Y
U C O I A O A L E
O L M G P M I T G
M O A I R C F Z O
O D N A I Z E R D
M U E S S O L O C
A O M P I E L M
W A P P A R G I E
T I I I E H A N T
S S N R A R M I E
A S S E I Z A R G
```

ALPS
AMORE
ARMANI
ARNO
CAESAR
COLOSSEUM
DOGE
"[LA] DOLCE VITA"
DUOMO
ETNA
FASHION
FELLINI
FLORENCE
GELATO
GENOA
GONDOLA
GRAPPA
GRAZIE
ITALIAN
LA SCALA
MICHELANGELO
MILAN
OPERA
PISA
PIZZA
POMPEII
ROMAN EMPIRE
ROME
SAN MARCO
SICILY
TRATTORIA
TREVI FOUNTAIN
UFFIZI
VATICAN
VENICE
WINE

Answer on page 269

Op-Position

The word list contains 24 pairs of opposites. One item in each pair appears in the arrow pointing left; the other appears in the arrow pointing right. It's up to you to figure out which goes in which position. For good measure, the word OPPOSITES connects the two arrows and appears exactly in the center of the grid.

```
                    C              I
                  O L            F O
                N P U          A E P
              F E O M          G S X I
            I T G S S          I E S P A
          D E K A N Y          L P T T E S
        E A R T T A T          E P O O R N T
      N N R E C I T N          L W H S M O S A
    T G Y D I B V D A          G Y T L I U G I R
  E R I N N O C E N T          N O A Y O T N M V V
  I Y O D S I T O H F R        I C N I N O I S Y E I
  U U S P E L G V W R E O      S I R F E F R V U T C N
Q H T N E I C N A I O P P O S I T E S U N W A V E R I N G
  H U E N R C I C S G L M      S O L M G O T P A N E O
    A G N R Y O O H A Y I      D F A F N R P Z T E R
      E E A U G L Y E R O      E P C L I K Y R E G
        M M W T F W H A O      H T T V Z S O H E
          P I U N A N T P      T N I C E V H O
            L O K S A N E      O A V T E N U
              O H H S E E      L S E R R S
                Y Y T D A      C M T E F
                  E Y E E      W E D A
                    D S Y      D O A
                      S W      M E
                      D        O
```

OPPOSITES

ACTIVE	SEDENTARY	GUILTY	INNOCENT
AGILE	CLUMSY	HUGE	TINY
ANCIENT	MODERN	IMPORTANT	TRIVIAL
ANGRY	CALM	INTROVERTED	OUTGOING
BOILING	FREEZING	MARRIED	SINGLE
CHEAP	EXPENSIVE	NASTY	NICE
CLOTHED	NAKED	NEGATIVE	POSITIVE
CONFIDENT	UNSURE	NOISY	QUIET
CRAZY	SANE	PLAYFUL	SERIOUS
EMPLOYED	OUT OF WORK	POOR	RICH
GIVING	SELFISH	SATED	STARVING
GORGEOUS	UGLY	UNWAVERING	WISHY-WASHY

Answer on page 270

People Who Work Outdoors

```
R R W O R F K F O R E S T R A N G E R I N G O
U E T D R A O O I R T S D I A M R E T E M C R
T T P E A R A L G R U B T A C E O N O F V O L
E N S P T M E P E N E B E O G P U R E T L O U
L I T U A E Y E T O U F W G G H N B F I U R M
A A T D R R T E R O E B I I N G D I A R B E B
V P S O R V T W W E O R E G N E S S E M R P E
G E H I E L E S E Y F C O O H H K N L L I E R
N S E N L C T Y E K C O J D E T E I N T C E J
I U D G A F E E O E S F O R E D E O C R K K A
K O C R H O S N S R I N M R R V P R G A L E C
R H B R W I D M R O T A V A C X E G E C A M K
A A P R O S K I E R N N G R E W R T A L Y A L
P Y T D I T C H D I G G E R A K E I S T E G S
C O N S T R U C T I O N W O R K E R T O R L L
```

BRICKLAYER
CAT BURGLAR
CHIMNEY SWEEP
CONSTRUCTION
 WORKER
COWBOY
DITCH DIGGER
EXCAVATOR
FARMER
FIREFIGHTER
FISHERMAN

FOREST RANGER
GAMEKEEPER
GARDENER
GROUNDSKEEPER
HOUSE PAINTER
JOCKEY
LUMBERJACK
MESSENGER
METER MAID
MOVER
PARKING VALET

PIT CREW
PRO SKIER
RIGGER
ROOFER
SAILOR
SERF
STEVEDORE
STREET VENDOR
SURVEYOR
TRAPPER
WHALER

Answer on p

Word-Search Pu

Honorable Mention

Shaped like a plaque, the grid below contains references to awards, prizes, and honors.

```
      F E L L O W S H I P L K U D O S L
      E T T H M T H I S E B E Y R T O A
      U U R E O C E R T I F I C A T E V
      M L D E O N T Y G B T O N W R K O
      P A L M E D O R M O E D E A L N R
      L S Y M O N A R Y M I O B P U I P
      R N S Y E N L T A N A F O V F G P
      P U L I T Z E R G R O R L M R H A
      U G E W T S A O T A Y H G E I T F
      R E T U H E V P R C C D N B T H O
      P N R H Q A S H E S I P E R I O L
      L O Z A T A I Y E O T T D G B O A
      E Y E I G O L D S T A R L A R D E
      H T O N Y D V P R K T I O P B E S
      E N B O N O E R A T I H G U R O E
      A E N E Z I R P Y B O O B C E C T
      R W H E V I P C T O N R I G S R H
      T T E S U A L P P A F O D N U O R
      E T O P K C A J W H O L C I A W D
        N M E R I T B A D G E G V O N
        Y I T A T L T O N B E O A
          B L U E R I B B O N L
          J O R O T H N N R
            D I P L O M A
            S L E A G
            X C E
```

...ST	GRAMMY	PHI BETA KAPPA KEY
...BBON	GRANT	PLAQUE
...IZE	HONORARY DEGREE	PULITZER
	JACKPOT	PURPLE HEART
	KNIGHTHOOD	ROUND OF
	KUDOS	APPLAUSE
	LOVING CUP	SEAL OF APPROVAL
	MEDAL	SILVER PLATTER
	MERIT BADGE	STANDING OVATION
	MVP AWARD	TITLE
	NOBEL	TONY
	OBIE	TROPHY
...BE	OSCAR	TWENTY-ONE-GUN
	PALME D'OR	SALUTE

Answer on page 271

Take It Like A Man

In the man-shaped grid below, every item in the word list contains the letters MAN in consecutive order. When these letters appear in the grid, they have been replaced by a ♟. We hope you'll ♟AGE just fine.

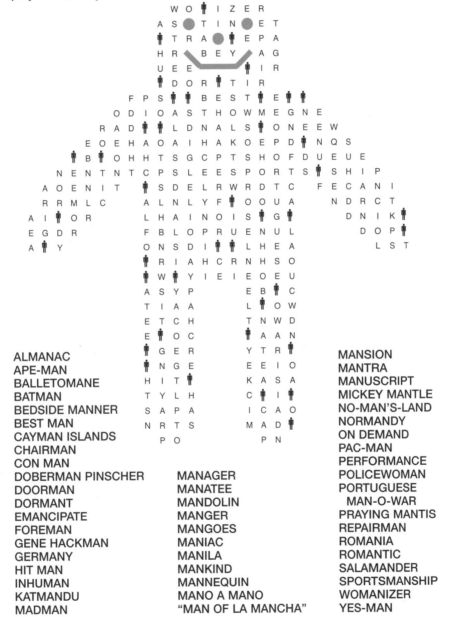

ALMANAC
APE-MAN
BALLETOMANE
BATMAN
BEDSIDE MANNER
BEST MAN
CAYMAN ISLANDS
CHAIRMAN
CON MAN
DOBERMAN PINSCHER
DOORMAN
DORMANT
EMANCIPATE
FOREMAN
GENE HACKMAN
GERMANY
HIT MAN
INHUMAN
KATMANDU
MADMAN

MANAGER
MANATEE
MANDOLIN
MANGER
MANGOES
MANIAC
MANILA
MANKIND
MANNEQUIN
MANO A MANO
"MAN OF LA MANCHA"

MANSION
MANTRA
MANUSCRIPT
MICKEY MANTLE
NO-MAN'S-LAND
NORMANDY
ON DEMAND
PAC-MAN
PERFORMANCE
POLICEWOMAN
PORTUGUESE
 MAN-O-WAR
PRAYING MANTIS
REPAIRMAN
ROMANIA
ROMANTIC
SALAMANDER
SPORTSMANSHIP
WOMANIZER
YES-MAN

Answer on page 271

That Really Hits The Spa

```
I U S T A I H S F M A N I C U R E S Y T O U M
E A N N K R O W P E T S A T O K S E E S E P A
S O U W Y P E I L L I A S T H G I E W T F I L
S A I P P R A M O H T A B D U M C S S R I E D
S B L D A E E M C T H G P E L R R E S E O S S
C Y C I R O U I P T H E I A P U E N O T N E K
I S I N E A A N K E D T A W R B X H A C O B U
B M T C H T C G T I R F H Y O W E R I H U O N
O A S E T R H E C N O I T A T I D E M K A R W
R S I N A L T U H T R T N H E S T E B E E T O
E S L S M M R R O L F I N G X T I E E S R S D
A A O E O E R O P E R S O N A L G R O W T H M
L G H I R V E O R F A C I A L S H R W E A A I
N E O D A E O L O L H O S W E A T S U I T E L
B O D Y A L I G N M E N T L R M S E S S S R S
```

AEROBICS
AROMATHERAPY
BODY
 ALIGNMENT
CARDIO
DIET
EXERCISE
FACIALS
GET FIT
HOLISTIC
INCENSE
LEOTARDS
LIFT WEIGHTS
MANICURES

MASSAGE
MATS
MEDITATION
MUD BATH
NATURE HIKES
PAMPERING
PEDICURE
PERSONAL
 GROWTH
REIKI
RELAX
RESORT
ROBES
ROLFING

SAUNA
SEAWEED WRAP
SHIATSU
SLIM DOWN
STEAM ROOM
STEP WORK
STRETCH
SWEAT SUIT
SWIMMING
TAI CHI
TIGHTS
TONE UP
WHIRLPOOL
YOGA

Answer on page 272

Abbr.-Ations

The list below contains abbreviations for common words and phrases that are hidden in the grid. It's up to you to figure what those spelled-out entries are. Two hints: the numbers in parentheses tell you the number of letters in the words; and the list is in alphabetical order based on the spelled-out versions. If you need help, the complete list can be found on page 68.

```
A F M Y I O E S R U N D E R E T S I G E R L G
H S I E R E U O S A R S N M D O T O M B N I N
N O S R E P T N A T R O P M I Y R E V O L M I
E C T O O C M E C E E H U A A O R V O A I I N
P D E M O C R A T E M A O T P G W P R S A T O
P P R D G N O R T R U O H R E P S E L I M E I
O G U L T R A V I O L E T N S A N E Y O A D T
S S A T U U L S G E O T C A E E M D E O I G I
T T I L Q N S E P C V Y O T G I P N T S U H D
E E H D L N O Y K O R E B O T C O O Q G E O N
X L A G T O K A N O S E N T M C B U W A Z Z O
C E J Y I O N I O A G S R S Q U A R E E T J C
H R N A A E O M C A P A I C O L A R N R R U R
A R N D D B W E K C P M O B I H O M E R U N I
N A M N E I N C O T S P O F L R E H S O A I A
G B N O I T A L U D O M Y C N E U Q E R F O N
E D C M E P S E T U N I M R E P S D R O W R O
```

AC (3,12)	Gen (7)	pkg (7)
aka (4,5,2)	HQ (12)	pd (4)
ASAP (2,4,2,8)	Hz (5)	p/t (4,4)
bbl (6)	HR (4,3)	PX (4,8)
c/o (4,2)	hp (10)	R.N. (10,5)
co (7)	IOU (1,3,3)	rte (5)
Dem (8)	Jr (6)	sq (6)
DQ (10)	KO (8)	tsp (8)
Dr (6)	Ltd (7)	UV (11)
doz (5)	mph (5,3,4)	VIP (4,9,6)
ER (9,4)	Mr (6)	vol (6)
FM (9,10)	Mon (6)	wt (6)
gal (6)	Oct (7)	WPM (5,3,6)
	oz (5)	

Answer on page 272

It's A Mystery To Me!

Shaped like a keyhole, the grid below contains references to mystery and detective stories.

```
            S U S P E C T
          I M O T I V E R D
        H W O W R C I R E I O
      R W A I R O W D T I T M R
      C A S E V T S E M L O H E
      E T F E R E C N A D R G P
      S A R M N T R C A P I L A
      S U A L I U A E S U O L C
      P U M V K S O L V E P N Y
      A N E P A O S E C R E T S
        E D G E D E I I S L E
          V R R V E V N I U
          S I B A A C U G C
          R E C T F G D I R
        T F O E T L T P R E I
        S S E N T I W O N H S
        L Y M V N A M I N E C
      P E N T U I R N S D A E L
      L U S D G R T T O H S N A
      O T O E E D D E N P T E L
    E T H E B U T L E R D I D I T
    C W T I V E L O O R S T O B R
    Y A G A T H A C H R I S T I E
```

AGATHA CHRISTIE	EVIDENCE	SCENE
ALIBI	GUILTY	SECRETS
BREAK-IN	HERCULE POIROT	SLEUTH
CAPER	HOLMES	SOLVE
CASE	"I WAS FRAMED!"	SUE GRAFTON
CLOUSEAU	LEADS	SUSPECT
CLUES	MISSING	"THE BUTLER DID IT"
COLD TRAIL	MOTIVE	TWISTS
CORPSE	MURDER	VICTIM
COVER-UP	PLOT	WEAPON
CRIME	POISON	WHODUNIT
DETECTIVE	PRIVATE EYE	WITNESS

Answer on page 273

Things That Make You Sweat

```
F G H W A W A I T I N G A V E R D I C T H I F
I F N S E B R O W I R I S K Y B E T O S E E P
R W I I E D D M A X E L A N I F B V N T A W U
E I N R C E D T H H J T E O N E T S E R V T B
F S T W S N E I E A S O T V H E S E P F Y S L
I A E E R T A N N I N G B O O T H S A N L S I
G W R R H A D D M G E T E I E T R H L I I E C
H T R C U A L A N A N M D L N Y S O A O F K S
T S O L G N I T T E G S A T H T E T J W T Y P
I H G O L E N W O E T A L G N I E B O R I R E
N S A U N A E I L D S I N T G D H R E H N R A
G F T A C E S F N O R T R O P I C S V H G U K
E O I E R A M T H G I N W E S M B N O I D C I
T P O C A Y B R E V O D E L L U P G N I E B N
A T N E M S S A R R A B M E N H Y M T A N W G
```

AUDIT
AWAITING A VERDICT
BEING LATE
BEING PULLED OVER
  BY A COP
BIG GAME
CURRY
DANCING
DEADLINES
DEBTS
DESERT
DETAILS

EMBARRASSMENT
FEAR
FEVER
FINAL EXAM
FIREFIGHTING
FIRST DATES
GETTING LOST
HEAVY LIFTING
HOT STOVE
HUMIDITY
INTERROGATION
JALAPEÑO

JOB INTERVIEW
MISTAKE
NIGHTMARE
PUBLIC
  SPEAKING
RISKY BET
RUNNING
SAUNA
TANNING
  BOOTHS
TROPICS
WEDDING

Answer on page 273

All Bottled Up

The bottle-shaped grid below contains things found in a bottle.

```
                R S L
                E U I
              Y E N O H
            E K B T S E M
          M U S T A R D E A
          N L O W N A N S T
          D G H E L G W S F
          I T R S O E O A M
          U A L L T N S G T
        O Q L O I I I A E I E
      M L I C O C O V R S T R R
      A P L A N A N E D P I H S
      P E G I D T O G V D S N E
      L A N D Q S E A S I E K C
      E R I T I U S T L S L L U
      S S H A M P O O A I N O A
      Y D S E T H P R M N G I S
      R S A H C E E A I F E D Q
      U D W D O I M D E E N N B
      P Q H H O U U E O C I L B
      T W S E I S F J S T E A M
      G N I S S E R D D A L A S
      E S D N S A E G C N E I N
        A B O E T P H T T L E
```

BBQ SAUCE	HONEY	PILLS
BEER	JUICE	SALAD DRESSING
BLEACH	LIQUOR	SHAMPOO
CATSUP	MAPLE SYRUP	SHIP
COLOGNE	MESSAGE	SHOE POLISH
DISHWASHING LIQUID	MILK	SODA
DISINFECTANT	MOUTHWASH	SUNTAN LOTION
GATORADE	MUSTARD	VINEGAR
GENIE	OLIVE OIL	WATER
GLUE	PERFUME	WINE

Answer on page 274

Making Connections

Help! A gap separates the two sections of the grid! To connect those sections, fill in the gap by writing in letters from the word list that are missing in the grid. When you're done, read those filled-in letters across the gap and you'll find out the name of the connection you've just made.

```
N  A  E  N  A  R  R  E  T  I  D  E  M  W  S  H  O  E  P  O
E  E  N  N  H  U  D  S  O  N  B  A  Y  I  C  O  L  N  E  I
Z  R  L  U  G  O  M  B  N  I  A  P  R  R  E  I  F  A  R  R
T  I  R  S  L  L  A  F  A  R  A  G  A  I  N  U  D  S  S  A
G  O  E  D  N  T  I  E  G  C  I  C  R  Y  M  R  S  F  I  T
N  D  O  R  A  T  H  S  I  T  I  C  A  R  I  B  B  E  A  N
A  E  R  I  E  E  P  F  H  T  R  B  R  A  O  J  E  C  N  O
Y  L  T  T  C  H  I  E  C  C  A  U  T  H  A  M  E  S  G  S
S  A  E  N  O  C  T  R  I  P  H  I  T  R  I  M  O  O  U  P

S  L  S  E  A  T  O  A  E  O  R  I  N  O  C  O  E  Z  F  P
E  A  A  S  I  N  T  S  K  C  I  A  M  N  C  A  S  F  O  R
T  T  E  S  D  E  G  D  A  I  O  T  F  I  E  E  D  R  F  N
A  A  O  S  N  N  M  C  L  O  G  R  T  E  B  L  E  L  A  O
R  M  B  O  I  I  A  S  R  U  R  N  A  U  L  E  R  E  L  A
H  B  A  R  E  N  T  S  S  E  A  N  N  L  S  E  G  N  A  G
P  R  E  P  E  I  N  D  D  L  N  A  G  O  S  E  T  T  S  O
U  B  B  U  I  L  D  T  T  H  D  E  C  A  A  E  N  A  K  L
E  N  I  E  S  T  L  A  W  R  E  N  C  E  S  E  A  W  A  Y
```

ADRIATIC	ERIE	PERSIAN GULF
AEGEAN	EUPHRATES	RED SEA
AMAZON	GANGES	RHINE
ARCTIC	GULF OF ALASKA	RIO DE LA
ARNO	HUDSON BAY	PLATA
ATLANTIC	HURON	RIO GRANDE
BARENTS SEA	INDIAN OCEAN	ROSS SEA
BERING SEA	LAKE MICHIGAN	SEINE
CARIBBEAN	MEDITERRANEAN	ST. LAWRENCE
CORAL SEA	NIAGARA FALLS	SEAWAY
DANUBE	NILE	TAMPA BAY
DNIEPER	ONTARIO	THAMES
ELBE	ORINOCO	TIGRIS
ENGLISH CHANNEL	PACIFIC	YANGTZE

Answer on page 274

Taking A Stand

Shaped like a painting held by an easel, the grid below contains references to the world of art.

```
R F I N G E R P A I N T I N G
O T H O A E I S T M Y L E H R
L I S S C P O R T R A I T E S
O T E E O S N R Y A N E H D A
C L R S U N E V F O H T R I B
R H T S T R R R I S O T H C E
E L C I P A A M F M L A N K S
T R A T C A R T S B A E I A I
A P M A E F O R G E R Y U A M
W I O M N K E T Y I U N G O P
G I N M P L S O R N M T U A R
A V A N T G A R D E I L A N E
T B L S L U T D T O I G G O S
C C I R E M B R A N D T H O S
B H S E P T R M R V U A U T I
W A A V A N G O G H I P R L O
Y G S R H O U N P I C N C P N
D A L I C G A E S A P S C D I
O L S A E O I T N D I I A I S
T L C A N V A S M U C D S T M
        I       L       A
        T       B       S
    E S         L       S E
    X I         O       O P
  L A S T S U P P E R E
    N L         V       E I
  G I           R       L M
  O S           E       I K
  Y                     V
  A                     E
```

ABSTRACT ART
AVANT-GARDE
"[THE] BIRTH OF
   VENUS"
CANVAS
CHAGALL
CHARCOAL
DA VINCI
DADA
DALI
EASEL
FINGER PAINTING
FORGERY
FRESCO
GAUGUIN
GOYA
IMPRESSIONISM
KLEE
"[THE] LAST SUPPER"
LOUVRE
MATISSE
MIRO
"MONA LISA"
MONET
MOULIN ROUGE
MURAL
OILS
PICASSO
PORTRAIT
PRADO
REMBRANDT
RENOIR
"[THE] SCREAM"
SEURAT
SISTINE CHAPEL
SKETCH
SOUP CANS
"[THE] STARRY NIGHT"
VAN GOGH
WATERCOLOR
"WHISTLER'S MOTHER"

Answer on page 275

Taking It Hard

```
K C I R B T Y O F B U E O H S E S R O H A R R
N E S O N E L L O R R E N N I D D L O K E E W
A A N O T L C H I A Y N G A H P A P L M H V A
R E I D D L G U Y S W I H E C N E E M Y O O U
S C A L C U L U S S S M N N N A A A H T C C L
A H B E S B O O K K I A N G U D H C R E D E L
F I R E H Y D R A N T R E B P E O H B L M L E
E I H T E E A D R U O B T I G A H P E E A O H
T S O S F B N T M C E L P D N S I T W T H S
Y H A R M O R A A K I E E N I G H T E A B N E
G O U T M U L H M L I L M I X S S N H I S A L
L F T A B L L A B E S A B C O C O N U T R M T
A O I N E D T T E S L E T H B T A H D R A H R
S D R T U E T E R C N O C K S A M E C A F N U
S E S S E R T T A M E M O S Y O N H E L M E T
```

ACORN
ARMOR
BASEBALL BAT
BONE
BOULDER
BOXING PUNCH
BRASS
 KNUCKLES
BRICK
BULLET
CALCULUS
COCONUT
CONCRETE

DIAMOND
ENAMEL
FACE MASK
FIRE HYDRANT
FRYING PAN
HARD HAT
HELMET
HORSESHOE
LEAD PIPE
MALLET
MANHOLE COVER
MARBLE
NAILS

PEACH PIT
PEARL
SAFETY GLASS
SHIELD
SLEDGEHAMMER
SOME HEADS
SOME
 MATTRESSES
STEEL DOOR
STONE WALL
TURTLE SHELL
WEEK-OLD DINNER
 ROLL

Answer on page 275

Fish Tale

The fish-shaped grid below contains names of fish and ways to prepare or eat them.

```
            I H N
          C S C O A
        T I H C M D H       S D
      F E F I E O F     R T M M                   P E
    D F T I E Y E L L A W M U L L E T         G I I S
  S S A L H H P F O E T H O H S E I L Y     P R N R K E
E T C H I F A U I E A R O N N L E W T Y G R O P I A E S
W I L R I R O N M T L T N A H A N C H O V Y U A T T
T H O E Y H D R I I R L P S P H L L I D E P A C E I U E D
    D S S E S T B H H P E I E O O C T P E R C H L H N N O
T A R T A R S A U C E E A A T M A C K E R E L S     W E O A
    T M A E T S S R N O M L A S B O F               B B
        V T H R               E A I I
          O R I T             A S I
          D N L               H S
            G S
```

Word List

ANCHOVY	HALIBUT	SKATE
BONE	HERRING	SMELT
BONITO	LEMON	SNAPPER
BROIL	MACKEREL	STEAM
CATFISH	MAHIMAHI	SUSHI
CHILEAN SEA BASS	MULLET	TARTAR SAUCE
DEEP-FRY	PERCH	TILAPIA
DILL	PIKE	TROUT
DOVER SOLE	POACH	TUNA
FILLET	PORGY	WALLEYE
FLOUNDER	SALMON	WHITEFISH
GROUPER	SCROD	WHITING

Answer on page 276

Winding Down

Shaped like a stopwatch, the grid below contains references to time.

```
                    Y E A R
                    T T T H
                    I   O
                    U   M                           E
    I                                       
        S T     M E R N I E I S       A D
        R E M I T G G E C G P M R E A A
          M G T L T E V C A M I O C R
          P C A H H E E L R I B E N E
        B U S U E C N R O O D D T C T U
        Y S P L I T S E C O N D S N E H
        A F F O U A U R K A I G T O M S
        N U U R N W A N H T G E A L O I
        D G Y S Y L I E I T H K I G N N
        B I L U L A L S A M T L L A O I
        Y T T N B T O M O R R O W W R S
          L P D T I U P I S L I E S H
          B I I E G G R A D N E L A C
          L A R I L B I K K O O Z
          L D D Y L E T A L E
          R I G H T N O W
```

AGES	EGG TIMER	NEVER
ATOMIC CLOCK	EONS	RIGHT NOW
BIG BEN	HOURGLASS	SOON
BY-AND-BY	IN A WINK	SPLIT-SECOND
CALENDAR	LATELY	SUNDIAL
CENTURY	LITTLE HAND	"TEMPUS FUGIT"
CHRONOMETER	LONG AGO	TIMEPIECES
DAILY	MIDNIGHT	TOMORROW
DECADE	MINUTE	WEEK
DIGITAL WATCH	MONTH	YEAR

Answer on page 276

Photo Finish

Shaped like a camera with a flash, the grid below contains references to cameras and photography.

```
                              T H S T R E
                              P L M H O O O M
                              D T I E I O O U L G
                              E L R D N H G A I L
                              E B U C H S A L F P
                              P T H D H D C O E N
                              S M O O Z N S A O N
                              T R T E B A S K P T
                              N E G A T I V E
                              O R T N E T
                                  T I
                  E                 E O
            S P H                   R P
  S O A U E C E L S R P A Y A Y S P S T P
  P U Y O B A U T E E H S T C A T N O C R
  O T C L A N T D T D T L E P S R N T R O
  T E H O S D N T A A O P H O T O D I H C
  L M E A F I T W C N M M B L H B A A T E
  I U E T F D I G I T A L C A M E R A R S
  G L S W N T A M L I O S E R E H K A I S
  H S E S L I D E P W E X P O S U R E P I
  T I S A P E R T U R E T L I F I O N O N
  V O D E E E D P D E X K A D O K O I D G
  S N S T E D C I T A M A T S N I M A G E
```

APERTURE	IMAGE	PRINT
BATTERY	INSTAMATIC	PROCESSING
BLOW-UP	KODAK	ROLL
CANDID	LENS CAP	"SAY CHEESE!"
CONTACT SHEET	LOUPE	SEPIA
CROP	MATTE	SLIDE
DARKROOM	MINOLTA	"SMILE!"
DIGITAL CAMERA	MODEL	SPEED
DUPLICATES	MUG SHOT	SPOTLIGHT
EMULSION	NEGATIVE	STROBE
EXPOSURE	NIKON	STUDIO
FILM	PHOTO	TINTYPE
FILTER	POINT-AND-SHOOT	TRIPOD
FLASHCUBE	POLAROIDS	VIEWFINDER
FOCUS	POSE	ZOOM

Answer on page 277

End So It Goes ...

```
T T H O E E I N D O F C A L L I T A D A Y A L
H L I T A I N T O V E R T I L L I T S O V E R
A O H I O U A T S I V A L A T S A H R E N A G
T H A N K S F O R C O M I N G Q X P L O L E N
S R L I I N A I G E U N O I S U L C N O C N I
A W T F C I T L N L P R B E T I O A H R K R D
L I E N O G L L A A V P T H A T S A W R A P N
L C E O W G A I R H L E A A R T O E I D P W E
F E L M N S D T G T A E R C I I T O N N U E Y
O D H O P E Y O U H A D F U N N A N D E T A P
L D L R S S S O G O T E M I T G S S U L D K P
K O N E O I I O W T H S E P L T O A P I E P A
S C E V F O N L A S T W O R D I R T E A O O H
B Y E B Y E G G H E F I R U D M S U T T T I O
M R E A L L S W E L L T H A T E N D S W E L L
```

ADIEU	FINALE	[THE] PARTY'S
ADIOS	FINITO	OVER
ALL GONE	HALT	QUITTING TIME
ALL'S WELL THAT	HAPPY ENDING	SO LONG
ENDS WELL	HASTA LA VISTA	STOP
ALOHA	HOPE YOU HAD FUN	TAIL-END
BYE-BYE	IN CONCLUSION ...	THANKS FOR
CALL IT A DAY	IT AIN'T OVER TILL IT'S	COMING
CAPPER	OVER	THAT'S ALL,
CIAO	IT'S CURTAINS	FOLKS
CLOSING	KAPUT	THAT'S A WRAP
DONE	[THE] LAST WORD	TIME TO GO
[TILL THE] FAT LADY	LIGHTS OUT	TOODLE-OO
SINGS	NO MORE	WINDUP

Answer on page 277

Word List

6. MOVIE SEQUELS
NINE MEN OUT ("Eight Men Out")
SIXTH ELEMENT ("The Fifth Element")
SIX EASY PIECES ("Five Easy Pieces")
FORTY-NINE HRS ("48HRS.")
FORTY-THIRD STREET ("42nd Street")
FIVE WEDDINGS AND TWO FUNERALS ("Four Weddings and a Funeral")
FRIDAY THE FOURTEENTH ("Friday the 13th")
MAGNIFICENT EIGHT ("The Magnificent Seven")
NINE AND THREE-QUARTERS WEEKS ("Nine fi Weeks")
TEN TO SIX ("9 to 5")
OCEAN'S TWELVE ("Ocean's Eleven")
TWO-EYED JACKS ("One-Eyed Jacks")
ONE MILLION AND ONE B.C. ("One Million B.C.")
EIGHTH SEAL ("The Seventh Seal")
EIGHT YEAR ITCH ("The Seven Year Itch")
SEVEN DAYS EIGHT NIGHTS ("Six Days Seven Nights")
SEVENTEEN CANDLES ("Sixteen Candles")
SEVENTH SENSE ("The Sixth Sense")
ELEVEN COMMANDMENTS ("The Ten Commandments")
FOURTH MAN ("The Third Man")
FORTY STEPS ("The 39 Steps")
FOUR AMIGOS ("¡Three Amigos!")
FOUR FACES OF EVE ("The Three Faces of Eve")
FOUR MEN AND TWO BABIES ("3 Men and a Baby")
THIRTEEN ANGRY MEN ("12 Angry Men")
ONE O'CLOCK HIGH ("Twelve O'Clock High")
THREE FOR THE ROAD ("Two for the Road")

18. WHAT A BEAST!
AMULET
BATHING SUIT
BEARDED
BOOKWORM
BOWLER
BULLET
CANTER
COMMANDEER
CROWN JEWELS
DANDELION
EXCLAMATION POINT
FLAMBÉ
FOX TROT
FROGMAN
GOATEE
GUACAMOLE
HAS-BEEN
HOT DOG
INTRAVENOUS
JAY LENO
LEAVE IT TO BEAVER
LOTTERY
POOL SHARK
SAWHORSE
SCATTER
SCOWL
SEALING WAX
SHARES
SIGN UP
SPIGOT
SPREAD-EAGLE
STIFFLY
TIGER LILY
TOADSTOOL
VIDEOTAPE
WRATH

32. WORD GURDY
1. ALL FALL
2. BAD AD
3. CHOSE FOES
4. CLAW LAW
5. DEAR EAR
6. EYES PRIZE
7. FETCHES SKETCHES
8. FREE TEA
9. GET NET
10. GRAY DAY
11. HEAT SUITE
12. I LIE
13. JAGGER'S DAGGERS
14. KEEP JEEP
15. LANCE'S DANCES
16. MAID STAYED
17. NEW CUE
18. NO SNOW
19. ON SWAN
20. PEER FEAR
21. PRETTY CITY
22. QUEEN'S JEANS
23. RARE PAIR
24. REFERENCE PREFERENCE
25. SPIN PIN
26. TOP COP
27. TRYING SPYING
28. USHER RUSHER
29. VINDICATION INDICATION
30. WAX SAX
31. YELLOW CELLO
32. ZOO CREW

50. ABBR.-ATIONS
AIR CONDITIONING
ALSO KNOWN AS
AS SOON AS POSSIBLE
BARREL
CARE OF
COMPANY
DEMOCRAT
DISQUALIFY
DOCTOR
DOZEN
EMERGENCY ROOM
FREQUENCY MODULATION
GALLON
GENERAL
HEADQUARTERS
HERTZ
HOME RUN
HORSEPOWER
I OWE YOU
JUNIOR
KNOCKOUT
LIMITED
MILES PER HOUR
MISTER
MONDAY
OCTOBER
OUNCE
PACKAGE
PAID
PART TIME
POST EXCHANGE
REGISTERED NURSE
ROUTE
SQUARE
TEASPOON
ULTRAVIOLET
VERY IMPORTANT PERSON
VOLUME
WEIGHT
WORDS PER MINUTE

Crossword Puzzles

Wedding Traditions

ACROSS
1 Old Roman robe
5 Homeric epic
10 Beer containers
14 Track shape
15 Bart Simpson's mom
16 Tra ___
17 SOMETHING OLD
20 Answers questions in school
21 Fished with a net
22 Paddle
23 Helsinki citizen
24 Affront
28 "Little Man ___" (Jodie Foster film)
29 Tour vehicle
32 SOMETHING NEW
34 Used e-mail

35 ___ one's ways (stubborn)
36 Yes, in Montreal
37 City on the Mohawk River
38 Work on words
39 SOMETHING BORROWED
41 Comic actor Louis
42 Sahara feature
43 Least civil
44 Parrot or sparrow
45 John Macdonald's title
46 Peace Nobelist of 1994
49 In a skill-less way
53 SOMETHING BLUE
56 Gumbo thickener
57 Brittle fragment

58 Jason's ship
59 Fuel source
60 Musical sounds
61 Journey segments

DOWN
1 Youngster
2 Finished
3 Strong air current
4 One of the Baldwins
5 Copy
6 High-tech beam
7 Showy flower
8 In the past
9 Compression increases it
10 Calvin of fashion
11 Merit
12 Sticky stuff

13 Make smooth
18 String instrument
19 Parti Quebecois founder Lévesque
23 Model for novel covers
24 Norwegian playwright
25 Unprosperous
26 French composer Erik
27 College credit
28 Mole-colored
29 Light brown
30 Last of the Mohicans
31 Beginning
33 Tied up
34 Cleat
37 Commandeers

39 Least loquacious
40 Twentysomethings sitcom
42 Ape studier Fossey
44 Soundalike of A sharp
45 Drum in a marching band
46 Individually
47 Deal with fallen leaves
48 Atmosphere
49 "___ Old Cowhand"
50 Greenish blue
51 Early harp
52 B-movie crook
54 Reporter's question
55 Maritime distress signal

Answer on page 278

Color Commentary

ACROSS

1 Each
5 Apt. ad info
8 Goldman, ___ (investment firm)
13 LaMotta, the "Raging Bull"
14 Tinted
16 Guesstimate word
17 Highfalutin manner
18 "All ___" ('30s tune)
19 Effigy, e.g.
20 They're blue
23 Workweek start: Abbr.
24 Adam's madam
25 Smudge on a crossword
27 Outdoors, to a diner
32 Macintosh image
33 It's bellied up to
34 Public uprisings
36 Mr. Kringle
39 Tantrum thrower
41 "Ars gratia ___"
43 Jacob's biblical twin
44 Informal farewell
46 Netanyahu defeated him
48 Cable channel
49 i finishers
51 Gives a pink slip to
53 Salon workers
56 Slithery fish
57 ___ Ramsey ('70s Richard Boone role)
58 They're green
64 PDQ , to Shakespeare
66 Fritzi Ritz, to Nancy
67 Medieval defense
68 Prefix with grade or fit
69 Eliot's "Adam ___"
70 In one's birthday suit
71 Sonora simoleons
72 It may be around a buck
73 "Make it snappy!" initials

DOWN

1 "Stronger than dirt" cleanser
2 Two queens, e.g.
3 Gumbo vegetable
4 Be a noodge
5 Zimbabwe, once
6 Fail to catch
7 Highway hauler
8 Comics soldier, with "The"
9 ___ Dhabi
10 They're red
11 Bookstore section
12 "Funny Girl" composer Jule
15 Take out, editorially
21 Anon's partner
22 Hosp. scanner
26 Like some losers
27 Israel's Eban
28 Cooking fat
29 They're yellow
30 Fortune 500 abbr.
31 Aquatic mammal
35 Kingly address
37 Having one's marbles
38 Phoenix hoopsters
40 Black & Decker item
42 Draft-notice recipient
45 Sound systems
47 Tarot reader
50 Madrid Mrs.
52 Barnard College grad
53 The key of G has one
54 Conical dwelling
55 Clean the poop deck
59 Felt sorry about
60 Within: Prefix
61 Debtors' notes
62 A bit of vocal fanfare
63 Recipe part
65 ___-Magnon

Answer on page 279

Great!

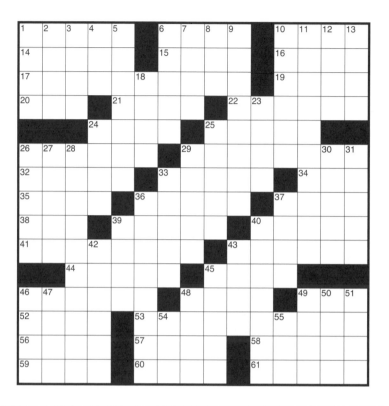

ACROSS

1 "Caution" color
6 "___ Slidin' Away"
10 Kind of hall or drunk
14 "Nervous pudding"
15 "Beloved" author Morrison
16 Pervasive glow
17 Great!
19 Detail
20 Wish undone
21 Homecoming attendee
22 Alcatraz inmate of the '30s
24 Formal order
25 Moll Flanders, e.g.
26 Positive potential
29 Fascinating allure
32 They're sometimes proper
33 Harbor sights
34 Scottish form of John
35 Run easily
36 None too pleased with
37 Meringue-making need
38 Diamonds, to hoods
39 Lets go
40 Shout of pleasure
41 "The Silence of the Lambs," for one
43 He played Ben-Hur and El Cid
44 Mason's private eye
45 "Make the ___ of it"
46 Like jam
48 Bagel shop
49 Toothpaste topper
52 Prunes
53 Great!
56 "Capeesh!"
57 Pequod skipper
58 Auspices
59 Hole numbers?
60 Cross-legged exercises
61 Underground event, briefly

DOWN

1 Half-open
2 Diner's card
3 Color, or off-color
4 Slippery ___
5 Jason of "Max Dugan Returns"
6 Walk of the cock?
7 Impend
8 Public house
9 Business picture for Mrs. Smith?
10 Capitol of Nationalist China
11 Great!
12 Small songbird
13 Tom, Dick, or Harry
18 1986 Nobel Peace Prize winner Wiesel
23 Snobs put them on
24 Beef bourguignon ingredient
25 Oakland team, to fans
26 Not turned on
27 Bowwow
28 Great!
29 Autumnal quaff
30 Myopic Mr.
31 Williams of "Happy Days"
33 Gay city?
36 Luminous band in the night sky
37 "It is the ___, and Juliet is the sun!"
39 Black key, maybe
40 Sammy Davis Jr.'s autobiography
42 Flowers in a record-setting Van Gogh painting
43 Keep in reserve
45 The toast of the opera world?
46 Go gaga
47 Sub ___ (secretly)
48 Bummer
49 Nicolas of "Leaving Las Vegas"
50 "Warts and all"
51 "Hey, over here!"
54 "So that's your game, eh?"
55 "___ the games begin"

Answer on page 281

Giver of Gifts ...

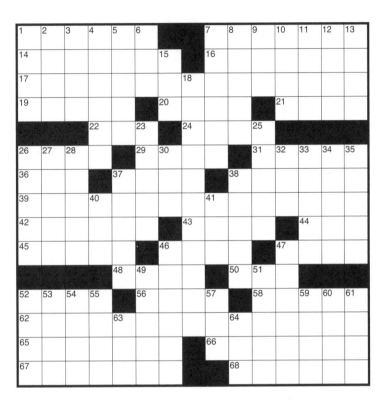

ACROSS

1 Jockey Eddie
7 Quivering dessert
14 Make a boo-boo
16 Either of two continents
17 ... in winter
19 Geographical regions
20 Alphabetize
21 Dispatched
22 Part of AARP
24 Musical silence
26 Aladdin's find
29 Landlord's take
31 Part of REM
36 Past
37 Leaf in a book
38 City with wet streets
39 ... in spring

42 Just know
43 Auctioneer's cry
44 U-turn from SSW
45 It may give you hail
46 Pesky flier
47 Dresses, with "out"
48 43,560 square feet
50 Refueled the body
52 New York City district
56 Defeat
58 Overact
62 ... in autumn
65 Emergency plane transport
66 Practical, as science
67 Hamsters, e.g.
68 Handsome horses

DOWN

1 A in code
2 The sound of Simba
3 "Don't get ___ with me!"
4 B flat equivalent
5 Pee Wee of baseball
6 Beginning of the Lord's Prayer
7 Room at the top
8 Gives off
9 Bandleader Brown
10 Painting and sculpture
11 Game-stopping cry
12 "___ Get It for You Wholesale"
13 Cartoonist Thomas

15 Digital devices: Abbr.
18 Heap of trouble
23 Pamphlet or parcel
25 Fad
26 ___ lazuli
27 Representative
28 "Semper fidelis," for one
30 Inflated self-image
32 Hill dweller
33 Victor Borge's instrument
34 Cake spread
35 Xs out
37 Donna's first name?
38 River of Ghana
40 It's north of Afr.
41 ___ man (unanimously)

46 Oat grains
47 "Indiana Jones and the ___ of Doom"
49 Chin indentation
51 Attract
52 Have top billing
53 Song by Crosby, Stills, Nash & Young
54 Common people, with "the"
55 Eye amorously
57 Health club
59 Tulsa dweller
60 Like the score when the game starts
61 Purposes
63 ___ Tin Tin
64 Good times

Answer on page 283

Seeing Red

ACROSS
1 Navel blockade?
5 Border on
9 Attack in force
14 First word of many tales
15 It's often red in government
16 "My Cousin Vinny" Oscar winner Marisa
17 Brightly coloured birds
20 Disgrace
21 Commerce sci.
22 Inner, as a feeling
23 Written Jewish authority
26 Like the Marx brothers
27 Dorothy's footwear in "The Wizard of Oz"
32 Two-tone cookie
33 Simpson's judge
34 Stationed
38 Hard drive maker
40 Legal taking of property
42 Sappy stuff
43 Neither's partner
44 ___ Saturn (game system)
45 Cultivated shrub
49 Boxed in
52 Elaborately decorated
53 First Latin verb?
54 ___ d'oeuvre
55 Office copy, commonly
60 Prudence, justice, temperance, and fortitude
64 Multiplication word
65 Even-steven
66 Unwritten
67 Thick slices
68 Gorillas
69 Jules Verne's captain

DOWN
1 Poor result
2 Part of a foot
3 Sports org. governing U.S. campuses
4 Contract stipulation
5 Put away
6 Cave dweller
7 Having a bouncy, jazzy beat
8 Amusement park ride container
9 Spider-Man creator Lee
10 ___ up (dress finely)
11 Greek horseshoe?
12 Summer television offering
13 Foggy
18 Tennis do-overs
19 Intersection
24 Landed
25 Dietetic, on grocery shelves
26 One of the Gabors
27 Singer Diana of "The Wiz"
28 1934 Nobel chemist Harold
29 Fuzzy Wuzzy was one
30 Cultural food?
31 Baseball stat.
35 Plaintiff
36 Therefore
37 Cain of "Lois & Clark"
39 GI's mail address
40 Couch potato's place
41 Formerly, in days of yore
43 Designed like a shower mat, perhaps
46 In a minute
47 List of printing mistakes
48 Mister, in Munich
49 Treaties
50 Internet message
51 ___ Jean Baker (Marilyn Monroe)
54 Make like a snake
56 College founded by Henry VI
57 Undiluted
58 Paper quantity
59 1952 Winter Olympics site
61 Society gal
62 Neckline shape
63 Drivers' licences, e.g.

Answer on page 285

All Saints Day

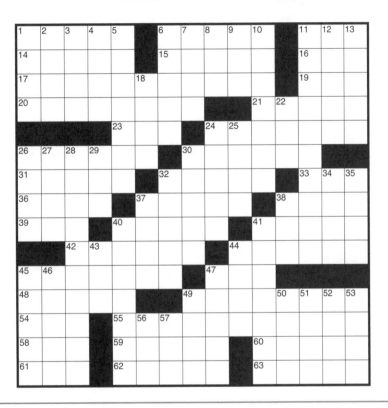

ACROSS

1 Traveled like a tennis lob
6 Vinegary prefix
11 Amtrak stop: Abbr.
14 Beetle Bailey's nemesis, for short
15 Olympic great Comaneci
16 Athenian T
17 Obsessed with the theater
19 A dancer may cut one
20 Certain bike
21 Utter nonsense
23 USNA grad
24 Wintertime auto accessory
26 Not in attendance
30 ( ), informally
31 Whipped, à la Kasparov
32 "Gay" city
33 Newsman Koppel
36 Shah's domain, once
37 '80s–'90s legal drama
38 Fruit cocktail chunk
39 Thieves' place
40 Wolfed down
41 Change lanes erratically
42 Rockies' home
44 Made java
45 Hirer's in-box filler
47 "Welcome" bearer
48 Newsboy's shout
49 Fall off
54 A.P. competitor
55 With a stellar cast
58 "___ blu, dipinto di ..."
59 Heroic tales
60 Evaluated, with "up"
61 90° joint
62 The bad guys
63 Minuscule

DOWN

1 Right-hand man: Abbr.
2 Assign a "PG-13," say
3 ___-Strawberry (Ocean Spray cocktail flavor)
4 Hen fruit
5 Dangerous part of the pool
6 Starts the pot
7 Topps or Fleer collectible
8 Part of a school's web address
9 Recurrent twitch
10 Acorn source
11 Cut from the short loin
12 Brownish gray
13 Boring tool
18 Dropped in the mail
22 Turned tail
24 See-through wrap
25 Scullers
26 In the center of
27 In the altogether
28 Deadlock in negotations, e.g.
29 Nightfall, in verse
30 Not so ruddy
32 Liver spreads
34 Roof overhang
35 Scott in an 1857 decision
37 Take a bath
38 According to
40 All together
41 "In God ___"
43 Where It.'s at
44 War ender
45 See the old classmates
46 Boot out
47 Like Oscar Madison
49 Tiny weight
50 Adams or McClurg
51 Wood-dressing tool
52 "... ___ and not heard"
53 Circular current
56 Give a whipping to
57 Improve, as wine

Answer on page 287

Off to a Rocky Start

ACROSS
1 Drop from above
8 Fervor
15 Freeze on the surface
16 She helped Theseus through the Labyrinth
17 Maiden voyage, perhaps
19 Place for an ace?
20 "Bear of very little brain"
21 Like most colleges today
22 "Politically Incorrect" emcee Bill
24 Miss Boop
25 Twoness
29 Nowhere near
31 Motionless

32 Singer Tori
33 Pan pal?
36 Hiking peril
39 Talese's "___ Neighbor's Wife"
40 Pale as a ghost
41 Soldier's outfit, perhaps
42 Toy with a tail
43 She should get what's coming to her
44 Raved like a raven
47 Critic who's all thumbs?
49 On
50 Copycat
51 "___ above all ..."
55 It'll keep you dry
59 Hot spot
60 Humor

61 Frat party fixture
62 Judges establish it

DOWN
1 Chef's serving
2 Bounce back
3 Whiskered clapper
4 Furnace fuel
5 Madam Adam
6 Simpsons' neighbor ___ Flanders
7 Stanley Cup, e.g.
8 Wide view
9 Sole support?
10 Peppermint Patty, to Marcie
11 It'll hold a cup
12 Knucklehead
13 Opening foray
14 Down and out
18 Tale of ___
22 Lost

23 Swear (to)
24 Perfect game spoiler, for one
25 Move quickly
26 Jazz locale
27 Dilettantish
28 Gershwin's "___ 'Em Eat Cake"
30 Red Baron's plane
32 "Unsafe at ___ Speed"
33 Sweet Betsy's home
34 Soul singer Redding
35 "Guarding ___" (1994 movie)
37 Collie, on the job
38 Cocktail lounge
42 "The Father of Modern Astronomy"

43 Deserving a medal
44 West Indies Indian
45 Observe Yom Kippur
46 Stout sleuth Nero
48 Nectar collector
50 Prince Charles's sister
51 Stranger than fiction?
52 Room between rooms
53 Swenson of "Benson"
54 Goulash
56 Where Mork and Mindy spent their honeymoon
57 Gene material
58 Goes overboard, slangily

Answer on page 289

Ate Times Eight

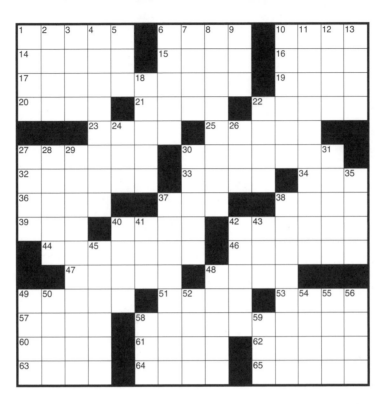

ACROSS

1 Give a tongue-lashing to
6 Org. that defended Thomas Scopes
10 "Anna and the King of ___"
14 Uninvited pool guests
15 Sound from "The Lion King"
16 Bear above the air
17 ATE
19 FDR or JFK
20 Leak
21 Snaky swimmers
22 Vertical, as an anchor cable
23 Fig leaf wearers' former home
25 Intense desires
27 Invalidated, as a check
30 ATE
32 Invalidates, as a marriage
33 Not very much
34 Spot for experiments
36 F-___
37 Female sib
38 Type of ranch
39 Tic-___-toe
40 June honorees
42 Witch-baking girl
44 ATE
46 Go back (to), as a habit
47 "See ya"
48 Circle of angels
49 Overhand tennis stroke
51 "Layla" singer Clapton
53 "___ us a son is given"
57 Try to roll the ball into the hole
58 ATE
60 Away from the wind
61 Bar mitzvah or baptism
62 Take care of
63 Foxx of "Sanford and Son"
64 First grade lesson
65 Sum kind of snake?

DOWN

1 Gives in to gravity
2 Board game that became a movie
3 Look at flirtatiously
4 ATE
5 Ruby or Sandra
6 Eve of "Our Miss Brooks"
7 Hep, as cats
8 Attire for attorneys?
9 Vase in a verse
10 ATE
11 Lacking determination
12 On the Caribbean, e.g.
13 Jim Carrey flick, with "The"
18 Real estate papers
22 Ripened
24 "Runaway" singer Shannon
26 Part of a gene's makeup
27 Sweeping, but not using a broom
28 Available from a keg
29 Used a syringe on
30 Donald Duck's girlfriend
31 "Unsafe at Any Speed" author Ralph
35 It goes to waist?
37 Eve, at first?
38 ATE
40 Hiking trail
41 Have unpaid bills
42 Actress Kelly or singer Slick
43 Concern of the Nat. Council of Churches
45 ATE
48 Walks in the woods, perhaps
49 Practice, to pugilists
50 Its daddy is a donkey
52 Campus mil. group
54 Require
55 London gallery, with "The"
56 Scent
58 Bathing suit top
59 Young men's org.

Answer on page 291

Location, Location, Location!

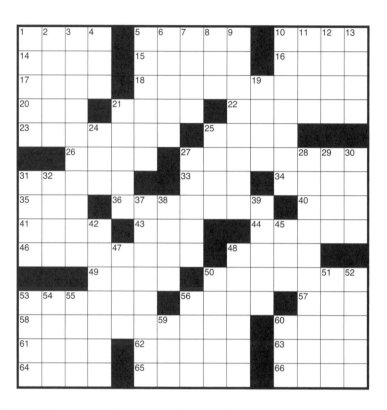

ACROSS
1 Make angry
5 Island of the Blue Grotto
10 Sword handle
14 Region
15 Pacific, for example
16 Opera highlight
17 Nimble
18 Unduly lofty
20 Small colonist
21 Kennedy and Danson
22 Defeats
23 Listens to new evidence, perhaps
25 Spice made of nutmeg covering
26 Poker pot basis
27 Collected
31 Family of African languages
33 Unrefined metal
34 Urgently desperate
35 Mature
36 Corn Belt locale
40 Card game for two
41 It's below TUV on a phone
43 Boxing promoter King
44 Barbecue remnants
46 They make miniatures
48 Move like a butterfly
49 Vietnam neighbor
50 Character in Uncle Remus stories
53 Fall upon
56 Stocking stuffers?
57 Indignation
58 Inconspicuous
60 Not very nice
61 "Woe is me!"
62 Blokes
63 Singing voice
64 "Remember this"
65 Breadmaker's ingredient
66 Churchill successor

DOWN
1 "M*A*S*H" corporal O'Reilly
2 "Goodnight, ___"
3 Like Babe Ruth or Bill Clinton
4 Nibble
5 Stick
6 They turn litmus red
7 Cribbage markers
8 Word of cheer
9 Adds air
10 Yokel
11 Ornamental flower
12 Spiel
13 Auto plates
19 Lomond, for example
21 Ryan O'Neal's daughter
24 Med. specialty
25 Stable parent?
27 Fancy dresses
28 Al Kaline's domain
29 Buffalo's lake
30 Cub Scout groups
31 Period of economic growth
32 Kal-Kan rival
37 Political agenda, maybe
38 Diana, the "blonde bombshell"
39 Stories
42 Backslide
45 Title for Chaplin
47 Hideaway
48 Least encumbered
50 Fastening devices
51 Speak from a soapbox
52 Gas used in strobe lights
53 Actor Thicke
54 Flight student's test
55 Spank
56 Singer Turner
59 Charge
60 Actress Clarke of "Public Enemy"

Answer on page 293

K Rations

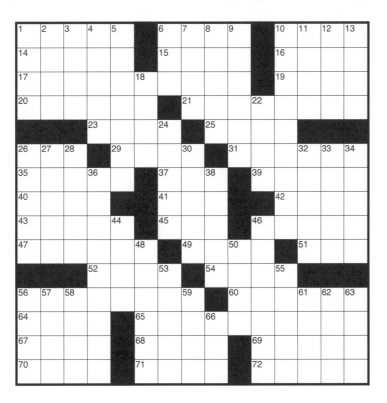

Crossing Safety

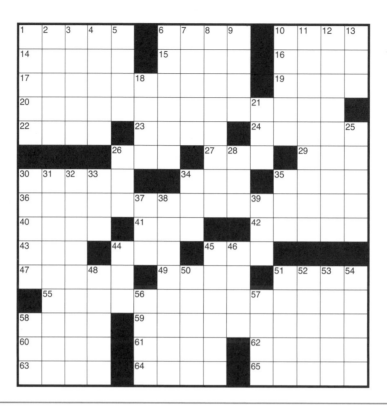

ACROSS

1 King-size kiss
6 "Yeah, right!"
10 She was born free
14 He played Ugarte in "Casablanca"
15 Author Angelou
16 "Serpico" author Peter
17 Where to find Neptune?
19 ___ up (put on some beef)
20 "Go no further!"
22 "Take this"
23 Chihuahua change
24 Name of two Presidents
26 "___ Girls" (1957 Gene Kelly musical)
27 Quiche base
29 "Spring forward" letters
30 Playing marble
34 Fork-in-the-road shape
35 Gymnastics coach Karolyi
36 "Reflect on yourself!"
40 Sicilian simoleons, once
41 What little lambs eat, in song
42 Author who went through Hell
43 Had a bellyful?
44 Like Leroy Brown
45 One who looks at books: Abbr.
47 Kind of blockade
49 Cuba or Aruba
51 Pink-slips
55 "Don't be so pigheaded!"
58 Ruckus
59 Vail vehicle
60 "... ___ open fire" (seasonal lyric)
61 ___ up (in the bag)
62 First name in 1976 gymnastics
63 Soccer legend
64 Buried treasures?
65 Stylishly smooth

DOWN

1 Winter nuisance
2 Three-card game
3 Emotional intensity
4 Parisian pancake
5 Deborah of "The King and I"
6 Some are spitting
7 Darkroom dunks
8 One way to see
9 Bakery bite
10 Stick in the mud
11 Ellie Sattler in "Jurassic Park"
12 Stephen King thriller
13 Set as a price
18 Use a sponge
21 Broom Hilda, e.g.
25 Much more than a glance
26 Hula hoop?
28 Small wonder
30 Detective Pinkerton
31 Proceed independently
32 "Myra Breckinridge" author
33 Tina's ex
34 A question of motive
35 Suntan spoiler
37 Actress Vardalos
38 Microwaveable meal
39 Gilbert & Sullivan's "Princess ___"
44 Short-order order, for short
45 They'll put on a happy face
46 Salon set
48 How two hearts may beat
50 "Uncle Tom's Cabin" penner
51 Scheming bunch
52 In reserve
53 "I'm really serious!"
54 Furtive fellow
56 Standard Oil, once
57 Many millennia
58 "___ Gun" (Cruise film)

Answer on page 278

At's Something Else

ACROSS

1 Time in a classroom
7 S&L assets, maybe
10 Neato, today
14 Amos ___ Stagg, of football fame
15 Not to mention
17 Wickerwork
18 Light musical drama
19 Your spouse's lawyer?
21 Sandra of "A Summer Place"
22 Beer bust delivery
23 Dove utterance
24 Nabokov novel
27 "Giant" writer Ferber
29 Escape, with "away"
31 Hold back
32 Chemical reaction
35 Sheepless shepherdess
37 NCOs getting hugs?
41 Sings "White Christmas" maybe
42 Andretti's auto
43 Astronaut Shepard
44 Grover Washington's instrument
45 Jack, once of HUD
49 Type of school for doctors
50 Seasoning meas.
52 Cries of surprise
55 ___ tai
56 Halt like a streaker?
60 Carrot nutrient
62 Plays possum, for example
63 Simon Legree, e.g.
64 Bring to light, with "out"
65 Prefix with wolf
66 Pro-prohibition
67 Main channel

DOWN

1 Strut like a peacock
2 Pleased as punch
3 Suspicious, as in Hamlet's Denmark
4 Very much a fan of
5 Range in Arkansas
6 "Death Be Not Proud" author
7 Satiate
8 Characterize
9 One subject to a dictator?
10 Type of bargain
11 Serious trouble
12 Animated insect of DreamWorks
13 Leaves beverage
16 Singer Woody's son
20 Provoke
25 Hold, as an opinion
26 Rock band blasters
28 Vacuum tube filler
30 Movie crowd member
31 Fire from a plug
33 Adverb in verse
34 Gov't. lawyers
35 Often flicked pen
36 Smallest bill
37 Con game
38 Perry's creator
39 Auto with a rumble seat
40 S of WASP
44 Data portrayer Brent
46 Settler in a foreign land
47 Bearing
48 Spot that isn't spotless
50 Guy gobblers
51 Gathered intelligence
53 Nicholson role
54 Drove participant
57 Container weight
58 Not, before "a one"
59 "Java" trumpeter Al
60 Nonvulgar swearing
61 "___ Got a Secret"

Answer on page 279

Movie Marathon

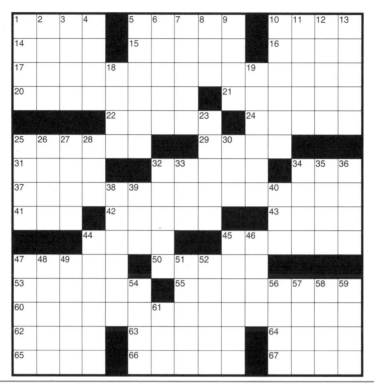

ACROSS
1 Wax-coated cheese
5 Withdraw from office
10 Introduction to physics?
14 Main character of "The Clan of the Cave Bear"
15 Sect that settled in Pennsylvania
16 Tennis call
17 1970 Richard Thomas coming-of-age film
20 Outlaw
21 Class list
22 ___ rarebit
24 Neat? Not!
25 European capital
29 Sees red?
31 Get out
32 Kitchen gadget
34 USO visitors
37 1950 Barry Jones thriller
41 Pub order
42 Usher's walkway
43 Aware of
44 Sword developed in the 19th century
45 Trinket
47 Kind of bull or cross
50 "The Three Musketeers" author
53 Takes down a peg
55 Relative of a stencil
60 1941 Elia Kazan musical melodrama
62 Hawk
63 Drives the getaway car, maybe
64 Rug's coverage, perhaps
65 Speaker of Cooperstown
66 French Revolutionist assassinated by Charlotte Corday
67 NFL team in St. Louis

DOWN
1 Wyatt of O.K. Corral fame
2 Batik artisan
3 "Battle Cry" actor ___ Ray
4 Prepare avocado for guacamole
5 Convertible couch
6 Modern messaging method
7 Gloves for diamond workers?
8 Doctrine
9 Hammer-throwing deity
10 Parsons' houses
11 Works on words
12 Pitchfork features
13 Teed off
18 Small, flightless bird
19 The Joker portrayer, on TV
23 Gym apparatus
25 City east of Phoenix
26 Skater's leap
27 Deliberate loss, in boxing
28 Map abbr.
30 All ___ (completely wrong)
32 Looked over, as a joint
33 Popeye's Olive
34 "Get off the stage!" signal
35 It follows theta
36 Winter fall
38 Italian city with a view of Mount Vesuvius
39 Shaping tool
40 "Right away!"
44 Stands in the studio
45 Most plucky
46 TV choice for armchair athletes
47 Miller rival
48 Having more skill
49 Son of and successor to Catherine the Great
51 Say
52 "The Three Tenors" conductor Zubin
54 "Anna and the King of ___ "
56 Word before "pants on fire"
57 Where the Taj Mahal is
58 1954 mutant-ants film
59 Flight board postings, briefly
61 Shaq's org.

Answer on page 281

A Gnawing Issue

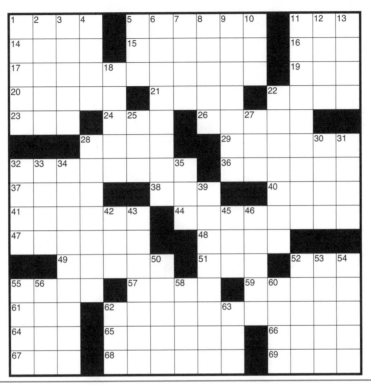

ACROSS
1 Comic Carvey
5 St. Francis's home
11 Dickens alias
14 Pupil surrounder
15 Warehouse platform
16 Swellhead's excess
17 They're belted for homers
19 The whole enchilada
20 Drive forward
21 European auto
22 Eye layer
23 Thumbs-down vote
24 Ex-G.I.
26 Teammate of Snider and Hodges
28 Craps pair
29 Bob Cratchit and Uriah Heep, for two
32 Debuts in society
36 ___ lit (book genre)
37 Andy's partner
38 Same old same old
40 Wedding dessert
41 Not as slack
44 Disraeli or Spock
47 At the scene
48 Grouchoesque look
49 Pass, as a law
51 "Ben Hur" novelist Wallace
52 Tally up
55 Xerox
57 Intense craving
59 Like a beaver, maybe
61 Gardner of film
62 Abrasive tool
64 Unburden
65 ESPN commentator Dick
66 Pub pints
67 Classifieds
68 Does in, biblically
69 Marge Schott's team, once

DOWN
1 "Mangia!"
2 Bakery enticement
3 Chilly, like winter air
4 1975 Wimbledon champ
5 Tax mo.
6 Virus planter, e.g.
7 Duel invitation, perhaps
8 Greener around the gills
9 Magnum portrayer on TV
10 "___ the economy, stupid"
11 Wisconsin city
12 Eye amorously
13 "Nana" author Émile
18 Oft-impersonated singer
22 Want-ad purchase, perhaps
25 Environmental prefix
27 Yalie
28 Manifest ___ (19th-century doctrine)
30 Hall of Famer Cuyler
31 "... ___ and not heard"
32 Roman known as "The Elder"
33 Middle East sultanate
34 Common desk items, these days
35 Place to soak
39 Rat fink
42 Greek H
43 Take back, as land
45 Maiden-name preceder
46 Tiara inset
50 ___-frutti
52 Quick on one's feet
53 Removed from print
54 Get togged up
55 Irene of "Fame"
56 "The Art of Love" poet
58 E.R.A. or B.A.
60 Way, way off
62 Homes on wheels, for short
63 -y, pluralized

Answer on page 283

Trifecta

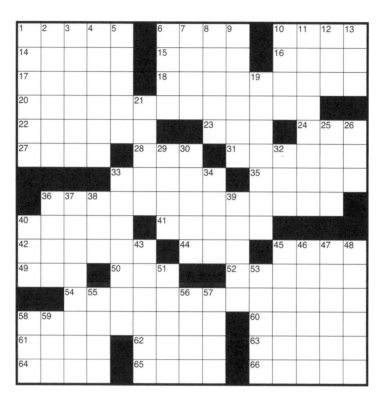

ACROSS

1 Sonia of "Kiss of the Spider Woman"
6 Projects
10 Fail to include
14 "Falcon Crest" playboy Lorenzo
15 007's alma mater
16 Conquering ___
17 In the open
18 Like Mad
20 Milne character
22 Start a paragraph
23 Club ___
24 Path of a pendulum
27 Acid ___
28 "Surfin' ___" (1963 hit)
31 Bring under control
33 Sacred cows
35 Hunter of myth
36 Patient's improvement, possibly
40 Bouillabaisse base
41 Wall-system part
42 Divulge
44 Kwik-E-Mart owner on "The Simpsons"
45 ___ spumante
49 Whiskey variety
50 Satchel
52 Get ready for market, perhaps
54 '50s variety show featuring Jack Benny and a deluge of luminaries
58 Prolonged family struggle
60 Cartoon coyote
61 Cravings
62 Took advantage of
63 First set of invitees
64 "Postcards from the ___"
65 "___ is more"
66 Mommies' mommies

DOWN

1 Botch the job
2 Gully's big brother
3 Reparations
4 January birthstone
5 Gomez Addams portrayer John ___
6 "Surely you ___!"
7 Four Corners state
8 Tribal trademark
9 Potshot taker
10 Baltimore's railroad partner
11 Pit crew member
12 Nest-egg letters
13 "My mama done ___ me ..."
19 Headed into the sunset, perhaps
21 Chopin practice piece
25 Funny fellow
26 Larry King employer
29 Has a bawl
30 Hilo hello
32 Dander
33 Sleepy Hollow schoolmaster Crane
34 Creep through the cracks
36 Sheep, to wolves
37 Serenade
38 Enjoyed the buffet
39 Actor's error
40 "Baby, it's cold outside!"
43 Legit
45 Number-one Hun
46 Yalta's Joseph
47 Mother ___
48 Maps of Alaska and Hawaii, often
51 They fly in formation
53 Lake Nasser's dam
55 Hydrant hookup
56 Bemoans
57 Chances
58 Tournament pass
59 Conducted

Answer on page 285

Ethane Allen's Dictionary

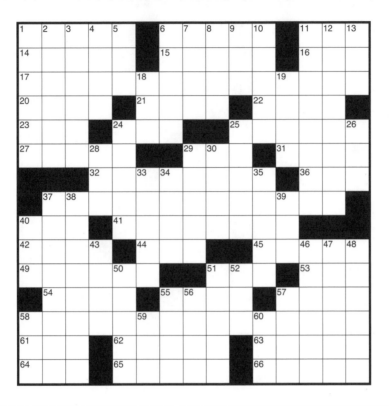

ACROSS
1 "Me and Bobby ___"
6 Part of a big name in fashion
11 Class for EMTs
14 Employ a silver tongue
15 Hunter of the stars
16 Flirt with persistently, with "on"
17 Giving up just a little?
20 Just like you see it
21 It helps you get a grip
22 Sherwood Forest friar
23 It carries a small charge
24 Cabbage forked over
25 Throw shadows on
27 Splendid
29 I, as in personality
31 Nimble
32 Ed Asner title role
36 Common Mkt.
37 Elegant renaissance?
40 Evidence type
41 Unflagging
42 Hugging limbs
44 Turner of channels
45 Guitar sound
49 City near Pompeii
51 Might
53 ___ Aviv
54 Irreverently, after "in"
55 Chicken ___
57 Bangkok tongue
58 On-topic animal keeper?
61 Ctrl + ___ + Del
62 Moved on hands and knees
63 Gifted person
64 Papers: Abbr.
65 C&W singer Tucker
66 Courts at college

DOWN
1 Goat garment
2 Friday's friend
3 Shooting craps, e.g.
4 Long E's in Greek
5 Adverb in verse
6 Former talk show host O'Donnell
7 Time periods
8 "___ goin'!"
9 Rocky top
10 Hill of hearings
11 Hummus source
12 Walleye
13 66, for one: Abbr.
18 Name from Hebrew for "life"
19 Hairy garments
24 Ice cream drink
25 "Valediction Forbidding Mourning" poet
26 U.S. capital, 1789–90
28 Linen vestment
29 Went off course
30 Celt or Highlander
33 Platoon and company
34 "First Knight" actor
35 Thin-skinned
37 Frees from complication
38 Fortifications
39 U-turn from ENE
40 Rather newsworthy?
43 Unlikely, as chances
46 Minerva, on the Acropolis
47 Got closer to
48 Flies without a motor
50 Make applicable
51 Conductor Zubin
52 Caesar's salutation
55 "Neato!"
56 Cosby espionage program
57 Ten C-notes
58 Leg
59 FDR program
60 "Immediately, if not sooner!"

Answer on page 287

It's (No Longer) Element-ary

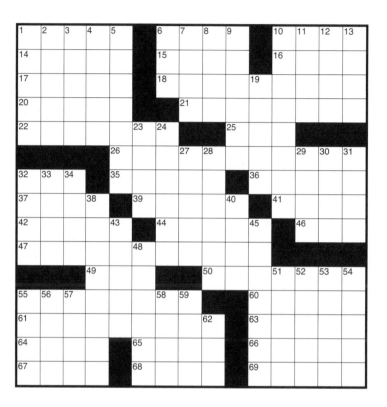

ACROSS

1 Lingerie items
6 Let it out?
10 Fugue master
14 Vietnam city
15 Head of France?
16 Jai ___
17 Knock down a peg
18 Umber, for example
20 Times Roman, Helvetica, and so on
21 Argued against
22 Bridge support
25 It's between the U.S. and the U.K.
26 1997 Harrison Ford film
32 Bankroll
35 Whey
36 Regular routine
37 Sir Guinness
39 "Billions and billions ..." scientist
41 TV's warrior princess
42 "Cosmicomics" author Calvino
44 Pitchfork parts
46 "That's affirmative"
47 Dalmatian's hangout, stereotypically
49 Pass with flying colors
50 Laugh up one's sleeve
55 Help
60 Accra's nation
61 Olympic team game
63 Navigation system
64 State emphatically
65 Celebrity, often
66 Put up
67 Good Queen ___
68 "Uh-uh"
69 Big tops

DOWN

1 Mine opening
2 Woman's work?
3 Pointless
4 Sends, as to a bulletin board
5 Nogales naps
6 Joan of Arc's title: Abbr.
7 Fruit a lute is shaped like
8 Raison d'___
9 Fixture for home mixologists
10 Domineering, sharp-tempered woman
11 "What ___ of baloney!"
12 Walking stick
13 Took off fast
19 Storage chest
23 "sex, ___, and videotape"
24 List of mistakes
27 Tempus ___ (time flies)
28 Muscat-eers?
29 Toe the line
30 Diamond crew
31 Cockpit guesstimates, for short
32 Street child
33 High: Prefix
34 Expensive
38 Ward, June, Wally, and Theodore
40 Plymouth auto
43 Coveted statuette
45 Rich Hall's "a word the language needs" coinage
48 Split part, sometimes
51 Task
52 Valentine of "Room 222"
53 Pass on the Hill
54 Carries on
55 Q-Tip, for example
56 Icicle holder
57 AAA suggestions
58 Pother
59 Feed the pigs
62 "Rah!" in Madrid

Answer on page 289

Kick Me!

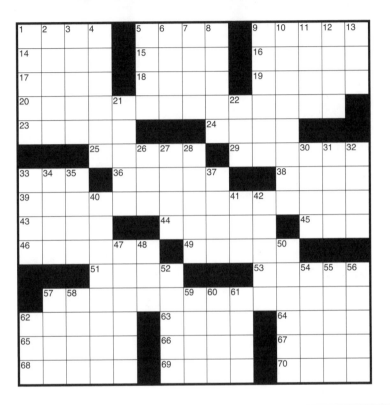

ACROSS

1 Names
5 Recipe guesstimate
9 Prior's superior
14 About, in memos
15 ___ breve
16 Pickling solution
17 Greasy-spoon side
18 Sax man Sims
19 Cube creator
20 KICK ME
23 Evil eye
24 Jean Arp's movement
25 Job for an aging AL player, perhaps
29 City of northern Illinois
33 Blow away
36 Like a house ___
38 Pennsylvania port
39 KICK ME
43 Newsman Sevareid
44 Flip-chart holder
45 Kind of block or deck
46 "Volare" singer Bobby
49 "Who's on First?" catcher
51 Sherwin-Williams layer
53 Luncheonette handouts
57 KICK ME
62 Procreate, biblically
63 Cavity detector
64 Chamber music group, sometimes
65 Big name in talk
66 Mallard's cousin
67 (ding-dong) "___ calling"
68 Words in a fairy tale intro
69 Ticked
70 New Year's word

DOWN

1 Brake parts
2 Blacked out
3 Sonia of Hollywood
4 Negotiator of an 1867 "folly"
5 Punchy state
6 Zillions
7 Nickelodeon opening
8 Couldn't stomach
9 Use sandpaper
10 1980 Redford film
11 Netanyahu, familiarly
12 "I'll get right ___, chief!"
13 Toothbrush brand
21 Get off the sauce, perhaps
22 Hornswoggled
26 "___ Only Had a Brain"
27 "Swoosh" logo company
28 "___ Caesar's ghost!"
30 Liberal pursuits
31 Stead
32 Capital on the Aare
33 U.S.
34 Like an Airedale's coat
35 Bagnold or Blyton
37 Former pump sign in the U.S.
40 Sandwich filler, maybe
41 Mack of old TV
42 Crockett's Waterloo
47 Can't stomach
48 Back muscle, in gym lingo
50 Nosy Parkers
52 Primers
54 Full of chutzpah
55 Kind of shop or suit
56 14 pounds, in Britain
57 Hung on to
58 Introduction to culture?
59 Hydrox lookalike
60 Allen successor
61 War correspondent Ernie
62 Feathered scarf

Answer on page 291

One at a Time

ACROSS

1 Dash of panache
5 Rascal
10 Basie's specialty
14 "Star Wars" princess
15 Big top headliner
16 Natural balm
17 Rich Little's opening bit?
20 Where Van Gogh lost his ear
21 Fight finish, often
22 S&L convenience
25 The whole shebang
26 Slow cooker popular in Boston?
30 Dastardly dude
32 Rock's ___ Jovi
33 Root word?
34 It exists only after it's expired
38 Comic-strip news editor
39 "___ he drove out of sight ..."
40 Artist's pad?
41 Result of a too-intense grilling?
45 Crime boss
46 Flamenco dancer's shout
47 "Children of a ___ God"
48 Musical Cat
51 Take a bough
52 Common Market initials
53 "... ___ woodchuck could chuck wood"
54 Gaseous mist
56 Time, relatively speaking
63 Emulate the Blob
64 "Burnt" color
65 Show of hands
66 River that starts in Pittsburgh
67 Civil rights leader Medgar
68 Final stroke, usually

DOWN

1 Leprechaun
2 Kauai keepsake
3 Melody
4 "The Right Stuff" org.
5 Hushed
6 "Ship of the desert"
7 Rock concert gear
8 Mal de ___
9 Fake it
10 "Friday the 13th" villain
11 He floated like a butterfly
12 "If I Ran the ___" (Dr. Seuss book)
13 Meditative discipline
18 Like circus animals
19 Jamaican music
22 Mornings, for short
23 It's a drive, usually
24 Breadmaker, perhaps
26 Big boo-boo
27 Bountiful
28 Where to tie a yellow ribbon, in song
29 Most common English word
31 King Hussein's Queen ___
32 Harbor hauler
35 Dorothy clicked hers to go home
36 Consider overnight
37 Hordes
41 QBs' objectives
42 Former TV host Phil
43 Romeo and Juliet, for two
44 Atomic energy org.
49 Olive-green songbird
50 Newt, but not Gingrich
51 Worse, as excuses go
54 Slangy feeling
55 Letters of invitation?
56 Egg ___ yung
57 Sound of pain or pleasure
58 Commando weapon
59 Tag renewal payee: Abbr.
60 Chit
61 Giant of a Giant
62 Basketball champion's "trophy"

Answer on page 293

Fast Food, Hasty Reading

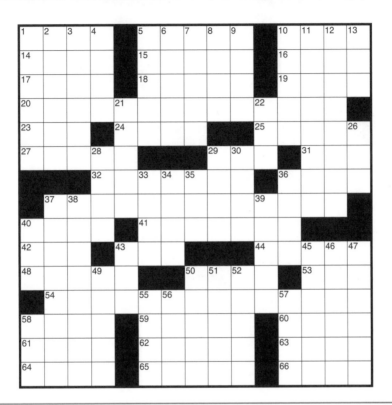

ACROSS

1 Type of board or joint
5 The Man at the monastery
10 Quickly applies
14 Jay on TV
15 Comb projections
16 Angry
17 "Tell ___ the judge!"
18 Deal with
19 Selects, with "for"
20 Coin stamper?
23 Bar symbols, collectively: Abbr.
24 Peter & Gordon's "True Love ___"
25 Like kings and queens
27 Makeup maker Lauder
29 Johnny Reb's country: Abbr.
31 Take in
32 Bring forward
36 Contends
37 Little white lie?
40 Healthy cereal ingredient
41 Good for the heart and lungs
42 Finish'd
43 Nightmare street of film
44 "Otello" composer
48 '92 Wimbledon winner Agassi
50 "Sighted sub, sank ___"
53 Layer, but not a stratum
54 Cowardly caretakers?
58 "Stop pouring"
59 Gulf of the Red Sea
60 Jacob's hairy brother
61 The point of mountain climbing
62 Part of RFD
63 "The Ghost and Mrs. ___"
64 Gets sum
65 Lists
66 Man, for one

DOWN

1 Exclusive circle
2 Pauses
3 Not broken
4 Word with box or boy
5 On the ocean or in a fog
6 Noah of "The Sea Wolf"
7 Pager sounds
8 Director Preminger
9 .001 mil
10 Current path
11 Broken chord
12 Judas Iscariot, for one
13 Radical '60s org.
21 Insignificant individual
22 Advocate of those that can be fired?: Abbr.
26 Slow-spinning records
28 Town on the Thames
29 Movie about a St. Bernard
30 Check remainder
33 Silicon dioxide stone
34 Swarm
35 '67 NHL Rookie of the Year
36 Type of squad
37 Injured by twisting
38 Stubborn person
39 David of "The Pink Panther"
40 Nonpoisonous but dangerous snake
43 Continental trade group: Abbr.
45 Monkey used in research
46 Knock off the tracks
47 Get a policy on
49 Skating areas
50 Vocalize vociferously
51 On offense, on a diamond
52 Board in a rooming house
55 Small rec vehicle
56 Lateral opening?
57 Moore of movies
58 Agency under FDR

Answer on page 295

Good Sportsmanship

ACROSS
1 Chess "soldier"
5 Fundamental knowledge
9 First name of the writer quoted in this puzzle
14 Puccini highlight
15 Certain tide
16 It might be diminished
17 ___ Picture Studios ("Jeopardy!" taping site)
18 Stong wind
19 Main artery
20 Start of a quote from "An Ideal Husband"
23 Prefix meaning "gas" or "atmosphere"
24 Dogpatch's Daisy ___
25 Part 2 of quote
31 Medicos
35 Defame in writing
36 Della of "Touched by an Angel"
38 Buddy
39 Early producer of video games
40 Give ___ go (try)
41 ___ firma
43 Old boat
44 Polite refusal
46 Hilton competitor
47 October's stone
49 Part 3 of quote
51 Raw material
53 Josh
54 End of quote
63 ___ in on (approached)
64 Zone

65 Flabby ... not!
66 Making a mockery of
67 Stitch together
68 "Headlines" comic
69 Last name of quoted writer
70 Verbal connective tissue
71 Distort

DOWN
1 El ___, Texas
2 Presley's middle name
3 Spritzer ingredient
4 Skeptic
5 Knitter's choice
6 Belle's boyfriend
7 Stock option
8 Got the lead out

9 City in north-central Florida
10 ___ up (exposed)
11 Mrs. Dithers
12 Pretentious
13 Abbrs. on vitamin bottles
21 Actor Van ___ of "Patterns"
22 Carter and Grant
25 Teacher of Aristotle
26 Beamed
27 Addis ___, Ethiopia
28 Coffee descriptor
29 Lace again
30 Discover
32 Competitor of Geraldo and Ricki
33 Magna ___
34 Thin strips of wood
37 Word with food or neighborhood

42 Looks over
45 "The Virginian" author Wister
48 Relatively cheap, as merchandise goes
50 Lofty instruments, sometimes
52 Oak ___, Tennessee
54 Defrost
55 Pueblo dweller
56 "___ and the Detectives" (1964 Disney film)
57 It means nothing to Carlos
58 Tabriz's country
59 Dweeb
60 Exude, as charm
61 "Hamlet" extra
62 Reason to get a better antenna, maybe

Answer on page 278

From C to Shining C

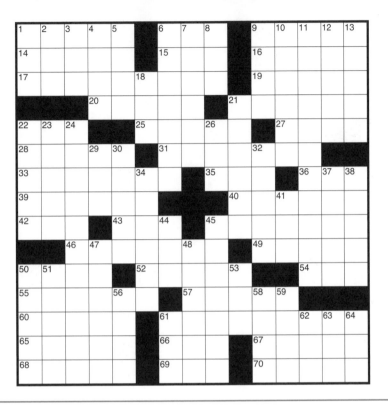

ACROSS

1 Tom of "The Seven Year Itch"
6 Abe Lincoln's boy
9 Colorful parrot
14 Sylvester's frequent costar
15 10% of a sawbuck
16 Chip away at
17 Idle talk
19 Conceded putt
20 Are able to, biblically
21 Fought for air
22 Rambler mfr.
25 ___-Croatian
27 Beachgoers' acquisitions
28 Taj ___
31 Builder of the McDonald's empire
33 Peeper protectors
35 Excellent, bond-wise
36 Kiltie's cap
39 Playful chitchat
40 Amp schlepper
42 "Do ___ say, not ..."
43 "___ to worry"
45 Dumbbells
46 "Piece of cake!"
49 Gets whupped
50 Kemo ___ (the Lone Ranger)
52 Not so loco
54 React to spilled milk?
55 Enticement
57 Playful pinch
60 Barrel slat
61 OK
65 Matisse or Rousseau
66 Pizzeria ___ (restaurant chain)
67 Emulate Mr. Kotter
68 Slow-pitched a softball
69 Perfecta or trifecta
70 Went on the stump

DOWN

1 End of a list, often
2 "Do ___ Diddy Diddy"
3 New Haven collegian
4 Continental or Town Car, to a car buff
5 Himalayan holy man
6 Salad mixers
7 "Peer Gynt" dancer
8 Yule mo.
9 Prefix with bucks or bytes
10 Noble Brit, briefly
11 Stereo input
12 Madison Avenue types
13 Unwanted vegetation
18 Young ___ (backwoods tots)
21 Motorized mini-vehicle
22 Single-celled critter
23 Yucatán peoples
24 White wine grape
26 Lose ___ whisker
29 Spacebar neighbor
30 Bank claims
32 "Eating ___" (1982 movie)
34 Be half-asleep
37 Assistant
38 Like many a teen's room
41 Sgt.'s address
44 Quaff from Snapple
45 Hasenpfeffer maker's need
47 Hors d'___
48 San ___ (Texas city, familiarly)
50 "Peter and the Wolf" bird
51 Do some tailoring
53 Stephen of "Citizen X"
56 1967 Tony winner Beryl
58 Intermissions separate them
59 Stay fresh
61 Wrigley Field denizen
62 Lao-tzu's "way"
63 "That's disgusting!"
64 Compadre of Fidel

Answer on page 279

Crossroads

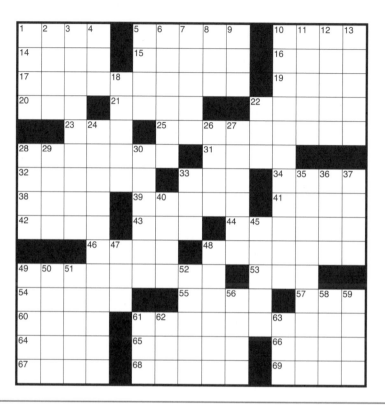

ACROSS

1 They fly by night
5 Savory jelly
10 Ford and Lincoln, but not Clinton
14 Diamond of song
15 Erie Canal city
16 Straddling
17 Fat City
19 Cry of success
20 Feat of Klee?
21 Cry of derision
22 Spread around
23 First lady
25 Professor Henry Higgins, to Shaw
28 Wide-ranging cultural series on '50s TV
31 Passion or fashion
32 Hallucinogenic cactus
33 Business transmission
34 Prohibitionists
38 Radiate
39 Futuristic fantasy, for short
41 Offend olfactorily
42 It's the wrong thing to do
43 Passes, in "Variety"
44 Tropical rum cocktail
46 Perlman of "Pearl"
48 Cambridge campus
49 Axis Sally's counterpart
53 Come together
54 Poker comment
55 Quartet member
57 Suppositions
60 Hindu honcho
61 Evidence of embezzlement, e.g.
64 Cop who inspired "The French Connection"
65 Khaki twill
66 "Beetle Bailey" pooch
67 Hockey feint
68 Nasser's successor
69 Gusto

DOWN

1 "Every ___ winner!"
2 Put on
3 Uses a bug
4 Canny
5 Cougar or Jaguar
6 Sharpens a razor
7 High fidelity?
8 Sorbet
9 Nap or nip preceder
10 "City Slickers" undertaking
11 Nintendo forerunner
12 The Calgary Stampede, for one
13 Generate
18 "Come Back, Little ___"
22 Droop
24 Post-Indy site
26 '95 Wimbledon champ
27 Nissan model that's tops?
28 Harbinger
29 Note to the staff
30 Long, heavy overcoat
33 Pickle
35 Get even
36 Vintage
37 Warehouse pallet
40 "Arrivederci"
45 Underworld lingo
47 Coal scuttle
48 Capital of Montana
49 Out of gas
50 Mead's "Coming ___ in Samoa"
51 Lollipop cop
52 Savory
56 Race pace
58 "If the shoe ___, ..."
59 Job opening
61 Laptops, e.g.
62 "Caught ya!"
63 Frasier's call screener

Answer on page 281

Mixed-Up April Fools

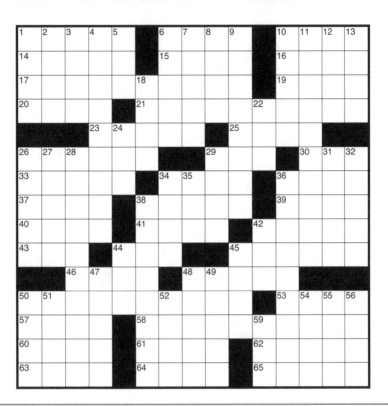

ACROSS
1. Got out of bed
6. Dirty, as a joke
10. Non-Gingrich newts
14. Syrup source
15. Skin lotion plant
16. Away from the wind
17. LEAKY BOAT
19. Environmentalists' pal Al
20. Disappear, like a snowman
21. SUPERMAN LOSES THIS WHEN HE STANDS
23. Author of "Uncle Tom's Cabin"
25. Prophet
26. O-ring
29. Ullmann of "Autumn Sonata"
30. He raved about a raven
33. Les of government
34. "Button your lip!" with "up"
36. Dance for Cinderella
37. Othello, for one
38. Offends the olfactories
39. Tick off
40. Moon ___ (Frank Zappa's daughter)
41. Facility
42. Fragment of the cross, e.g.
43. Business card abbr.
44. Bug killer: abbr.
45. Saucers, cups, and a pot
46. Gladly, old-style
48. Forms a puddle
50. VERY FAVORABLE OPINION SAMPLING
53. Scarlett's home
57. Owl's call
58. NAVAL FAILURE
60. Writer Pound
61. Sharp side of a blade
62. Creator of Friday
63. Erode, with "away"
64. Property paper
65. Second or sixth president

DOWN
1. Radio type
2. Infrequent
3. Iridescent gem
4. Garment allowing free leg motion
5. Slimmer swimmer
6. Bochco legal drama
7. Descend ladder and wed
8. Canine comment
9. Accumulations on a river bank
10. Lunar lander
11. MOP BUCKETS
12. Garr of "Tootsie"
13. Investigates, with "about"
18. "Coin-eating" part of a vending machine
22. Minister, for short
24. Lowest card in a royal flush
26. Entire range
27. In unison
28. RUIN VEGETATION
29. Skywalker of sci-fi
31. Stan's partner in comedy
32. Vote in
34. Give a chair to
35. "___ So Fine"
36. Nursed without a bottle
38. Aglow, à la Rudolph
42. Univ. course in Islam, e.g.
44. Bad-mouth, to rappers
45. Matador's opponent
47. Promising location?
48. Satchel of diamonds
49. Lubricated
50. "That was close!"
51. Dispense pretentiously, as charm
52. Disappear gradually, in movies
54. Communications word for A
55. Board companion
56. Tarzan's neighbors
59. Nutritional minimum: Abbr.

Answer on page 283

Suits Me!

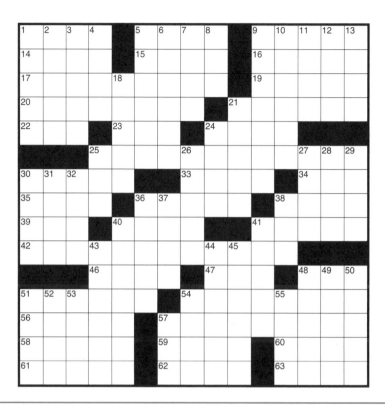

ACROSS
1 Jab, for most boxers
5 Church area
9 Film promos
14 PAC-10 inst.
15 Pear plant
16 Sophia of film
17 Beef cut
19 ___ barrel (in an awkward position)
20 New York's ___ Mountains
21 Expended
22 Suffix meaning "resident"
23 Inventor Whitney
24 Work without ___
25 Nickname for Delaware
30 Language for the masses?
33 Military division
34 "The Company"
35 It may be final
36 Saw
38 Brand spanking new
39 Supermodel Carol
40 Carrying a grudge
41 Underlings
42 Deepest emotions
46 Drinks near a dartboard
47 PBS benefactor
48 She played Maude
51 Cracker-like breads
54 Oater hats
56 Subaru competitor
57 Gathering of data as a project starts, perhaps
58 ___ Vanilli

59 Short-legged dog, shortly
60 Succulent plant
61 Capri, Man, and so on
62 Hardly blasé
63 Unadorned

DOWN
1 Emmy winner Susan
2 Dazzling effect
3 Galway's instrument
4 Bills
5 Hun king
6 Bout before the main event
7 Symbolic medallion
8 "A mouse!"
9 Most familiar
10 Musical Lyle
11 Ticked off
12 Inca's land
13 Simplicity itself
18 Yarn buy
21 Loosened
24 Mother of Elizabeth I
25 ___ sum (goodies in a Chinese restaurant)
26 Ear or space descriptor
27 Litmus test chemical
28 Fork part
29 Puts away
30 Wife of Jacob
31 Cart spindle
32 "See ya," in England
36 Quantities of medicine
37 Crafts' partners

38 Prefix meaning "wrongly"
40 City in which to "Meet Me"
41 Colored quartz
43 Dazzle lead-in
44 Food, for example
45 Had more than a thirst for
48 Start of a Yale Bowl cheer
49 Get on the register
50 Interrogated
51 "La Bohème" soprano
52 Words on a sale sign
53 Progressive rock group Jethro ___
54 Erupt
55 Mop
57 Stairmaster site

Answer on page 285

Pay Up!

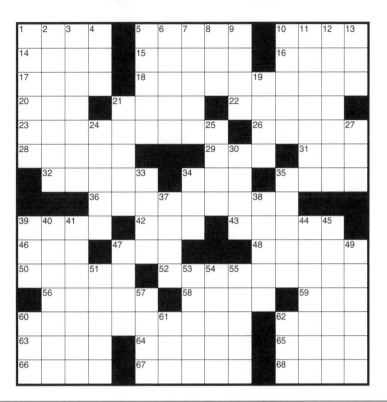

ACROSS
1 Central points
5 "Peachy-keen!"
10 Does some darning
14 Mil. school
15 Open courts
16 Military group
17 Acts the masseur
18 They've got things to do
20 Schnozz extension
21 La ___ Tar Pits
22 Ellington's "___ Doll"
23 Parting words
26 Martinique volcano
28 "Band of Gold" singer Payne
29 Hippie's home
31 Snaky shape
32 "Goosebumps" author R.L. ___
34 ATM code
35 Aide: Abbr.
36 "Damn Yankees" star
39 Talc-to-diamond scale
42 Arrid rival
43 Abs tightener
46 Santa ___, California
47 Immigrant's subj.
48 1965 Moody Blues hit
50 Modify, as a soundtrack
52 Cookie variety
56 Family auto
58 Benjamin Moore layer
59 London's Paddington, for one: Abbr.
60 Emmy-winning TV documentarist
62 Don ___ (womanizer)
63 Garfield's foil, in the comics
64 "The Wreck of the Mary ___"
65 Go ballistic
66 Reading rooms
67 More clearheaded
68 Flexible Flyer, e.g.

DOWN
1 Way in the distance
2 Eyepieces
3 1972 Liza Minnelli movie
4 Psyche parts
5 Mollusk-shell material
6 Mrs. Mertz
7 "He's ___ nowhere man ..." (Beatles lyric)
8 Recurrent twitch
9 Symbols of sturdiness
10 Hotel accommodation
11 Stores, as grain
12 Testimony giver
13 N.Y.C.'s 42nd, et al.
19 Sgt. Friday's employer
21 Safari boss
24 Wields a blue pencil
25 Drive to nowhere in particular
27 Superlative suffix
30 Pantry pests
33 Peters out
34 Knock-knock joke, essentially
35 ___-Detoo ("Star Wars" android)
37 Cry from the guardhouse
38 Number on a black ball
39 Spray graffiti on
40 "Outta my way!"
41 Rat-infested town of legend
44 Out of the ordinary
45 Pitney-Bowes meter filler
47 Course finale, often
49 Withdrew, as from a habit
51 Twiddles one's thumbs
53 The deep
54 Peter of "Casablanca"
55 Kind of disk or printer
57 Silent assents
60 Physique, in gym lingo
61 Vote of endorsement
62 Some H.S. students

Answer on page 287

Captive-ating Leaders

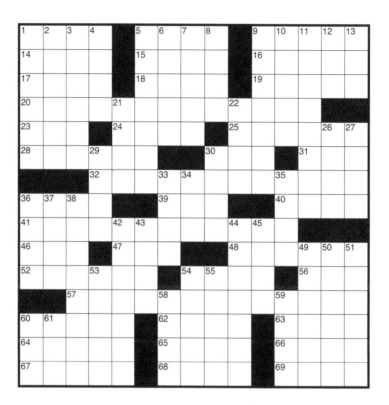

ACROSS

1 Compulsion
5 Much-used pencil
9 Visibly happy
14 Civil offense
15 Galileo's home
16 Hogwash
17 Hodgepodge
18 Colorado Indians
19 Jousts
20 "Awakenings" director
23 Summer Games gp.
24 Plenty of time?
25 Do what's asked
28 Art school or depth charge
30 Andy Capp's wife
31 Glutton
32 First governor of Utah
36 Cork's locale
39 Attention
40 Obedience-school command
41 '50s British sportscar racer
46 Helping hand
47 Eagle on a par 3
48 Key of two Brandenberg Concerti
52 Peerless
54 Well-protected
56 Big galoot
57 Murphy Brown portrayer
60 Came upon
62 Storm
63 Nefertiti, to Tut
64 Every señorita has one
65 Horne solo
66 Significant other
67 Easy to understand
68 Egg holder
69 Egg on

DOWN

1 Thomas More's "nowhere"
2 Loggers' tourneys
3 Dr. Seuss villain
4 Captain Hook's alma mater
5 Colorful Italian dessert
6 Saturn's largest moon
7 Manipulative types
8 Opera villain, usually
9 "Way to go, guy!"
10 Cross-examine
11 Gulliver's landfall
12 Elect
13 "Nightmare on Elm Street" director Craven
21 Sophomore, e.g.
22 "Gentleman's Agreement" Oscar winner Celeste
26 Yul's "Solomon and Sheba" costar
27 Like French toast
29 Radio-active trucker?
30 Orwell's "Animal ___"
33 Kelly or Krupa
34 Witch
35 Greek peak
36 Biblical birthright barterer
37 Pack ___ (quit)
38 Mockery
42 Make ill-gotten gains well?
43 Clinched
44 Unconventional
45 Captain Hook's henchman
49 Largest American cat
50 Willing to try
51 Like many a tux
53 Interview format, for short
54 Close call
55 Protection
58 Mideast theocracy
59 Way off the highway
60 Truth in Lending org.
61 Black gold

Answer on page 289

Some Wear Out There

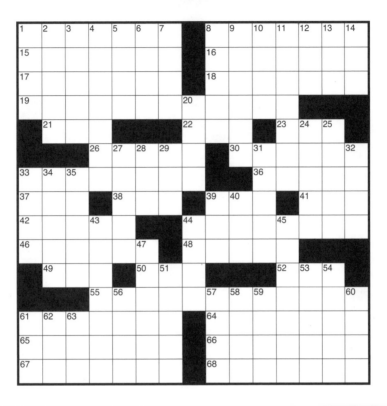

ACROSS

1 Thought the world of
8 Some mimosas
15 It's sought in vein
16 Like Kool Aid in water
17 Show the ropes again
18 12-year-old, but not for long
19 Planet-orbiting bands
21 Yours truly, facetiously
22 67.5°
23 Bothersome bambino
26 Desserts, to dieters
30 Drag kings?
33 Apparent change in a star's color
36 Guided from the outside
37 Transport for 38-Across
38 TV E.T.
39 Ryan or Tilly
41 "___ little teapot ..."
42 Skillet user
44 Planet's icy area
46 Type of parsley
48 Farewell
49 Loud lion letters
50 Hellenic H
52 Org. of eagles
55 Rock group beyond Mars
61 Most slow-witted
64 Writing that can be felt
65 In the distant past
66 Trireme crew
67 Gets over it
68 Cast a spell over

DOWN

1 What the haughty put on
2 Bobby Darin's "___ Lover"
3 "Be prepared," for one
4 Reduced to rubble
5 Laugh loudly
6 Land of leprechauns
7 Animal lairs
8 Former secretary of defense Les
9 Situation without escape
10 Words following shake
11 Matters
12 "How Can ___ Sure" (Young Rascals song)
13 Malted drink without ice cream?
14 Counterpart of Rep.
20 Symphony silence
24 Battlefield doc
25 Donna's first name?
27 Chicago terminal
28 Not a lick
29 Switch option
31 Uninvited pool "guests"
32 Picture or pod
33 Dog of Dennis the Menace
34 Zimbalist of "The F.B.I."
35 "Nothing ___!"
39 Like bell-bottoms
40 Whitney or Wallach
43 As one body
44 Jack of TV talk
45 "Nonsense!"
47 "Come on!"
51 Wyoming range
53 Town of a civil rights march
54 Tim of "Home Improvement"
56 Waters numbering seven
57 Double-reed instrument
58 Coward's confession?
59 Jeanne ___
60 Circus or revival shelter
61 Hoover, for one
62 Self-centeredness
63 Neighbor of Cal.

Answer on page 291

Spice World

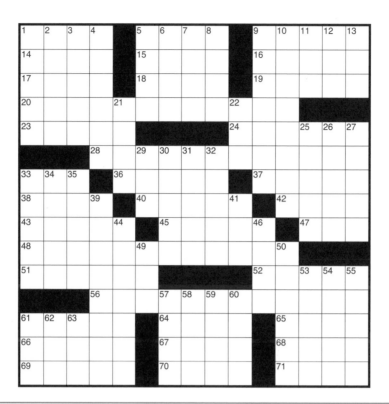

ACROSS

1 Double-___ trailer
5 Tries to catch apples
9 "Terrif!"
14 Eros's counterpart
15 Jump on the ice
16 Name on a 1945 bomber
17 Convertible, to a Spice Girl?
19 Drop in on
20 Gymnast's perfect score
21 Economy watcher Greenspan
22 Son of Adam and Eve
23 Qualified voters
25 Religious pamphlets
28 Auditioner's hope
29 Disgusting sight
30 Tabula ___ (clean slate)
33 Start of a Shakespeare title
34 Sister
35 PC key
36 Mind, to a Spice Girl?
39 ___ Plaines
40 "One Day ___ Time"
41 Fifty-fifty
42 Singer Feliciano
43 Ricocheted, like a billiard ball
45 Certain ski lift
48 Make an attempt to obtain
49 One who's fast with a one-liner
53 Two-dimensional, essentially
54 Coffee servers
55 ___ de France
56 Pakistani or Thailander
58 Soda choice for a Spice Girl?
60 "The Prince of Tides" star
61 Prefix for eight
62 Made angry
63 Like the Capitol
64 Ring decisions
65 Indefinite large number

DOWN

1 Pour down the drain, perhaps
2 Force to move
3 Fictional Lorna
4 Drop the ball
5 Texas's oldest college
6 Beast of burden's burden
7 Lima and pinto
8 35mm camera type
9 Most austere
10 Hall of Fame quarterback Johnny
11 Penthouse, to a Spice Girl?
12 Yale student
13 Mouse's cousin
18 "So long"
22 Recording-industry needles
24 H&R Block supervisor
26 Aligns properly
27 It may be common
29 City lines
30 Acknowledge a stimulus
31 "___ Is Born"
32 "Alien," to a Spice Girl?
33 Author Rand
36 Expressed distress over
37 Deflect
38 Garden area
42 Some sons, briefly
44 Not long ago
45 "Who Can I ___?" (Tony Bennett favorite)
46 Church gambling games
47 Church area, but not for gambling
49 Fast
50 Jeweled headpiece
51 DeGeneres's sitcom
52 Thin-sounding
56 Common connective
57 Jack of "Barney Miller"
58 Acquired
59 Canyon area

Answer on page 293

Drink Up!

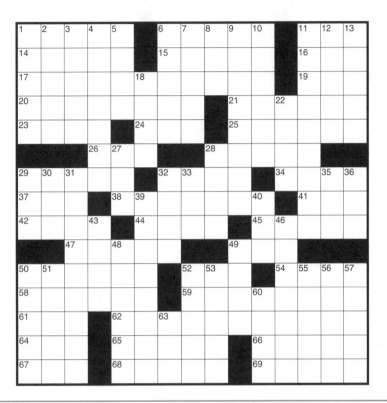

ACROSS

1. Invited to one's apartment
6. Rock bottom
11. Family docs
14. Layer with a "hole"
15. Have ___ to pick
16. Enjoy the buffet
17. Knockout blow, perhaps
19. Lennon's widow Yoko
20. Angels' perches, around Christmastime
21. Confession taker
23. Nostradamus, for one
24. Pumpernickel alternative
25. Get underhandedly
26. "___ whiz!"
28. Singer Lenya
29. Captain's superior
32. German coal region
34. Pepper's partner
37. Pub pint
38. Painter ___ Moses
41. Bummer of a grade
42. Prepares to feather
44. "Holy smoke!"
45. Ballplayer's rep
47. Jack, in cards
49. Wheels, so to speak
50. Word on a dog-owner's sign
52. Model of honesty
54. Nile snakes
58. ___ with (equal to)
59. Ostentatious, academically
61. Hall of Famer Mel
62. 1988 Michael Keaton film
64. 10-point tile in Scrabble
65. Silicon Valley giant
66. Comedian Sherman
67. Boot one
68. Be gaga over
69. Della or Pee Wee

DOWN

1. Party throwers
2. Sky shade
3. Gift getter
4. Experience
5. Fuel from bogs
6. Fuzzy, like a carpet
7. Treat like dirt
8. "GoodFellas" boss
9. Critter that moves in measured intervals?
10. Prepare, as leftovers
11. "Fables in Slang" author
12. "What's My Line?" guessers
13. Five-and-ten, e.g.
18. Days gone by
22. Aardvark's meal
27. Work unit
28. Cheryl of "Charlie's Angels"
29. Ring covering
30. ___ carte
31. Remote, as a town
32. Cooking herb
33. Santa ___, California
35. Novelist Deighton
36. Vietnamese New Year
39. Jesse Jackson, for one
40. Excellent bond rating
43. Piece of cake
46. Bit of sugar
48. Qatar's peninsula
49. Sign away
50. Hard stuff
51. "Come on in!"
52. More suitable
53. Slugger Albert
55. Subway entrance
56. Typesetters' measures
57. Part of an act
60. Not shut tight
63. DDE's command

Answer on page 295

Striking Changes

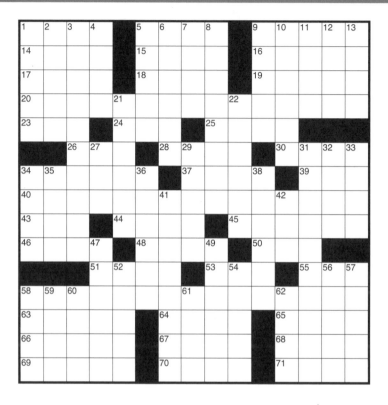

ACROSS

1 "___ of the Flies" (Golding novel)
5 Pearl Harbor villain
9 Resilient strength
14 Mrs. Paul Simon, née Brickell
15 Erelong
16 Pale purple
17 Rewards for waiting
18 Mickey's maker
19 "You Can't Get There From Here" author Nash
20 Swimming against the tide
23 Big bird
24 "Bill ___, the Science Guy"
25 Duel tool
26 The ___ (British rule in India)
28 Take it from the top
30 NFL broadcaster
34 Drive-in employee
37 Hollywood and Holliday
39 "The ___ of Pooh"
40 Showing originality
43 Dusk, to Donne
44 "On the Waterfront" director Kazan
45 Valuable weasels
46 A dime a dozen, e.g.
48 Eggshell
50 Comic Charlotte
51 Jeff MacNelly comic strip
53 HBO alternative
55 Washington Wizards' org.
58 Going cold turkey, perhaps
63 From the top
64 Eurasian range
65 Frontiersman Boone, to pals
66 Leader of the Mel-Tones
67 "___ Cassius has a lean and hungry look": Shakespeare
68 On the main
69 Black-and-white munchies
70 Warms the bench
71 They play at Shea

DOWN

1 Do not disturb
2 Intense dislike
3 Dangerous outflow
4 Roll top, e.g.
5 Brownish yellow
6 Wild ass
7 Sudden shock
8 Punctual
9 Dealt a mighty blow
10 "You said it!"
11 Skinny-dipper
12 Neck and neck
13 Make (one's way)
21 A select few get it
22 Times to remember
27 "Bingo!"
29 Mystery writers' award
31 Diamond heist?
32 Beyond the ___
33 Auction actions
34 "Good buddy"
35 Bailiwick
36 Overburden with, as work
38 Use AltaVista, e.g.
41 Leo Durocher said they finish last
42 Finance grad
47 Kind of dog or pie
49 Dag Hammarskjold's successor
52 "Tap" dancer Gregory
54 Pinochle putdowns
56 IQ test developer
57 Greek strongman
58 The Green Hornet's sidekick
59 Frankenstein's flunky
60 Kind of package
61 "Star Trek: The Next Generation" counselor
62 First bone donor?

Answer on page 278

Nay Sayings

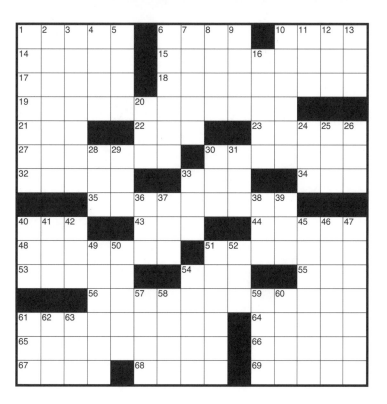

ACROSS

1 Nasser of Egypt
6 Free verse rhyme scheme?
10 Hoopla
14 ___'s Pieces candy
15 They manage beasts of burden
17 Clarinetist Shaw
18 Damns
19 Pickup basketball rule
21 Club for GIs
22 High USN rank
23 Allen of the Green Mountain Boys
27 They rent quarters
30 Restaurant rule, with 35- and 48-Across
32 Borden's bovine
33 Plane without propellers
34 Long, in Morse code
35 See 30-Across
40 Nile biter
43 Charged particle
44 "A Tale ___ Cities"
48 See 30-Across
51 Garfield's grub
53 Excited, with "up"
54 Regrettable behavior
55 "Blow" director Demme
56 Weightlifter's rule
61 Favorite
64 Kind of alarm or step
65 Type of gene
66 Former students
67 Etching fluid
68 At any time
69 Backs of necks

DOWN

1 Small particle
2 Spray in a can
3 Techniques
4 Cambodia's continent
5 Lascivious look
6 Modifies, as legislation
7 Like a Rubens model
8 Bass or treble
9 Art ___
10 Toasters drink to this
11 Still
12 Beginning for fix
13 Sink trap shape
16 Answers on some tests
20 Deface
24 Put out of sight
25 Coach Parseghian
26 Utmost
28 Cardplayer's cry
29 Fair-hiring policy: Abbr.
30 Maiden name preceder
31 Extra periods in sports: Abbr.
33 Actor Voight
36 Command to Rover
37 Dirt chopper
38 "___ if I can help it!"
39 Light switch option
40 Request
41 "What did I tell ya!"
42 Be nosy
45 Get sum numbers
46 "I'm sunk!"
47 Peculiarity
49 Having air holes
50 The golden calf and others
51 Bit left from a blaze
52 Landers of letters
54 One strains when using this
57 Sit before a lens
58 Tel ___
59 In the wink ___ eye
60 Festive celebration
61 Bathing suit top
62 Common Mkt.
63 ___-fi

Answer on page 279

Old Wine, New Bottles

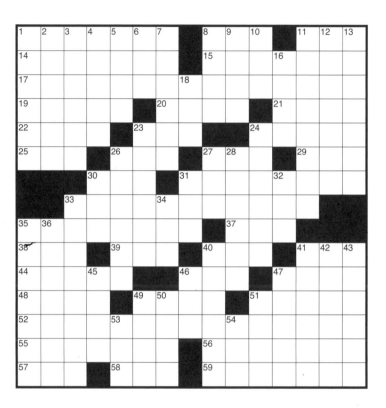

ACROSS

1 God of wine and revelry
8 Toward the stern
11 Media svc. based in Ottawa
14 Most sore
15 Shoe material
17 Vintner's favorite sax player?
19 Actress Lisa
20 It's right on the map
21 Bone-dry
22 WWII craft
23 The height of fashion?
24 "The Tempest" role
25 Road curve
26 Janitor's implement
27 Eddie Rabbitt's "___ a Cheater"
29 Anticipatory time
30 San Diego attraction
31 Preying "prayers"
33 California vintner's favorite city?
35 Put the kibosh on
37 Blockade
38 Ref's ring call
39 Mork's home planet
40 Ride the wind
41 Have a little drink
44 Lost a lap?
46 Female rabbit
47 ___ cava (blood vessel)
48 Carry on
49 BSA part
51 "The Threepenny Opera" composer
52 Vintner's motto?
55 Natural resistance to change
56 Possible reply to "Take out the garbage, please"
57 Turner or Knight
58 Beret's cousin
59 Fill the bill

DOWN

1 Run off at the mouth
2 Puzzle heading
3 Some are Gregorian
4 Motion pictures
5 Test the weight of
6 GI's club
7 Oscar winner Meryl
8 Help for the needy
9 Tour de force
10 Roofing sealant
11 Most suspicious
12 Swallow, so to speak
13 Babes' beds
16 Former Russian ruler
18 Horse's mother
23 Owl, at times
24 In error
26 "The Seven Year Itch" lead
27 Prince of Broadway
28 Authorize
30 Use a stun gun
31 TV hosts
32 Ending for cash or cloth
33 Pampered, in a way
34 One way to get information
35 Like clear, moonless nights
36 Kiev's country
40 Raids
41 Fishing nets
42 Green, as trees
43 Picayune
45 Ending for young or hip
46 Last mo.
47 "Rigoletto" composer
49 Korea, China, and so on
50 Word of greeting to a lady
51 Mae or Adam
53 "The Addams Family" cousin
54 She was Maude

Answer on page 281

Spooked

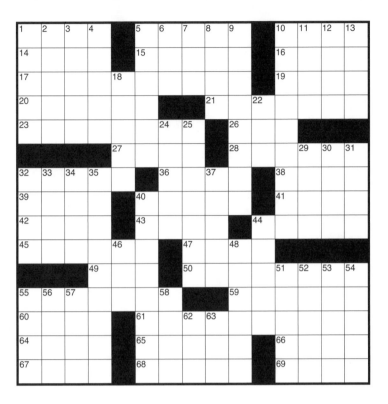

ACROSS
1 Crow's-nest support
5 Wearied
10 Took a shuttle
14 Big name in petroleum
15 ___ Lodge (motel chain)
16 Superman, to Reeve or Reeves
17 Greg Kihn novel about B movies
19 Kinds
20 Fine fiddles
21 A word that should exist, according to Rich Hall
23 Ineffectuality, as excuses go
26 Ordinal number ender
27 MacLachlan of "Twin Peaks"
28 Houston nine
32 Build up, as a fortune
36 Prominent donkey features
38 Wax's opposite
39 Coll. math course
40 Transplant, in a way
41 Ancient Andean
42 Nepal's continent
43 Apiece
44 Adult tent caterpillar
45 Eagerness
47 Shipping dept. stamp
49 Post-grace exhortation
50 Junk mail destination, usually
55 Underwent chemical change
59 Got up again
60 Abu Dhabi bigwig
61 Rastafarian's do
64 Generic dog's name
65 One way to eat ham
66 Bit of burlesque
67 Ragout or burgoo
68 Star-___ mole
69 Nine-digit IDs

DOWN
1 Taj ___
2 Coffee emanation
3 "Get lost!"
4 Pastry from Linz
5 Certain dairy cow
6 They're rated in BTU's
7 Play-___ (kids' sculpting stuff)
8 Seth's son
9 Maine, colloquially
10 Halloween headwear
11 Take it easy
12 Sommer of film
13 Division in many sports leagues
18 Porkers' patter
22 "___ now or never!"
24 Grab some shuteye
25 Liner's terminus
29 Summoned, as the butler
30 Second word of many limericks
31 Burn the surface of
32 "... way to skin ___"
33 Prepare potatoes
34 Et ___ (and others)
35 Cornfield presence
37 Dogie catcher
40 Fingered, as a criminal
44 Ford flop
46 Was successful at musical chairs
48 Checked for valid ID
51 ___ Perot
52 Gets ready to fire
53 Invite for coffee
54 Hatchlings' homes
55 Ring officials
56 Throw off
57 Man Friday
58 Foe of 007
62 Hosp. units
63 Nautical assent

Answer on page 283

Four-In-Hand

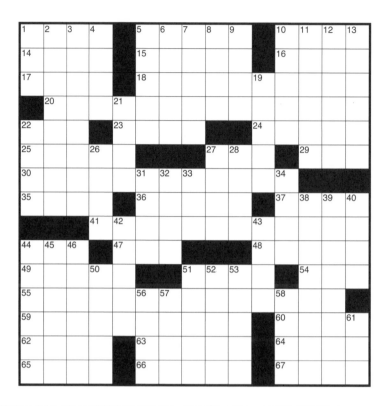

ACROSS

1 Arched recess
5 Smeltery refuse
10 Painter Chagall
14 Jezebel's idol
15 "Walk Away ___"
(1966 hit)
16 Penultimate fairy
tale word
17 Coffee brewers
18 "Here I Go Again"
band
20 Whodunit queen
22 Billy the Kid
portrayer Gulager
23 Caftan
24 Civil rights gp.
25 "The dog ate my
homework," e.g.
27 "Surfin' ___"
(1963 Beach Boys
hit)

29 "King Kong" studio
30 "Let's Be Buddies"
Ethel Merman
musical
35 The yoke's on them
36 It's connected to
the knee bone
37 "Back in the ___"
(Beatles hit)
41 Sparkle Plenty's
mother, in "Dick
Tracy"
44 Inclined
47 Summer cooler
48 Welsh woofer
49 Fowl pole?
51 Scotch water
54 Raggedy ___
55 '50s kidvid puppet
star
59 Princess Leia's
android

60 Outer limits
62 Times Square
flasher?
63 First American
orbiter
64 First name in
moon-walking
65 Helen's home
66 Belgian WWI battle
site
67 1962 Bond
baddie

DOWN

1 "Aladdin" monkey
2 "The ___ View"
(1974 Beatty
thriller)
3 Ruddy, as a
complexion
4 "Lohengrin"
soprano

5 BBC cult sci-fi
series
6 Detox center
7 In the bag
8 Member of the first
family?
9 Crystal gazer
10 The brainy bunch?
11 Incarnation of
Vishnu
12 Second chance at
three points, e.g.
13 He may make your
flesh crawl
19 Moses's mount
21 In shape
22 Mafia kingpin
26 Whimper
alternative, in an
Eliot poem
27 Water Wks. or Elec.
Co.

28 Unaccompanied
31 Hardly any
32 Bee flat?
33 Copper head?
34 ___ Disney
38 Colander
39 Registered
40 Free ___ (carte
blanche)
42 Ten-to-one, e.g.
43 Canyon comeback
44 Unmitigated
45 Wedding-vow word
46 La-di-da
50 Unemotional
51 Down the road
52 Endangered layer
53 Masked critters
56 Uptight
57 Seaweed
58 Look after
61 Pavement caution

Answer on page 285

Race Relations

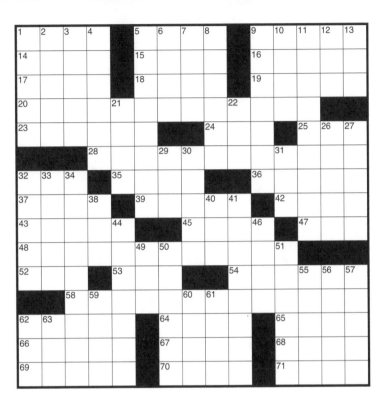

ACROSS

1 Stats derivable from birthdates
5 Applies hastily
9 Crimson-clad
14 Rob of "Wayne's World"
15 Considerably
16 Gets closer to
17 Game show host Trebek
18 Mexican pyramid builder
19 1978 Nobel Peace Prize recipient
20 Racer Michael's father
23 Beginnings
24 U-turn from WSW
25 Wednesday forehead marker
28 Racer Kyle's father
32 Atlanta Olympics flame lighter
35 Diamonds, for one
36 Used indelicate language
37 Barrett of gossip
39 Flight unit
42 Moran of "Happy Days"
43 Open-mouthed
45 Told a tale
47 Health club
48 Racer Donnie's brother
52 FICA funds it
53 Night before
54 Practice pieces
58 Racer Ralph's son
62 Frontiersman Jim or his knife
64 Disorderly demonstration
65 Insert into other people's business
66 Tests without pens
67 Lawyer Perry's creator
68 Red Skelton's Kadiddlehopper
69 Vast chasm
70 ___-in-the-wool
71 Wings that don't flap

DOWN

1 San Antonio mission
2 Heights on the Israeli border
3 Pitchers that aren't mine?
4 More alluring
5 World's oldest continuously existing city
6 Lawyer Dershowitz
7 Woody's surname on "Cheers"
8 Intense looker
9 Shoe parts
10 Straight, as a drink
11 Water-coolers
12 NOW-supported proposal
13 Syst. of late sunsets
21 Redding of blues
22 The last word in some stories
26 Prefix with tease
27 It's cry is a laugh?
29 Bat successfully
30 Whatsoever
31 Fleeceable female
32 "Aladdin" extras
33 Shirt alligators
34 Really hurting
38 Message to all police stas.
40 Egotist's three conversation topics?
41 Took umbrage at
44 Like a peeled potato?
46 Performs for King James
49 Madison or 5th: Abbr.
50 Cast a sidelong glance
51 Subtle distinction
55 Oddly amusing
56 Unfortunate Ford model
57 Checks, as the tide
59 Is laid up
60 Open to breezes
61 Part in a play
62 Crawling crusher
63 Sphere

Answer on page 287

Don't Be Greedy

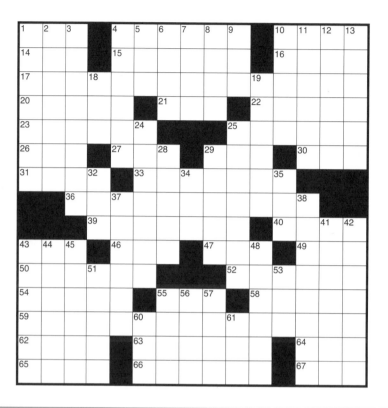

ACROSS
1 First-grader's trio
4 Theatrical company
10 Tickle Me Elmo and Nehru jacket
14 Bart, to Lisa
15 Show derision for
16 Vicinity
17 Start of a quote from Oprah Winfrey
20 "Hit the road!"
21 "___ Loves You" (Beatles hit)
22 Fathered
23 Densely packed
25 Decorated anew
26 Summer quencher
27 Catch on
29 Shannon lander ___ Lingus
30 Signify approval
31 Suffix meaning "not having"
33 Make clear
36 Middle of the quote
39 Book before Jonah
40 Base on balls
43 "This minute!"
46 Roll call response
47 T. follower
49 "The Bells" author
50 International waters
52 Clean the waterway
54 Long-time football coach Amos Alonzo ___
55 Nothing
58 Another time
59 End of the quote
62 Across
63 Make certain
64 Funny ___ (dragster)
65 Joins
66 Joined forces
67 They loop the Loop

DOWN
1 Unfathomable
2 Rich fabric with raised designs
3 It may be professional
4 London's river
5 Director Howard
6 "What wonderful fireworks!" squeals
7 Arches National Park state
8 Put down asphalt
9 Summer along the Seine
10 Predetermined
11 Catherine of ___
12 Roosevelt's middle name
13 Enriched fradulently, as a mine
18 Garfield, for one
19 Spain and Portugal together
24 Some disco employees
25 Got through to
28 Display, as charm
29 Ritual center, often
32 ___ Canals (ships' connection between Lakes Superior and Huron)
34 Greek letter
35 U-turn from SSE
37 River to the Zaire
38 Emulate Gregory Hines
41 Making sense
42 Professional mourners
43 Unexpected absentee
44 Do-to-do interval
45 Drove erratically
48 Like "Midnight Cowboy," originally
51 Stress and trauma, for some
53 "I" trouble
55 "Code of the West" author Grey
56 "Casablanca" role
57 Cushy, as a job
60 Asian observance
61 "We ___ not amused"

Answer on page 289

Four of a Kind

ACROSS

1 Sprat's restriction
6 Puts together
11 Swiss accompaniment, often
14 Wt. system
15 Actress Verdugo
16 High dudgeon
17 1998–2000 Series-winning manager Joe
18 One way to dive
20 Militaristic city-state
22 Get the feeling
23 Middle America
26 Old TV detective Peter
28 Brass et al.
29 Self-denying one
32 Logical beginning?
33 Having a key
35 "The Name of the Rose" author
36 Theme of this puzzle
40 Circular filler
43 Falsely incriminate
44 Spumante city
48 Quickie buildings
50 Big name in yogurt
52 Dabbler
53 With absolutely no trouble
56 Zagreb resident
59 Playground gizmo
60 Where losers may be winners
62 Clarence's accuser
65 Diner sandwich
66 Characteristic
67 Type of tube
68 Cheer for the toreador
69 Scorekeeper's mark, perhaps
70 Brewer's offering

DOWN

1 "Unforgettable" name
2 Lacto-___-vegetarian
3 On the block
4 Tightly sealed
5 Ghent document of 1814
6 Conductor Zubin
7 "... ___ and hungry look"
8 Mauna ___
9 Tackles' neighbors
10 Ahead of the tag
11 Shaggy
12 "Old Lace" companion
13 Expansion player of '62
19 "Bus Stop" dramatist
21 "Treasure Island" monogram
23 "Bali ___"
24 Antiquity, in days past
25 Monkey or Watusi
27 Sgt., e.g.
30 Gal of song
31 Actor Gulager
33 Pan, and then some
34 Omega symbolizes it
37 "Scent ___ Woman"
38 City area, informally
39 Hippie's headwear
40 Well put
41 Kind of battery
42 Saw-toothed
45 Flurrying
46 Drive a wrecker
47 Bed-and-breakfast
49 Noodlehead
50 HST's successor
51 Lace into
54 Jellied garnish
55 Not o'er
57 Memo abbr.
58 "Comin' ___ the Rye"
60 Cable initials
61 Watched junior
63 Placekicker's aid
64 Sheet music abbr.

Answer on page 291

Down the Line

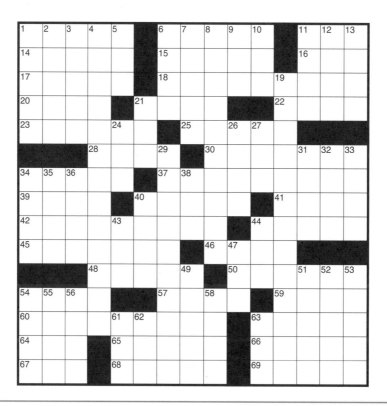

ACROSS

1 Tees off
6 Code of conduct
11 The Red Baron, for one
14 Communications that are always "monitored"
15 Defeat decisively
16 "MAD TV" network
17 Inferior
18 San Francisco arena
20 ___-league (inferior)
21 "___, Nellie!"
22 Gets one's goat
23 Head Hun
25 Image doc
28 Undercover cop
30 "So what?"
34 One of five in a children's rhyme
37 Clams to clam up
39 Heaps
40 Lets up
41 Solitary
42 Lovin' Spoonful singer John
44 "The Wreck of the Mary Deare" author Hammond
45 Kind of label
46 Frisbee, e.g.
48 Checkers' double-deckers
50 "Cocoon" Oscar winner Don
54 Jazzman ___ "Fatha" Hines
57 "___ the Roof" (1963 Drifters hit)
59 "Hud" Oscar winner Patricia
60 Emir or raja
63 Pong producer
64 Bum ___
65 Motown founder Gordy
66 Assail
67 Exploit
68 The Dow, e.g.
69 Sweet liqueur

DOWN

1 Peach ___
2 Poker player's last words?
3 He sold his soul
4 Gar gear
5 Wily
6 Cut glass
7 Bunch of Brownies
8 E.M. Forster novel and 1992 Oscar-winning movie
9 Little rascal
10 April is his cruelest mo.
11 A ways away
12 ___ of the walk
13 What people get when they're divorced
19 "Mostly Mozart Festival" site
21 Kind of bride or chest
24 Give, as odds
26 Minerals' hardness-scale inventor
27 Use the crosshairs
29 Pedal-pusher protector
31 By and by
32 Auberjonois of "Deep Space Nine"
33 The Eagles' "Lyin' ___"
34 Head-'em-off site
35 "___ Her Go" (Frankie Laine song)
36 Mongolian for "place without water"
38 It's a free country
40 It's across the Thames from Windsor
43 Something to do in a jump suit
44 Belief
47 "Society's Child" singer Janis
49 Tower topper
51 Cool it
52 Group that wears oda cologne?
53 Chosen few
54 Color of raw silk
55 Puzzle solver's cries
56 Plump and juicy
58 Layered chalcedony
61 Org. that got Dillinger
62 Half a score
63 1970 Jackson 5 hit

Answer on page 293

Retirement Speech

ACROSS

1 Sadat of Egypt
6 Reef material
11 It often follows "Ooh!"
14 Control mechanism, for short
15 Comedian Kovacs
16 Bride's words
17 Speech before retiring, with 29-, 45-, and 59-Across
19 Dancer Reagan
20 Former rival of the USA
21 Reverend's subj.
22 Horse house
24 Play segments
25 ___ chair (comfortable seat)
27 Dozes
28 Strong wind
29 See 17-Across
32 U-turn from WNW
33 Letter before tee
34 Move briskly
35 Layers
37 Trapped by routine
41 Complains continuously
43 ___-fi
44 Suffix for benz, but not Mercedes
45 See 17-Across
49 Ali ___
50 Butterlike spread
51 Division made by a comb
52 Guinness of "Star Wars"
53 Wrote one's John Hancock on
56 Slinky squeezer
57 State of the Great Salt Lake
58 Actress Gardner
59 See 17-Across
62 Leave, with "out"
63 Let out a long howl
64 Gantry or Fudd
65 Before
66 Zero-wheeled vehicles
67 Adolescents

DOWN

1 Soothes
2 Current events program
3 Hulk Hogan, for one
4 Disinclined
5 Nonsense
6 Flakes and pops
7 End of a threat
8 Chem. in cells
9 Uses crosshairs
10 For fear that
11 Auto safety device
12 Former Kentucky coach Rupp
13 Like Abe
18 Horse-training method
23 Hill of hearings
26 Still
30 Source of sticker shock
31 "Love Will Keep Us Together" singer Tennille
33 And others: Abbr.
36 Singer Susan
38 Hours actually elapsed
39 Without a single defeat
40 They may have pets
42 Fuel additive
43 Covers up
45 Medicine amount
46 Master Twist
47 Render ineffective
48 Used a computer key
49 Gaudy trinket
54 Recedes
55 Start a card game
60 Color for fabric
61 Congeal

Answer on page 295

Open for Inspection

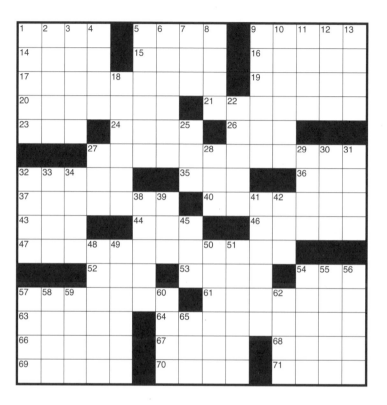

ACROSS
1 Queens counterpart to Yankee Stadium
5 Office communication
9 Editorial piece
14 Sermon inspiration
15 River to the Caspian Sea
16 Oil source
17 Gregorian chant
19 Polytheist, to a monotheist
20 Considering everything
21 Female warriors
23 Small child
24 Deportment
26 Granada article
27 Funt's show
32 Golfer Sam
35 ___ choy cabbage
36 Fancy move on the dance floor
37 Having worse laryngitis
40 Absolute rulers
43 Often-vilified org.
44 "So that's it!"
46 Speak up
47 Inventors' mecca
52 Jazz singer Williams
53 Provide a common bond
54 Vent opening?
57 Editing room techniques
61 Like some events
63 Baldwin and Waugh
64 Discerning
66 Nick of "Lorenzo's Oil"
67 Light
68 206, classically
69 Ballpark figure
70 Kettle of fish, so to speak
71 Quaker pronoun

DOWN
1 Mar. honoree
2 "What was that?!"
3 Raise high
4 Busy
5 Cotton fabric
6 Wore down
7 Cutoff ___ (baseball relayer)
8 Gymnast Korbut
9 European nación
10 Captain Marvel's magic word
11 Starch-yielding palm
12 Broadway's ___ Jay Lerner
13 Hankerings
18 Wanderers
22 Covered with gunk
25 Pen point
27 Pace or prowl follower
28 Internet address component
29 Crime novelist Buchanan
30 "Norma Rae" director Martin
31 Basilica section
32 Send out
33 "Sleepless in Seattle" director Ephron
34 Defender in bridge columns
38 Packed away
39 Greek letter
41 Porch perch
42 "We ___ Family"
45 CIO's partner
48 Throws out
49 Attention getters
50 Hemp products
51 Works with mosaic tiles
54 ___ out (win a mind game)
55 "Deathtrap" star
56 "Frasier" dog
57 Pit viper's weapon
58 Felipe of baseball
59 Take out
60 Racket
62 Splinter group
65 Rough problem?

Answer on page 280

Easy Does It

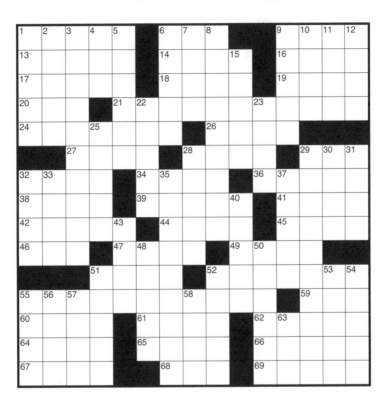

ACROSS
1 Finely chopped, as potatoes
6 Slangy "certainly!"
9 Whole bunch
13 Earthy tone
14 "___ the Roof" (Drifters hit)
16 Prefix with legal or normal
17 "Ta-da!"
18 Succotash bean
19 Oscar-winning role for Julia
20 Fotomat abbr.
21 "Easy!"
24 Marathoning legend Bill
26 "Rag Mop" brothers
27 Intro for -footed or -handed

28 Buttonhole, e.g.
29 "___ see here!"
32 Stare stupidly
34 1949 mil. alliance
36 Love to pieces
38 Is green around the gills
39 Fix, as text
41 Did a takeoff on
42 High dudgeon
44 La ___ Tar Pits
45 Abbr. in many business names
46 Skater's need, once
47 Writing on the wall
49 Timber wolf
51 Go a few rounds
52 Up to the task
55 "Easy!"
59 Ban-___ (shirt material)

60 New York theater award
61 Geritol's got it
62 Like helium or neon
64 Thespian's gig
65 Right-hand man
66 Touted rookie
67 Have a skull session
68 Salty sauce
69 Expressionless

DOWN
1 Generic pooch name
2 Likeness: Prefix
3 "Easy!"
4 Fish sans pelvic fins
5 Dealer in cloth
6 Year-end seasons

7 Of majestic proportions
8 Macaulay Culkin smash
9 Glasses, slangily
10 "Doctor Zhivago" heroine
11 Composer Satie
12 Peter out
15 A musical Judd
22 Cara or Castle
23 Greek salad topper
25 B&B visitor
28 "Private Parts" star
29 "Easy!"
30 Hydrox clone
31 Gets hitched
32 Rubberneck
33 Suffix for the well-to-do
35 Perfume fixative

37 "Yabba ___ Doo!"
40 ___ Lama
43 Kachina doll-making Indian
48 Suffix with Beatle or Wrestle
50 Study of light
51 Hatemonger's garb, perhaps
52 Brooklyn's ___ Island
53 "Two Women" Oscar winner
54 Contest submission
55 Average guy?
56 Tubular instrument
57 Bit of mosaic
58 Brouhaha
63 Word in a petal-plucker's phrase

Answer on page 282

Sandwich Islands Recruits

ACROSS
1 Catchall abbr.
5 Football coach Mike
10 Dogpatch designer
14 Absorbed by
15 Cleveland Indians
16 One side of the Urals
17 Straight-arrow link
18 "Hey, Good Lookin'" songsmith
20 Beatles bandleader recruited by 33-Across?
22 Plunder and pillage
23 The eighth mo., once
24 Russell of "Gypsy," for short
26 "Once In Love With ___"
27 Bolshevik bug?
30 Buster Brown's dog
31 Faux pas
32 Pitcher's bagful
33 Sandwich Islands discoverer
36 Keaton of "Annie Hall"
38 Muzzle
39 Nightclub bits
40 Dastardly looks
42 Go downhill fast
45 Kitten's cry
46 Pinky or Peggy
47 Lean against
49 Murder suspect recruited by 33-Across?
53 Warhol can contents, presumably
54 Piece of fencing?
55 Flair
56 Celebrity ribfest
57 The Fed's Greenspan
58 Ferber of fiction
59 Llama land
60 The Planet's strongest man

DOWN
1 Poisonous atmosphere
2 Jeans line
3 ___-eyed (overly romantic)
4 "1-2-3-kick" dance
5 Like the eaters of rich chocolate desserts?
6 Kind of horse or maiden
7 Slant
8 Continue
9 Slant
10 Bellyache
11 Star of "M*A*S*H"?
12 Polish dumpling
13 Botch a birdie
19 Go (for)
21 The other side of the Urals
25 Branch of Buddhism
28 Crack Justice gp.?
29 Come up
30 Blow the whistle
31 Forbids
32 Shakes awake
33 Sometime resident of 32 Pussyfoot Road
34 Lisbon-to-London dir.
35 Taints
36 Leave it to beavers
37 Freezing
40 Lady of Spain
41 Schindler portrayer
42 Centerfold sight
43 Seoul proprietor?
44 Move over five spaces, perhaps
46 Parking place
48 Chow from a cow
50 Turner of "Peyton Place"
51 Fill, as the bases
52 Calliope, for one
53 Pebble Beach peg

Answer on page 284

Role Reversal

ACROSS

1 Nest eggs
5 Landlocked African republic
9 Bad-mouth
13 Emperor that fiddled around?
14 "The Firebird" composer Stravinsky
15 Low-voiced lady
16 At least once
17 Easily-split mineral
18 Petticoat
19 With 35-Across, appropriately named self-help book?
22 ___ of Good Feeling
23 Hard water?
24 Program-installing command
26 Silences in the orchestra
28 "Cocoon" director Howard
30 Muhammad in the ring
31 Entered
34 Grand closing?
35 See 19-Across
37 They're often inflated
39 A, as in AWOL
40 ___ Aviv
41 Wanted poster letters
42 Best of the artichoke
46 Specter of the Senate
48 Slugger's stat
50 Chinese chairman
51 Author of the self-help book?
55 Expendable one
56 Start of a plea
57 Kazan of "On the Waterfront"
58 Burden
59 Kukla's companion
60 Peroxide, to would-be blondes
61 Secreted salt water
62 Multicolored stone
63 Meat-flavoring mint

DOWN

1 "Well!"
2 Patriot Paul
3 Spots for sports
4 Rather, with "of"
5 Do a take-off on
6 Well-coordinated
7 Prefix with weed or motion
8 Baghdad's country
9 Count in jazz
10 Team from many teams
11 They provoke
12 Beer plant
20 Stair tread connector
21 PT boats are in it
25 Snaps
27 "Terrible" age
28 Rolls off the hoop, with "out"
29 At the expense of yours truly
32 Neighbor of Can.
33 Sousaphone, for one
34 Rose or Rozelle
35 Additional question, often
36 "He's Got the Whole World ___ Hands"
37 Hellenic H
38 Pertinent
41 One with "high hopes," in song
43 Air Earhart
44 "___ to go" (gung-ho)
45 So far
47 Dadaist Max
48 Race with a baton
49 Type of cheer
52 Dope, but not an idiot
53 Break of day
54 Shrimping tools
55 "Batman" fight scene word

Answer on page 286

Rated PG

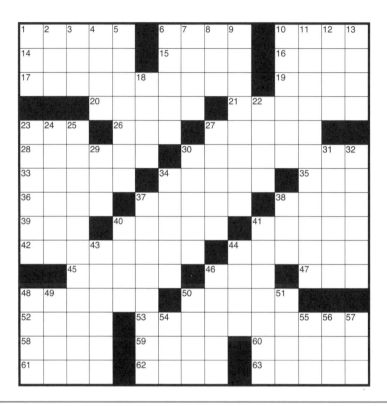

ACROSS
1 Off the mark
6 Interclan hostilities
10 Barbecue gadget
14 Tendon
15 "So what ___ is new?"
16 High-___ (state-of-the-art)
17 Window material
19 Suit to ___
20 Long-necked wading bird
21 Luncheonette
23 Dance noisily
26 Review harshly
27 Fraternal or religious community
28 Blotted out
30 With a lot of affection
33 "___ words were never spoken"
34 Usual egg-purchase quantity
35 Caviar, for example
36 Stir up
37 Helped with the dishes
38 "Endeavor" org.
39 GPA part
40 Talked like hipsters
41 Fido's friend
42 Added some pepper
44 Like some servants
45 Overturn
46 Snow White's bespectacled friend
47 Ave. crossers
48 Actress Pier of "Somebody Up There Likes Me"

50 Had offspring, in the Bible
52 Libertine
53 Charades, for example
58 Spread out, as plaster
59 Israel's airline
60 Wore out
61 "Alas!"
62 Musicians' jobs
63 Old enough

DOWN
1 Egyptian cobra
2 1,000 gees
3 "___ pig's eye!"
4 NFL linebacker Joyner
5 Soccer position
6 Criminal
7 Oomph

8 Initials on an American vessel
9 Merited
10 ___ Island (New York City borough)
11 Star of TV's "Mission: Impossible"
12 Bakery employee
13 Unnamed authorities
18 Reunion attender
22 Tennis score after "deuce"
23 Aquarium fishes
24 Get in
25 Artist who spent time in Tahiti
27 Exuded moisture
29 Meet a poker bet
30 Ran easily
31 Throw a hissy fit
32 Longs
34 Tried a jackknife

37 Manitoba's capital
38 Fall mo.
40 "Piano Man" player Billy
41 Arnaz's sitcom name
43 Bathing suit brand
44 Nike's "swoosh," for one
46 Small valleys
48 Guthrie of music
49 Early visitor to Ararat
50 Speak highly of oneself
51 End-of-the-week exclamation
54 Pugilist nicknamed "The Mouth That Roared"
55 Palindromic Oklahoma town
56 Russian fighter jet
57 WSW's opposite

Answer on page 288

Cheese It

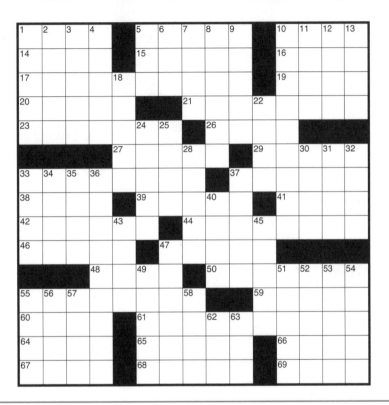

ACROSS

1 Hairpieces, slangily
5 Command to a junkyard dog
10 Male porker
14 Concerning, in legalese
15 "What's in ___?"
16 Pakistani tongue
17 BRICK
19 Shake hands with
20 Cashed, as a doctored check
21 Bark growth
23 Not so dense
26 Consult the crystal ball
27 Clear the tape
29 Brainstorms
33 Beachgoer's need
37 Like a mammoth
38 Aunt Bee's charge
39 Farm gear pioneer
41 ___ Bator, Mongolia
42 Crescent-shaped
44 Word on many dictionaries
46 Inundation
47 Cash on hand, e.g.
48 "If We Only Have Love" composer Jacques
50 Part of an eighteen-wheeler
55 Makes angry
59 Oil-yielding rock
60 No walk in the park
61 COTTAGE
64 '20s Oscar winner Jannings
65 Ouzo flavoring
66 Invited a ticket, perhaps
67 Say it ain't so
68 Big Three meeting site
69 Start of a selection process

DOWN

1 Insurers assume them
2 Nerdy
3 Persona non ___
4 Passover meal
5 ___ Paulo, Brazil
6 Baseman's milieu: Abbr.
7 Horse preceder, aphoristically
8 Exit one's cocoon
9 Jason's wife, in myth
10 BLUE
11 Nabisco bestseller
12 Fruit drinks
13 Dead-end jobs, e.g.
18 Ford flop
22 Operatic Pinza
24 Whittle away
25 Triathlon, e.g.
28 Applies a fudge factor to
30 Vogue competitor
31 Banned apple spray
32 Thesaurus entries: Abbr.
33 Scale notes
34 "___ and Away"
35 Santa Maria companion
36 CREAM
37 Magnetic flux unit
40 Catch one's breath
43 Jimmy Carter had one
45 Secret supply
47 Barnard College grad
49 Op-ed offering
51 Picked out
52 Neutral shade
53 Daily Planet cub
54 Like an oboe's sound
55 Place for the lawn mower
56 Subdue
57 Word in a March 17 slogan
58 McKinley's "full dinner ___"
62 Omaha Beach vessel
63 Grazing ground

Answer on page 290

All in the Family

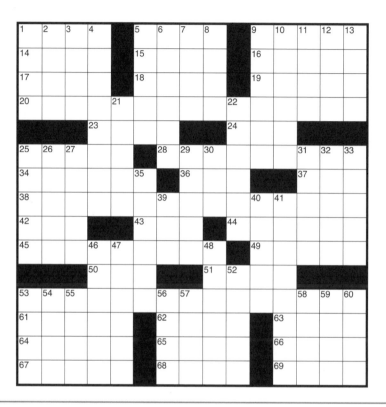

ACROSS
1 Make like the Big Bad Wolf
5 Ducks' docs
9 Home
14 Pluckable
15 Jon Arbuckle's pooch
16 Fixed fritters
17 Flight from Israel?
18 Bistro
19 Flush out
20 Best Director for "The French Connection"
23 Glamour rival
24 "No ___" (Chinese restaurant sign)
25 Emerson's middle name
28 Agra, from New Delhi
34 Stimulate
36 Coast Guard VIP
37 Seashore seashell seller
38 Grimm name-game guy
42 Where to find Cavs and Mavs
43 Mop-topped Stooge
44 Moola, Mexican-style
45 Certainly, in Montreal
49 Pulitzer poet W.H. ___
50 Listening device
51 Action word
53 First U.S. Congresswoman (1917–19)
61 Montezuma, for one
62 Cry of dismay
63 Greek liqueur
64 Spring bloomers
65 Data-speed unit
66 Put your foot in it
67 "On the Waterfront" director Elia
68 Cry of dismay
69 Breaks off

DOWN
1 Witch's ___
2 Film on which "Carnival" was based
3 Iridescent gemstone
4 Surged to the surface
5 Outspoken
6 "My Cup Runneth Over" singer
7 Squabble
8 Nostradamus, e.g.
9 From square one
10 Troll's charge
11 Sow sound
12 He loved Lucy
13 Idyllic place
21 "How can ___?" (gambler's query)
22 "So they say"
25 Tips off
26 Caribbean getaway
27 Miller's salesman
29 Square dance group
30 AP rival, once
31 Popped the question
32 English county
33 Dovetail piece
35 "Get Shorty" author Leonard
39 Not worth a ___
40 Pageant prize
41 .38 feature, perhaps
46 Tribe of the Iroquois Confederacy
47 1978 Fosse musical
48 Bring into balance
52 Lose ground?
53 "City Slickers" Oscar winner Palance
54 Book after II Chronicles
55 Dictionary range
56 Mug shaped like a stout man with a cocked hat for the brim
57 Asian cuisine
58 Former baseball commissioner Bowie
59 Polo shirt label
60 Refusals

Answer on page 292

Scents You Asked

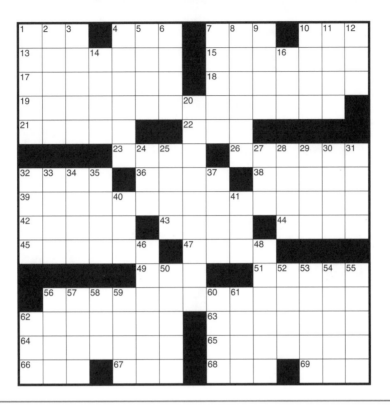

ACROSS
1 Veer to the side
4 Destroy the interior of
7 Hosp. honchos
10 X to Xenophon
13 Terrestrially
15 Clear up
17 Where "away" appears in most dictionaries?
18 Dragon of "Kukla, Fran, and Ollie"
19 Coins phrases?
21 Really impresses, as a lover
22 Gal. fourths
23 River on the Korean border
26 The boss's "echo"
32 Dips in gravy
36 "I kid you not" sayer
38 River of Cologne
39 Microfiche segments?
42 Peace Prize winner Sadat
43 Jacob's brother
44 Garment close to cards, for some
45 Sacred music genre
47 Little devils
49 Chicken preceder ... or not
51 Licorice flavoring
56 "Olé!" and "Rah, rah, rah!"?
62 Tavern
63 Non-rent-paying residents
64 Accelerate
65 Delta, but not alpha, beta, or gamma
66 Venom source
67 Pig's digs
68 F of FSU
69 A Chicago nine

DOWN
1 Closeup shots, maybe
2 Horseshoes rest on it
3 Davis of "Thelma and Louise"
4 Lush, like a pasture
5 Spy plane or rock band
6 "So what happened ___?"
7 Central part
8 Nodding but not saying yes
9 Ford, in "Star Wars"
10 128 cubic feet, to a woodchopper
11 Shades
12 Tag antagonists
14 Bohemian
16 "Neither" companion
20 Two short horizontal lines
24 Fitting
25 Forgetful of the clock, perhaps
27 Go off course
28 Switchblade
29 Wartime harbor hazard
30 Hill habitants
31 Hornet's home
32 Six-pointer, sometimes
33 "Well, hell!"
34 Supporters of the congregation?
35 Mild censure, when on the wrist
37 Scold, with "out"
40 Anger
41 Little Lab
46 Released
48 Bogie war flick
50 Like an injured leg
52 Salt on a chemist's table
53 Vonda Shepard's "It's ___ Kiss"
54 One who works for a dictator
55 County in England
56 Drains, as energy
57 Type of school
58 Bauxite, for one
59 Lightning drawers
60 1988 Wimbledon winner
61 "... shuffled off this mortal ___"
62 Tenderfoot's org.

Answer on page 294

Dann Party

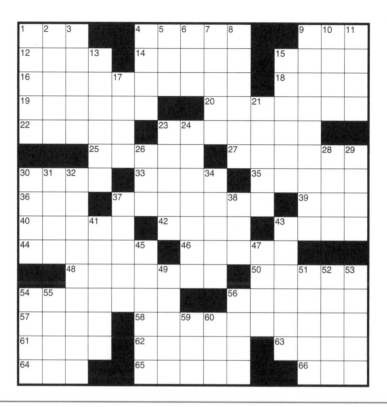

ACROSS
1 Sitcom ET
4 Model builder's wood
9 Marsh area
12 Attractions at San Diego and Chicago's Lincoln Park
14 Pertaining to birds
15 Lounge about
16 Folk dance of southern Italy
18 Meat-inspecting agcy.
19 Works with acid
20 Went by, as time
22 Swindle
23 Compound used in smelling salts
25 "The Mary Tyler Moore Show" spin-off
27 Won a rummy hand
30 ___ California
33 Entertainer Minnelli
35 Like Santa's suit on December 26th
36 Onassis's nickname
37 "Begin the ___" (Cole Porter standard)
39 Rock's ___ Halen
40 Have an effect on
42 First name in detective fiction
43 Word in many detective fiction titles
44 Lustrous fabrics
46 New Hampshire city
48 Intellectual highbrow
50 Saddam Hussein, for one
54 Confirmed
56 Aspen attraction
57 E.g., e.g.
58 Flapper's dance
61 Entre ___
62 TV journalist Couric
63 Italy's Villa d' ___
64 Beer barrel
65 Links great Sam
66 Suffix with law or bow

DOWN
1 Montezuma subject
2 Reluctant
3 "May the ___ be with you"
4 Comes to the plate
5 Blvd. crosser
6 ___ Abner
7 Oregon's capital
8 Counterpart of "digital"
9 Dance from Brazil
10 Shoppe descriptor
11 Lighthearted
13 Northern Africa, west of the Nile
15 Ida of film
17 Neighbor of Belg.
21 Liqueur flavoring
23 Verona's river
24 Folk dance of Poland
26 "¡Bravo!"
28 Hellenic letters
29 Newton's smaller cousin
30 "Paper or plastic?" items
31 Neighborhood
32 Jazzy two-step dance
34 Was under the weather
37 Beatnik's drum
38 Word before a maiden name
41 Siegfried and Roy's cats
43 Moderate red
45 "'tweren't nothin' "
47 Big name in court shoes
49 "Raising Arizona" filmmaker Coen
51 ___-craftsy
52 Provide, as a stock price
53 Word with city or tube
54 Count (on)
55 Orchestral reed
56 Malamute's burden
59 Had a little something
60 Fjord's kin

Answer on page 280

Dollar Daze

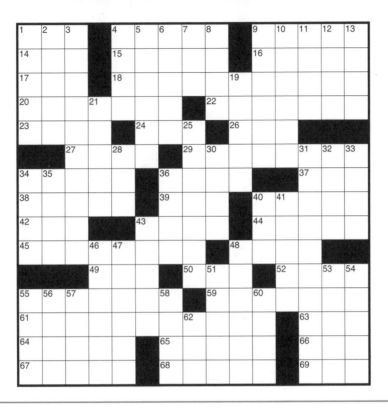

ACROSS

1 Mineo of movies
4 Stinkweed emanations
9 Hide away
14 Thrilla in Manilla winner
15 Delhi dough
16 ___ Carlo
17 Jazz style for Gillespie
18 Hearty soup
20 Set up for use, as a computer program
22 Becomes fond of
23 Jules Verne captain
24 Problem letter for lispers
26 Tierra ___ Fuego
27 Parts of some chairs
29 Pole vaulter's hurdle
34 De ___ (actual)
36 Aspirin's target
37 Numero ___ (first-rate)
38 Aggravated
39 CPR expert
40 Formal pronouncements
42 Improve, as steak
43 "___ Time, Next Year"
44 Alan of "Catch-22"
45 Race winner of fable
48 Poet ___ Khayyám
49 Fix, as a fight
50 "___ Rosenkavalier"
52 Durante's protuberance
55 "Winnie-the-Pooh" author
59 Offspring of a deity and a mortal
61 Texas leaguer
63 Lilly of pharmaceuticals
64 Singer Ronstadt
65 Teammate of Snider and Hodges
66 Stoolie
67 Moth-___ (timeworn)
68 Everglades bird
69 AARP members

DOWN

1 Oral vaccine developer
2 By oneself
3 Flavored gloss for kids
4 Shamu or Willy
5 Washington-area airport
6 October gems
7 Dreamy acronym
8 Religious offshoot
9 Enjoys a cheroot
10 "His" and "Hers" items
11 "No ifs, ___, ..."
12 Leave in, to a proofreader
13 Hefty sandwich
19 Wore
21 Rich cake
25 Took to the cleaners, so to speak
28 Fashionable, '60s-style
30 Baptism or confirmation
31 Spaceman portrayed by Buster Crabbe
32 Not in favor of
33 Colorful horse
34 Italian automaker
35 Golden Fleece ship
36 Green Giant spheroids
40 Water gate
41 Persian, today
43 "Open" and "Out to Lunch," e.g.
46 Vacuum tube type
47 Crankcase bottom
48 End of a blackmailer's threat
51 Lawn neatener
53 Kind of energy or battery
54 Cuts and pastes
55 Up to the job
56 Inter ___ (among others)
57 Wyo. neighbor
58 Sinn Féin's land
60 Track contest
62 Battery term.

Answer on page 282

Glee Club

ACROSS

1 Penny prez
4 Composure
10 River to the underworld
14 Capote, on Broadway
15 Coffee maker
16 Furry critter in "Return of the Jedi"
17 Brussels-based trade gp.
18 More than happy
20 1995 Baseball Hall of Fame inductee Mike
22 Down to the ___
23 With 57-Across, more than happy
25 It ain't worth a dime
29 WWII gun
30 Flange
32 Wee wand wielder
33 Intimidate
36 Pooch of primers
38 Berliner's article
39 More than happy
44 Cote comment
45 Longest river entirely within Spain
46 Malaprop or Miniver
47 Impressionist painter Degas
49 First zoo?
51 Instrument with a triangular frame
55 Tank battle?
57 See 23-Across
60 Downwind
62 Brian of "Presumed Innocent"
63 More than happy
67 XXX center
68 "Days of Grace" author Arthur
69 "Empty hand" skill, literally
70 Bull or fool follower
71 Mutant Marvel Comics supergroup
72 Cured, in a way
73 Korean-American comedienne Margaret

DOWN

1 Bikini tryouts
2 "The Threepenny Opera" writer Bertolt
3 32-card trick-taking game
4 Bubbling, as hot water
5 Gearshift sequence, often
6 Cannibal Hannibal
7 Pal of Pooh and Piglet
8 Socks sound
9 Boston Garden skater
10 Largest of the Finger Lakes
11 Light or night beginning
12 Hither and ___
13 Classic Jag
19 Gadabout
21 Subdivide minutely
24 Warp
26 City near Chernobyl
27 Barge canal of song
28 Coal miner's daughter
31 Dashboard letters
34 On the whole
35 World-wide phenomenon
37 Electrician's mantra?
39 "___ to differ!"
40 Zip, to Zapata
41 Loses rigidity
42 FDR's Blue Eagle gp.
43 Ghostly
48 Come to
50 Alaskan brown bear
52 Vinegary
53 Cover old ground
54 Hitchcock classic
56 Smells up the place
58 Five-in-a-row board game played with stones
59 Signed on the dotted line
61 Wax-coated appetizer
63 Customs duty, e.g.
64 Ideology
65 Ernesto Guevara
66 Old hand

Answer on page 284

Closed-Door Policy

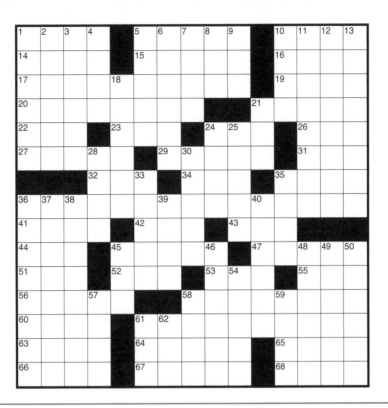

ACROSS

1 Expressed, as farewell
5 Pre-tax-audit feeling
10 Bible book after John
14 And others, for short
15 Lunar landing module
16 Anecdotal knowledge
17 Capillary coil
19 "Put a lid ___!"
20 In the books
21 Make more lean
22 Sgt. or cpl.
23 Brewed beverage
24 Edible paste
26 Dogleg shape
27 Columbus's home town
29 Out of ___ way (safe)
31 Prefix with dent or cot
32 Salutation for Caesar
34 Woody's ex
35 Nonlethal phaser setting
36 Streak in a stormy sky
41 "Breaking ___ Hard to Do"
42 ___ Tin Tin
43 "So!"
44 U.S. Grant's rank
45 Discharge from the service, in British slang
47 Snowy bird, perhaps
51 "You ___ There" ('50s documentary drama)
52 Diamond judge?
53 From 300 to 3000 MHz
55 Egg fragment?
56 Apply juice, as to a turkey
58 Diplomatic etiquette
60 Where the joke may be
61 Consume consecutive Camels
63 Lofty poems
64 Rock's ___ and the Dominos
65 On the rocks
66 Becomes eligible for repentance
67 Peach pits, e.g.
68 Commotion

DOWN

1 Fit in
2 Right now
3 Wrinkle-resistant material
4 Sommer of "A Shot in the Dark"
5 Crusoe's creator
6 Having the old school spirit
7 "Yikes!"
8 MacGraw of "Love Story"
9 Article written by Martin Luther?
10 Skin lotion source
11 Ticker-tape parade "rain"
12 Shakedown cruise
13 Paying the bill, with "up"
18 Book size
21 Put down, to P. Diddy
24 Pointlessly precise person
25 Beach at Normandy
28 Feedbag contents
30 Kind of acid in protein
33 Zimbalist of "The F.B.I."
35 Hosiery hole
36 Hobgoblins
37 Modus ___
38 They assist referees
39 Walk with a wobble
40 Burglaries
45 Subject to collection
46 Underground, as treasure
48 Ornate architecture style
49 Produced a vivid impression of
50 "Holy" Ohio town
54 Sounds the horn
57 Della on "Touched By an Angel"
58 Remove by cutting
59 Leave out
61 Tape alternatives
62 "___ Haw"

Answer on page 286

Hitting for the Cycle

ACROSS
1 Fix some potatoes
5 "Hey ___" (Beatles hit)
9 Tony, for one
14 Pre-Columbian Peruvian
15 "If ___ a Hammer"
16 Spock portrayer
17 Without a date
18 Indicate by signs
19 Wears down, in a way
20 Unassisted
23 Section of "Hamlet," for example
24 Northern Ireland, informally
28 Experiencing diplopia
33 Tummy muscles
36 Low point
37 They divide Europe and Asia
38 "Nota ___" (note well, classically)
40 ___ Taylor of "The Nanny"
42 Worry
43 Overeats
45 Worries
47 Alums-to-be
48 Multitalented one
51 Bravery, in Canada
52 Quagmire
56 "Fog Warning" artist
61 Pre-Columbian Mexican
64 Bus alternative
65 Stick around
66 Joie de ___
67 Accompanying, in Montreal

68 "That's clear enough"
69 Make ___ at (hit on)
70 Safe place?
71 "Faster ___ a speeding bullet"

DOWN
1 Beethoven's "___ Solemnis"
2 Shenanigan
3 Marginally enough
4 Traditional Scottish dish
5 Dovetail
6 "Oops!"
7 The world according to Arp?
8 "Tree of knowledge" garden
9 Non-Pre-Columbian Maya?
10 Ride a sailboard
11 GP's gp.
12 Rank or file
13 Prefix meaning "bad"
21 Legal claim
22 Hardly a success
25 Some ski lifts
26 Aunt ___ ("Oklahoma!" role)
27 Takes five
29 Dumbo's "wing"
30 Clarifying phrase from Cato
31 Last inning, usually
32 Feminist Germaine
33 Where to see Peter Jennings
34 Oft-quoted ballplayer
35 Slow critter
39 Authorizes

41 Its gestation period is 147 days
44 Floodgates
46 Ambassador's ceremonial accessory
49 West ender
50 Small-time
53 "Give me the simple life" advocate
54 She helped Jason get the Golden Fleece
55 Strut with pride
57 Attempt
58 Source of obsidian
59 Farm team
60 Candle component
61 Gardner of "Mogambo"
62 Get-up-and-go
63 Bldr. of dams

Answer on page 288

The Yoke's on Us

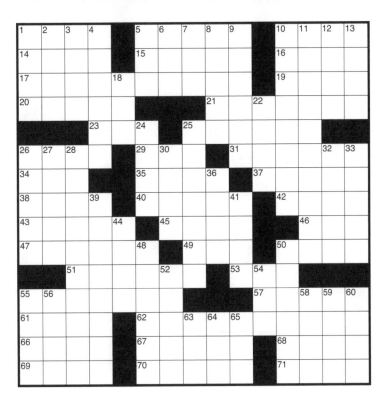

ACROSS

1 Picket line crosser
5 With Begin, 1978 Nobelist
10 Electrical letters
14 Stretch out on the couch
15 Cleveland team, in headlines
16 Perlman of "Cheers"
17 Site of Lee's surrender
19 Use a harrow
20 Kind of jar
21 Ultra-left-winger
23 Faddish '90s collectible
25 Rudolph's master
26 LP's
29 Attorneys' org.
31 Like many oaths
34 "___ bin ein Berliner"
35 Fuji flow
37 Adorée of old films
38 Annapolis mascot
40 Addis ___
42 Disgorge
43 Words before fritz or lam
45 "Ah, me!"
46 Sugar suffix
47 More than chubby
49 Burrows of the theater
50 Tara Lipinski feat
51 Keys in
53 Fuse rating unit
55 Andalusian city
57 In bad company, according to Bierce
61 Singer Lane
62 Breaking with tradition
66 "Let's Make a Deal" choice
67 Bar mitzvah scroll
68 Cole's "___ Lisa"
69 Appealing, in a way
70 Like some winter days
71 ___ Bones (Sleepy Hollow bully)

DOWN

1 Shut loudly
2 Nightclub in a Manilow tune
3 Mont Blanc range
4 Softly-hit singles, maybe
5 RR depot
6 Museum pieces
7 E, to Morse
8 Scrub, NASA-style
9 Alamo defenders
10 Newspaper fillers
11 Childhood malady, usually
12 Boxer Oscar ___ Hoya
13 Ump's decision
18 Touch-tone 6
22 Christian of fashion
24 Big bash
25 Telly on the telly
26 Inflexibility
27 ___ Lodge (motel chain)
28 Motor-mouth
30 Rum cake
32 Reagan Attorney General Edwin
33 Stairway post
36 Quatrain rhyme scheme
39 Booming
41 On a clipper
44 Within: Prefix
48 Enters society
50 Self-confidence
52 Talked and talked and talked ...
54 ___-jongg
55 They're no gentlemen
56 Bassoon relative
58 Dumpster emanation
59 Forbidden thing
60 Oral or physical
63 "___ y Plata" (Montana's motto)
64 Like steak tartare
65 The Lord's Prayer pronoun

Answer on page 290

Let There Be Light Humor

ACROSS

1 Dracula's alter ego
4 Tear into
10 High point
14 "Do Ya" rockers
15 Villain
16 Frolic
17 Big dog, for short
18 Part 1 of a quote by Flannery O'Connor
20 Thurman of "The Truth About Cats and Dogs"
21 "It's no ___!"
22 Bodies of art?
23 Part 2 of quote
25 "Hold the ___" (deli request)
27 For example
29 Lush sounds
30 Guff
31 Berlin article
32 Part 3 of quote
37 Shellacking
38 "Stick ___!"
39 Part 4 of quote
46 Exchange barbs or jabs
47 Sussex suds
48 First name in household humor
49 Wheaton of "Star Trek: The Next Generation"
50 "___ on the Wild Side"
52 Part 5 of quote
54 Business biggie
56 "___ With Dick and Jane"
57 Uris hero ___ Ben Canaan
58 End of quote
61 Witticism
62 Thrilled
63 Lack of musical ability
64 "To the max" indicator
65 Famous last words
66 Brogue, e.g.
67 Mommy deer

DOWN

1 "Animal House" star John
2 El ___, Egypt (WWII battle site)
3 Plantation product
4 Liaison
5 Have a hunch
6 End of the year event
7 Even the slightest
8 It comes after Sr. and Jr.
9 Southpaw
10 Parodist
11 Historically memorable
12 Trench in the West Pacific
13 Private ___
19 Court
24 Shylock
25 A thousand Gs
26 Individually
28 Itch
30 Murderous
31 Caught sight of
33 ___ v. Wade
34 On the other hand
35 Philips of comedy
36 Giant syllable
39 Detroit-to-Denver dir.
40 Nickname
41 Conspicuous
42 Yellowstone beast
43 Lambasted
44 Tenderly, in music
45 Gulf of Mexico pirate Jean
50 Obi-___ Kenobi
51 Baker of the blues
52 Lazy lady?
53 More than lethargic
55 "Dying swan" attire
56 Priceless?
58 "Cats" monogram
59 Damone of "Kismet"
60 In this pkg.

Answer on page 292

Sorry

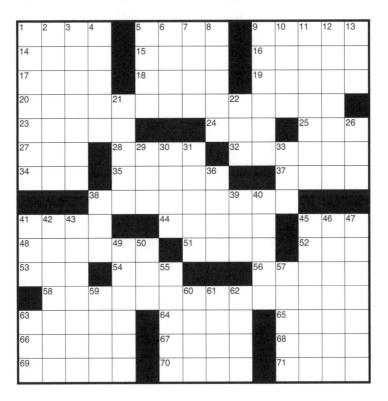

ACROSS
1 Wight, for one
5 Warsaw agreement
9 Bitterly pungent
14 Moon walker Armstrong
15 Dull pain
16 Demi or Dudley
17 Piece of soap
18 Noisy impact
19 Wrinkle-resistant textile
20 "Sorry!"
23 Tucker of "Nickel Dreams"
24 Sung syllable
25 Hours of sunlight
27 Language suffix
28 Tremendous
32 Hold without proof
34 One-eighty from NNE
35 Put in two cents worth
37 Matrimonial escapees
38 Sorry!
41 Perimeter contents
44 Gregg Allman's brother
45 Trig. ratio
48 Paul Simon's "El ___ Pasa"
51 "Giant" writer Ferber
52 Ecology org.
53 E of EEC
54 Commanded
56 "Unsafe at Any Speed" author
58 Sorry
63 Loud blow
64 Type of lens
65 North Sea feeder
66 Dog, to a mailman's leg, perhaps
67 Feline female of film
68 Greenspan of interest
69 Dictation taker
70 Beginning to do-well?
71 Blowgun missile

DOWN
1 Urges, as to riot
2 Saltwater swimmer
3 In seemingly mint condition
4 Plaintive poem
5 "El ___" (Marty Robbins # 1 hit)
6 Scopes Trial org.
7 Scorch
8 Offer a bad choice to
9 Without principle
10 Firewood measure
11 Circular file?
12 Era after Bronze
13 Cub scout unit
21 AltaVista alternative
22 Coach Parseghian, of Notre Dame fame
26 "That's right"
29 ___ tree (stumped)
30 Encircle
31 Bestow
33 "Uncle Robert" of the Confederate army
36 "Holy cow!"
38 Michael Jackson chart topper
39 Landers of letters
40 Should have said
41 Crack fighter pilot
42 Forgo creature comforts
43 On the way
45 Soft c mark in "français"
46 Where drinks are on the host
47 "Madame X" painter
49 Veteran
50 Sports judge
55 Thirteen, to some bakers
57 Leading
59 Serious sign
60 Part of a play
61 Narrow victory margin
62 Shariff of "Funny Girl"
63 Ted's network: Abbr.

Answer on page 294

Theatric Antics

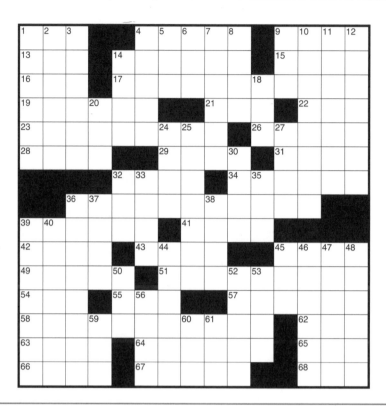

ACROSS

1 Locomotive part
4 Change, hopefully for the better
9 Humane org.
13 Power hitter's stat
14 Gum arabic source
15 Impetuosity
16 Word in the Three Musketeers' motto
17 Headline after a Wells Fargo holdup?
19 Yogi Bear's sidekick
21 Fidel's friend
22 Gretzky's gp.
23 UPS drop-off location?
26 Calf in a range herd
28 Give off
29 Sunday ___ (finery)
31 Coin factory
32 Mare's babe
34 Reddish tree-dwelling apes, commonly
36 Absolute zero?
39 Rum cocktail
41 Pollution you can see
42 ___ Domini
43 "¿Cómo ___ usted?"
45 Bringing up the rear
49 Heredity elements
51 Outing for fly-fishing enthusiasts?
54 "___ Yankee Doodle dandy ..."
55 Musical ability
57 Axle cover
58 Leno's substitute?
62 "Sting like a bee" boxer
63 In a little while, to Juliet
64 Start on the links
65 Cub Scout subgroup
66 Time to give up?
67 Piggish proboscis
68 Fraction of a joule

DOWN

1 Buster of Flash Gordon serials
2 In full flower
3 Mississippi city
4 ___ God (unpreventable occurrence)
5 Ewe's cry
6 Heart test's printout, briefly
7 Family reunion attenders
8 6 drops, in recipes
9 Sun. speech
10 Dropping like a rock
11 Using computer memory effectively, perhaps
12 Short socks
14 From
18 Turner or Williams
20 Plant-life sci.
24 Building beam
25 Keyboard instrument
27 Mideast sultanate
30 Kind of list
32 The Sunshine State, briefly
33 Jon Arbuckle's dog
35 Oil-drilling machinery
36 Cappuccino flavoring, often
37 Siouan speaker
38 Bit of Latin conjugation
39 Giving a feeling of enchantment
40 Windflower
44 Block (from view)
45 Where experiments may take place
46 Amusement center
47 Less fresh
48 At the keyboard
50 Min. fraction
52 Ripoff artist's crime
53 Dragon's name, in a song
56 ___ and crafts
59 Passbook abbr.
60 August sign
61 Promissory note, of a sort

Answer on page 280

Old Testament Revisited

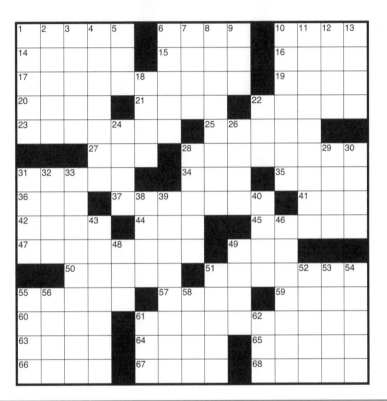

ACROSS

1 ___ one's ways (obstinate)
6 Busboy's pickup
10 Obsolete VCR format
14 Egg producer
15 Bob of "Road" films
16 Menswear brand
17 Old Testament cookie maker?
19 Flip-a-coin test answer
20 Deuce follower, maybe
21 Place for ChapStick
22 Absorb in class
23 Tightens the oxfords
25 Scout unit
27 George Burns role
28 Policeman, slangily
31 Truman veep Barkley
34 "Mr. October" Jackson, for short
35 Noxious vapor
36 China's Chou En-___
37 Folks to keep up with?
41 "... ___ a lender be"
42 Scatter Fitzgerald
44 Cambodian's neighbor
45 Intense feeling
47 Reported to the home office, in a way
49 Cellular phone co.
50 Tyrolean's tune
51 Lacking color
55 Bosc cousin
57 ___-trigger temper
59 Opposed to, in Dogpatch
60 "Arf!" equivalent
61 Old Testament national park?
63 Daredevil Knievel
64 "Not to mention ..."
65 Annoyance
66 Tyne of "Cagney & Lacey"
67 Uncle ___ (rice brand)
68 Fragrant compound

DOWN

1 To date
2 Steer clear of
3 Sri Lankan native
4 Period starting about 1400 B.C.
5 Big Apple sch.
6 Bangkok residents
7 Lopsided win
8 Jesus's twelve
9 Marv Albert shout
10 ___ more than one can chew
11 Old Testament poet?
12 Sightseeing trip
13 Mideast gulf
18 Gravity-powered vehicle
22 Place to park
24 "And" or "or": Abbr.
26 Go ballistic
28 Refrigerator coolant
29 Melville classic of 1847
30 Guam, for one: Abbr.
31 Baldwin or Waugh
32 In ___ land (spacey)
33 Old Testament singer?
38 Shoppe sign word, often
39 Spackler's target
40 Fill to excess
43 In a standoffish manner
46 Has a connection
48 Part of a school's web address
49 Spiritual mentor
51 Ritz alternatives
52 White-plumed bird
53 Sifting utensil
54 Villain's look
55 Thunderstruck
56 Chevy of yore
58 Org.
61 Sharp left from Ali
62 Big brute

Answer on page 282

Tops

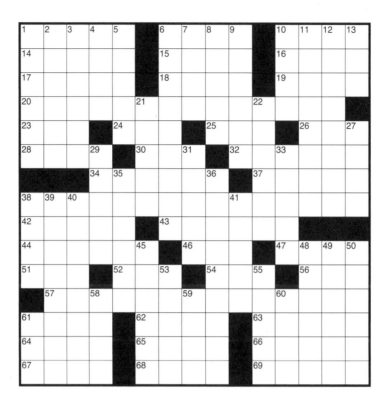

ACROSS
1 Climbs
6 They're radio-active
10 Altar area
14 Call off, as a mission
15 Moises of the Cubs
16 Climb
17 Historic Alabama city
18 Sylvester's trademark
19 Lohengrin's bride
20 Top choice
23 Target the target
24 Deposited
25 Blow it
26 Cartoon collectible
28 "Sweater Girl" Turner
30 Third numero
32 Am-scray, old-style
34 Gushes
37 Bedevil
38 Top dog
42 Throw around
43 Largest city of the West Indies
44 Stage whispers
46 It isn't gross
47 Ivory source
51 Machine gun syllable
52 Give the go-ahead
54 ATM-making co.
56 Herd word
57 Top deb
61 Cubist Joan
62 Without question
63 Ho Chi Minh city
64 Goody two shoes
65 "Let Us Now Praise Famous Men" author James
66 Vacuum tube gas
67 Down Under greeting
68 It's a question of time
69 Dill swill

DOWN
1 Scamp
2 Airline to Madrid
3 Extremely earnest
4 Anecdotal Bombeck
5 It's canceled when it's accepted
6 Twice-told, it's still a tale
7 Came down to earth
8 Israeli statesman Dayan
9 Splendiferous
10 Antiquing element
11 Explorer Marco's outerwear?
12 Hitchcock's genre
13 Pollution police: Abbr.
21 ___-body experience
22 Stupid clod
27 Unwelcome glance
29 Invited
31 Hawke of "Reality Bites"
33 Imply
35 Gulf War general
36 Girls' magazine
38 H.S. exam
39 "Superman" intro phrase
40 Yardsticks
41 Glom (onto)
45 It has its ups and downs
48 Lip-stretching woman
49 Oater bar
50 Tiger great Al
53 Hard-nosed
55 Post-op therapy
58 Sluggish
59 Complimentary
60 Roseanne, once
61 Fuel economy letters

Answer on page 284

They Called My Number

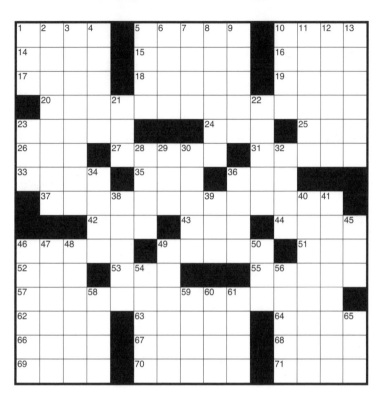

ACROSS

1 Von Trapp family escape route
5 "Angel of the Battlefield" Barton
10 Portend
14 Liquid container
15 Takes a shine to
16 Trebek, in "Jeopardy!"
17 Singer Fitzgerald
18 Baja buddy
19 Out of work
20 Cupid triumphed again?
23 Stopwatch or hourglass
24 Superman's nemesis Luthor
25 Lawyer, briefly
26 Natl. news network
27 Remove chalk dust from
31 Takes the hook
33 Tush
35 One sixth of an inning
36 Edible part of a snow pea
37 Overly sharp blade?
42 "___ you sleeping, Brother John?"
43 By means of
44 Pugilist Spinks
46 Mrs. Butler's maiden name
49 Speaks in sport
51 Aladdin's monkey
52 Egg drink
53 Golf supporter
55 Satirist Nash
57 Carpet golf?
62 Word with sesame
63 Drab color, sometimes
64 "The joke's ___"
66 Toast topper
67 Huron and Erie
68 Antiaircraft fire
69 Bits
70 Jerry Maguire, for one
71 Last word on December 31, maybe

DOWN

1 Hail, to Maria
2 Land with a small population?
3 Golden-coated horse
4 Work one's fingers to the bone
5 Type of hammer
6 Long car, for short
7 Related by blood
8 Delight
9 In unison
10 ___-and-switch
11 Passé
12 Computer key
13 Brings to bear
21 Before
22 "The ___ Incident"
23 Bath basin
28 ___ herd on (managed)
29 Mo. named for a Caesar
30 Comedian Martin
32 Golden calf, for one
34 Skyrocket
36 Introductory exam: Abbr.
38 Muse of love poetry
39 Bad-mouth, to a rapper
40 Unchangeable, like a CD
41 Short-haired dog
45 Woman under a vow of poverty
46 Without a horse or car
47 Commotion
48 Came to terms
49 Flying fatigue
50 Sun deity
54 Name on a bomber
56 Makes mistakes
58 Son of Seth
59 March or move up
60 Get ___ (retaliate)
61 Suffix with gab or slug
65 Barely make, with "out"

Answer on page 286

Get Packing!

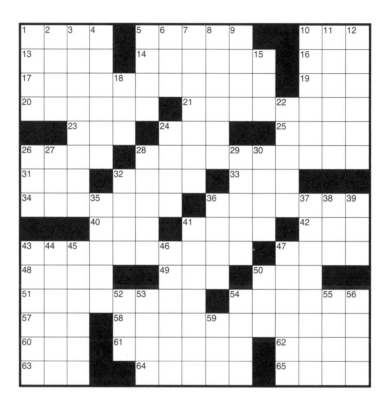

ACROSS

1 Easy victory
5 Arrived
10 Rink official
13 Girder resembling a letter
14 Ark's ultimate resting place
16 Bush, collegiately
17 Item in Holyfield's locker
19 Do some damage
20 Grabs hold of
21 Patellas
23 Kittenish cry
24 GI's entertainment supplier
25 Lean to one side
26 Oklahoma city
28 Main phone circuits
31 "The ___" (Diana Ross film)
32 Defeat soundly
33 Convent figure
34 Pensive poems
36 Michael or Stonewall
40 Verse intro?
41 Unsteady, as a tone
42 Bygone Eur. realm
43 Deep body of water in the Cascade Range
47 Be in accord
48 Ages and ages
49 It's unrefined
50 Race, as an engine
51 Rigging ropes
54 Funt's "Candid ___" show
57 Cassowary's cousin
58 Saddam Hussein's capital
60 Fam. member
61 Big name in potato products
62 Restaurant handout
63 NFL gains
64 Colorado resort
65 "Un bel di," for example

DOWN

1 Pokes fun at
2 Reed instrument
3 Make the most of
4 Treasured highly
5 Comic's stock in trade
6 The "O" of NATO
7 Promotes
8 Like some clothing patches
9 Church part
10 Stay
11 Go by, as time
12 Earliest occurrences
15 Area at one end of a fairway
18 Just out
22 Hoosegow
24 "Battle Cry" author
26 Pasture parent
27 Nothing at all
28 Others'
29 Scalawag
30 Inept outfielder, in "Peanuts"
32 Dinner accompaniment, for some
35 Valiant
36 "Raging Bull" pugilist LaMotta
37 "Brr" sayer, perhaps
38 Spherical symbol of authority
39 Born
41 Aircraft carrier, for one
43 Waldorf salad ingredient
44 Was a wanderer
45 Makes void
46 Resort hotels
47 Aunt ___ syrup
50 Cool, nowadays
52 Blood system, for short
53 ___ avis
54 "Misery" star James
55 Rajah's wife
56 Water color
59 President after HST

Answer on page 288

Hue Asked for It

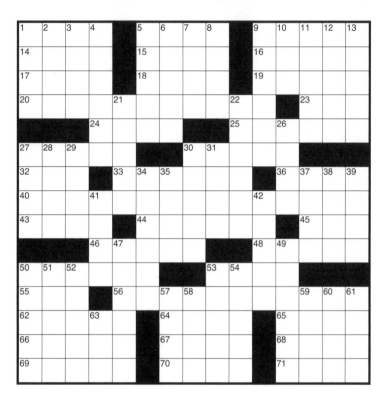

ACROSS
1 Put into cubbyholes
5 Dory or dinghy
9 Decrease gradually
14 Cowlick's composition
15 Opposed
16 Give the slip to
17 Kett of old comics
18 Place to build
19 Distressed feelings
20 Elm, for one
23 Joey of "Peppermint Twist" fame
24 School on the Thames
25 Meal
27 Cattail locale
30 Build up
32 He dethroned Foreman
33 Morale
36 Used the cuspidor
40 Some broadcast booth banter
43 Hide's partner
44 Iroquoian language
45 Fizz ingredient
46 Gave an "X" to, perhaps
48 Iced up
50 Bookish one
53 "___ each life ..."
55 Sinn Féin's org.
56 Rotary phone's incapability
62 Make dry
64 "Sit ___!" ("Happy Days" catchphrase)
65 Ill-mannered one
66 Lauder of cosmetics
67 Skunk's defense
68 Golden Rule preposition
69 Shorten again, as pants
70 Baseball's Hideo
71 Fling the pigskin

DOWN
1 The Beatles' "___ a Woman"
2 Swearing-in highlight
3 Comic Rudner
4 Gets this for that
5 Low man in the chorus
6 Burger-joint freebie
7 Westernmost Aleutian
8 Stadium level
9 Great Plains homes
10 Gardner of film
11 Black and white beast
12 Beats by a hair
13 Alley-clearing button
21 Early anesthetic
22 Prepared for shipping
26 "Hey, you!"
27 Big ___ (popular burgers)
28 Skin soother
29 Rub the wrong way
30 ___ and dangerous
31 Maurice Chevalier song
34 Soprano Renata
35 Corn bread
37 When doubled, a Samoan port
38 Calif. neighbor
39 Newcastle-upon-___, England
41 Gumbo veggie
42 Measure signed by Clinton on 12/8/93
47 Tune preceding the first pitch
49 Make into a ball
50 St. Patrick's Day musician
51 Wipe clean
52 ___ Vader
53 Figure of speech
54 Explosive stuff, for short
57 Factory whistle time, often
58 Prefix with skeleton
59 New Rochelle college
60 Cocktail party munchies
61 Classic Pontiacs
63 Middling mark

Answer on page 290

Reel Fruit Flavor

ACROSS

1 Japanese seaport or dog
6 Invigorate
11 Watering hole
14 "Lady Love" singer Lou
15 Sun screen?
16 Receiver abbr.
17 Malcolm McDowell satire of '71, with "A"
20 Party animal?
21 Sudden invasion
22 Their man in Havana
23 Here-there connector
24 Open-books exams
25 Godfrey Cambridge serio-comedy of '71

31 Short art course?
32 Send through channels
33 Steely, as nerves
36 Meet moguls
37 Piece of history
39 Discern
40 Crony
41 Cheated, so to speak
42 Europe's highest volcano
43 Henry Fonda film of '40, with "The"
47 Jerry's ex, on "Seinfeld"
49 Cry of discovery
50 Attack
51 Africa's most populous capital city
54 Dazzle

57 Bob Hope film of '51
60 Audio receiver
61 Cox of "Beverly Hills Cop"
62 Like a new penny
63 Fourth-yr. folks
64 Rip off
65 "Fatha" of jazz

DOWN

1 Keystone structure
2 Headless cabbage
3 Triumphant taunt
4 Mom's forte, for short
5 Solicit
6 Shoddy
7 II Chronicles follower
8 Dawdling

9 Crazy Eights cousin
10 It makes scents
11 Revolutionary of '79
12 Sound of Seattle
13 Skaters' 540s
18 Spineless one
19 Ethiopian of opera
23 Basketball trophy of sorts
24 Chip in chips
25 Waist variety
26 "My Way" lyricist
27 Aggressive drivers, often
28 Get the lead out
29 Takes long strides
30 Show up
34 Copper
35 One-third of a Fab Four refrain
37 Sports fans, often

38 Optimist's asset
42 Gay Nineties, e.g.
44 Omani money
45 Klinger player
46 Rushing sound
47 Rob of "Melrose Place"
48 "The Merry Widow" composer Franz
51 Heavenly Hash holder
52 "I" of "The King and I"
53 Romantic interlude
54 Cut from the same cloth
55 Khayyám quaff
56 Ben & Jerry's alternative
58 Bon ___
59 Fraternity letter

Answer on page 292

Tie It, You'll Like It

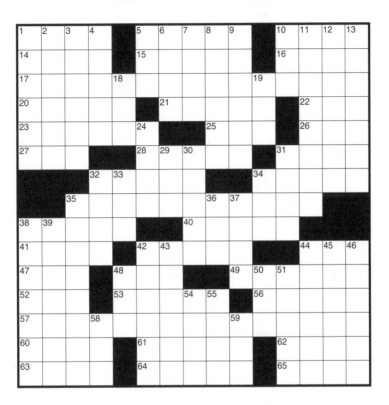

ACROSS

1 Batman portrayer West
5 Open, as a bottle
10 Got older
14 Warsaw Pact opponent: Abbr.
15 Man from Mecca
16 Raft "oar"
17 Having practical experience
20 Like some truck beds
21 Take care of
22 Chou En-___
23 In ___ (held on condition)
25 Disencumber
26 The A of "Q and A"
27 "___ Done Him Wrong" (Mae West flick)
28 Merlin of "Father Murphy"
31 ___-free
32 Devastation
34 Layers
35 "What pretty clothes!"
38 Unconventional offspring
40 Silver-screen feature
41 Shoved off
42 Elf
44 On the authority of
47 Cry in a stuffy room
48 NFL player, for one
49 Queen's title
52 Greek letter
53 The way to anyone's heart?
56 Argument
57 Exercise influence
60 Creator of courtroom Perry
61 "His" towel owners
62 Test-drive vehicle
63 Father of Lucie Arnaz
64 Type of preview
65 It's wrapped in a red rind

DOWN

1 Leg joints
2 Cheese pastry, perhaps
3 Right this minute
4 Blade shortener?
5 An adm. serves in it
6 Mediocre mounts
7 "Don't get ___ with me!"
8 Stay attached
9 Cobbler container
10 Part of a mil. address
11 Come up in the world
12 Rigby of song
13 Ceases
18 Words of a single ending?
19 Steiger or Stewart
24 Made rugs, maybe
29 Parcel of land
30 Blockhead
31 Type of dish or arm
32 Helpful suggestion
33 Pet detective Ventura
34 Half a drink?
35 Bare-bones
36 CD-___
37 At any time
38 Showed appreciation manually
39 Free time
42 Stable employees
43 1066 invader of England
44 Defeated, in wrestling
45 World War II encoding machine
46 Mel Gibson flick
48 Mates of mas
50 Go astray
51 Your conscience, hopefully
54 Scope opening
55 Supported by saltwater
58 A blooming necklace?
59 Condescending cluck

Answer on page 294

Measuring Up

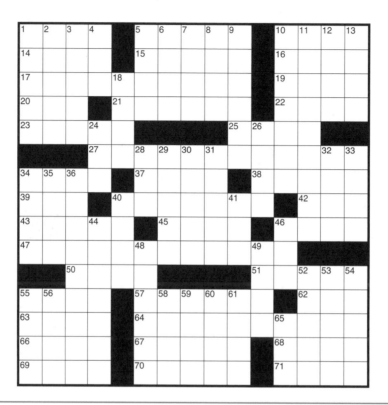

ACROSS

1 Ashen
5 Face concealers
10 They're spotted in casinos
14 South Yemen port
15 Dickensian clerk Heep
16 City in Oklahoma
17 Limited in size or scope
19 One who opposes
20 Gratuity
21 Chemical compound of more than one form
22 Work for four hands
23 Baffled
25 John Paul II, for example
27 Double-entry ledger listing
34 Firefighter's gear
37 Algonquian language
38 Finish
39 Docs' org.
40 Slows down
42 Kimono sash
43 Hawaiian island
45 After-lunch sandwich
46 Brief time per.
47 Insulating adhesive material
50 Trolley car
51 Dominating
55 Female friend of Françoise
57 Capital of Texas
62 Reverence
63 ___ Strip (Mediterranean coastal area)
64 Stadium bylaw
66 Without ___ to stand on
67 Takes in
68 More than ajar
69 Go by bus
70 Frozen rain
71 Goes to the track window

DOWN

1 Penne or rigatoni
2 Acknowledge
3 Abrupt transitions
4 Darkroom abbr.
5 Rumple
6 Sacramento's ___ Arena
7 Thailand, once
8 Curly-leafed cabbage
9 Himalayan guide
10 Poker-faced
11 Veiled hints
12 Repeat a passage from
13 Censor, perhaps
18 Perjurer
24 Summer along the Loire
26 Hispanic hurrahs
28 Motel freebie
29 First name of a "Star Wars" android
30 Find out
31 Soft cap
32 Third power, in math
33 Larger-than-life
34 College basketball period
35 Actor Sharif
36 Cleaned up
40 Hollywood's Hayworth
41 1950 film noir classic
44 Land area
46 Almost 50% of us
48 Figures of speech
49 Golden or Walden
52 Brownish gray
53 Young hooter
54 Parts of hammer heads
55 Culture medium
56 Timbuktu's country
58 River of western Russia
59 Huffy
60 Tommy of Broadway
61 Part of MIT
65 Director Reiner

Answer on page 280

Knice Knames

ACROSS

1 Pipe parts
6 Sprinter's event
10 Drops for a ten-count
13 Sylvester's "Rocky" costar
14 Actress Lenska
15 Change the decor of
16 Coeur d'___, Idaho
17 Kenton-era singer Anita
18 Cameo stone
19 Best Supporting Actor of 1988
21 Gives the green light to
22 Suffix with journal or computer
23 "My gal" of song
24 "Shame on you!"
26 Guinness suffix
28 Faxed or e-mailed
30 Bodybuilder's iterations
32 Meddlers' probes
34 "___ the World"
36 Poopdeck Pappy's son
37 Big name in unauthorized bios
39 Cochise or Geronimo
41 ___ fours (crawling)
42 One with seniority
43 Butterfly collectors' gear
44 Washday woe
48 Mork's planet
49 Sugar suffix
51 "___ bad boy!" (Lou Costello)
53 Text-scanning acronym
54 Charisse of "Silk Stockings"
56 "Roots" hero
59 Workbench adjunct
60 Lake bordering Kazakhstan
61 Classic monster movie of '57
62 Change machine input
63 London art gallery
64 Upturned, as a box
65 National anthem contraction
66 Musher's transport
67 Nostrils

DOWN

1 Preakness ___
2 "Honor Thy Father" author Gay
3 A natural, in craps
4 Revealing skirt
5 "Danse Macabre" composer Saint-___
6 Dry humor
7 BMW competitor
8 Biases
9 President before Garfield
10 "One Flew Over the Cuckoo's Nest" author
11 Homer epic
12 Fenway Park crew, for short
15 "Winnie-the-Pooh" baby
20 Tae kwon do relative
25 Small hill
27 Lao-___
29 "Once bitten, ___ ..."
31 Tea type
33 German autos
35 Prefix with centric
36 Emergency room supply
37 Dean of the "Kollege of Musical Knowledge"
38 Gave the right
39 Hubbub
40 Swinish
43 Of the spinal cord
45 Consider at length
46 Gas pump datum
47 Election return patterns
50 Three-player card games
52 Rubber center
55 ___ Plaines, Ill.
57 Thurmond or Archibald of the NBA
58 New Rochelle college
59 "Hinky Dinky Parlay ___"

Answer on page 282

You Can't Miss It!

ACROSS
1 Scandal suffix
5 "Over here!"
9 Arbor Day time
14 C&W showplace
15 Klutz's cry
16 Jostle
17 Mayberry moppet
18 Come-on
19 "Later!"
20 Basketball call
23 Guys
24 British Parliament outrage of 1765
28 Proposes
30 Mother of Pearl in "The Scarlet Letter"
31 With 41-Across, the central concept in Thorstein Veblen's "The Theory of the Leisure Class"

36 Hayworth hubby ___ Khan
37 Bounders down under
38 Nile nipper
39 One of Woody's kids
40 Hems and haws
41 See 31-Across
45 Corkscrew
47 Tallow ingredient
48 Action flick, usually
51 Cavern
55 "Dewey Defeats Truman" headline, for example
57 "Key ___"
60 Screenwriter/reviewer James
61 Out-of-this-world org.
62 It's the last word in Tours

63 Seal in the juices
64 O.T. book
65 Have the ___ on
66 Angled annexes
67 Shouts of approval

DOWN
1 Explode
2 Northern Spy, for one
3 Due process process
4 Spectacle
5 Polish hero of the American Revolution
6 Give the cold shoulder
7 Puts first things first
8 It's a steal
9 Takes on

10 Graves's role on "Mission: Impossible"
11 Future fry
12 What a kid'll eat, in song
13 Gamboling spot
21 Grate upon
22 Where to find Sunset Beach
25 Home entertainment pioneer
26 Ma's instrument
27 Check for fit
29 Riffle (through)
31 Outer layer of the earth
32 Get-up-and-go
33 Private disagreement

34 Carrier letters
35 Magnum follower
39 Mason, for one
41 Unsympathetic
42 Stewpot
43 Street thugs
44 ___ Noël (Santa Claus, in France)
46 Fixed
49 Clear the boards
50 Orion's left foot
52 Smidgen
53 Puccini opera
54 Verbal grillings
56 "The Subject Was Roses" star Patricia
57 Determine who breaks, in billiards
58 Big deal
59 Carnival city

Answer on page 284

Wild Animals

ACROSS

1 Beam or boatperson
7 Ticket remnant
11 ___ City (easy street)
14 Peter of "Lawrence of Arabia"
15 Get behind
17 Runway surface
18 Lid edger
19 Soothing, like ointment?
21 Dirt chopper
23 Tree with yellow ribbons, in song
24 "Night" author Wiesel
25 Port of Belgium
28 "Hear" a voice with the eyes

31 More frost-covered
32 Gaucho's weapon
33 Preparing to dress for the forum?
40 Sweet-talk
41 "Throw in the ___"
42 Cutting tools
46 Marked the iambs
48 The last word in worship
49 The drink
50 Nest egg
51 May registration?
57 Scout gathering
58 Does a Latin-American dance
61 Cause hostility in
62 Roll out
63 Serve to be replayed

64 Dire sign
65 Visit briefly

DOWN

1 Nonsense
2 One ___ time
3 "Never mind!"
4 Large volume
5 Pizzazz
6 Parish pastor
7 Well-groomed
8 "Wot's It ___?" (Robbie Nevil song)
9 Purposes
10 Dracula portrayer Lugosi
11 Last movement
12 Pilot Earhart
13 Designated
16 River of Rome

20 Locale for a small computer
21 Former secretary of state Alexander
22 Without repetition
26 Allowing alcohol
27 "Fear of Flying" author Jong
28 Chaney "of a Thousand Faces"
29 ___ de France (Paris and vicinity, once)
30 Vermicelli, for example
32 Fight with fists
34 Right this minute
35 Speeders step on it
36 Huge amount
37 Confessing

38 Will of "The Waltons"
39 Pierce on "M*A*S*H"
42 Mischief-maker
43 Pierce on a point
44 Beginning driver's certificate
45 Prey in a mock hunt
46 "Told ya!"
47 Desert flower
49 Charlie or Martin
52 "___ Nanette"
53 About 15 grains
54 Group of badgers
55 "Critique of Pure Reason" writer
56 Dope
59 Eyeball or Earth
60 Like a fox

Answer on page 286

In the Black

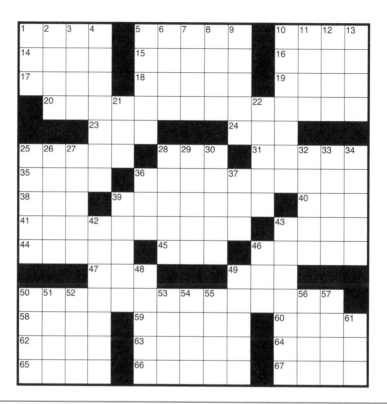

ACROSS

1 Atmospheric mist
5 Ginger cookies
10 Recipe amt.
14 Give ___ for one's money
15 Librarian's warning
16 Simba's warning
17 Desire
18 Subordinate to
19 Data, briefly
20 RAVEN
23 Provide help
24 Señora, in the USA
25 Unbroken
28 Trucker's space
31 A little push
35 It's a click away
36 PITCH
38 Father
39 Second in command in the sky
40 Leno's standout feature
41 CARBON
43 Asta's mistress
44 Computer programming language
45 Jeanne d'Arc's title: Abbr.
46 Garden flower derived from the Johnny-jump-up
47 Envy or gluttony
49 Long lunch?
50 JET
58 Become agitated
59 Swedish import
60 Realtor's sign
62 Sicilian peak
63 Out of line
64 Soft drink
65 Godiva's title
66 Suspicious
67 Give approval to

DOWN

1 "Hee ___"
2 Sinai dweller
3 New Mexico native
4 Go aboard, in a way
5 Ten-armed sea creature
6 Georgia pol Sam
7 Opera set in Egypt
8 Look-see
9 Senator Thurmond
10 Causes to stumble
11 Singer/politician Sonny
12 Ump's call
13 Dance for seniors
21 Accomplished
22 "Heaven Can Wait" director Lubitsch
25 Lesser-played half of a 45 rpm platter
26 Florida city
27 Mineral veins
28 Mil. officers
29 "He's making ___ ..."
30 Contradict
32 Mustard city
33 First, second, and reverse
47 Super Bowl winning quarterback John
36 Michael, to Kirk Douglas
37 Nickname for a Chicago baseball team
39 ___ B. DeMille
42 Error
43 SnackWell's company
46 Boxer
48 Of warships
49 Kind of owl or egret
50 One of Eve's boys
51 Kappa follows it
52 Lemon zest, really
53 Kind of dive?
54 Actress Sommer
55 Anon's partner
56 Cranny's cousin
57 Jazz singer Fitzgerald
61 "The ___ of the Jackal"

Answer on page 288

The Pits

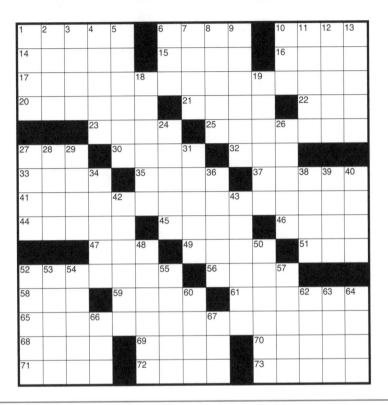

ACROSS
1 Joyce Kilmer poem
6 Petri dish stuff
10 Make fun of
14 Lunar valley
15 Kemo ___
16 Hellenic H's
17 They're the pits
20 "That's My ___"
   (doo-wop classic)
21 "Dracula" author
   Stoker
22 Grassy meadow
23 Feudal flunkie
25 Way across the
   Brooklyn Bridge,
   once
27 VH-1 rival
30 Shoulder muscle, in
   gym lingo
32 Laurel and Hardy,
   e.g.
33 Transvaal settler

35 Tourney bigwig
37 ___ the Riveter
41 They're the pits
44 Uncle Tom's creator
45 Flaw in the two-by-
   four
46 Cubs slugger
   Sammy
47 G.P. gp.
49 Olden days
51 ___ TURN
   (road sign)
52 Merchant ship
   capacity
56 Longtime senator
   Claiborne
58 ___-Locka, Florida
59 Philosopher
   Immanuel
61 Moocher
65 They're the pits
68 Zhivago's love
69 Appear to be true

70 Catalogue issuer of
   yore
71 Get fur all over the
   rug
72 Vexes
73 One way to eat ham

DOWN
1 Trampled
2 Vex
3 "Boola Boola"
   collegians
4 "The King"
5 Fume
6 Louisville Slugger
   wood
7 Duds
8 Scratch, to NASA
9 Word on a lost-dog
   poster
10 Wandering ___
   (common
   houseplant)

11 "Any Time ___"
   (Beatles tune)
12 Name on a check
13 English exam
   finale, often
18 Charitable
   Mother
19 Illicit affairs
24 Patch of color
26 Joins in the rioting
27 Many Wall St. types
28 Racetrack figure
29 Literally, "I forbid"
31 Pint-sized
34 Martin's "Laugh-In"
   partner
36 Hang like a walrus
   mustache
38 In a jiff
39 ___ facto
40 Jacob's twin
42 1976's "King
   Kong," e.g.

43 Kind of test or
   fracture
48 1992 Wimbledon
   winner Andre
50 City on the Rio
   Grande
52 Ax and adz
53 First name in talk
   TV
54 Mother-of-pearl
55 Sign up
57 Sophia of the
   screen
60 Cruise with Kirk
62 In the
   neighborhood
63 Cooper of "High
   Noon"
64 In ___
   (existing)
66 Was afflicted
   with
67 Early hrs.

Answer on page 290

Roll Call

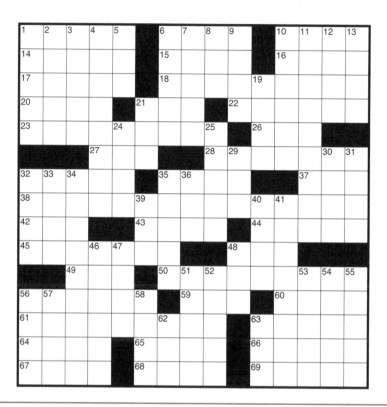

ACROSS

1 Based on base eight
6 "___ Good Men"
10 Headline
14 Weeper of myth
15 Welles's tycoon publisher
16 Flash or sugar follower
17 "The Great Forest" painter Max
18 A couple of rolls
20 Hankering
21 George Bush was one
22 It's distilled from wine
23 Two more rolls
26 Suitable
27 Clunky dory
28 Attentive
32 Grim Grimm guys
35 Scottish terrier
37 Coiled choker
38 Three more rolls
42 Cool, in the '50s
43 Warmonger
44 Tipped rapiers
45 Scorpio's brightest
48 Rock and Roll Hall of Fame architect
49 Pier gp.
50 Yet another two rolls
56 Recently
59 Animal house
60 Counter's opener
61 The last two rolls
63 Picture
64 "Out of Africa" author Dinesen
65 "Breathless" star Richard
66 Rather risky
67 1169 erupter
68 Symbols of strength
69 Palette pigment

DOWN

1 Get the better of
2 Wispy clouds
3 The Friendly Islands
4 No-show
5 "___ the Good Times Roll"
6 Cub Scout pack leader
7 "Oliver Twist" baddie
8 He was attached to his brother
9 Friday on TV
10 Predicament
11 Lazy Susan
12 Sacked out
13 Put your money (on)
19 Sea east of the Caspian
21 Go with the flow, perhaps
24 Unseat
25 Rapids transit
29 Moon unit?
30 Characterization
31 Pipes up
32 Workplace watchdog: Abbr.
33 "Damn Yankees" dancer Verdon
34 Cold-bloodedly treacherous
35 Cash cache
36 Royal Botanic Gardens site
39 "___ Bop" ('84 Cyndi Lauper hit)
40 Scoff
41 Contagious, as laughter
46 Baked state?
47 Compile a top-ten list
48 Cutesy trailer
51 Country rock's ___ Mountain Daredevils
52 "The Highwayman" poet Alfred
53 Gunslinger's command
54 Fastidious Felix
55 Skeptical response from the Cyclops?
56 "The Grapes of Wrath" figure
57 Firmly fixed
58 Hence
62 Toy ammo
63 Veiled comment?

Answer on page 292

You Wanna Piece O' Me?

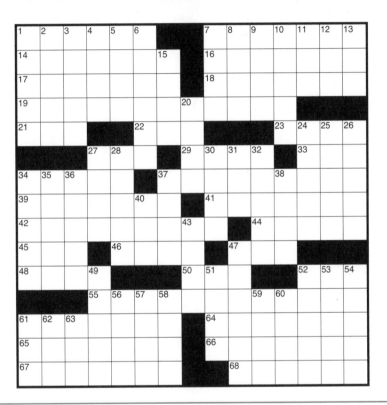

ACROSS

1 Sticks it to
7 Town known for a bar
14 Secure, as a professor
16 Basically
17 Ship sunk 12/7/1941
18 Got stronger, in a teapot
19 Blow up
21 67.5°
22 Slugging meas.
23 Clothing joint
27 Links org.
29 They may be black-eyed
33 Sch. supporter
34 Line on Mars
37 Listen
39 Birmingham resource
41 Begin, for example
42 Assist
44 Way of the theater
45 Nutty fruitcake center?
46 Pulled apart
47 Rinks org.
48 Virginia dance
50 Fuss
52 Exec's degree
55 Tender help to a walker
61 Permanently
64 Neighbor of Latvia
65 Now applicable
66 Vivaldi's foursome
67 Back in Washington, for example
68 Toothy swimmers

DOWN

1 Like cut-rate bread
2 Aquatic fowl
3 Ouzo flavoring
4 Detonator
5 Helen's home away from home
6 Mexican ma'am
7 Sauteed leftovers, perhaps
8 Female "tail"
9 Carla portrayer on "Cheers"
10 Players ranked in a tournament
11 Luck
12 Before, in the past
13 From Jan. 1 to now
15 Apply artlessly
20 Ready for plucking
24 Blades with guarded tips
25 Whatsoever
26 Cake advocate Antoinette
27 Window division
28 Rub it in
30 Oklahoma town
31 Paper rectangles?
32 Isaac's mother
34 Reward for doing better than "close"
35 "Get thee up!"
36 Bright stars
37 Regan's father
38 Polished part of a pinky
40 P on fraternity row
43 In the vicinity of
47 Horse opera neckties
49 Shirt alligators
51 Vat colors
52 Stately Wayne ___ of "Batman"
53 Critical point
54 Pile up
56 Y intersection
57 Central points
58 Forbidden fruit garden
59 Beach near Omaha
60 Parks on a bus
61 Source of needles
62 Three Dog Night hit
63 Mayberry mail serv.

Answer on page 294

Twisted Crosswords

Introduction & Instructions

Angling (pages 166, 186, 206)
Each answer is to be entered *diagonally* in the grid, with its first and last letters in the given numbered squares (in one order or the other), and the answer's path turning once at a 90° angle. Letters in the outlined area, reading left to right, will spell a quotation from director Woody Allen in puzzle on page 166, from humorist Erma Bombeck in puzzle on page 186, and from comedienne Judy Tenuta in puzzle on page 206.

Around & About (pages 147, 167, 187, 207)
Answers to Around clues are to be sequentially entered counterclockwise, starting in space 1 and ending in space 100. Answers to About clues will completely overlap the Around answers, reading clockwise instead.

Catching Some Z's (pages 155, 175, 195, 215)
Answers to each set of clues 1–8 run sequentially, starting in the northwesternmost numbered triangle, then going right, then down left, then right again, following the path of same-numbered triangles to form a Z pattern.

Crazy Eights (pages 154, 174, 194, 214)
The eight-letter answer to each clue is to be entered in the eight squares that surround the numbered square; the first letter's square is for you to determine. Direction of the answer is indicated after the clue: a "+" means clockwise, and a "–" means counterclockwise.

Crossing Paths (pages 163, 183, 203)
Answers to each set of clues 1–4 run sequentially, starting in the numbered square, then going down to the right, then up to the right, and so on, turning 90° every time a border is reached, finishing in the square southwest of the numbered square. Answers to the Fours clues are four-letter words to be entered reading inward in the circled areas, in no particular order.

Crushword (pages 151, 171, 191, 211)
Answers are to be entered as they would be in a standard crossword puzzle, except that each square will accommodate at least two letters.

Cubism (pages 157, 177, 197)
Answers are to be entered as they would be in a standard crossword puzzle, except in three directions as indicated, Down Left, Down Right, and Across. In puzzle 31, watch out for that smaller cube that's been cut out of the big cube! In puzzle 51, each row consists of three or four answers, separated by bars, and each set of clues is given in random order.

Helter-Skelter (pages 156, 176, 196)

Each answer begins in the correspondingly numbered square and reads in a straight line, finishing at or beyond the square with the next higher number.

Honeycomb (pages 161, 181, 201)

The six-letter answer to each clue is to be entered in the six cells that surround the numbered cell; the first letter's cell is for you to determine. Direction of the answer is indicated after the clue: a "+" means clockwise, and a "–" means counterclockwise.

Intersections (pages 164, 184, 204)

This puzzle is a standard crossword, with one difference. Each clue number is followed by two clues, whose answers intersect at the numbered square in the grid. (Either the Across or the Down answer may be clued first.)

Jigsaw (pages 165, 185, 205)

Across and Down clues yield 15-letter answers, to be entered in the standard fashion. Placement of these answers will help you enter the 72 five-letter answers, clued in random order within each section.

Marching Bands (pages 149, 169, 189, 209)

Answers to Rows clues read across, two per line, consecutively from left to right. Row 7's words are separated by a black square; in all other rows, you must determine where one answer ends and the next starts. Answer to Bands clues read sequentially starting in the lettered square and running clockwise.

Maze (pages 159, 179, 199)

Answers to Across clues read two per line, consecutively from left to right. Answers to Path clues read sequentially, starting in square 1 and following the trail outlined by the black bars, ending in the lower right square.

Pathfinder (pages 150, 170, 190, 210)

Each answer begins in the numbered square and winds through the grid, taking at least one right-angle turn somewhere along the way. The letter following the clue's number indicates the initial direction (north, south, east, or west) of the answer. The enumeration of the answer is given in parentheses at the end of the clue. The completed grid will use each square exactly twice.

Quadrants (pages 153, 173, 193, 213)

The diagram's bars roughly divide it into four sections, each to accommodate eight six-letter answers, four across and four down. In addition, there are another eight six-letter answers to be entered in the center section of the diagram. Within each of these five sections, the clues are listed randomly.

Round the Bend (pages 162, 182, 202)
Answers to Across and Down clues (each five letters long) are to be entered normally. Answers to Bent clues begin in the numbered square and read counterclockwise, finishing at the puzzle's border (except for 12-Bent, which reads clockwise in a full circle).

Siamese Twins/Triplets/Quadruplets (pages 160, 180, 200)
Each clue number is followed by one clue for each diagram, in no particular order. Where you place the answers for 1-Across is up to you, but thereafter everything must link up properly, of course.

Target Practice (pages 158, 178, 198)
Each six-letter answer is to be entered, one letter per ring, starting in the numbered space and reading inward (clockwise or counterclockwise, as indicated) in adjoining spaces.

Tops & Bottoms (pages 148, 168, 188, 208)
Each answer's letters are to be entered two per square, starting with the top triangles and finishing with the bottom triangles. (For example, if the answer word were ENIGMA, the first box would have E/G, the second would have N/M, and the third would have I/A.)

Trivia-Cross (page 216)
After solving the crossword, arrange the letters in numerical order on the dashes to produce a quotation from Sir Arthur Conan Doyle's *The Adventure of the Mazarin Stone*.

Weaving (pages 152, 172, 192, 212)
Answers to Weavers clues form a continuous chain, with the first letter in the starred space, the next four letters in the numbered spaces, the next letter in the semicircular space adjoining space four, and so on, shuttling back and forth across and around the diagram. Answer to Ring clues run sequentially in the corresponding ring; the numbered space will contain one of the letters from the answer to Clue a (not necessarily the first letter).

Around & About

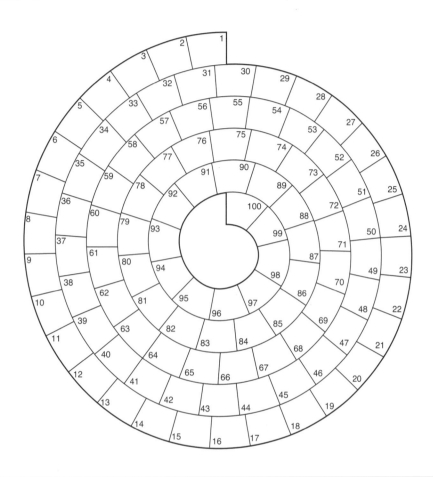

AROUND

- **1-5** Won every game
- **6-11** Collar
- **12-17** "That's enough!": 2 wds.
- **18-21** Tennis tactics
- **22-32** Host of PBS's *Reading Rainbow*: 2 wds.
- **33-43** Brides keep them more often nowadays: 2 wds.
- **44-47** ___ dixit, assertion without proof
- **48-51** Ricky's portrayer
- **52-56** Bug
- **57-63** Poisonous mushroom
- **64-70** Small bouquet
- **71-78** Cloudy
- **79-81** Bad hairpiece
- **82-87** "He was a bold man that first ate an ___": Swift
- **88-95** Chiricahua chieftain invoked by jumpers
- **96-100** Bracelet locale

ABOUT

- **100-98** Wapiti
- **97-93** Wynonna's mom
- **92-84** 1936 Tommy Dorsey recording for the uncontrite?: 2 wds.
- **83-77** They're enhanced by *Lactobacillus bulgaricus*
- **76-73** 6,272,640 square inches
- **72-67** "Bon ___!" ("Have a good trip!")
- **66-59** Simplified musical composition for one or two instruments
- **58-49** Rémoulade base
- **48-42** Hate
- **41-36** Having a crew of at least one
- **35-30** Rejoinder to "You are too!": 3 wds.
- **29-27** Difficulty
- **26-15** Classical piece featured in the movie *10*: 2 wds.
- **14-5** Island devastated by the Soufrière Hills volcano since 1995
- **4-1** Congregation's stations

Answer on page 296

Tops & Bottoms

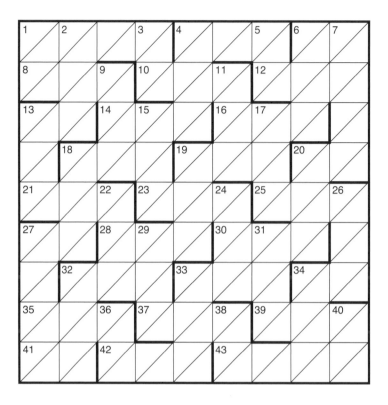

ACROSS

1 House on a rancho
4 Phone book datum
6 Large land mass
8 Grand Rapids's county
10 On the blue side
12 Film time?
13 Sheltered nook
14 Rock band, the Violent ___
16 Soprano Maria
18 Sports jacket
19 Person who is in bondage
20 Jacques Cousteau's middle name
21 Way up north
23 "___ he-e-e-ere!"
25 In a bloody manner
27 Teens' mecca
28 Least cultured
30 39-Across hires them
32 He has nothing to hide

33 This way
34 1957 Nabokov novel
35 King's dinnertime aide
37 Little lampreys
39 Entrepreneur Ford
41 "A Holly Jolly Christmas" singer
42 City on the Willamette
43 Factor of the area of a triangle

DOWN

1 Wastes no time
2 Promptly: 2 wds.
3 Desert Storm territory
4 Rain cloud
5 One of Rosie's inspirations
6 *Hogan's Heroes* heroes
7 Help
9 Burning
11 Actor Maximilian of *Judgment at Nuremberg*

13 Tie
15 Restaurant
17 Wild sheep with spiral horns
18 Runner-up in the 1998 World Cup finals
19 Frustrate
20 Tyrolean music
22 Las ___, NM
24 Toastmasters
26 *Guys and Dolls* writer
27 Wreck a keypunch card
29 "___ Fideles"
31 End of a blackmail note: 2 wds.
32 They're all at sea
33 *Earth in the Balance* writer: 2 wds.
34 Commiserated with
36 Withered
38 Enormous
40 Profession

Answer on page 297

Marching Bands

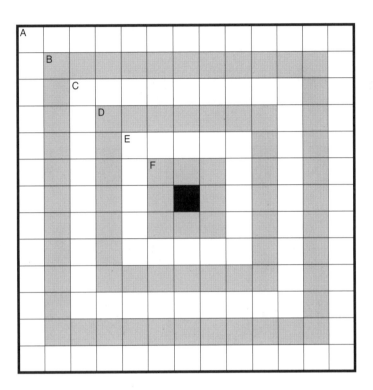

ROWS

1 a Rudolph's cousin?
  b Spasmodic movement
2 a Clan-related
  b Handcuff
3 a *Futurama*'s Bender, for one
  b General Mills product introduced in 1941
4 a State unequivocally
  b Some full-figured women's sizes
5 a Attendant to Charlemagne
  b Burns around the edges
6 a Sprung up
  b Theater seating under the balcony
7 a Kin of actor Buddy
  b Surpass in a pie contest
8 a ___ *Dearest*
  b Naturals in a crap game
9 a Certifies
  b Attack with vigor: 2 wds.
10 a Hardly subtle
  b Recording one's arrival: 2 wds.
11 a Archaic pronoun
  b Sour-tasting
12 a Will topic
  b Elastic fabric
13 a Vestige
  b Hand out

BANDS

A a Antillean native
  b Get the better of
  c They're in pieces: 2 wds.
  d Cameo stones
  e Massage
  f Motorcyclist's cocktail?
  g Vietnamese holiday
  h Break: 2 wds.
B a Umbrella spoke
  b Annually updated publication
  c Hermit
  d McCarthyistic
  e Afternoon quickie?
  f Mount an attack on: 2 wds.
  g Plumed cap
  h "Wonderful show!"
C a Bungle
  b Preternatural
  c Small, round, tangy plum
  d Actor David of *The Pink Panther*
  e Mosque official
  f Helpless?
D a Determine the gravitational force
  b Group opinion
  c Growing like ivy
  d Show that earned Cosby three Emmys: 2 wds.
  e Arizona city founded by Mormons
E a Cacophony
  b In ___ (in the original place)
  c Inventor Howe
  d Cosecant's reciprocal
F a They've gotten out early

Answer on page 298

Pathfinder

CLUES

1E Taking a circuitous path (9)
2E St. Louis team (4)
3E Entry in Baby's agenda (3)
4E It's usually left to your accountant (3)
5S Justin Wilson's favorite cuisine (5)
5S Southern constellation with the star Canopus (6)
6S Played for a patsy (10)
7S Monkey bars (6,3)
8S "That deaf, dumb, and blind kid [who] sure plays a mean pinball" (5)
9S Earring's locale (4)
10S Talk discursively (6)
11W Almond-paste confection (8)
12N Hemophiliac (7)
13S Championship (5)
14E Type of toothpaste or shaving cream (3)
15S 1968 Classics IV hit (6)
16N Rental car company (5)
17N Stand for (9)
18S "Dying swan" portrayer (7)
19N ___ Oscar (4)
20N Skunk's defense (4)
21W 1940 JFK book, *Why England ___* (5)
22N Fog or mist (5)
23S Drop on a rope (6)
24N Kind of insurance (5)
25W Cockatoos and lories (7)
26E Dr. Frank N. Furter was one (12)
27E Go places (6)
28E Vacationing (3)
29W Computer language created in 1956 (7)

Answer on page 299

Crushword

ACROSS
1 Big dog
4 Reassure
6 Will Smith, e.g.
8 At the top of the decibel scale
9 Battle of Bull Run locale
11 Reagan Cabinet member
12 Took another meeting
13 "Will you walk into my parlor?" said he: 2 wds.
14 Frank criticism has been directed at her: 2 wds.
16 Chuck Connors as Lucas McCain
18 Potato chip dare: 2 wds.
19 Post-Christmas store activity
20 Diplomatic minister and staff
21 Following teens' fads
23 More than sufficient
24 Queenly quarters
25 Composure: Hyph.
26 Chicago suburb: 2 wds.

27 11/11 honoree
28 William I was one
30 *Master Class* playwright
31 Japanese form of fencing
33 Tune
34 1992 Spike Lee movie: 2 wds.
36 She's having a ball
37 Chants
38 Computer storage code
39 Stephanie's father

DOWN
1 Mrs. Bob Hope
2 Eerie Atlantic area: 2 wds.
3 "'Tis good to keep ___ egg": Cervantes: 2 wds.
4 Authority figure
5 LBJ appointee who resigned in 1969
6 Talk show host or Ninja Turtle
7 Orbital point nearest Earth

10 City of southwest Canada
13 Actor
15 Cole Porter's "Were ___ That Special Face"
17 First host of *Jeopardy!*
18 5-Down et al.
19 Title relinquisher: Hyph.
20 In most states, 18: 2 wds.
21 Classic comedy movie of 1974: 2 wds.
22 Endocrine gland
24 Like *X-Files* subjects
25 Skewered Indonesian appetizer
26 Light beer
27 In a mercenary way
28 Limitation
29 Rey or Luis of '80s baseball
30 When Clinton beat Bush
32 Document file
35 Coke and Pepsi
36 Circle dance

Answer on page 303

Weaving

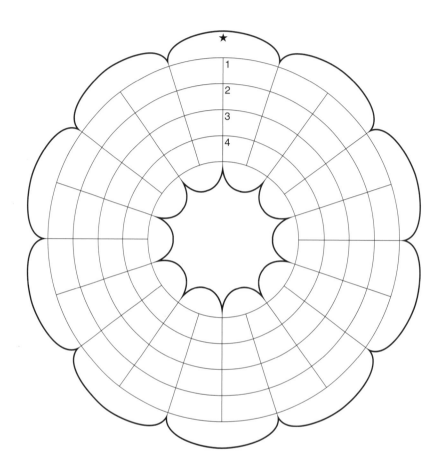

WEAVERS

a Actor whose uncle is Francis Ford Coppola: 2 wds.
b Shake in the grass?
c A silk hat brought him to life
d He had a Top-10 hit with 1994's "Loser"
e Much loafing is done there
f Most silly
g Pearl Mosque locale
h Wherewithal
i Bet both ways
j Sign painter's skill
k Montaigne output
l Turns the ignition key: 2 wds.
m Navy mascot
n *To Kill a Mockingbird*'s Radley
o Goolagong of tennis
p All ___ (clumsy)
q Tall, slender champagne glasses

RING 1

a Item on a tourist's itinerary
b Large body of troops
c Orderly
d Austrian opera conductor Karl

RING 2

a Inasmuch as
b Worker who uses glossy paint
c Correct a correction

RING 3

a Time piece?
b Had brunch
c Indication of a possessive woman?
d Most debonair

RING 4

a Cough syrup dosages, often
b Where to find the USA's only diamond mine

Answer on page 301

Quadrants

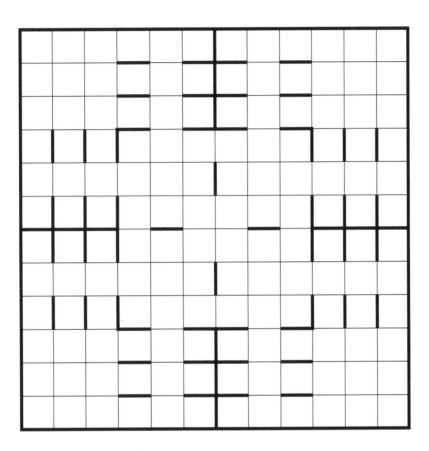

NORTHWEST
a About 3.5 million square miles, mostly sand
b Athabaskan language
c Bearse of *Married ... With Children*
d Fast-growing softwood tree
e Hardly dense
f Moore's hubby in *Ghost*
g Singer/actress Pia
h Stocky, burrowing marsupial

NORTHEAST
a Bad news for the manufacturer
b Finally: 2 wds.
c Gracefully slender
d Main thoroughfare
e Nauseatingly coy

f Passes along
g Petty organization?
h Red Bordeaux

SOUTHWEST
a Baby
b Edberg of tennis
c Enter hostile territory
d Feel a strong need (for)
e Philippines' "Iron Butterfly"
f Punctual: 2 wds.
g Use Scope
h Welsh dogs

SOUTHEAST
a *Cabaret* venue, the ___ Klub: 2 wds.
b Crooner Julius: 2 wds.

c Like T-shirts and jeans, e.g.
d Nocturnal lizards
e Octogenarian's next milestone
f One of Lucille's costars
g Opposite of "Attention!": 2 wds.
h Sentence structure

CENTER
a *Beach Blanket Bingo* outfit
b Book following Acts
c Calm
d Drawing pen
e Liable to erupt
f Shul staff
g Swap commodities
h Try hard

Answer on page 302

Crazy Eights

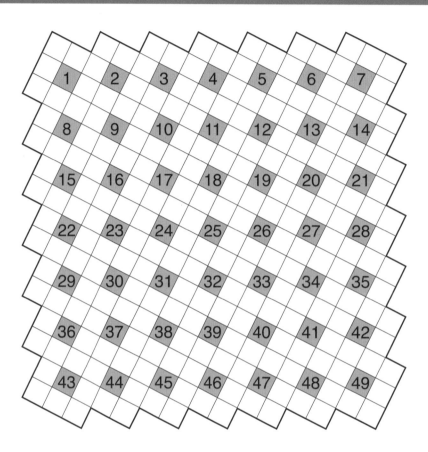

CLUES

1 Empathic, loving partner (+)
2 Blondie and Tootsie's business (−)
3 Competitor of Uncle Ben's (+)
4 The Land of Opportunity (−)
5 *War of the Worlds* invaders (+)
6 *Strangers on a Train* author Highsmith (+)
7 Inability to sleep well (+)
8 Buys (−)
9 Criminal activity (+)
10 Specific place (+)
11 UPS truckload (+)
12 Wedlock (−)
13 Repeated word for word (−)
14 AKC concern (+)
15 Intimate apparel (+)
16 Old coin equal to $\frac{1}{4}$ penny (−)

17 Burrito's outside (+)
18 Scheming individuals? (−)
19 Cartographer (+)
20 In need of Viagra (+)
21 Casey Jones was one (+)
22 Cosmetic item (−)
23 Having a bad reputation (+)
24 Bug from the Caribbean coast? (−)
25 Obi-Wan Kenobi's portrayer (+)
26 Individually wrapped desserts (−)
27 Arousing pity (−)
28 Interjections from the Seven Dwarfs?: Hyph. (+)
29 ___ bars (gymnastics equipment) (+)
30 Alternative to tablets (+)
31 Bushy-tailed rodent of suburbia (+)
32 Camouflage (−)
33 Mock (+)

34 Gifted (−)
35 Fused together, in a way (+)
36 Calculates comparatively (−)
37 *Raging Bull* director (−)
38 In police custody (−)
39 Rosie O'Donnell's kids, e.g. (−)
40 Wine made chiefly from one type of grape (−)
41 Pertinent (+)
42 One of the original *60 Minutes* crew (+)
43 Toothed wheel (+)
44 Fish of the genus *Hippocampus* (+)
45 Bought stock (+)
46 Corn field? (−)
47 Indulge in Dungeons & Dragons, for example: Hyph. (−)
48 One way to see who's at the door (−)
49 Shame (+)

Answer on page 303

Catching Some Z's

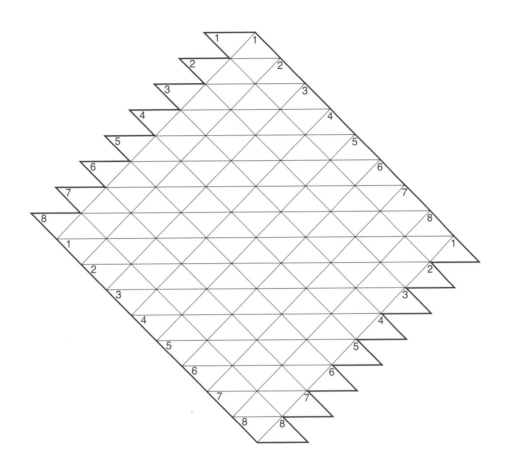

CLUES

1 a Aroma, to a viniculturist
   b Port city on Honshu
   c The role of Don Giovanni is generally sung by one
   d Use an S.O.S pad
   e Stimpy's pal
   f Sisters
2 a Fire a water pistol
   b Expunge
   c Bleakly pessimistic
   d "I await your reply, good buddy"
   e Danced with a glide
3 a Swiss state
   b Singer Young

   c Leisurely stroll
   d At ease
   e Navy clerk
4 a Mediocre novel written for the money
   b Abominable Snowman
   c One of the As in "AAA": Abbr.
   d Assess
   e Director Bergman
5 a Without difficulty
   b *Jurassic Park* beast: 2 wds.
   c Knave of Hearts' booty
   d Boca ___, FL
6 a Go on a brief break: 2 wds.
   b Anyone's game?

   c Pertinacious: Hyph.
   d Former colt
7 a Brunhoff's pachyderm
   b Tryst
   c Grassy plain
   d Do some cultivating
   e Knot on a tree trunk
   f Inferior
8 a Watergate Plumbers' equipment
   b Debonair
   c Park in New York City, for example
   d Admiral who devised the Pearl Harbor attack
   e Car whose old TV ads featured a liar named Joe

Answer on page 314

Helter-Skelter

				16	15
1	2				
8		21	22	17	
	19		18	11	
	9	20			
	23		5	14	
7	3			4	26
	10	24		25	
	6	13	12		

CLUES

1 Website address start
2 Receptionist, e.g.
3 Wireless inventor
4 Without much wiggle room
5 Wile E. Coyote's supplier
6 Mouse-spotting cry
7 Act obsequiously
8 One of Chekhov's *Three Sisters* sisters
9 Viticulturist's concern
10 *The Scarlet Letter* heroine
11 C.S. Lewis kiddie-lit locale
12 Replies
13 Hourglass fill
14 Victorious admiral at Manila Bay
15 Cowardly
16 Perry Mason's field
17 City in Uttar Pradesh
18 Bacterium
19 BLT spread
20 Jason's craft
21 *Children of a Lesser* ___
22 "Heavens to Betsy!": 2 wds.
23 They cost $200 each in Monopoly: Abbr.
24 Ride a windjammer
25 Cover
26 Sort

Answer on page 305

Cubism

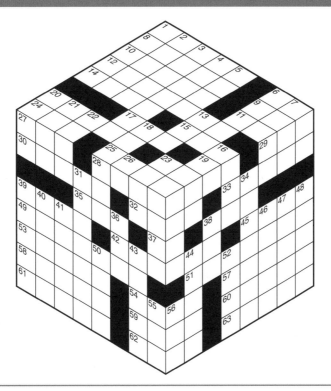

DOWN LEFT

1 Stationery units
2 Ill-deserved
3 Beauty's love
4 Ape
5 Kevin's wife
6 Pretend
7 This parlor item ...
13 ... may have this surface
16 Wild excitement
18 Manufacturer of "the dogs kids love to bite"
20 Variety of butterhead lettuce
21 Soliloquy in song
22 Unwilling to exert
23 Staff leader?
26 O.R. hookup
31 Accommodates
36 Balaam whipped his
39 Gold unit
40 Spry
41 Arrested: 2 wds.
43 Unqualified
50 "With malice toward ___, ..."
55 It's for horses

DOWN RIGHT

1 He got people to do the twist
6 Humor writer Lebowitz
8 Hostile opponent
9 Ecu's successor
10 Alphabetically first county of Iowa, Kentucky, Missouri, or Oklahoma
11 Lab assistant?
12 Small, hardy horse
14 Stiff hair
15 Re Aconcagua's range
17 Eavesdropping device
19 Type unit
20 Farm machine
23 Coagulate
24 401(k) alternative
25 Vigorously combative
34 *Hogan's Heroes* expletive
38 Infuriation
44 He played Barnaby Jones
46 Obey reveille
47 Fourth-anniversary gift
48 Mob scene member
52 Blue hue
56 ___ *Today*

ACROSS

27 Field, for short
28 Additional quality
29 Mouths: Latin
30 Marshy water
32 Automaker's decree?
33 Tori's old man
35 A couple of cups?
37 185-member org.
38 Corporate abbr.
39 Flying Wallendas' patriarch
42 Fort where the Civil War began
45 "One life to lose" claimant
49 Con
51 Kiddie-lit writer Potter
53 Richard Starkey's a.k.a.
54 In such a manner
57 *The Turn of the Screw* ghost
58 *Men in Black* figure
59 Relaxation
60 Family name at Indy
61 Grammarian's concern
62 Jeri of *Star Trek: Voyager*
63 Satellite launcher

Answer on page 314

Target Practice

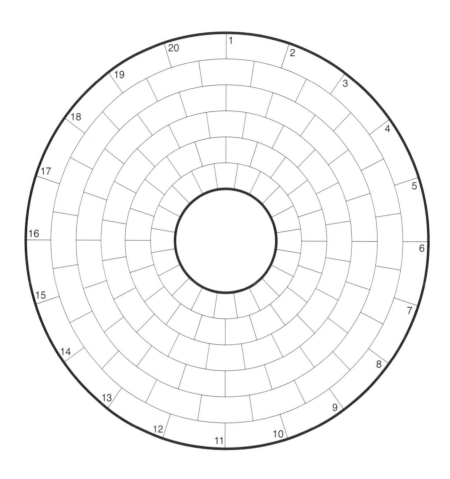

CLOCKWISE

1 Individual
2 Erstwhile grape
3 Water slides
4 Has confidence in
5 Irascibility
6 More acidic
7 Starbucks orders
8 She played Princess Leia
9 Rent payer
10 Bump up and down roughly
11 24ths of pure gold
12 Shade of yellow
13 Form of high-speed skiing
14 Become a tenant: 2 wds.
15 Hard, chewy candy
16 Ransacked
17 Money holder
18 Brand of fabric softener
19 Former chairman of the Joint Chiefs of Staff
20 Wheedle

COUNTERCLOCKWISE

1 Sold temporarily
2 Turn thumbs down on
3 King or Lombard
4 1936 song, "___ Make You Whistle"
5 His work was done by Friday
6 One confined by infirmity: Hyph.
7 Untie
8 Imperfections
9 Brits' near-quarts
10 Crown clown
11 Labeled with a U
12 Freedom fighters have them
13 Pop ___ Junior League Football
14 Threaten
15 Until now: 2 wds.
16 Nomadic types
17 Befitting the Mrs.
18 Canadian island in the Arctic Ocean
19 Hay fever stimulus
20 Gulch

Answer on page 307

Maze

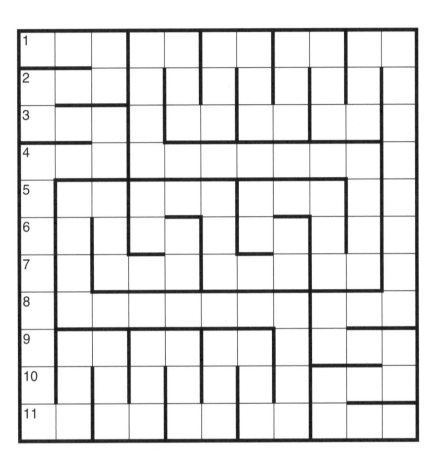

ACROSS

1 Thing
  Condo, co-op, cabin, or cave
2 Spiral-tusked arctic denizen
  Frat party outfit
3 Actress Holm
  It can provide zest
4 Portrayer of 007
  Tentacled sea creatures
5 1955 Inge play: 2 wds.
  SportsCenter's milieu
6 Cry of exasperation
  Endured
7 100 Turkish kurus
  Small noncommercial aircraft
8 Civil War general Burnside

Writer Janowitz
9 Antioxidant food preservative: Abbr.
  Miami Heat coach: 2 wds.
10 Story set in the 10 years after the
  Trojan War
  Megalomaniacal captain
11 Stench
  Home improvement expert: 2 wds.

PATH

1 Way in
2 Weaving need
3 Harped on
4 Actress Salma
5 Twitch
6 Take another whack at it

7 Limited quantities
8 Scepter ornament
9 It elicits a negative reaction
10 Nuncupative
11 Hearty enjoyment
12 Game in which players might "shoot
  the moon"
13 "Pieces of eight" piece
14 Danger
15 By means of this
16 Don't nod off: 2 wds.
17 Response to an ump's blunder
18 Cul-de-sac: 2 wds.
19 Mexican entree
20 Kippur preceder
21 Way out

Answer on page 312

Siamese Twins

ACROSS

1 Bill's wife ...
 ... and daughter
8 Mongol tents
 Played manicurist
13 Glowing
 Mud deposits
14 Cerulean
 Have ___ to grind: 2 wds.
15 Abjectly submissive
 Acute suffering
16 Eyes, slangily
 Galileo, by birth
17 Govt. grp. that OKs chem.
 substances
 Rice or Curry
18 Comes into sight indistinctly
 Toaster's word
20 Derek and Diddley
 Stashed
21 ___ even keel: 2 wds.
 Novice
23 A billion years
 NAFTA signatory
24 Docket entry
 Suddenly Susan cast member
25 Piercing tool
 Unmatched
27 Bandleader Cugat
 Over there
29 *Familia* member
 The Minister's Wooing author
32 Lakeside structures
 Put one's feat in one's mouth
33 *Ayer, hoy,* ___
 Microscope view
35 Buddhist discipline
 Clearasil target
36 Acceptable
 Salacious
37 Actress Balin
 Do some weeding
39 Enervates
 Napoleon and Nero: Abbr.
43 Refrain syllable
 Slugger Williams
44 Re Roman Catholicism
 Toss
46 British drivers' counterpart of AAA
 Mork's home planet
47 Songwriter Carmichael
 The ___ Sanction (Eastwood film)
49 1878 song a.k.a. "Farewell to Thee":
 2 wds.
 1953 Monroe/ Cotten movie
51 Act part
 Sign up

52 Shameless hussy
 Young star?
53 Kent portrayer
 Like some seals
54 Greg, Peter, or Bobby, to
 Carol
 Water between
 Kazakhstan and
 Uzbekistan: 2 wds.

DOWN

1 Must: 2 wds.
 Work requiring manual
 skill
2 Accessible
 Foolish, in rap slang
3 Painter Degas
 Peruvian pack animal
4 Lucy of *Ally McBeal*
 Valentine solecism
5 Compete in a regatta
 Hertz rival
6 Give life to, in a way
 Put on the line
7 Pal of D'Artagnan
 Popular search service
8 Barks snappishly
 Hair extension
9 9mm submachine gun
 "What's ___ name?":
 2 wds.
10 "The forbidden dance"
 Writer targeted by
 Khomeini
11 Park abode?
 Tabloid writeups, often
12 Baked Alaska, e.g.
 Return-address names
19 Physicist Planck
 Wool quantity?
22 "Fuhgged-aboudit!": 2 wds.
 Propelled a boat
24 Political writer who "can't say that,
 can she?"
 Ten sawbucks: Hyph.
26 Hideaway
 Symbol of intrigue
28 Butterfly's belt?
 Gibbon or orangutan, e.g.
29 From Valletta
 Overdo on the onions,
 maybe
30 Patriotic song
 Sign on a "samples" table:
 2 wds.
31 Stately older woman
 When challenged: 3 wds.

34 "Eureka!"
 Feel under the weather
35 Big fan
 More buffoonish
38 Lacteal rocks
 Mercenary martial artist
40 Gulf War participants
 Watery trenches
41 City Cole Porter wrote about
 Original: Prefix
42 Dagger
 Ladder, in Livorno
44 Basset hound of the comics
 Nabors role
45 Mediterranean seaport
 Traditional tales
48 Compass dir.
 Head of st.
50 Come together
 Start of a cadence count

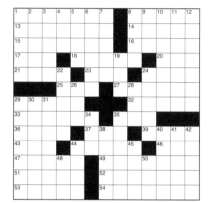

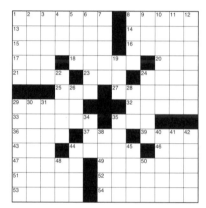

Answer on page 309

Honeycomb

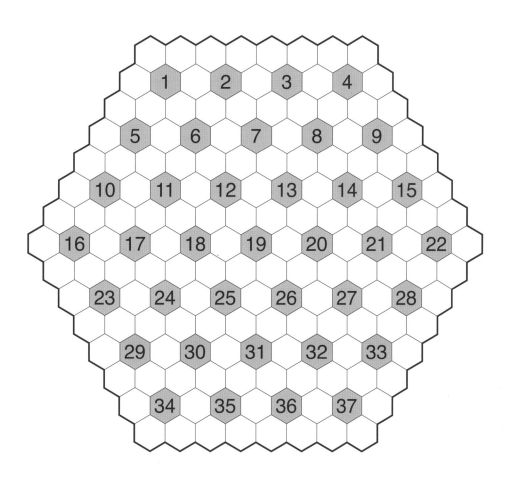

CLUES

1 Bill with the White House on the back (+)
2 It covers about 3.8 million square miles (−)
3 Lucy : Ethel :: Alice : ___ (+)
4 Season for pasta primavera? (+)
5 Maneuver through the tulips (+)
6 Celebrity status (−)
7 Imperative (−)
8 Richard's *Pal Joey* collaborator (−)
9 Sensational publicity (+)
10 Comment from Don Rickles, often (−)
11 Nun's headcloth (+)
12 Reaction to the villain's entrance (+)

13 Football officials, slangily (−)
14 Guppy troop (−)
15 The Japanese "picked" this name for Korea (−)
16 Bishop's subordinate (−)
17 Mental grasp (+)
18 *The Magic Flute* composer (+)
19 Antidepressant brand (−)
20 *American Beauty* Oscar winner (+)
21 Beaten to a pulp, as potatoes (−)
22 KFC piece (−)
23 Fate (−)
24 He's known for making long-distance calls (+)

25 Mideastern marketplace (+)
26 Munch depiction (−)
27 Air (−)
28 LBJ's press secretary who hosted PBS's *This Week* (−)
29 Restless (−)
30 City near Chicago that shares its name with a Roman goddess (−)
31 Third place award (−)
32 Contemptible person (−)
33 Shiver-inducing (+)
34 "Annus Mirabilis" poet (−)
35 Dowager's pet, typically (−)
36 Hay fever cause (−)
37 Hawaii, e.g. (−)

Answer on page 310

Round The Bend

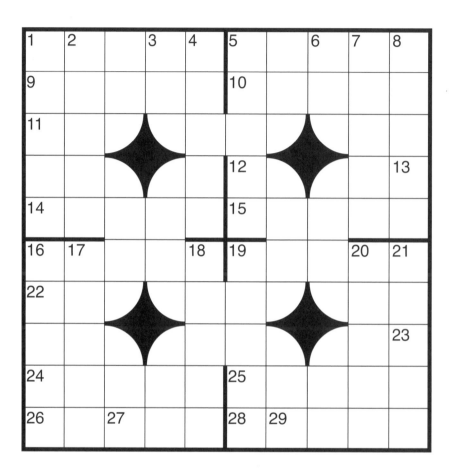

ACROSS
1 Cushioned
5 Second brightest stars
9 Astrologer Dixon
10 Put on the qui vive
14 Past or present, e.g.
15 Midway alternative
16 Honey bunch?
19 Between, in Boulogne
24 Subdued, to Stokowski
25 Soap opera extra, often
26 Poorly kept
28 Game show hosted by Chuck Woolery

DOWN
1 Bail out
2 Lookout point
4 Colonial lawyer Silas
5 Dueling instrument?
7 Intense devotion
8 Strunk & White's subject
16 Dance lessons
17 *Trivial Breath* poet
18 He often said, "He's dead, Jim"
19 Surveillance work
20 Awaken
21 Over

BENT
3 Complicate
6 Rushmore figure
11 *Aunt ___ Cope Book*
12 Late-night legend:
   2 wds.
13 Key factor when starting a
   business
22 Unjustly cruel
23 Barbizon landscapist
   Jules
27 Ace on a par-3
29 Reddish

Answer on page 311

Crossing Paths

CLUES

1. Their real names were Julius, Arthur, Leonard, Herbert, and Milton: 2 wds.
   The Bonfire of the Vanities author
   Heads out in a sloop
   Its last episode ended with the four leads in jail
   Considered
   Circle of light
   Ancient region that was part of the Balkan Peninsula
   One millionth: Prefix
   Suburb of New Haven
   Something wicked?
   The south of France
   Move on momentum
   CONTROL's Agent 86

2. Medley that starts a musical
   Oscar winner for Nicholson and Hunt: 5 wds.
   Norms
   Middle name of our 21st president
   Matrimony
   Appropriately, a four-letter word
   Capital of Latvia
   Collapse: 2 wds.
   The yoke's on them
   Wisconsin city on Lake Michigan
   17th-century mock-epic poem by Samuel Butler that satirized the Puritans
   Motorcycle brand

3. Pants
   Electrolytic coating for tableware: 2 wds.
   First victim
   Diamondbacks, Dodgers, Giants, Padres, and Rockies: 3 wds.
   Andrew Jackson's unofficial advisers: 2 wds.
   Beethoven's "Pastoral" Symphony
   Rude
   King Fahd's domain: 2 wds.
   Noted name in talk show lore

4. Emphasize
   Banners suspended from crossbars
   Wear away
   L.A. suburb founded by Standard Oil: 2 wds.
   More passionate
   Vain
   Loose, colorful African pullover
   Fad-following '40s teen girl

FOURS
Exchange premium
Kojak's first name
Qualifying race
To boot

Answer on page 312

Intersections

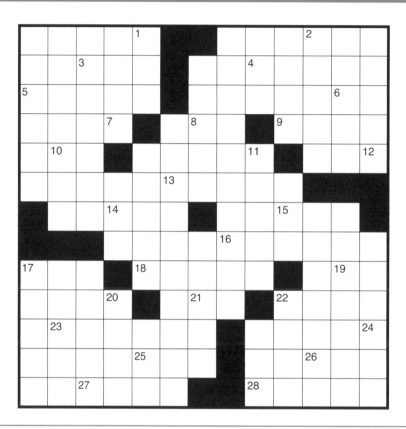

Answer on page 313

CLUES

1 Majorette's prop
Videogame initials
2 Ankle joint
Nun, in Nantes
3 Home of the Blue Jays
Moonstruck subject
4 Early pds.
The Music Man song, "Goodnight My ___"
5 Capital of Mali
Paddock parents
6 Jordanian king, 1953–1999
Song on Queen Latifah's *Black Reign* album
7 City near Provo
Molecule part
8 Abode of the dead, in Judaism
Belg. neighbor
9 Breathing: Abbr.
Positions

10 Dilettante
Suspense writer Follett
11 Danish money
Disembogues
12 Catcher's place?
Just know
13 Liberace prop: 2 wds.
MacLaine book: 4 wds.
14 Flaubert's birthplace
Group pronoun
15 Dracula, sometimes
Silklike nylon
16 He played a *Poseidon Adventure* survivor: 2 wds.
It's wound on a wound
17 Emeril's expletive
Highly successful, in *Variety*
18 An elephant has four
Antonio Prohias's battlers
19 Model airplane, pre-assembly
Work for Hanna-Barbera

20 Couturier Cassini
World Trade Org.'s old name
21 Jag
Passbook abbr.
22 Popular drink
"Prisoner of Love" singer
23 Pinkerton or Sherman
Run-down hotel
24 Birth month symbols
Posthumous John Lennon hit
25 Acknowledge applause
Strategem, when "pulled": 2 wds.
26 "Daughter of the Moon" who raised Hiawatha
Pica alternative
27 Attorney General under Reagan
Left jab followed by a right cross: Hyph.
28 Diamond corners
Entanglement

Jigsaw

ACROSS
3 1913 Arthur Wynne creation: 2 wds.
4 *Rebecca* author: 3 wds.

DOWN
1 Of great consequence: Hyph.
2 Hook-jawed reptiles: 2 wds.

TOP LEFT
a Be
b Couric companion
c Dragsters' arena
d Repairman
e Show biz union
f Stationer's quantity
g Takes it easy
h Went on all fours

TOP CENTER
a Carter who played Wonder Woman
b Dustin's *Kramer vs. Kramer* costar
c Greek consonants
d "Like ___ through the hourglass, ..."
e Piano man?
f Same old story?
g Swiss cheese features
h "Where the goblins go"

TOP RIGHT
a Clapton classic
b Give a leg up
c Leans to one side
d 1938 DuPont invention
e Page of music?
f Red-dog
g Roughly
h *Wait ___ Dark*

CENTER LEFT
a Blue Grotto locale
b Centerfold photo, maybe
c Golden State: Abbr.
d Helsinki residents
e How POSSLQs live, some say: 2 wds.
f *Murders in the Rue Morgue* culprit
g Tropical climbing vine
h What *tempus* does

CENTER
a Bare minimum
b Comic strip Viking

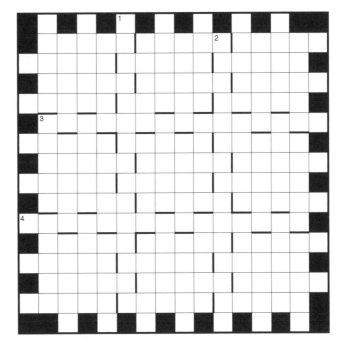

c Get ___ of (grasp)
d Lewis Carroll's "slithy" creatures
e Make a play for: 2 wds.
f Mr. T series, with *The*: 2 wds.
g Pointed arch
h Refuse

CENTER RIGHT
a Brownish-gray Asiatic cat
b Clear up congestion
c Defeats à la Deep Blue
d Dogpatch lad
e Greek physician
f Grotesque *Star Wars* gangster
g Kind of ink or rubber
h Mongolian for "ocean"

BOTTOM LEFT
a Actress Barkin
b Actress Berry
c Elsa Klensch's subject
d He activated a Tripp wire
e Jackie Robinson pal/teammate

f Kilmer masterwork
g Michaelmas daisy
h President after Harrison

BOTTOM CENTER
a Command
b Exasperated
c *Family Matters* nerd
d Insurrectionist
e Senator Hatch of Utah
f Student loans, e.g.
g Thin layers of aurum
h Yellow fever mosquito

BOTTOM RIGHT
a Captain Rickenbacker
b Enthusiastic, plus
c Liquor-and-hot-water drink
d Mary's pal
e One of the Magi's gifts
f Saw
g Supermarket section
h "You ___ at 'Hello'" (*Jerry Maguire* catchphrase): 2 wds.

Answer on page 296

Angling

1	2	3	4	5	6		7		8	9
10					11		12	13		14
					15	16		17		18
19	20		21	22	23			24		25
26	27	28	29				30			31
32			33	34		35	36			37
38			39	40	41	42	43		44	
45		46			47				48	49
50				51		52	53			54
			55	56	57			58	59	
60	61	62	63			64	65	66	67	68

CLUES

1-5 Cagney, Coco, or Caan
2-29 Big production number?
3-17 Gurus
3-20 Goya's *The Naked* ___
4-10 Prompted
4-34 Goosebump-inducing
5-33 Henley Royal Regatta venue
6-10 Investigated
7-14 A little lower?
8-24 Mexican sandwich
9-23 Human trunks
11-31 Grape that's seen better days?
12-18 Central points
13-44 Reveal by removing a covering
15-55 Produce

16-18 Intensely hot
16-28 Bridget : Peter :: Jane : ___
19-45 Groups of cattle
21-40 Monetary penalty
22-24 Dalai Lama's territory
25-49 Second rock from the Sun
26-50 Just a face in the crowd?
26-60 Ex-rival of Phil and Oprah
27-61 Aridity
30-64 Meadow
32-63 Fail to follow suit
34-35 Well-known family surname of vaudeville
36-58 Place for outdoor furniture
37-59 Worth
38-56 He made his last TV appearance on May 22, 1992

39-61 Chastity's dad
40-42 Cone-bearing tree
41-43 Vacationing
43-65 Dubious, like a "one that got away" story?
44-67 Radiuses' neighbors
46-57 Singer Nina, actress Uta, or golfer Walter
47-48 Go downhill powered by momentum
48-66 Evidence in the Watergate case
51-52 Sermon subject
53-62 Harsh, ironic derision
54-68 Mighty Joe Young, e.g.
65-67 Opinion

Answer on page 308

Around & About

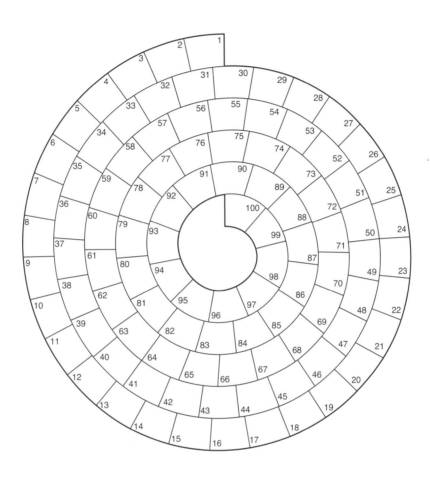

AROUND
1-4 Iditarod finish line
5-9 The big dipper
10-16 Blew the story
17-21 Senior member
22-27 Richard of *St. Elsewhere*
28-34 Spicy bit used to flavor ouzo
35-40 Pest
41-48 Timber tree also known as buttonwood
49-53 Code name?
54-56 Some of the bad stuff in cigarettes
57-62 Take out a loan, but not alone
63-71 Bigoted
72-76 Bandleader who was married to Charo
77-83 Starving artists' quarters
84-88 Greek vowel
89-93 Pulled some strings?
94-100 Query in ubiquitous dairy ads: 2 wds.

ABOUT
100-96 Austrian muralist Gustav
95-87 It's about 33 miles north of Salt Lake City: 2 wds.
86-80 Spackle's cousin
79-74 Motley
73-70 The Bruins of the NCAA
69-61 Changing the cast list
60-52 Athenian orator
51-46 Nicholson : Keaton :: ____ : West
45-42 He played the car salesman in *Fargo*
41-38 Scrape, as a knee
37-32 Hogan's hero
31-25 Vocalist on the #1 song on *Billboard*'s first published chart
24-19 Capital of New South Wales
18-12 Quantities of stock under 100 shares: 2 wds.
11-6 Noted name in Philippine history
5-1 Dud

Answer on page 298

Tops & Bottoms

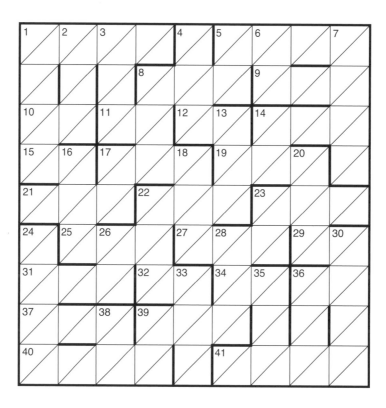

ACROSS

1 Musical starring Danny Kaye as Noah: 3 wds.
5 1990s line dance fad
8 Of inferior quality
9 Fix
10 Libertine
11 Head of the Sûreté?
12 Fascinated by
14 Stab
15 Footnote abbr.
17 Miss Piggy's skill
19 Actress De Carlo
21 Kipling boy raised by wolves
22 Name shared by teams in the NFL and NHL
23 Use a hypodermic syringe
25 He's got a case
27 Untenanted
29 Nickname of astronaut Donald Slayton
31 Playwright Albee
32 "Candy is dandy ..." writer
34 Ukraine city
36 Singer Campbell
37 High-IQ
39 Add (something) to a sketch: 2 wds.
40 The Wright stuff
41 Meteorologists' topics

DOWN

1 Recipe involving a soy sauce marinade
2 "___ worry?": 2 wds.
3 Steal a march on
4 Sudden terror
5 Creche figure
6 Floor space
7 Showed up
8 Silver service, perhaps: 2 wds.
13 Legwear in short supply during WWII
14 Director Reitman
16 Captain Kirk's infinitive-splitter
17 Titular river in a 1957 movie
18 Former daytime talk show host
20 Next up: 2 wds.
22 Deed holders
23 Rapper who starred in *New Jack City*: 2 wds.
24 Big current?
26 Impressed, and then some
28 AA spinoff group: Hyph.
30 Earth, air, fire, and water
33 Two-time Heisman winner Griffin
35 ___ Underground (Lou Reed's band)
36 Mourn
38 Rover's playmate
39 Advent

Answer on page 299

Marching Bands

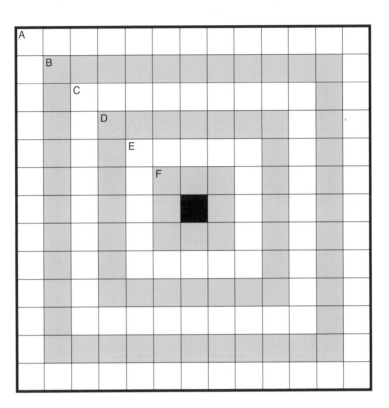

ROWS

1 a Andy Capp's wife
  b Get someone to do the work of two?
2 a Bits and pieces
  b Take on
3 a TV's "Mistress of the Dark"
  b *An Officer and a Gentleman* Oscar winner
4 a Single: Prefix
  b Polish sausage
5 a Sans sensitivity
  b Snug and warm
6 a Where to board a boar
  b Visible in X-ray photos
7 a Destroys
  b 1971 Nobel-winning Chilean poet
8 a He solved the Sphinx's riddle
  b Named, old-style
9 a Spark
  b Sniggler's quarry

10 a Compendium
   b Seeker of satisfaction
11 a Bury
   b Implore urgently
12 a "What happened when" charts
   b Pseudoaesthetic
13 a Specialized vocabulary
   b Symphonic piece: 2 wds.

BANDS

A a Struggles clumsily
  b Lustrous fabric
  c Abbey Theatre cofounder
  d What cats and rats do?
  e Admitting clients
  f Sergeant Snorkel's dog
  g Wasn't mellifluous
  h Restaurant employee: Hyph.
B a Old clothing dealers
  b Casual garment: Hyph.
  c Variety of poker

  d Guitar picks
  e Losing one's marbles
  f Short skirt
  g One east of Mountain
C a Shrews
  b Where to find buoys and gulls together
  c Glass cleaners?
  d *Chicago* lyricist
  e Pithy remark
  f Mustang's accelerator?
D a Father of the Midgard serpent
  b Portoferraio's island
  c Francis or Dahl
  d Dye tank
  e Prom attendees
E a Surreptitious
  b Overindulge at the bar
  c Coin toss command: 2 wds.
  d Cause of royal insomnia
F a Bacchus's a.k.a.

Answer on page 300

Pathfinder

CLUES

1E Following a tortuous path (12)
2E Former capital of Pakistan (7)
3S One engaged in mocking (5)
3S Internet language (4)
4S Consider making major changes (7)
5S Call forth (6)
6N Crowd together, archaically (5)
7N Croupier, at times (5)
8E Half the SAT test (6)
9S Carelessness? (6)

10N One who's not satisfied with straight A's (12)
11N Mars's counterpart (4)
11S John Steed or Mrs. Peel (7)
12W Ready for surgery (4)
13N Designated (6)
14S Whodunit author Marsh (5)
15S Blue-and-white earthen pots (6)
16W Broadway villain who sings "Alive" (2,4)
17W Summit (4)
18S Moviegoer's memento (4)

19N *The Lion King* baddie (4)
19S Easy mark (6)
20E Arrow poison (6)
21S The college in *Animal House* (5)
22S Cigar manufacturing city (5)
23S Use a chamois (3)
24W Stuck (7)
25W Scold severely (6)
26W A welcome sight? (3)
27N It doesn't mean they're *not* out to get you (8)
28E Oxidize (4)

Answer on page 301

Crushword

ACROSS
1 He gives a dam
3 Italian sheep's-milk cheese
6 Entry in *TV Guide*, e.g.
8 Open shelving
10 They get started in Indianapolis
11 Oktoberfest orders
12 Like some really bad headaches
14 Chattel
16 Their work is quite a strain
18 Lion-goat-serpent hybrids
19 Someone stimulating?
20 Cheerios?: Hyph.
22 Served raw
25 Bought and sold: 2 wds.
27 Train à Grande ___
  (superfast train)
29 Omphalos
30 Predicts

32 Very cold storage
34 Like
35 Actress Peters
36 Semisynthetic fabrics
37 San Diego football player
39 British show biz family
42 Workweek starts
43 Quarterback-turned-sportscaster
  Boomer
44 Impedes

DOWN
1 Borscht vegetable
2 C
3 Smoothing with a hammerhead
4 Welsh dog
5 Not yet senescent: 3 wds.
6 Permission to go ashore
7 Brandy cocktails

9 Answer
13 Implicit
15 Andrea Bocelli, e.g.: 2 wds.
16 Match
17 Sideways
18 Picks
21 One of the tribes of Israel
23 Scarlet songbird
24 Disclosure
26 Sheet metal?
28 Woo with song
31 Tracks down facts
33 Wasted little by little
34 Playground game: 2 wds.
35 *Hollywood Squares* host Tom
36 *Everybody Loves* ___
38 15-Down's renditions
40 Auto racer Hill
41 Evening service

Answer on page 300

Weaving

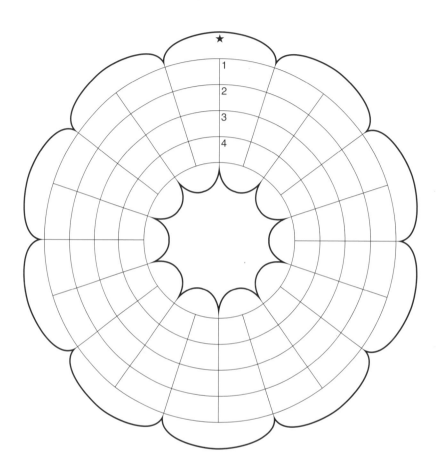

WEAVERS

a Resort island near Nantucket: 2 wds.
b Paper used for legal pads
c Standards
d Massachusetts city where volleyball was invented
e 1952 Eddie Fisher song: 2 wds.
f Contour
g Gentlewoman
h Pompous
i Pastoral Kenyan tribe
j Unbroken
k Shuffleboard stick
l Crossword diagram
m Signaled, as on *Win Ben Stein's Money*: 2 wds.
n Half a Steinbeck title: 2 wds.
o Home of Henry VIII's first wife
p 1954 mutant-ant movie

RING 1

a Red, white, green : Hungary :: black, red, gold : ___
b Paulo preceder
c Triangular street sign
d Capital of Bangladesh: Var.

RING 2

a Shot from above?: 2 wds.
b Seeing things?
c Goldfinger's first name

RING 3

a Rembrandt's ___ *Watch*
b Count loved by Anna Karenina
c Tacit

RING 4

a Fluttering insects named for a woman in Greek myth: 2 wds.
b Judge who framed Roger Rabbit
c Designating

Answer on page 303

Quadrants

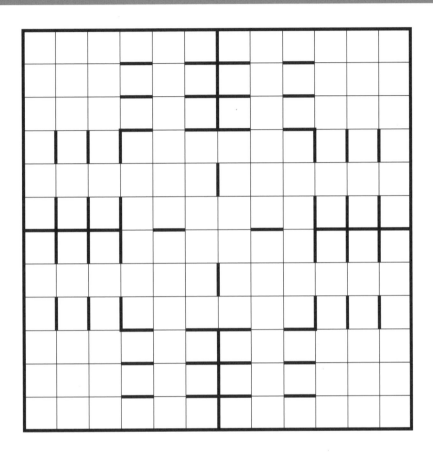

NORTHWEST
a Eggs: Spanish
b Grave
c June 6–7 endurance race site: 2 wds.
d Marathon runner Joan
e Maximally: 2 wds.
f Picture made of inlaid bits
g Run-down
h Vent

NORTHEAST
a Angora
b Blow reveille
c Croupier's task
d Frisbee prototype: 2 wds.
e Jim Varney character
f 1912 Olympian in a Burt Lancaster biopic

g One of Gilligan's co-islanders
h Singer Morissette

SOUTHWEST
a Electronics nut
b ___ K. Le Guin (sci-fi writer)
c 1975 James Clavell novel
d MacArthur said he would
e *My Favorite Year* star
f Playground piece
g Spectrum producers
h "That's putting it ___"

SOUTHEAST
a Declare positively
b *Growing Pains* star
c Hercules's companion

d Hit the road
e Leader of the Grateful Dead
f "Nearer, My God, ___": 2 wds.
g Religious Friend
h Vocation

CENTER
a Charlie Brown's creator
b Dag Hammarskjöld's successor: 2 wds.
c Dan who played the father in *The Wonder Years*
d Executor's responsibility
e Handled roughly
f Imam's place
g Shine brilliantly
h Silicon dioxide

Answer on page 304

Crazy Eights

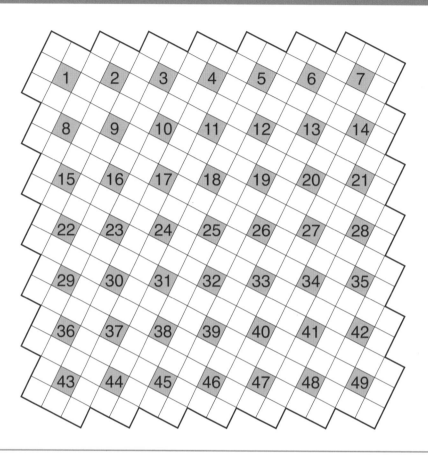

CLUES

1 Printed summary of a ball game: 2 wds. (+)
2 Button below the 8 (−)
3 Verdure (−)
4 Business involving quite a few spot checks? (+)
5 Bathrobe fabric (−)
6 Dug further down (+)
7 End of the time limit (+)
8 Iconoclastic philosopher Russell (+)
9 Company that gets goods from overseas (−)
10 Lab sample (+)
11 Group parodied in the 1999 sitcom *Thanks* (−)
12 Sandy Koufax's skill (+)
13 Capital of Manitoba (+)
14 Matilda's recreation? (−)

15 C-note portrait (−)
16 Hellish (+)
17 Moves forward (+)
18 It's found at the X (+)
19 Quibble over trifles (−)
20 Zamboanga resident (−)
21 Gem cutter (+)
22 Salivating (+)
23 British currency (−)
24 Onetime *Vogue* editor Diana (−)
25 Late-'90s dance craze (−)
26 Peru-Bolivia border lake (+)
27 Campaign for votes (−)
28 One way to start a family (−)
29 Got the computer going again (−)
30 Battles for prizes (+)
31 Pennsylvania Dutch pork recipe (−)
32 Streetlight support (−)
33 Quite hot and humid (−)

34 Criticizes the unimportant stuff (+)
35 Tie holder (anagram of Answer 34) (+)
36 Ham hocks, black-eyed peas, chitlins, etc.: 2 wds. (+)
37 Flees prosecution (−)
38 Braincases (+)
39 Brand of hardboard (−)
40 Spectacular view (−)
41 They're nothing new (+)
42 Zest (−)
43 Suspends a meeting (−)
44 Kept on talking nonsense (+)
45 Coolness comparison (−)
46 Found "x − y" (+)
47 Maneuvering a canoe (−)
48 Twilight zones? (+)
49 Actor and martial arts expert Jean-Claude: 2 wds. (+)

Answer on page 314

Catching Some Z's

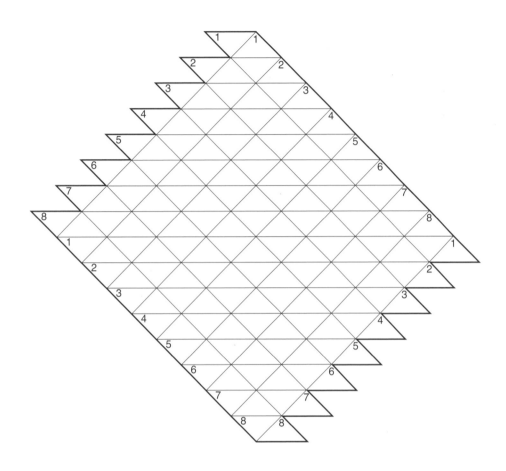

CLUES

1 a Its motto is "Eureka"
b Doesn't even get a D–
c ___ oblige (moral duty of the wealthy)
d Five-time World Cup finalist, three-time winner
e Cudgel

2 a *Sexual Politics* author Kate
b Imitation
c Rick Blaine's portrayer
d 1922 German film version of *Dracula*

3 a Use Snuggle
b Treated sacrilegiously
c Neptune or Poseidon: 2 wds.

d Casting no vote
4 a Lacking an MPAA designation
b Basil-based sauce
c ___ *a Wonderful Life*
d Scotland Yard inspector often shown up by Sherlock Holmes
e Objet d'art
f *An American in Paris* actress Nina
5 a Diner employees
b Why a store may be closed for two weeks
c Fasten your seat belt
d Michael Keaton/Teri Garr movie: 2 wds.

6 a Stupid person

b Tree in the pine family
c Small circles of friends
d Rice recipe
e Aristophanes's forte
f Bud's partner
g Navigator's stack
7 a Act of bringing forth
b Concealment
c Kidney-shaped
d *Saturday Night Live* alumnus
8 a Implicit
b *Born Free* lioness
c Adder or asp
d Re Brunei's leader
e Repetitive rhythm from the brass section: Hyph.

Answer on page 306

Helter-Skelter

24		22				21	11
			18		19		
23	16			17		20	
15			14		7	3	12
25			9			8	
			5			4	
	10						
1		2			6		13

CLUES

1 Comic strip that inspired a Broadway musical
2 Alabama university
3 Kentucky Derby wreath
4 Day of rest
5 Basic unit of computer information
6 Wrenching experience
7 Thick mass of hair
8 The James gang, e.g.
9 Desk accessory
10 Wild duck
11 ___ Moore (Hormel brand)
12 Compositor's selections
13 Home base of Nordstrom, Inc.
14 *Wind in the Willows* character
15 1971 Spielberg TV movie
16 Extreme
17 Deli loaf
18 88 days, on Mercury
19 Performance
20 Exclaim
21 Fred Gipson's "Old" mutt
22 Always, in verse
23 Encouraging word?
24 Oppression
25 ___ "The Man" Musial

Answer on page 307

Cubism

DOWN LEFT
1 Approximately
2 Stench, in Staffordshire
3 Temple address
4 Affirmative action?
5 Maryland border river
6 Baltimore partner
7 Engrossed
13 *Mad About You* star
16 Doggy bag minutia
17 Ring or rink
18 Titular soprano in a Massenet opera
20 Old type of photo equipment:
   2 wds.
26 Vegetable stalk often made into pie
27 Precept
39 Modern-day messages: Hyph.
41 Boeing products
42 Stroller
43 Tear down
44 Radio talker Don
45 "___ Valentine": 2 wds.
49 Guitar pioneer Paul

DOWN RIGHT
1 Puppeteers Bil and ___ Baird
5 Gershwin hero
8 Bad day at the Forum
9 *Butterfield 8* author
10 Holds up
11 Kind of table: Hyph.
12 4 and 7, to 64 and 343:
   2 wds.
14 Political philosopher Hannah
15 Octave components
16 Golfer Snead
19 Sebastian in *The Little Mermaid*
22 Score 72, perhaps: 2 wds.
30 Shun the TelePrompTer: Hyph.
32 M, in Morse code: 2 wds.
34 He has all the answers
36 Gas-X rival
37 Sri ___
38 Mystery fiction award
40 Corresponded
46 Gone prostrate
47 Kon-Tiki Museum city

ACROSS
21 Battle Born State city
22 High-tech hookup
23 O.R. goings-on
24 Strong as ___: 2 wds.
25 Works devoid of aesthetic value
28 Suffer the consequences
29 Max Factor creation
31 Timetable: Abbr.
33 *Fideles* preceder
35 Skill-less
42 Most important
45 Dolt
48 Japanese noodles
49 Spot check?
50 "Consarn it all anyhow!"
51 Cloudless sky
52 Character who sings "Some
   Enchanted Evening"
53 His biggest hit was 1959's "Lonely Boy"
54 Southwestern terrain features
55 Churchly council
56 Frost

Answer on page 308

Target Practice

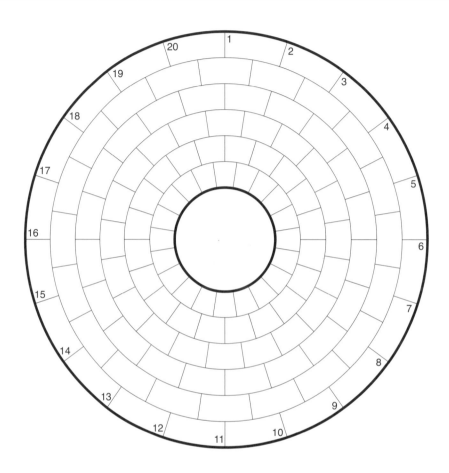

CLOCKWISE
1 Prepared, with "up"
2 Fireman's jacket?
3 Did some woodworking
4 Incriminated fraudulently
5 Long, curling ocean wave
6 Michigan's Lower Peninsula looks like one
7 Piece of lettuce?
8 *A Doll's House* surname
9 "Peanuts" character who raises dirt wherever he goes
10 Lacks: 2 wds.
11 "Water Music" composer
12 Pleasure trip
13 Summer TV fare

14 Last bit: 2 wds.
15 Environment
16 ___ Thursday (Easter minus three)
17 Emergency prioritization
18 Speed skater Blair
19 Pleasure trips
20 Pornographic: Hyph.

COUNTERCLOCKWISE
1 Run-down and dirty
2 Skullcap
3 Nebraska river
4 Bell-bottoms
5 Deranged
6 Sounded anguished

7 Rheostat
8 Place of rapid growth
9 Threw stuff at
10 *Love Story* director, onetime AMPAS president
11 J.R. Ewing's portrayer
12 National park in Alberta
13 Hall carpet, maybe
14 One was named for Achilles
15 First little piggy's destination
16 Cervantes's first name
17 *Gong Show* display
18 Boston hockey team
19 Became a member
20 Site of Kubla Khan's pleasure dome

Answer on page 309

Maze

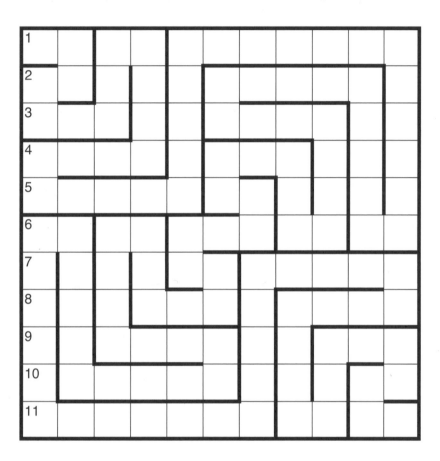

ACROSS
1 Decorous
  An infamous Jack
2 Deserter
  Nine-sided figures
3 Flat-bottomed coaster
  Madhouse
4 Win out
  Principal
5 University briefly attended by
  Howard Hughes
  Administers a vaccine, e.g.
6 Typewriter key
  Bunk
7 Excluding meals
  Vandalize

8 Hands : clocks :: ___ : sundials
  Singer Braxton
9 Tennyson's Mr. Arden
  Rival of Monica
10 Extraordinary
  Filch
11 Frodo Baggins's uncle
  Waterproof boot

PATH
1 Word at one end of a maze
2 Get
3 Impose a high markup
4 Enemy of Desdemona
5 Form icicles
6 Man, woman, and child

7 Bigfoot's Asian kin
8 Woman honored in "Woman"
9 Jets or Sharks
10 Down Under soldier
11 Many party favors were bought here
12 Hot stuff
13 Oft-tattooed word
14 Pin
15 Become obsolete
16 Pet rodent
17 Oscar winner as Charlie Allnut
18 Europe's oldest independent country:
   2 wds.
19 He got the point across to his son
20 Reaction to a punch in the gut?
21 Word at the maze's other end

Answer on page 310

Siamese Triplets

ACROSS

1 Seinfeld pal ...
... and another ...
and the other
7 Baby's first word, often
Boarding school
Uncategorized: Abbr.
11 Interstellar cloud
Victors in 1945
World's third-largest island
12 On crutches
Sigmund Freud's daughter
Terrorist's arsenal
13 Brunch entree
Fetches
Hard stones
14 Company that tries harder
The New Yorker founder Harold
Woodwind instr.
15 Clan symbol
Hit, on a 45: 2 wds.
Venom spigots
16 Bender
Silhouette
Steps over a fence
17 "Hurry up!": 3 wds.
Tall Californians?
Tom or Dick
19 ___-Magnon man
Ninny
Rubber-stamped
22 ___ disadvantage: 2 wds.
Gist
The Crying Game org.
23 Method: Abbr.
State of India
Toper's ailment
24 Apparitions
Lonesome Dove author
Mammal with a long tongue
27 Arouse heebie-jeebies
Fire men?
River of central England
28 Costume
Is well acquainted with
___ salts (MgSO$_4$•7H$_2$0)
32 Last writes?
Streamlet
Trig function
33 Group of actors
Light, loose smock
Prisoner of Zenda princess
34 Actress Swenson
Faxed
Qualified
35 Angles off the perpendicular
Rhododendron's cousin
Word that may accompany a
handshake

36 Cartesian conjunction
"___ magnifique"
Ostensibly be
37 Ari of *Kate & Allie*
Castle and Dunne
Courage and fortitude

DOWN

1 Shoelace problem
Swindle
Undergoes recession
2 Actress Singer
Big name in scat
San ___, Italy
3 Help a hood
Ken of *thirtysomething*
Saharan
4 Fifth-day Christmas gift
Horse-donkey offspring
Mystery writer Michael
5 Minus
Tom Lehrer listed them to a G. & S.
melody
TV series that spoofed 007 movies:
2 wds.
6 Aurora's counterpart
Informer
Ogee shape
7 Exuding virility
Newscaster Brown, to her cohorts
Socrates's student
8 Delirious
Like mosaic tiles
Portuguese island group
9 Couturier Pucci
Stephen King book
Try to grab suddenly: 2 wds.
10 Affectionate touch
Evaluate
100 Spanish centimos
16 Go down
Small firework
Use a telescope
18 Detergent brand
Giant of Cooperstown
Status follower
19 Assault troops' vehicle
Black currant used in making liqueur
Go up against
20 Amanuensis
Pass joining Afghanistan and
Pakistan
Wisconsin city
21 A secondary color
Bloodhound's evidence
Brave
25 Night vision?
"... or ___ be": 2 wds.
Vacant, as a flat

26 Have on
"... rosebuds while ___": 2 wds.
Tarts purloiner
29 Fat
It takes the cake
Mah-jongg piece
30 Bygone car model
PC operator
Stratagem
31 Ancient Iranian
Lip
Look-alikes, idiomatically
33 Freeh agents: Abbr.
Neely of hockey fame
Skye cap

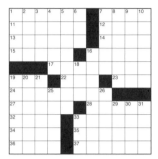

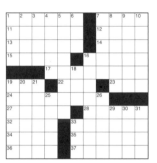

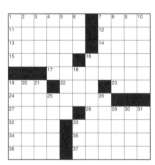

Answer on page 311

HoneyComb

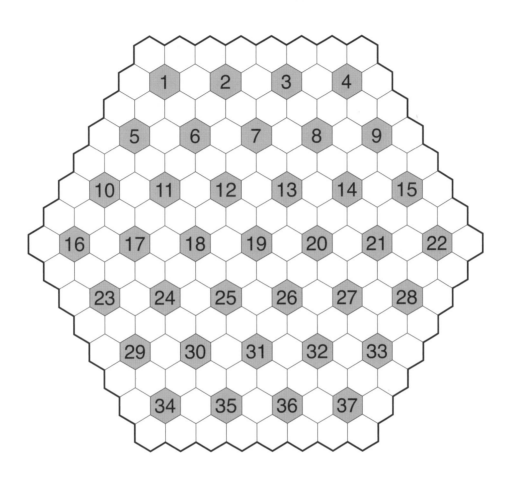

CLUES

1 Comedian known for his "seven words" (–)
2 Boring tool or gin cocktail (–)
3 Rook (+)
4 Give counsel (–)
5 Ally McBeal, e.g. (–)
6 Talk show host Williams (+)
7 Speaker of the House, 1977–1987 (–)
8 Go to bed (–)
9 She turned 40 on March 1, 1999 (–)
10 Car, in slang (+)
11 Cadence (+)
12 With Word 26, variety of American violet (+)

13 Seymour's love interest in *Little Shop of Horrors* (–)
14 Hospital vessel (–)
15 "As I live and breathe!" (–)
16 Alibi (–)
17 In good spirits (+)
18 Béchamel sauce with cheese added (+)
19 Controversial *Phantom Menace* character: 2 wds. (+)
20 Regal hue (–)
21 Fatal (+)
22 Nullify (–)
23 Hangouts (+)
24 Llama's cousin (+)

25 Sartre novel that may make you sick? (+)
26 See Clue 12: Hyph. (–)
27 Oughta (+)
28 Neurotic person (+)
29 Penalize (–)
30 *The Taking of ___ One Two Three* (–)
31 Old Testament sesquicentum (–)
32 Streisand signature song (–)
33 Orb (–)
34 Popeye or Sinbad (+)
35 Showed one's pearly whites (–)
36 Send to the guillotine (–)
37 *Star Trek* weapon (–)

Answer on page 312

Round The Bend

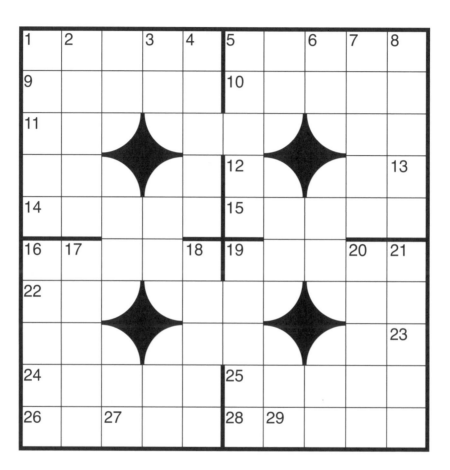

ACROSS
1 Grifter's ideas
5 *Maltese Falcon* tec
9 Hyundai headquarters
10 Whimpered
14 Boxer Liston
15 Lie
16 Canticle group
19 Topiarist's canvas
24 Belong: 2 wds.
25 Engage in blackmail
26 Criteria
28 Mysterious Psalms word

DOWN
1 Irving Berlin's "Blue ___"
2 Co-op's counterpart
4 Bygone mag for teen girls
5 Gushes forth
7 Exclude
8 Enlighten
16 Kirk Douglas trademark
17 *Wings on My Feet* autobiographer
18 Horseman's handful
19 Competition for Capriati
20 City in New York on the Mohawk River
21 Pullman accommodation

BENT
3 Created a snafu:
 2 wds.
6 Out of sorts?
11 Prefix for red or
 structure
12 Popular carol: 3 wds.
13 Pet
22 Drink that can be pink
23 Emulate
27 *Natural Born Killers*
 director
29 Described in detail

Answer on page 302

Crossing Paths

CLUES

1. Especially fine or beautiful
   Marquee datum
   Disappointments
   Apollo 13 VIP
   Are You There, God? It's Me, Margaret writer
   1935 Top-10 hit for both Xavier Cugat and Louis Prima: 4 wds.
   Face down
   Black Beauty's "chronicler"
   Sign of something big?
   Sidelong look
   They'll do the hole job
2. "In my opinion, ...": 4 wds.
   Was there
   Neck of the woods
   1952 Winter Olympics site

Go off the track
Italian variety of omelet
Disheveled
Marked with an X
Yours truly, thrice?: 4 wds.
Succumb to gravity
The world's longest river
Language of Pakistan
Intimately: 2 wds., Fr.

3. "Father of Modern Photography" Alfred
   The Stars and Stripes: 2 wds.
   Caper about
   At one's adversary's mercy: 3 wds.
   Base on balls
   Quentin Tarantino film of 1992 starring Harvey Keitel: 2 wds.
   Long, distressful cry

Type of sleeping accommodation
Book jacket paragraph
Behave: 5 wds.

4. Sexy style of footwear: 2 wds.
   Traffic pattern?
   Toy dog with long, silky, white hair
   Characterized by copycatting: Hyph.
   Mosque official
   Flips: 2 wds.
   Parasitic snakelike fish with a round, sucking mouth: 2 wds.
   Chase

FOURS

Anklebones
Church furniture
Hearty laughs
Lather

Answer on page 296

Intersections

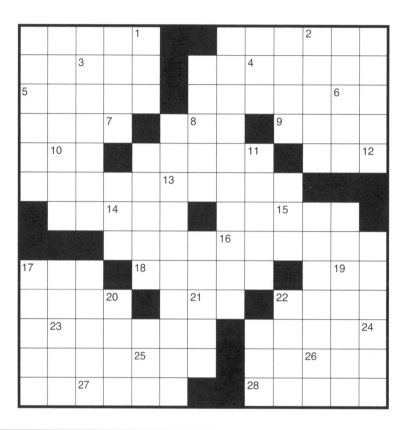

CLUES

1 Celtic sea god
   Shampoo brand
2 Exemplars of craziness
   False deities
3 *Jeffersons* actress Roker
   Show
4 Characterization
   Comet's path
5 Austro-Prussian War treaty city
   Have no stomach for
6 Rapper né James Todd Smith: 4 wds.
   Small bay
7 Cross-eyed Clarence, e.g.
   Profit
8 Flat: Prefix
   Initials at Narita Airport
9 *Dilbert* character
   Locale for dandling

10 Actor once married to Lauren Bacall
   Citified area, jocularly
11 Land of the Mau Mau uprising
   Leader of the Green Mountain Boys
12 Barrett of *Star Trek*
   Cards' home: Abbr.
13 *Damn Yankees* marked his Broadway debut: 2 wds.
   Opinion pieces
14 Australian isl.
   Harrison's band mate
15 Dagger concealer?
   Staff member?
16 African island group independent since 1976
   Gripes
17 Caen clerics
   Rudimentary lesson
18 Extraterrestrial
   Where people's fortunes are won?

19 Convention speech
   Sodium hydroxide
20 Gordius's poser
   Schnozz
21 Golfer Ernie
   "You're My World" singer Black
22 Home-perm name
   Triple this for a 1970 movie title
23 He gives a hoot: 2 wds.
   Its number is 666
24 Running out of: 2 wds.
   Trawler equipment
25 Indivisible
   Tallinn's land
26 Acceptable
   Mountain ridge
27 Magna follower
   Puts into writing
28 McBeal's field
   Tests the waters

Answer on page 312

Jigsaw

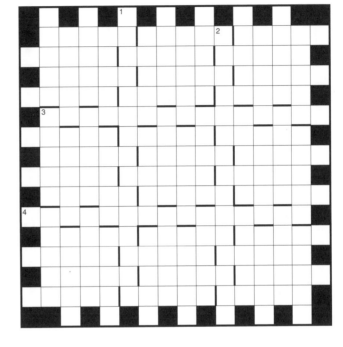

` ACROSS
3 1977 Ted Nugent album: 3 wds.
4 One kind is called "Samoa": 3 wds.

DOWN
1 Philatelists: 2 wds.
2 Liqueur made in St. Louis: 2 wds.

TOP LEFT
a Blackthorn fruits
b Fetal diagnosis method, for short
c France's longest river
d *Gandhi* setting
e Historical record
f Nonliteral expression
g Oil-well firefighting legend Red
h Surroundings

TOP CENTER
a Alternative to plastic
b Barbizon landscape painter
c Chilean units of currency
d Concealed
e Restraints
f Rio Grande feeder
g Spelling or Neville
h Word elongated by Ed McMahon

TOP RIGHT
a Alamo casualty
b Barbershop requests
c Barbershop tool
d Due (to)
e Half note
f Slow-witted
g Tolerate
h Victim of CFC's

CENTER LEFT
a ___ Aziz (cohort of Saddam Hussein)
b Brown-capped, edible mushroom
c Cartoon cat of note
d Close-fitting, brimless hat
e Cupid's yokemate
f Play-by-play counterpart
g Stopping all along the way
h The $50,000+ SC400, e.g.

CENTER
a Big name in talk shows
b Cultivated land, Southwestern-style

c Earliest: Prefix
d Harder to find
e MTV reporter Kurt
f Oteri of *SNL*
g Quinine water
h "___ You Glad You're You?"

CENTER RIGHT
a African grass-and-bush terrain
b Dweebs
c File for an appeal
d Netanyahu's successor
e Ryan's daughter
f Smoldering item in a fireplace
g *The Crucible* locale
h Type of radio: 2 wds.

BOTTOM LEFT
a Animal
b Baby bird?
c Cohort of Hawkeye and Trapper
d Emit, as through pores
e Film producer Adolph
f Mediterranean island near Spain

g Mr. ___ (handyman)
h Sputnik II passenger

BOTTOM CENTER
a Curmudgeonly Muppet
b Golf course transportation
c "I give up!"
d Mickey's pooch pal
e Pleasant Island, today
f Prognosticators
g Skiers' mecca
h Vietnam region whose capital is Hue

BOTTOM RIGHT
a Do tilework, perhaps
b Go from red to blue to green?
c New York hockey team, headline-style
d Nitrous ___ (laughing gas)
e Ohio city
f Pervades completely
g Skip a vowel
h Uses a rotary phone

Answer on page 298

Angling

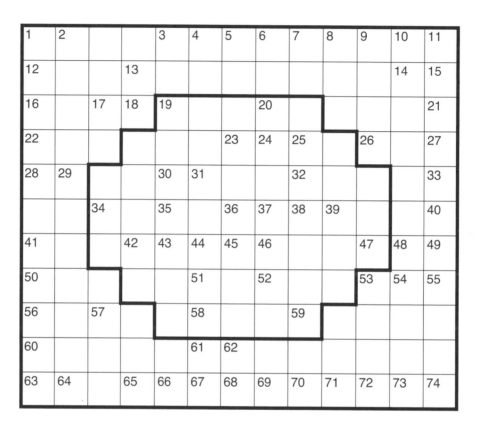

CLUES

1-56 Town on Long Island's south shore
2-35 Transported freight
3-7 Fill till full
4-8 Surname of the *Full House* twins
5-9 Companion of Porthos and Aramis
6-12 Thrive
7-24 "Phooey!"
8-26 No, in Nuremberg
10-48 Flock in the park
11-49 Kurt Cobain's band
13-43 *The Bell Jar* poet Plath
14-33 Famed operatic soprano Sutherland
15-53 High chairs?
16-19 Benjamin Siegel's nom de crime
16-30 Gray-barked tree bearing triangular nuts
17-41 "Pride ___ before destruction" (Prov. 16:18)
18-34 Grownup nits
20-27 Dugouts
20-38 Ohio nine
20-40 Sacred river of India
21-54 ___ War (1950–1953)
22-23 Least sensible, like one of the Seven Dwarfs?
23-50 Sullen in the extreme
25-31 Sheltered
28-56 Duke or Hearst
29-67 Sundance's partner
32-72 Roam aimlessly
35-46 Head light?
36-55 Dregs of society
37-39 Expected to arrive
38-44 Gray-sprinkled chestnut horse
42-64 Robbery
44-62 Ugly duckling, ultimately
45-56 Strength
47-70 Food supplied from heaven
51-59 Fox show that follows law enforcement workers on the job
52-74 Devastated
53-73 Thor Heyerdahl's *Kon-Tiki* was one
57-61 "Green-eyed monster"
58-60 Gave a shove
62-65 Toteboard numbers
63-66 "The Highwayman" poet
67-71 Full of current information
68-72 Hoarse
69-73 Basketball coach Pat

Answer on page 304

Around & About

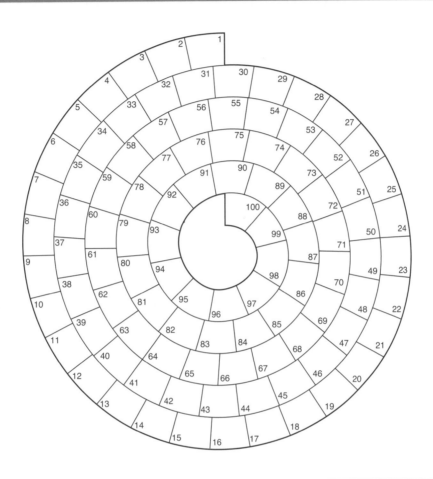

Tops & Bottoms

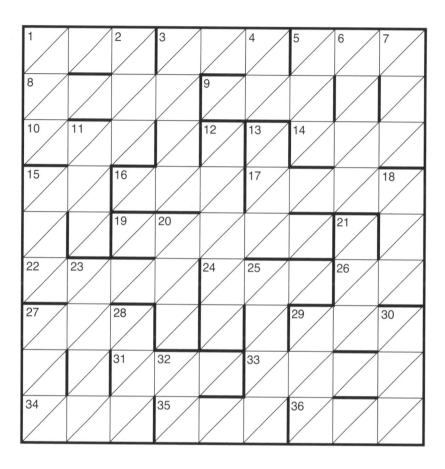

ACROSS
1 Rectangular game piece with dots
3 777 manufacturer
5 Pupil's coat
8 1973 Linda Blair horror film, with *The*
9 Big name at the U.S. Open
10 Knee injury
14 Dangles a carrot
15 Exceed 100° C.
16 Less attractive
17 First name of baseball Hall-of-Famer "Three-Finger" Brown
19 Honesty
22 Not needing an amp
24 Be a matchmaker?

26 Comic book superhero group: Hyph.
27 Umlauts turned 90°
29 Dashiell Hammett biographer Julian
31 Eric Blair's nom de plume
33 Talent
34 Actor in 27-Down
35 Cantankerous
36 Underwent oxidation

DOWN
1 *The Bicycle Thief* director Vittorio: 2 wds.
2 Gloomily ill-humored
3 Member of a Nielsen family?
4 Pantyhose packaging
5 Minty treat for Sylvester?

6 Friml's *The Vagabond King*, e.g.
7 A third of Antony's audience?
11 Duo
12 Speedster: 2 wds.
13 Flabbergasts
15 Intelligence
18 *The Omen* demon
20 Birthplace of two U.S. presidents
21 Water ingredient
23 Love at a rock concert?
25 Amount
27 1985 fountain-of-youth movie
28 Undo
29 Jolly Green Giant's li'l pal
30 Lost out on
32 Auditioner's desire

Answer on page 301

Marching Bands

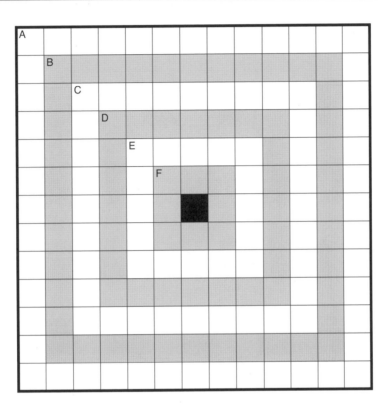

ROWS

1 a *Titanic* director
  b Second person to walk on the moon
2 a Home of a tall, tan, young, lovely girl
  b Looking intently
3 a *The Merry Widow* composer
  b *Like Water for Chocolate* author
4 a 1997 AL MVP Sandy or 1998 AL MVP Roberto
  b Popular takeout cuisine
5 a How used car dealers typically talk
  b Red wine recipe
6 a $C_{10}H_{14}N_2$, used as an insecticide
  b Dispensed medicine
7 a Symphony key: 2 wds.
  b Soft fur
8 a Sander of TV news
  b Less original
9 a Bright red

b Entangles or disentangles
10 a Star of 1979's *Dracula*
  b *Blues Suite* choreographer
11 a Cub, perhaps
  b Alien
12 a Needing something different: 3 wds.
  b Hodgepodge
13 a Light, downy particles
  b Fixed the roof, maybe

BANDS

A a Put in an appearance
  b George's predecessor
  c Head hood
  d Church council
  e Charles Lamb's pseudonym
  f Softball?
  g Satisfy
  h Trilby's hypnotizer
B a Windshield, e.g.
  b *Mode*, *Mad*, or *Mademoiselle*

c Mobster Bugsy
d Actress Samantha
e Travel on whitewater rapids
f Astronomers' Muse
g Writer Paglia
C a Long-eared lagomorphs
  b Stern companion
  c Artist's studio
  d Time and again
  e Stop-dime link: 2 wds.
  f "Singin' in the Rain" composer ___ Herb Brown
D a ___ orders (pink slip)
  b John's *Grease* costar
  c Brisk in tempo
  d Bible book with the shortest name
E a Naval hero of the Peloponnesian War
  b Soviet union
  c Barracks accommodation
F a Klutzy
  b Play with robots?

Answer on page 302

Pathfinder

CLUES

1S 1996 movie with a flying cow (7)
2W Put one over on (6)
3E Sequence (5)
4N Moo goo gai pan pan (3)
4S Search engines, e.g. (3,5)
5S Roy Orbison song covered by Linda Ronstadt (4,5)
6S Kofi grounds? (6,7)
7S Cushioned footstool (7)
8W He played Deep Throat in *All the President's Men* (8)
9W Rip a strip (5)

10N Sojourn (4)
11S Passive protest (3-2)
12S Disclose (4)
13N ___ the Hoople (early '70s band) (4)
14S 1992 Summer Olympics site (9)
15N Jaunty chapeaux (6)
16S Dairy-case item (4)
17W Polo equipment (7)
18N *Challenger* passenger, June 1983 (4)
19S Fame (6)
20N Cremona craftsman (5)

20S Hosni's predecessor (5)
21W He played Buck Rogers, Tarzan, and Flash Gordon (6)
22W Tenderize, in a way (8)
23S It's on after Conan (5)
24N Gadabout (6)
25S ___ *and the Art of Motorcycle Maintenance* (3)
26S *Titanic* message (3)
27S Riot act? (5)
28W Re an unborn child (5)
28E Hat named for a Moroccan city (3)

Answer on page 300

Crushword

ACROSS
1 Tonsillitis bug, for short
3 Two-way
5 Big blast?
8 Ain't right?
9 Plagiarized
10 Where-and-when news notations
11 1985 Emmy winner as Willy Loman: 2 wds.
13 Director of 1937's *Stella Dallas*
14 Silhouette on a lavatory door, e.g.
15 *Oklahoma!* choreographer: 2 wds.
17 Linguae
19 Mr. De Valera, Ireland's president from 1959 to 1973
21 Printed matter done in relief
23 Sinuous San Francisco thoroughfare: 2 wds.
26 Different
27 Acne marks
28 Governor Tony Knowles, e.g.

30 How cohabitating unmarried lovers live, according to some: 2 wds.
32 Pinnacle
33 Running fast, as a watch: 2 wds.
36 Ill-suited
38 Pirate ships
39 Uncultivated
40 Used wisely, as during a shortage
41 Soapboxers' spoutings
42 Newsman who hosted *What's My Line?*, 1950–1967

DOWN
1 Hoagy Carmichael classic: 2 wds.
2 With contrition
3 Prepare to reuse after some time: 2 wds.
4 Square dance maneuver
5 Shower participant?
6 C&W star Larry
7 Binary digits

10 Van Halen alumnus who recorded "California Girls": 3 wds.
12 Opium addicts
16 Feminist writer Kate
17 Color modifications
18 Many of them are educated
20 Team managed by Felipe Alou: 2 wds.
22 Washing dishes before using the dishwasher
23 Oil well city of Santa Barbara county
24 Fir coats
25 Vowels of Vathy
29 Jumping rodent of Mexico: 2 wds.
31 Palestinian Arabs' revolt
32 Gave the okay
34 Turnovers
35 In a laid-back way
36 Georgia city
37 High-tech surgery tool

Answer on page 305

Weaving

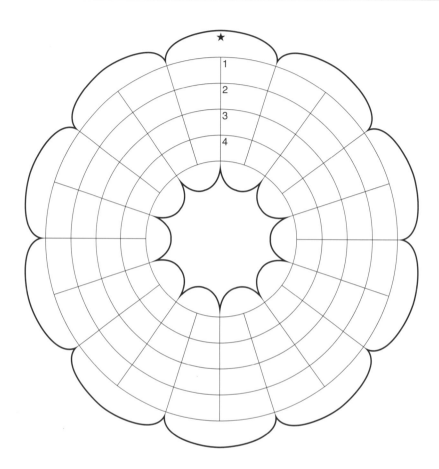

WEAVERS
a *Odd Couple*'s neat half: 2 wds.
b House Minority Leader (D-MO)
c Emblem of Erato or Terpsichore
d Breed of steed with speed
e Indispensable
f Hotel employee
g Refer (to)
h Bulletin board accessories
i Letter resembling a capital O with a superimposed hyphen
j Tropical monkey or embarrassing gaffe
k Piece of snooker equipment: 2 wds.
l Statement of religious belief
m Round of gunfire
n Young women, to Crocodile Dundee
o Arena supplanted by the Georgia Dome
p Mothers of Invention leader
q *Odd Couple*'s sloppy half: 2 wds.

RING 1
a Less bananas?
b Pinkerton Agency logo
c Gymnast Gaylord
d French-speaking Belgian

RING 2
a Do improv, psychotherapeutically: Hyph.
b Site of Northern Illinois University: 2 wds.
c Othello's lieutenant

RING 3
a Deliver the lines cold: Hyph.
b Take the wheel
c Outcry that turned Billy Batson into Captain Marvel

RING 4
a Paris street known for its retail stores: 4 wds.
b Zilch
c Title tec in a 1971 Donald Sutherland movie

Answer on page 309

Quadrants

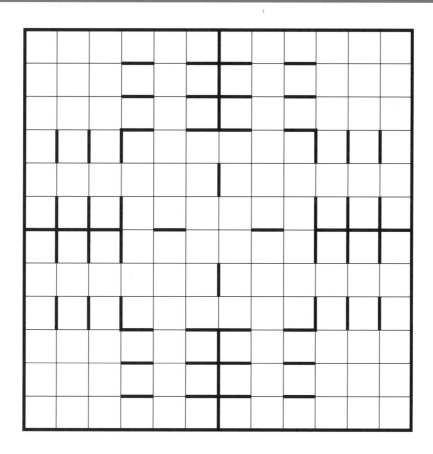

NORTHWEST
a Antonio's defender
b Golden-skinned, juicy fruit
c Green-lit
d ___-mâché
e Most mature
f Spain plus Portugal
g "___, That's My Baby": 2 wds.
h With hands on hips

NORTHEAST
a Corresponds
b Cowboy's ropes
c Debate participant
d Ice cream parlor supply
e Like most Manhattan streets:
  Hyph.

f Nashville-based TV series,
  1969–1992: 2 wds.
g Nova Scotia cape
h Went in search of

SOUTHWEST
a Cease
b Dumb
c Flyer out of Townsville, perhaps
d Harmful intent
e Highlander's plaid
f Occupation in an O'Neill title
g Party animal?
h Sunsweet product

SOUTHEAST
a Alternative to alpine
b Bluesy Cajun dance music

c Cultural agcy. of the United
  Nations
d German
e Just about
f Medical center
g Mountebanks
h Produce harmony

CENTER
a Follower of Lao-tzu
b Ingratiate
c In the neighborhood
d Long way to get there
e Monticello or Mount Vernon
f Off the blackboard
g Philippine ex-president
  Corazon
h Sunni's counterpart

Answer on page 306

Crazy Eights

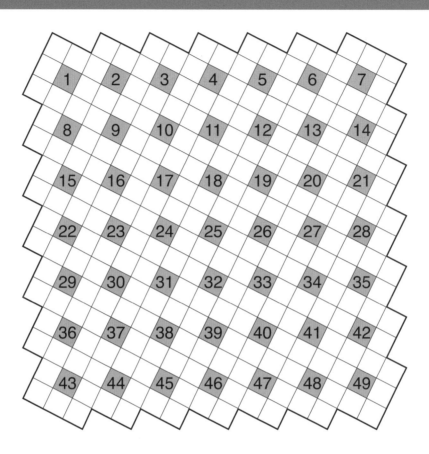

CLUES

1 Home of Lewis Carroll's cat (–)
2 Body of water divided by Taiwan: 2 wds. (+)
3 Booth, for example (–)
4 Part of Answer 5's menu (–)
5 Seaside picnic (+)
6 Carvings used to fasten obis (–)
7 Nickname for Idaho: 2 wds. (–)
8 Reinvest: 2 wds. (–)
9 Try (–)
10 Bedazzles (+)
11 Somewhat repetitious 8-line poems (–)
12 It may involve a 900 number: 2 wds. (+)
13 Willy Loman was one (–)
14 Discoverer of the Philippines (+)
15 Cave in (+)
16 Sinéad O'Connor's "Nothing ___ 2 U" (+)

17 North American reindeer (–)
18 Book owner's inscription: 2 wds. (+)
19 Driver's protection: 2 wds. (–)
20 Occupational hazard for an apiarist: 2 wds. (+)
21 Direct opposite (–)
22 Actions "above and beyond" (–)
23 ___ Day (late May event) (+)
24 Archie Bunker's is in the Smithsonian (+)
25 Year of Nixon's resignation (+)
26 Urban fleet (–)
27 Ski boot fasteners (–)
28 Potato chip enhancement: 2 wds. (+)
29 All set (+)
30 Re Mom and Dad (–)
31 Papeete denizen (+)
32 Sans paraphrasing (+)
33 Summoned back to the factory (+)

34 3,106-carat diamond found in 1905 (+)
35 Actress Loni of *WKRP in Cincinnati* (–)
36 Paginated (–)
37 Saddened by the death of a loved one (+)
38 Catholic prayer: 2 wds. (–)
39 Hollywood's "It Girl": 2 wds. (+)
40 Fire (–)
41 Summer squash (+)
42 Did a "three steps and a shuffle" dance: Hyph. (–)
43 Element 13; the British spell it with an extra "i" (+)
44 Sloping (–)
45 *Terms of Endearment* Oscar winner (+)
46 Advanced mathematics (+)
47 Like a nerd (+)
48 Pine, fir, and spruce, e.g. (+)
49 Design of letters, numbers, etc. (+)

Answer on page 307

Catching Some Z's

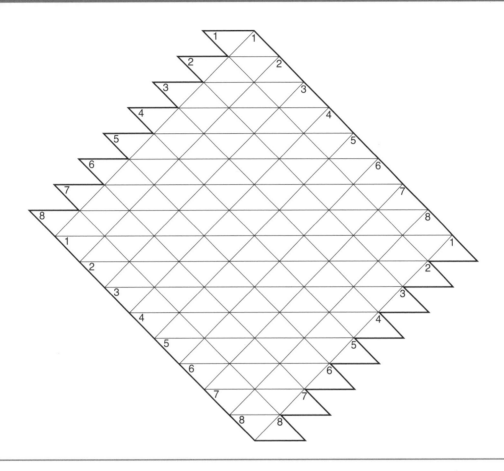

CLUES

1 a Baby boomer's kid: 2 wds.
  b Re Ra
  c Northern lights: 2 wds.
  d Ready for action
  e Black-and-white diving bird
2 a Veto, in pig Latin
  b Quick snooze
  c Like some 1998–1999 class action legislation
  d *The Music Man*'s Marian, et al.
3 a Hundred Years' War battle site
  b Stressed, as a syllable
  c Alimentary inflammation
  d Letter-shaped gripping devices: Hyph.
  e By inevitable predetermination
4 a Tubular, diagonally cut pasta

  b *Blanco*'s opposite
  c Composer of the opera *Fiesque*
  d Citrus spread
  e One of those "three little words"
5 a Fitness expert Jack
  b Home of *Venus de Milo* and *Winged Victory*
  c Supermarket shelfful
  d Wading bird with a down-curved bill
  e Mel Tillis's footstep-following daughter
  f Dot on a map
  g Cones' retinal partners
6 a Wall at the outer edge of a rampart

  b Buddhist doctrine of deliverance
  c It's divided in two by Goat Island: 2 wds.
  d Hippolyta was one
7 a Very dry, as champagne
  b Elbow
  c Part of Eden?
  d Abu Dhabi, for example
  e What the eighth season of *Dallas* turned out to be
  f Christmas carol
8 a Sexy
  b Quiche ___
  c Galápagos creature
  d Comedian who hung from a clock in *Safety Last*
  e Exude slowly through a hole: 2 wds.

Answer on page 297

Helter-Skelter

10		9		20	19	
	4		15		14	16
			18		17	21
	1		2		23	6
11						
		13	22	5		
	3	12	8			7
			25		24	

CLUES

1 Billfold
2 Inamorata
3 Samuel Butler's utopian satire
4 1955 Platters hit covered by Ringo 20 years later: 2 wds.
5 Nikkei factor
6 '60s jacket eponym
7 Beverage invented by pharmacist Charles Hires: 2 wds.
8 Life science
9 Sharp tug
10 He dove into Whitewater and came up empty: 2 wds.
11 Long, tiring trip
12 Perrier rival
13 Length ˘ width ˘ depth
14 Fruit tree considered sacred in India
15 Job application datum
16 Where thread goes through
17 Auto named for its country of origin
18 Run up the phone bill
19 Eastern tree, often with widespread branches
20 Parisian pal
21 Pianist/conductor José
22 Furrow
23 Saxophone range
24 Not so safe
25 One of the Trinity

Answer on page 308

Cubism

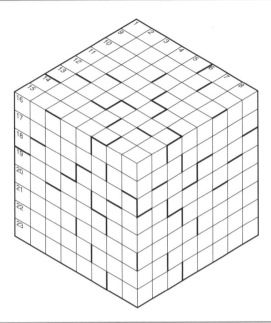

DOWN LEFT

1 a Centrifuge inserts
  b Macaulay's *Home Alone* role
  c Straight
2 a Mall of Macedonia
  b No-hit specialist Ryan
  c "___ the truth?": 2 wds.
3 a Calculator readouts: Abbr.
  b Family
  c Nail-trimming tool
  d Waterloo is there
4 a Binding datum
  b First Roman empress
  c 1950s sex researcher
5 a La Toya's sister
  b Leading man?
  c Wonder
6 a Feel nostalgic for
  b Great trepidation
  c Greco-Roman alternative
  d Singer Tori
7 a Foreign farewell
  b Kirk Douglas's dad, said Kirk's autobiography
  c Soothe
8 a Landscaping tool
  b *Marco Millions* playwright
  c Melancholy

DOWN RIGHT

1 a Oriental verse of 17 syllables, A trio of lines
  b Precincts
  c Sweaters?
9 a "I" trouble
  b Love, Italian-style
  c 7a, on the other side of the Pyrenees
10 a Actor Neeson
  b Burg
  c Defraud
  d *Dukes of Hazzard* boss
11 a Public square
  b Slander
  c Tape over
12 a Daytona competitors
  b One of Daisy Duck's nieces
  c Place in proper order
13 a Emulates Johnny Appleseed
  b Freud colleague
  c Obsessed captain
  d Siblingless
14 a Eucalyptivore
  b Soda shoppe orders
  c Used a blowtorch
15 a Cause of meteorological havoc: 2 wds.
  b Heavyweight champ, 1937–1949
  c Outfielder's aid

ACROSS

16 a Lawrence's venue
  b Treat with contempt
  c Trumpet piece
17 a First sign of spring
  b Spur
  c *Witness* sect
18 a Advertise
  b BLT enhancement
  c Move to the music
  d Nothing, in Nogales
19 a Kitchen fixture
  b Panorama
  c Siberian lake
20 a Chief port of the Balearic Islands
  b Small valleys
  c Weak
21 a Fetor
  b Henry ___
  c National park in Utah
  d Working diligently: 2 wds.
22 a Northern French city
  b Play Sherlock
  c Sorcerer
23 a Coasters
  b Hamstrings
  c Renders inflexible

Answer on page 310

Target Practice

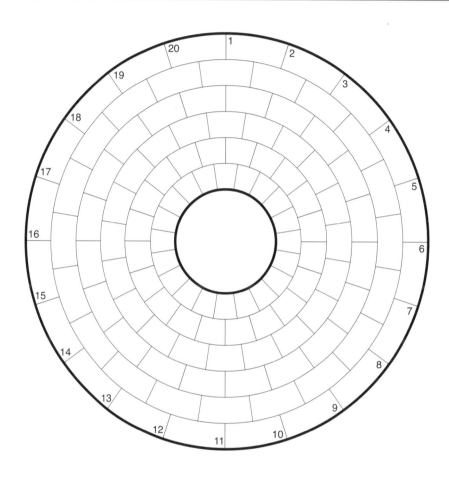

CLOCKWISE
1 Laid-back
2 Vegetable used in Chinese food: 2 wds.
3 Entireties
4 You, now
5 Stock footage?
6 Immobilized
7 West Point freshmen
8 Dubya's first name
9 Infantry members
10 Showing distress
11 Hang around
12 Someone who puts out?
13 To speak French?
14 Appropriate
15 Financial report acronym
16 "Unromantic as ___ morning" (C. Brontë)
17 Streisand standard
18 Shadowy
19 Tommy or Jimmy of Big Band days
20 Elton's metaphor for Marilyn

COUNTERCLOCKWISE
1 Patterned like fudge ripple
2 Reflection, to Rousseau
3 One who carries a torch?
4 Half a hyphenated word meaning "show indecision"
5 Bird with a fanlike crest
6 Do surveillance on
7 Verified
8 Equipment for Lennox Lewis
9 Eccentric old coot
10 Investigations
11 Polo man
12 What's happening?
13 *Grosse ___ Blank*
14 Fries lightly
15 Tried to cure
16 *The Naked and the Dead* author
17 Bill (punny synonym for the previous answer)
18 Elvis's "Return to ___"
19 Thingamajig
20 Rival of Dell and Gateway

Answer on page 310

Maze

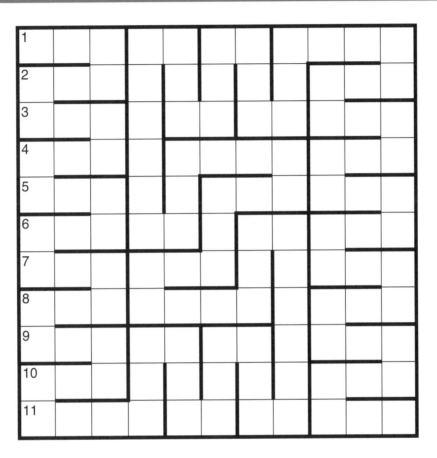

ACROSS

1 The beer in a boilermaker
  Extinguish
2 Broadcasting method: 2 wds.
  Capone nemesis
3 Bassett or Lansbury
  Walk daintily
4 Freebie
  John Buchan's *The 39 ___*
5 Come to pass
  Red Cross supply
6 Marty Robbins's biggest hit: 2 wds.
  Baserunner's tactic
7 Soprano parts
  Pinatubo output
8 In a perfect world
  Actress Lena

9 Show grief
  Clusters of petals
10 Hide the gray
  Sink
11 Monopolist's goal?
  Pretentious portrayal

PATH

1 Entrance
2 Phyllis Diller's "husband"
3 Moonshine ingredient
4 Newton's supposed inspiration:
  2 wds.
5 Don't follow orders
6 The Ewing saga
7 Judy Sheindlin's
  domain

8 Toxic element derived from ocean
  water
9 Dangles
10 Maine is the only state that has just
  one
11 Beginning
12 Tennis star with a palindromic
  surname
13 Mollified
14 Scottish landowner
15 Threatening
16 Perfumery products
17 OAS member
18 Howard Stern's self-proclaimed
  kingdom
19 Flavorful beans derived from orchids
20 Exit

Answer on page 311

Siamese Quadruplets

ACROSS

1 Unit of measure ...
  ... multiplied by 12, ...
  ... then again by 3, ...
  ... and then again by 1,760
5 Apprehends
  Dieter's target
  Goya subject
  Miserable state
9 Change for a five
  Really big show
  Track star Budd
  Vacationing
10 Felipe of baseball
  Singer Tori
  Soupçon
  Trygve Lie's birthplace
11 Bench occupants, maybe
  Card game for three
  Jackie Mabley's nickname
  Rollerjam track
12 Angry mood
  Deposited
  It's neither A.M. nor P.M.
  Penny-a-liner
13 Blowing up
  Cheap, concise telegram: 2 wds.
  Cheerfully irresponsible
  Supermodel of note: 2 wds.
15 Bamboozles
  Kimono tie
  Many millennia
  Stand in the way of
16 Bullies
  Distinguishing characteristics
  Highly seasoned tripe soup
  1992 Olympic skating star
22 Allies' foes
  In full bloom
  Iso-
  Make a statement
23 Musketeers or Stooges
  Picked up the check
  Sasquatch's kin
  Singer Mitchell
24 Appearance
  "King of the Nudies" director Meyer
  Let Us Now Praise Famous Men author
  Part of Caesar's boast
25 Analogous
  Coop group
  "I'll second that!"
  Prior to 12/8/28, it was the "WSM Barn Dance"
26 Crocheting equipment
  Dog owner's drudgery
  Jones of jazz
  Tackles' teammates

27 Egg container
  It's a long story
  Warmonger
  Year-end refrain

DOWN

1 Big do
  Happy Days cast member
  Sportswear brand
  Thanksgiving veggies
2 Black
  Draft animals
  MPs' quarry
  PBS science series
3 "___ Lama Ding Dong"
  Mad king of literature
  October birthstone
  "The Great Compromiser"
4 Found
  Indigestion
  Old West axes
  Some enchanted evening?
5 Disses a telemarketer, maybe: 3 wds.
  Hurler with 5,714 Ks and 2,795 BBs: 2 wds.
  Prince of old India
  2% shares
6 ___ for All Seasons: 2 wds.
  Lummox
  PDQ, on a memo
  Time Machine aristocrats
7 Athlete
  Minnesota's state bird
  Radar screen signal
  Where not to throw bouquets: 2 wds.
8 Breather?
  Circuit City supplier
  Sends out invitations
  TV's Jethro Bodine
14 Emeril's interjection
  Flow back
  Scott Joplin's style
  Tilling tool
16 Jodie Foster's alma mater
  KFC ingredient
  Macadamize
  Talk like an ass
17 Blue hue
  Cloverleaf feature
  Latvia's capital
  Mary Kay competition
18 Disposition
  Overwhelming passion
  Scot's ancestor
  Touch-tone abbr.
19 Lapdog, for short
  Linoleum measure
  Mafia bigwig
  Touched by an Angel's Downey

20 Bell sound
  Mayberry's town drunk
  Recognized
  Take on
21 McGwire's friendly rival
  Pastoral work
  Plummet
  Windshield option

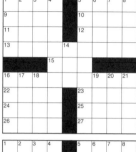

Answer on page 313

Honeycomb

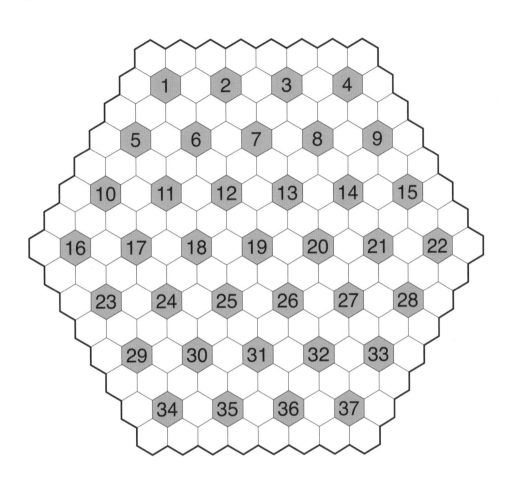

CLUES

1 Hair stylist's dessert? (+)
2 Unlikely trick-takers ... (+)
3 ... just beaten by these (+)
4 Comic book publisher (−)
5 Universal (−)
6 Sportscaster, author of 1985's *I Never Played the Game* (+)
7 Set up for a grand slam (−)
8 Found the value of x (−)
9 V-8 ingredient (−)
10 Piece of jewelry (−)
11 Honda model (−)
12 Fanatic (+)

13 Poor substitute (−)
14 Elaborately decorated (−)
15 Insurrection (+)
16 Where Clementine and her dad dwelt (+)
17 Cookwear? (−)
18 Esteemed highly (−)
19 A little night music? (+)
20 "Top" brand of TV set (+)
21 Gregarious (+)
22 Matthew, Mark, Luke, or John (−)
23 Offering a beautiful view (+)
24 Another V-8 ingredient (+)
25 City in northwest Iran (+)

26 Violinist Perlman (+)
27 Fabric sample (+)
28 Rap: Hyph. (+)
29 "Now is the ___ of our discontent" (−)
30 Pre-photocopy copy (−)
31 1973 musical based on a 1959 Lorraine Hansberry play (+)
32 Complain loudly (−)
33 The spirit of friendship? (+)
34 Aztec territory (+)
35 Paul's wife and frequent costar (+)
36 One of a kind (+)
37 A Britisher uses it when "hoovering" (−)

Answer on page 314

Round The Bend

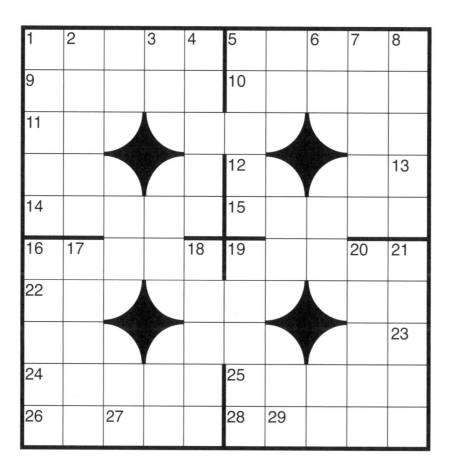

ACROSS
1 Made like a mole
5 Gilmore of basketball
9 Supercharger type
10 Garner's dad on *The Rockford Files*
14 "Spaghetti western" scorer Morricone
15 March VIP
16 Thickset
19 Asparagus serving
24 DKNY designer
25 Elbow
26 Burma-Shave trademarks
28 Windsor, Ontario's county

DOWN
1 Be quite conspicuous
2 Charade: Hyph.
4 "Tiny Bubbles" crooner: 2 wds.
5 Furthers felons
7 Von Bulow portrayer
8 Part of the UAR
16 Defrauds
17 Ex-premier Zhou
18 Sea dog's repertoire
19 Clapboard datum
20 Saw
21 Watchword?

BENT
3 *A Christmas Carol* name
6 "Danny Boy" singer, often
11 Videogame name
12 Pet store purchase: » 2 wds.
13 Snide suggestion
22 Patent holder
23 Splashes down
27 Interrogate
29 A famous high jumper

Answer on page 296

Crossing Paths

CLUES

1 Former Soviet republic whose capital is Baku
Canton in central Switzerland
Horseman?
6-time winner of the PGA Seniors Championship: 2 wds.
Egg white
Guest at a ranch
Scotch + sweet vermouth: 2 wds.
Variety of flatfish
Dismissal: Hyph.
Forms a single traffic flow
Supporter of Charles I of England
Thrash

2 Ethnic ___ (Milosevic's tactic)
Particular
Late-1990s welterweight champion: 4 wds.

Transportation company affected by Jay Gould's 1829 stock manipulations: 2 wds.
Citizen of Tabriz
Brass section's sounds: Hyph.
Michelangelo masterwork
Familiarizes with new circumstances
City in Santa Barbara County, California
Needle case
Gorky Park author Martin ___ Smith

3 Supreme happiness
Buckwheat pancakes often served with caviar
Heists
Jazz singer James, nicknamed "Miss Peaches"
Look Back in Anger playwright
From Here to Eternity role that earned Sinatra an Oscar
TV exec Arledge

Sock hop venues, often
Gloss targets
Frankish king, father of Charlemagne
Supervisor at a dock area: 2 wds.
Rocky of cartoons, for example: 2 wds.

4 Residents of what was once French Somaliland
Coverups for PJs
Greenish patina on copper or brass
NYC nickname: 2 wds.
Bob Keeshan role: 2 wds.
$\frac{1}{60}$ of a fluid dram
Spat

FOURS
Author Ferber
God, in Guadalajara
Libretto
Sound of contentment

Answer on page 298

Intersections

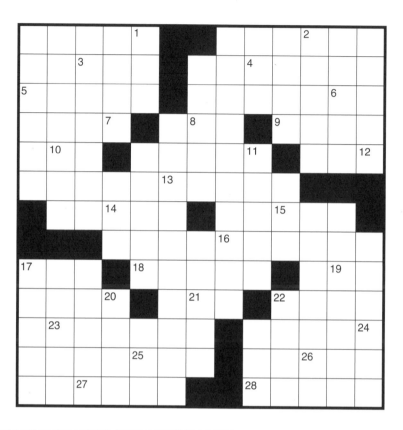

CLUES

1 It may include futomaki
  "... ___ pear tree": 2 wds.
2 From the Far East
  Singers' contributions to
  recordings
3 Bid entry to: 2 wds.
  "Get lost!"
4 Partner of *plata*
  Spray paint, e.g.
5 City near Rome
  Horse mackerel
6 Platitude
  Resort hotel
7 Disencumbers
  Sot's interjections
8 Roughly
  Sauce source
9 Freebie
  One side of a leaf

10 Oscar winner for *Spartacus*
   Remnant
11 Dunces
   Nestling pigeon
12 Bottom line
   Winter forecast
13 640 acres: 2 wds.
   Watch over: 3 wds.
14 Kin of "Presto!"
   Orphan in a Kipling tale
15 Author Santha Rama ___
   Fork options
16 Brazilian tennis star, three-time
   Wimbledon champ: 2 wds.
   Petrified: 2 wds.
17 Med. measures
   Wooden shoes
18 Re Helios's realm
   "Who Wants to Be a Millionaire"
   host

19 Has the wherewithal
   Popular soft drink brand
20 Cut of meat adjoining the ribs
   Prohibited act: Hyph.
21 Jim Croce's "___ Name": 3 wds.
   Stylish, à la Austin Powers
22 Ump's call
   Uses a straw
23 Milieu for the Williams sisters
   Unconscious: 3 wds.
24 At a reduced price: 2 wds.
   University of South Florida home
25 Muesli
   Watch chain
26 "___ the nerve!": 2 wds.
   What's the point of arithmetic?
27 High-speed photography device
   "Norwegian Wood" instrument
28 Free-for-all
   Nicole's hubby

Answer on page 299

Jigsaw

ACROSS

3 Lord Nelson looks out over it: 2 wds.
4 He goes after deadbeats: 2 wds.

DOWN

1 Company that acquired RCA: 2 wds.
2 Pre-opening practice sessions: 2 wds.

TOP LEFT

a Great sorrow
b Grinding tooth
c PR concern
d Scottish actor Williamson
e Stan's pal
f Truckers' loads
g Use Brillo
h World-weary

TOP CENTER

a *Bell, Book, and Candle* actress
b Major kitchen appliance
c Medium-size, coarse tea leaf
d Milne marsupial
e Okay for dieters: Hyph.
f Sofa bed style
g Took a shine to
h Transport for some Olympic events

TOP RIGHT

a ___ bear (arctic animal)
b Busch Gardens home
c "Bye!": 2 wds.
d Don Imus's medium
e Grenoble good-bye
f Put on the line
g Skiing star of the 1968 Olympics
h Wife on *The Bob Newhart Show*

CENTER LEFT

a A lot of it is just spam: Hyph.
b Apple cofounder Wozniak
c Colander
d Enjoys gum
e Get histrionic
f Heard the cock crow
g Reggie of NBA fame
h Tremor

CENTER

a About 35.2 cubic feet of cordwood
b Daytona car

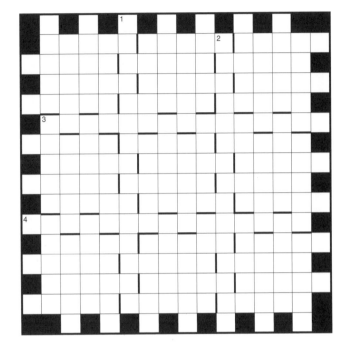

c "Halt!" on the high seas
d Honor, on a diploma
e Larynx output
f MTV offering
g Plaster for a tile wall
h Pupa-to-be

CENTER RIGHT

a Check how a garment fits: 2 wds.
b Groucho's role in *Duck Soup*
c High-pitched ring?
d *Just ___ Me*
e Right: Prefix
f Sacred: Prefix
g Singing cowboy of note
h Sleepyhead Jacques, e.g.

BOTTOM LEFT

a Alan Ladd title role
b *Alice* star Linda
c Dynamite inventor
d Excuse
e Factory
f *Inside the Actors Studio* channel

g Phil's onetime rival
h Steven Bochco series, 1986–1994: 2 wds.

BOTTOM CENTER

a Can't do without
b Certain to undergo: 2 wds.
c Curl the lip
d Island near the Statue of Liberty
e Ms. Meir
f One of the five senses
g Sportscaster Schenkel
h Throw really hard

BOTTOM RIGHT

a Acknowledges
b Hindu teacher's honorific
c Jack
d Long-time "center square"
e She minds more than her P's and Q's
f *The First ___ Club*
g Ungainly
h Wanderer

Answer on page 300

Angling

1		2	3		4	5	6	7	8	9	10	11
12	13				14			15	16	17	18	19
20			21					22				
23	24		25		26		27				28	
29			30		31		32	33	34	35	36	37
38	39		40		41	42	43	44	45	46		
47		48		49	50				51	52	53	
54	55	56		57		58	59					
	60	61	62	63		64	65		66			
		67		68	69						70	
	71					72	73		74			75
76	77	78	79				80	81	82	83	84	

CLUES

1-24 One of the Three Bears
2-7 Juliet called it "such sweet sorrow"
3-50 Means of transportation
4-8 Romanian round dances
5-33 Howard Stern's primary medium
6-19 Jay's predecessor
8-36 *The Scream* artist
9-35 "___ the Raven, 'Nevermore'"
10-15 She loved Narcissus in vain
11-28 *Candid Camera* creator
12-21 Farmer's territory?
12-31 Reclined lazily
13-14 Penn & Teller's specialty
14-24 "___ Monday" (first hit for the Bangles)
16-59 Country music?
17-53 Singer of "Taxi" and "WOLD"
18-27 The Teamsters, e.g.
20-47 Urge forward

21-23 Fencing tool
21-34 Southern belle's sunshade
22-59 Silver medalist's place
23-54 Vestibule
24-43 Algonquin nature spirit
25-40 Movie in which Mercedes Ruehl played Tom Hanks's mother
26-49 Parting words?
29-41 *The Leatherstocking Tales* author
30-32 Georgetown University team
31-44 Glaswegian girl
32-66 Soft drinks
35-73 Natural environment
36-66 Tends tears
37-64 Whim
38-76 Caesarean C
39-61 Castaway's new home
42-51 *The Empire Strikes Back* character
45-81 Instrument often in a St. Patrick's Day marching band
46-80 Protest strongly

48-79 Hitchcock classic
50-60 Glass, in Grenoble
51-82 *The Breakfast Club* cast member
52-67 Injuring à la Sleeping Beauty
54-57 Poultry selection
54-58 Someone of great beauty
54-69 Bart Simpson's "principal" nemesis
55-59 Those who endorse a petition, e.g.
56-78 Picture puzzle
58-62 Variety of poker
59-63 Spotted
61-77 "*Veni, vidi, ___*"
62-66 *Steel Magnolias* actress or her politico cousin
63-73 Bus fare, perhaps
65-72 Brand of cereal manufactured by General Mills
65-84 Comiskey Park squad, for short
68-71 Sharpen
70-83 Atheist's lack
74-75 Big commotion about nothing?

Answer on page 305

Around & About

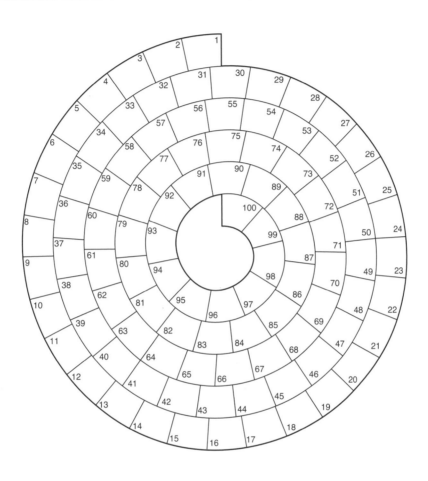

AROUND

1-4 Fast horse
5-9 Morocco's capital
10-16 With a twang
17-21 Place for seeing a hearing: Hyph.
22-30 As a diplomat would
31-37 Hire a decorator
38-42 Mijbil or Edal, in *Ring of Bright Water*
43-50 Enlivens
51-57 It's just beyond the delta
58-62 Mother-of-pearl
63-69 Union soldier in the Civil War
70-76 A mark below a C in French
77-81 Comedienne Butler or baseball player Butler
82-87 Wolf pack members, in the 1940s: Hyph.
88-92 Seat of Dallas County, Alabama
93-97 Again and again and again
98-100 School of whales

Ω ABOUT

100-95 Metal drawer?
94-87 Having no head
86-84 Benjamin Hoff's *The ___ of Pooh*
83-74 Turkey brand
73-66 Southern belle's surprised expression: 2 wds.
65-61 Yield to another's judgment
60-53 Ricotta-filled tubes
52-47 Spanish coin
46-40 Muezzin's perch
39-34 Holy city?
33-29 Goldie's rival in *Death Becomes Her*
28-25 Minnelli's half-sister
24-19 A few minutes in Morpheus's arms
18-13 Charybdis's counterpart
12-1 TV soap that originally starred Dame Judith Anderson: 2 wds.

Answer on page 302

Tops & Bottoms

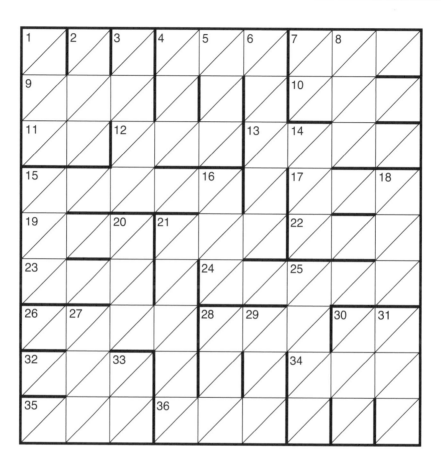

ACROSS
4 Give in
7 He played Mr. Chips 30 years after Donat
9 Creator of Meg, Jo, Beth, and Amy
10 TV role for Jenna
11 Frank Herbert trilogy
12 Twisted, like a phone cord
13 Krypton is one: 2 wds.
15 Prevailing (over)
17 Amphetamines
19 Owing: 2 wds.
21 ___-faire
22 Cave
23 Like bright white teeth
24 *The First Wives Club* costar: 2 wds.
26 Finished, *en français*
28 Calm
30 Anything but that!
32 Network that suffers during sweeps week?
34 Shields on the screen
35 Suffer from a glitch: 2 wds.
36 Constrictor type

DOWN
1 Apollo 11 crewman
2 Track
3 Benihana entree
4 Each
5 Frank
6 Patent sharer
7 Skunk's giveaway
8 R&B singer Houston
14 Prospector's bit
15 Marilyn's successor, so to speak
16 The youngest Simpson
18 Frequent whodunit weapon
20 Finger or toe
21 Kiwi product: 2 wds.
25 Retriever's home
27 *High Noon* star
28 1960 film classic remade in 1998
29 Sunblock, maybe
30 Three-horse carriage
31 Monopoly property enhancements
33 Doubled, a 1991 Amy Grant song; tripled, a 1992 TLC song

Answer on page 303

Marching Bands

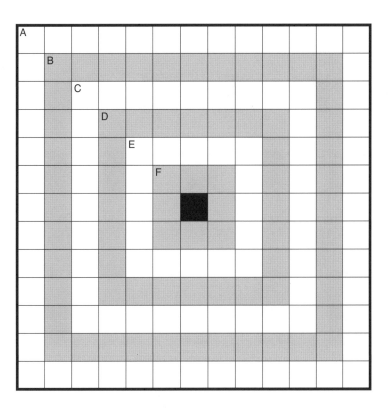

ROWS

1 a Recess in a wall for displaying a statue
  b Singer
2 a Famed maitre d' of the Waldorf
  b Distance from the y-axis
3 a Wet, spongy terrain
  b Rough, jagged tear
4 a Select: 2 wds
  b Work with antiques
5 a Suggesting subtly
  b Plays charades
6 a 1930s actress Landi
  b "Love Is Blue" orchestra leader Paul
7 a Rio Grande city: 2 wds.
  b Michael of *The Day the Earth Stood Still*
8 a Brief literary sketches
  b Big bash
9 a 1983 Rabbitt/Gayle duet: 3 wds.

b *The X-Files* creator Chris
10 a Spoke to
  b Staffer
11 a Jason Leigh or Love Hewitt
  b Switch positions: 2 wds.
12 a Sudden strong insight
  b Mona Lisa's countenance
13 a Playwright who coined the word "robot"
  b Supervisor

BANDS

A a Never mind, to Nikita
  b Ally's portrayer
  c Lipton competitor
  d Umpires
  e Withdraw
  f Wear a rut in the rug
  g Lower-level school athlete
  h Vagrant
B a Egyptian amulet

b Like some flycatchers: Hyph.
  c Apt to collapse
  d "Unh-unh"
  e Conveyed by cable, as Muzak
  f Crankcase stuff
  g 8th-century Chinese poet: 2 wds.
C a Candied
  b Use of reason and logic
  c Raw rock
  d Gulf of Bothnia dweller
  e Grooved on
  f Blood drive donation
D a 1994 Oscar-winning role for Tom
  b Prince Valiant's son
  c Report card data
  d Antitoxins
  e Tammany Hall foe
E a Starlets' parts
  b Tart quality
F a Almond-flavored liqueur

Answer on page 304

Pathfinder

CLUES

1E Slalomer's course (6)
2E Request on some magazine blow-in cards (7)
3E First state to ratify the Constitution (8)
3E No longer under the government's thumb (11)
4S He was in *Heat* (2,4)
5N Pink bunny's brand (9)
6S City near Salt Lake City (5)
7N Folklore fiend (4)
8N Extortionist (6)

9N He had a Ball (5)
10W Old salt's recount (4)
11N ___ *Breckinridge* (4)
11S Texas city that shares its name with BBQ fuel (8)
12S Edward Cox's in-laws (6)
13N Tin, copper, or gold (5)
13S Big bang units? (8)
14E Ashamed and a bit angry (9)
15W Austin Powers's pet verb (4)
16S Cross words? (7)
17N Laughing gas is one (5)

18N Fringe benefits (5)
19N Millie's successor (5)
20N Traditional first-anniversary gift (5)
21N Summoned into court (5)
21S Candice Bergen once did TV ads for this perfume (5)
22S Reading course, for short (3)
23S Sybil Fawlty's inept hubby (5)
24W City near Ciudad Juárez (2,4)
25W ___ del Fuego (6)
26E Dr. Smith's original intention, on *Lost in Space* (8)

Answer on page 297

Crushword

ACROSS
1 Capital of Western Australia
3 Aware
6 Small donkey
8 Entreaty
9 *Rosemary's Baby* writer: 2 wds.
11 ___ metabolism
12 Most radical
14 Reciprocated: 3 wds.
16 What steam shovels do: 2 wds.
18 Comprehension
19 Pangolin, for one
21 Emulator
23 Dwelling that shares a sidewall: 2 wds.
26 Mosaic piece
27 Garden of earthly delights?
28 Gondoliers at work
29 Wine-nutmeg-lemon beverage
31 Bach's Brandenburg six
33 Louisiana: 2 wds.
36 Lodging a protest
39 Tremble
40 Brilliant scarlet
42 *Essence* competitor
43 Like a toad's skin
44 Flimsy sleepwear
45 Moon vehicles

DOWN
1 Confound
2 Picture palace
3 At minimal power when driving a stick: 3 wds.
4 Examination format
5 Chopper at a MASH unit
6 City near Los Angeles
7 Orlando's love in *As You Like It*
10 Acura model
13 Greeks and Turks
15 Unfair shares, maybe
17 Flourished
19 Stud fees?
20 Rib
22 French city known for its lace
24 Intact
25 People with laptops, e.g.
30 *Madame Bovary* author Flaubert
32 Rites
33 Pakistan city near the Khyber Pass
34 ___-split
35 Ends
37 High-pitch range
38 They'll never be the same
41 "Blinded by the ___"

Answer on page 301

Weaving

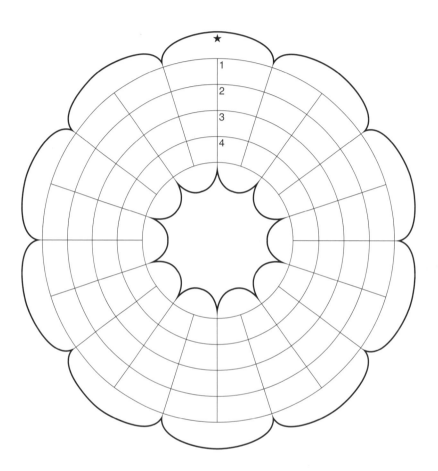

WEAVERS
a Pole staff?
b St. ___ (two-time Olympics site)
c Mencken and Hunt: Abbr.
d Cry from a surprised Brit
e Western horse
f Palindromic preposition
g Had the desired effect
h Soon-to-be non-bachelor
i *Rebel Without a Cause* actor
j Wintered with the birds: 2 wds.
k Dressy apparel: 2 wds.
l French article
m Clearasil target

n 100 decades
o Command to Rover
p Block and tackle, e.g.
q Mint condition
r Summertime quaff: 2 wds., var.

RING 1
a Rich
b Scintilla
c Verdict in *12 Angry Men*: 2 wds.

RING 2
a Power to cause bad luck:
2 wds.

b Bob who played Captain Kangaroo
for over 30 years
c Interlocks

RING 3
a Fenway Park's left-field fence:
2 wds.
b He's looking rather blue
c Fit of hysteria, to Bart Simpson

RING 4
a Periodic payments for life
b Kimono accessory
c Long-popular "Must-See TV" entry

Answer on page 212

Quadrants

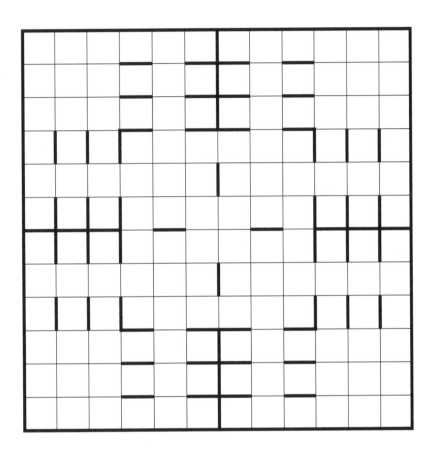

NORTHWEST
a Apply a T-shirt decal: 2 wds.
b California surfers' haven
c Ferdinand's kingdom
d Hogan occupants
e Love apple
f Measure of ft³ or dB
g Williams of *Poltergeist*
h WWII Pacific Fleet commander

NORTHEAST
a Cassius : Muhammad :: Lew : ___
b Duration
c He carries out orders
d Indulges in libel
e Leaves in the fridge overnight
f Stowe's cruel taskmaster

g Supreme Court justice, 1955–1971
h Surrey decoration

SOUTHWEST
a Big ___ (large WWI cannon)
b Goldfinger's hat-hurling aide
c "Handwriting on the wall" decipherer
d Hidden assailant
e Hot dog topping
f In abundance
g Missouri city named in "Route 66"
h Ransom note closing, maybe: 2 wds.

SOUTHEAST
a Batman's bailiwick
b Beat
c Brand of Mexican beer

d Country song?
e Unctuously servile
f White of *Family Matters*
g With cordiality
h Wizard-in-training Harry of kiddie lit

CENTER
a Exciting experience
b Fictional sleuth Queen
c Fourscore
d Late-'70s candy bar named for a ballplayer
e Nursery toy
f Pang
g Toro's offensive tactic
h Whoville killjoy

Answer on page 308

Crazy Eights

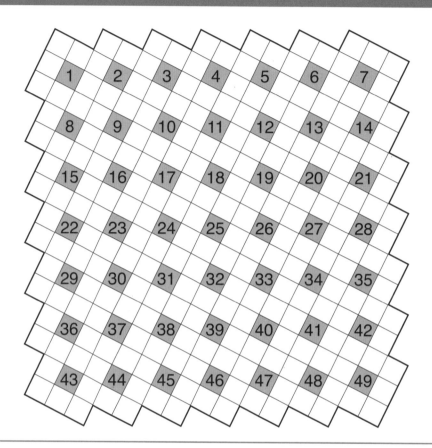

CLUES

1 Strong countercurrent (+)
2 Torments diabolically (−)
3 1st, 2nd, 3rd, etc. (+)
4 Volcanic glass (+)
5 Electric power reduction (−)
6 Eponym of a steelmaking process (−)
7 Asks (−)
8 Decorative paper ribbon (+)
9 Acting to halt a disease's progress (−)
10 Very quickly: 3 wds. (−)
11 First Jewish Supreme Court justice (+)
12 Re surface structure (−)
13 Whirlpools (+)
14 One who'll eat anything (−)
15 "The Velvet Fog": 2 wds. (−)
16 VIP (+)
17 Mythological figure also known as Agriope (+)

18 Santa's herd (−)
19 More corpulent (−)
20 France's flag, for example (+)
21 Cheese choice (−)
22 Breed of prolific egg-laying chickens (+)
23 Biting gnats also known as punkies: Hyph. (+)
24 O'Hara and O'Sullivan (−)
25 Union (+)
26 Zany 1980 movie spoof (+)
27 *Rocky* star (+)
28 Storyteller in a Danny Kaye biopic (+)
29 Songbirds (−)
30 Mary Poppins's transportation (−)
31 People of Luanda (+)
32 Three-striper (−)
33 Overhaul the decor (+)

34 Hardly sunny (−)
35 Copies (+)
36 New recruits in the Navy (+)
37 Piece of weightlifting equipment (+)
38 Copious source of profit: 2 wds. (−)
39 *The Red and the Black* novelist (−)
40 Legendary lost island first described by Plato (+)
41 Garrisoned fort (−)
42 Prop for Kojak (−)
43 *Strangers in a Strange Land* author (+)
44 An Alaskan glacier he discovered in 1879 was named for him: 2 wds. (+)
45 Most dirt-covered (+)
46 Annoyed repeatedly (+)
47 Aardvark (+)
48 Capital of South Australia (−)
49 London thoroughfare or cigarette brand: 2 wds. (−)

Answer on page 311

Catching Some Z's

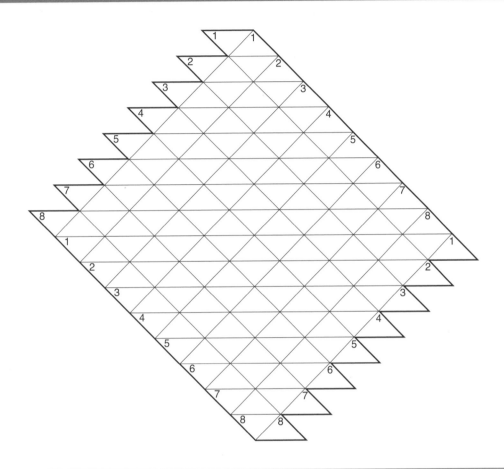

CLUES

1
a Tommy Smothers is skilled with this toy
b Queen of whodunits
c Fashion's Armani or music's Moroder
d Hand bone
e Nation on a Persian Gulf peninsula

2
a Captain Janeway's starship
b Floral emblem of the Mikado
c Morose
d *Plan 9 From Outer Space* vessel (truly!)

3
a Take it on the lam
b Aplenty
c *Liar, Liar* actress Tierney
d Baseball club?

e Compact: 2 wds.
f Saharan caravan

4
a Nylon tape fastener
b Capital of Tibet
c Defeat soundly; or, an old 78 rpm record
d A little night music?
e Male chauvinist's assessment of women: 2 wds.

5
a Bitter resin, an ingredient in perfumes (Makes a great gift!)
b Poor substitute
c Jack Ruby's defense attorney
d Ecclesiastic's office
e Sam Malone, e.g.

6
a Fruits used in Newtons
b Sweet potatoes' look-alikes

c She threw her hat into the ring
d Has a bug
e Seamen's org.
f Scrimshaw or decoupage
g Squashed square

7
a Monetary unit of Sweden
b *Lost in Yonkers* star
c Youngster in an aerie
d Birthstone for October (ancient) or March (modern)
e Muslim temple

8
a Popular variety of pocket billiards
b Unknowledgeable in a given field
c Idle companion?
d Iowa city on the Mississippi

Answer on page 299

Trivia-Cross

5	34		32	27	22	7
1	6	3	29		17	40
19		4	35	13	37	
39	14	30	8	38	23	28
	41	26	15	2		12
24	33		20	36	18	31
11	9	16	21		10	25

```
___  ___  ___  ___  ___  ___  ___  ___  ___  ___  ___  ___  ___  ___
 1    2    3    4    5    6    7    8    9   10   11   12   13   14

___  ___  ___  ___  ___  ___  ___  ___  ___  ___  ___  ___  ___  ___
15   16   17   18   19   20   21   22   23   24   25   26   27   28

___  ___  ___  ___  ___  ___  ___  ___  ___  ___  ___  ___  ___
29   30   31   32   33   34   35   36   37   38   39   40   41
```

ACROSS

1 One of the soprano seamstresses in the 1900 Charpentier opera *Louise*

4 Bishop's throne, at the eastern end of an ancient church

5 Character portrayed by Mr. T on *The A Team*

10 Abbr. of a first name shared by four U.S. presidents

11 The giant mutations running rampant in the 1954 movie *Them!*, for example

17 Abbr. of the state whose motto is "The Life of the Land Is Perpetuated in Righteousness"

20 Form of fencing in which the opponent's entire body is a valid target

24 *La ___ de bautismo*, Spanish for "birth certificate"

32 Cat, voiced by Bernadette Peters, partnered with the dimwitted dog Runt on TV's *Animaniacs*

39 Fast-food chain begun in 1960 in Ypsilanti, MI, by Thomas Monaghan

41 Lead character of the series whose first episode was titled "Sins of the Past"

DOWN

3 Titular Broadway heroine who marries Beauregard Jackson Pickett Burnside

5 He made a crucial steal during the last five seconds of Game 5 of the 1987 Eastern Conference Finals

7 Tridactylous member of the genus *Bradypus*

13 Redhead among Kellogg's noisemaking trio

14 Animals appearing on Chinese calendars for 1985, 1997, 2009, 2021, 2033, etc.

18 Initials of the magazine whose features include "News + Notes" and "Jim Mullen's Hot Sheet"

22 On a 1980s–1990s sitcom, he was Elvin Tibideaux's only brother-in-law

24 A long, long way for Maria to run?

28 Act of sliding one ski outward on its edge in preparation for making a turn

32 Synonym for "plunders"; anagram of the word that completes George S. Kaufman's pun, "One man's Mede is another man's ___"

34 0 : 15.999 :: ___ : 39.95

Answer on page 306

Cryptograms

Cryptogram Hints

1 J→S	58 C→F	115 C→M	172 T→W	229 G→S
2 Y→S	59 F→P	116 A→T	173 W→I	230 B→I
3 O→B	60 S→T	117 W→O	174 Z→L	231 B→G
4 O→Y	61 A→E	118 T→P	175 U→O	232 Z→C
5 Q→L	62 K→E	119 J→C	176 E→O	233 Q→I
6 H→L	63 M→I	120 P→D	177 K→U	234 W→H
7 T→E	64 H→P	121 A→E	178 O→T	235 K→O
8 M→W	65 U→K	122 V→P	179 L→A	236 N→H
9 P→E	66 C→A	123 C→G	180 U→S	237 Z→I
10 T→R	67 S→B	124 B→U	181 A→P	238 C→O
11 L→U	68 I→R	125 W→F	182 O→R	239 N→E
12 E→F	69 A→L	126 X→D	183 U→E	240 L→N
13 C→D	70 T→S	127 U→R	184 A→I	241 I→A
14 K→T	71 C→T	128 C→H	185 M→G	242 R→N
15 Y→E	72 K→S	129 V→L	186 E→H	243 X→M
16 S→E	73 J→R	130 G→E	187 D→T	244 T→F
17 Y→A	74 X→K	131 X→E	188 R→W	245 M→R
18 D→Y	75 A→G	132 B→O	189 Z→C	246 F→O
19 Q→N	76 T→O	133 W→N	190 I→S	247 K→M
20 N→L	77 G→L	134 W→T	191 X→P	248 V→I
21 N→V	78 O→E	135 Y→H	192 U→M	249 G→O
22 B→S	79 S→I	136 V→A	193 B→N	250 F→H
23 R→T	80 P→I	137 X→A	194 T→G	251 G→E
24 K→I	81 Z→H	138 D→I	195 B→K	252 X→Y
25 X→C	82 D→A	139 B→E	196 X→H	253 P→O
26 I→L	83 Q→W	140 K→N	197 V→H	254 A→O
27 C→L	84 B→H	141 D→C	198 L→E	255 M→C
28 F→C	85 F→O	142 E→W	199 L→H	256 M→T
29 G→M	86 R→H	143 K→B	200 C→E	257 V→N
30 Q→U	87 Z→T	144 F→W	201 Y→C	258 M→E
31 P→R	88 B→R	145 T→R	202 J→E	259 G→B
32 G→A	89 B→C	146 U→T	203 Q→M	260 Q→O
33 H→W	90 K→I	147 Z→F	204 S→M	261 U→N
34 V→I	91 I→Y	148 Y→L	205 S→T	262 N→T
35 E→Y	92 K→P	149 A→H	206 N→T	263 I→W
36 H→E	93 M→P	150 Q→R	207 W→R	264 H→T
37 Z→T	94 L→C	151 I→N	208 G→T	265 S→U
38 N→W	95 Q→I	152 M→N	209 J→B	266 F→D
39 J→O	96 L→E	153 F→A	210 Z→O	267 E→D
40 L→V	97 R→M	154 V→E	211 Y→U	268 X→T
41 J→N	98 O→E	155 Y→N	212 Y→T	269 N→I
42 H→U	99 K→E	156 L→P	213 N→Y	270 Q→E
43 O→S	100 H→I	157 A→S	214 Q→K	271 P→C
44 P→H	101 T→U	158 W→L	215 M→V	272 K→F
45 L→I	102 P→S	159 X→R	216 O→B	273 B→T
46 O→C	103 X→W	160 W→E	217 N→H	274 Q→G
47 G→H	104 P→W	161 N→O	218 N→P	275 G→R
48 V→R	105 M→S	162 Y→M	219 H→O	276 J→T
49 V→K	106 D→P	163 Z→N	220 A→C	277 W→Y
50 P→T	107 M→H	164 P→L	221 G→N	278 G→P
51 R→U	108 R→T	165 W→A	222 C→S	279 P→O
52 N→R	109 H→C	166 I→E	223 V→O	280 L→O
53 D→S	110 U→O	167 H→M	224 R→O	281 Z→H
54 H→R	111 O→L	168 K→D	225 S→A	282 R→E
55 J→L	112 Y→R	169 B→P	226 F→T	283 Z→O
56 B→L	113 V→Y	170 H→A	227 M→L	284 Q→W
57 R→E	114 Q→P	171 F→E	228 U→P	

Cryptograms

1.

IT IS UNWISE TO COMPLAIN LOUDLY
MK MC DWYMCL KN UNEOAZMW ANDIAG

ABOUT HOW THE BALL BOUNCES
ZHNDK TNY KTL HZAA HNDWULC,

ESPECIALLY IF YOU ARE THE ONE WHO
LCOLUMZAAG MQ GND ZXL KTL NWL YTN

DROPPED IT
IXNOOLI MK.

m—IALN-O

HINTS: 63, 69, 161

2.

JK HKT ZQKS MVBM SDNNDBF MBWM SBY

MVU WDIYM XIUYDJUQM MK FBZU IUATNBI

TYU KW BQ BTMKFKRDNU SVDNU VU SBY

OVDUW ULUOTMDCU?

HINTS: 256, 235, 183

3.

YNM RETOY DJNIXQJDYC RM SQJ ONER EIT

AMZZER STMQYITMO DO YE LM SEXWZMYMZC

DJFDAAMTMJY YE YNMDT JMMFO.

HINTS: 174, 217, 188

4.

NHXNQH AIX SBO SX TCMH CP KTNBHGGKXP

XWSHP LX; KS KG XWSHP PXS SIH MKPL XW

KTNBHGGKXP SIHO SBO SX TCMH.

HINTS: 218, 90, 60

Answers on page 315

Cryptograms

5.

CUFLS IZVIJZVO, EVMOFMH OB XVD AFC
JFUU EFOA V LAZLS, EVC OBUI JD EVFOZP
OAVO YVMVHZYZMO PNUZC PZWNFPZ
XVDFMH LAZLS EFOA V JFUU.

HINTS: 94, 31, 209

6.

GVZ CPEZ MZQQUC NUWQB MPIB OXZYG
NUIEUQYGPUI PI IZYXQA YIAGVPIO;
ETYQQZX EYQYXA TZYIE ETYQQZX GYKZE.

HINTS: 151, 208, 17

7.

LDZJO OXM ZQWE OXVQP OXLO PZMR LR TLH
OZFLE LR VO FVF OMQ EMLHR LPZ VR OXM
FVKM OXLO HZWWR JQFMH OXM DMF.

HINTS: 179, 266, 196

8.

HXLT OMJ VUQLUDX UMHWQRV UXL VUWQV,
OMJ YWO TMU QLWDX MTL, KJU OMJ HPSS
TMU LTR JN HPUX W XWTRGJS MG YJR,
LPUXLQ.

HINTS: 146, 4, 33

Answers on page 315

Cryptograms

9.

V IOVF FOVWOI SG DYO XKD EVY MZOGG
XKSEK XVQ NKO EIDXW XSFF CO MDSYM VYW
NKOY MON DZN SY JIDYN.

HINTS: 78, 185, 103

10.

UJI LJIFE OYD DNY KNJWD YME JB DNY
XGWOGQM QB UJI KNJIFE EYLQEY DJ DWGEY
JTTJWDIMQDU BJW KYLIWQDU.

HINTS: 39, 267, 187

11.

XNFYF RYF EFYG HFT FYYSYU IRQF AG R
ISXNFY-VB-KRT TNS VU RB FEFY-TVKKVBP
ARAGUVXXFY.

HINTS: 248, 112, 171

12.

ZTDN D KSNI NTDN KJYKBJ ZTY TDOJ
FBYGJL XSVLG QGQDBBI LYV'N TDOJ
XYQNTG NY XDNFT.

HINTS: 92, 243, 30

13.

EPDL QSZOUW XOD GYNWOA, PD PA
OWDPUOYC GSAAPHYO DS OWXSC ZPWWOU
PW NQOUPVN NWZ LNTO LONUDHJUW STOU
OJUSGO.

HINTS: 80, 193, 98

Answers on page 315

Cryptograms

14.

BLMQSKT H TJZQTG SO OSRSMHJ CL BHWSKT
H IZJJ SK ULZJ OBLG, ABSFB FHZOGO
GWGJU OCGY CL IG YHSKDZM ASCBLZC
OBLJCGKSKT CBG CJSY.

HINTS: 84, 194, 140

15.

SRIX U LZCXQ VZL FUGIY U VUFR ZD ROY
ZSX UMMZAN, OF OY U YCAI FROXQ RI OY
QZOXQ ZX ROY DOAYF NUFI.

HINTS: 274, 210, 86

16.

VRVZ LC SKZVT PWVI KZ UWVVA, AKSV
QVKQGV IKJGY FXRV UK IWLUV FKSV
MVUIVVZ FXWRVAUA CKW AKSV YKJPF.

HINTS: 114, 154, 263

17.

NSHKFV NLV EX GKJJSA AQS HFEOKX
NSFZCLCKH DLF SOKF YSVH-GEVLVDKH
QECQALU SV DFKHEZ DLFH CLXSJEVK.

HINTS: 141, 257, 123

18.

HEXCPXQ'H TXQZXMF EQCJXQ: "TLSS VJ
VYNFD ILFD EQYEXQ HFNTT, CMR MNRKX VX
IDXM L DCZX HCLR XMYNKD."

HINTS: 244, 131, 150

Answers on page 315

Cryptograms

19.

HBTN "DACR" LFNW BHIFQ JOTRF
OJJDMFQIR: DACNBLDRDQU, DACOIDFQJF,
DACTQDIW, OQM DACTXRDLFQFRR.

HINTS: 138, 40, 119

20.

BXLXJSW BGL BTXYWY, BXNBTWY BXSSGVY
BHQIQOXS; PQHYN BVIJWHYGIW
BGOPWYYQGO BSGYWY BXYW.

HINTS: 137, 2, 89

21.

BLSLJC MKB MBXRYBVYNKF OVXRLJ TC PNZP
TNDD MBKS JKOYKB: YPNFE KM HPVY VF
XFJLBYVELB HKXDJ OPVBZL.

HINTS: 212, 44, 88

22.

GAVTEAFTQ GPFOBA, GAILESZAB GR GLX,
GWLXZE GVOYWFPP, GVOLQZAQ GAQE, GTE
GWFYA, GAVT; GASFUAQ GVOYAW'Q GWLBA.

HINTS: 61, 164, 259

23.

O ERCSN KOTE WUFCWSUT O TZMFZRSOWE
FR FLU KZJWOWE VZFL FLU MRGGUSF, "ZF'X
FRR TZXMRSSUMFUT FR JU ZSFUWUXFZSN."

HINTS: 255, 237, 226

Answers on page 315

Cryptograms

24.

WUMJ SKGG UVFM HMVLUMC VCXGMPLMRLM
SUMR V DXJ RXWKLMP WUVW V AKHG
RXWKLMP WUVW UM KP RXWKLKRA UMH.

HINTS: 258, 134, 94

25.

VUIHYXNIL FPNSH LXDEYSZ DBJYH QUCPYX
NR FUIHYIBYH QNSJ FUQYB RXUQ EYXZ
BPUXC FUVB.

HINTS: 159, 203, 151

26.

MPGK ZACE GIMQ NK RKULMKR
LGGKRLCQKAB QP ZWKUKQ PWSCELFKR
YWLGK TWPG RLMPWSCELFLES MPYLKQB.

HINTS: 29, 207, 45

27.

ANCGB-CJQHU BQQECOQG GRVVQY ZRA
FCGQEBA VD CAUREO RK BZQD MAQY BL
GRYQ BL AHZLLJ LE BZQ VMNFD VCHUA LK
YRELACMGA.

HINTS: 81, 270, 66

28.

MEXW IPXGGQWR T CQIRXSJ KTKJ, HXPXUJ
RXS EDUI DC T KASSDW, SEXW MTQS AWSQU
SEX KASSDWEDUX LDHXG TPDAWI.

HINTS: 186, 229, 143

Answers on page 315–316

Cryptograms

29.

UXDG UBJB QJBZMPNTVA IDVVBW
GBVBZMTMPY TGDGMPY LJBDFT DJB YPU
OPJB PRGBY VMFB IPOQPNYW RJDIGNJBT.

HINTS: 253, 73, 139

30.

QXI KGEU UXLI HUK GFKIGAK MKIDXT
YISFKD USD EGI, XI SD HSKY LM ST
HIGQQSE, UK NKGFKD SH MGIBKY QXI
KNKFKT UXLID.

HINTS: 62, 264, 79

31.

BK EGGNE GXMA HGIEPJ ZPT NGGK MXJ
HIGEMIBRG X MTIG LPI KAG MPNNPJ MPWS—
RTK JPK ZPTI SPMKPI.

HINTS: 14, 279, 255

32.

QIU PWMJ-KQQU PWDALRQU TNVT LDT
KQOWTJDF WMZBQTDQP NZZWNUT JQ LNSW
RWWP JQIFLWK QYY RV NP QBK YBNOW.

HINTS: 160, 260, 70

33.

ZDN UFZ ZF JEUX AKDN IRGM VDFUS VEZM
NFRD GMEQXDKU. LKDMWLH ZMKN MWAK
LWZZKDUKX ZMKIHKQAKH WJZKD NFR.

HINTS: 99, 213, 156

Answers on page 316

Cryptograms 225

Cryptograms

34.

E O B   K E U O ,   D O G F P B   K E   G C C E H X   H G X G H   F D K
U Z Q M Z O R   K E   J D K   X E U O   E O   Q W B B X B H Q ,
M D O R   D W   K M Z Q   H E G X   Q Z R O :   " Q W B B X   K H G W
G M B G X . "

HINTS: 58, 32, 126

35.

J B M   Y M I I Q U   U B Q   Y S N O J   O H S Z   " H   L M K K V
Y Q N   V Q E N   J B Q E X B J O "   B H Z   M F S Z M K J I V
K M F M N   L H S Z   Y Q N   L O V A B Q H K H I V O S O .

HINTS: 276, 113, 258

36.

G T Y R S   P L   L R Y W H G P J X   O P U W   Z   J W W V O W   Z J V
H G S W Z V ,   Q R S ,   P Q   V W Q H O M   T L W V ,   P H   F Z J
C Z H F G   T C   C S Z F H P F Z O O M   Z J M H G P J X .

HINTS: 28, 41, 160

37.

E I U M D H I   H R I   S Y Z I V E Y A ,   H R I   X I A C   U R P A H I U H
V D O R H   P J   H R I   C I Y A   D U   S R A D U H K Y U   I X I —
J A P K   U N V E P G V   H P   U P V - N M .

HINTS: 180, 257, 86

38.

Q R Z I C   H T   Q   S E J I R J   Q V H N   J Y Q J   N E I T   O E C I
Y Q C O   J E   J Y Q J   H R   B Y H V Y   H J   H T   T J E C I N   J Y Q R
H J   V Q R   J E   J Y Q J   E R   B Y H V Y   H J   H T   S E M C I N .

HINTS: 135, 100, 176

Answers on page 316

Cryptograms

39.

NAWAWXAN, JQ AZAMJUTN TBANJUTN
WKCOU OJMA OKG YBG JQS STEQG, XYU OA
KG TQA TH UOA HAE BATBZA EOT VQTEG
EOANA OA KG CTKQC.

HINTS: 169, 142, 52

40.

CKB YRBMYAB VBMLEQ NEWUI FWZK VMBGBM
CE DB ZEFVUHFBQCBI GEM Y SEWCKGWU
YVVBYMYQZB CKYQ VMYHLBI GEM NHLIEF
YCCMHDWCBI CE YAB.

HINTS: 71, 245, 17

41.

WKVKURMEHB: AKJJTQ QDT QHU UT UIMK
RDKMK QKMK UREJJ H STIWJK TA PHJJTBU
TA PHU EB RDK SHM.

HINTS: 83, 55, 62

42.

BWZ MLSTZG LD U JPSREZ JSLMDEUCZ DUG
LXBMZPRWJ BWZ MPJTLQ LD U MWLEZ
XSPNZGJZ LD QZBZLGLELRPJBJ.

HINTS: 280, 234, 8

Answers on page 316

Cryptograms

43.

QZ IXRAFAPR AP Q XVYPIZ DOI AP PSYV OV
OQP OVQYM QTT IJ ROV OSFIYISP
MVJAZARAIZP IJ QZ IXRAFAPR.

HINTS: 108, 265, 184

44.

XCH MBP CWYX NHTMW EZ XCHB TEWO
GMWOPBL, DHR RNP RBCHDYP ICTPL GNPW
XCH LRMBR RC ZCYYCG ER.

HINTS: 42, 133, 236

45.

UPLV UOL, AYGO SJOWUTUOSOWM, PWO
YLIADOLFOC RV FTLCYSYTLM MDWWTDLCYLN
SJOU; SJO TSJOWM, AYGO SJOWUTMSPSM,
CT MTUOSJYLN PRTDS YS.

HINTS: 76, 192, 60

46.

HMDVABSBKZWA HBCWAMPHAOQ WBUO YOMD
QZNNZHPSA HMDVABKMRUW RCQ WAPUVOQ
CORMSD RSS WBSYOMW.

HINTS: 132, 109, 237

47.

QFN OMMC MYC CLXU—PFNI L QNNILONJ
PNIQ BIQM QFN OLJLON LIC TLEN MAQ
GAUFBIO QFN YLPI EMPNJ.

HINTS: 239, 13, 104

Answers on page 316

Cryptograms

48.

SC MGTY GDD SMGS ICN JGZS FGI RY
VHLMYU; MCJYTYV, SC RY LCFODYSYDI
LCZSYZS JHSM ICNV DCS HU JYGDSM.

HINTS: 205, 107, 238

49.

PNCXFEWQ—FMR KZF ZWH QZR WONXNQS QF
QWLR HFERQZNMU, WMP SRQ EWLR QZR
FQZRY CRYHFM ORXNRAR ZR NH UNANMU NQ
WKWS.

HINTS: 269, 57, 152

50.

ZPUAHCP NYBC APKAJP UBS, MPVS TPN
TKJDU YBMP XKVP XKQPS CYBQ CYPS DQKN
NYBC CK ZK NHCY.

HINTS: 38, 9, 181

51.

GFXKBP ZUOOQLOZ KZ TZTFAAH AKXO
ZUOAAKBP GKZZKZZKUUK; HJT GTZD XBJN
NLOB DJ ZDJU.

HINTS: 228, 101, 29

52.

ACK TQ LUGK VCHJTYBG NBBL FQ BUF
FCBHY NEHGUVC HG NJQA LQFHQG—HGUVC
XK HGUVC?

HINTS: 128, 221, 260

Answers on page 316

Cryptograms

53.

DWH SRCU RIIBCUJ XWABRMMD QSUO DWH
ARO XHAAUXXNHMMD SWMJ R AWAFVRBM ROJ
TMRVU WN ARORTUX ROJ ARIID WO R
AWOCUIXRVBWO QBVS WOMD VQW SROJX.

HINTS: 18, 220, 68

54.

URWES KTSW IRBB ZK UJCSGL RGK ESIRFDS
ZK URW LJK ES RGJFLC BJLH SLJFHT KJ ES
IRBBSC RLWKTZLH SBDS.

HINTS: 16, 56, 240

55.

SIRNV, KFLU ENTNAQAUC YLEH QAI TIRVN
XZIX WZN YLU TLIX LP WIRVN YAXZ PISLKW
FIEAW VIRNV, WXIEXNH HIUTAUC IXLF
XIRVN.

HINTS: 129, 268, 241

56.

EINLKSYXOQ, VXNKH YXOQAK LEXOQ, DFW
MSKWWZ EIOQZ XVH GFV PANBKEC BWXOQ
FC YXOQ GPAEK MEXZAVD LEXOQYXOQ.

HINTS: 46, 214, 137

Answers on page 317

Cryptograms

57.

ETYTYATE, CWT BKSCKNUVEI KM CWT NUGI
XGVST PWTET INQ'GG OKUB MQSSTMM
SNYTM ATONET PNED.

HINTS: 7, 162, 105

58.

LMH LA CRNMI VMAJ LZR JSOLNXRO AV
ALZRMO. HAQ KSCC IAL CSPR CAIE RIAQEZ
LA JNXR LZRJ NCC HAQMORCV.

HINTS: 254, 27, 282

59.

LZPJT ZHX QDUZ V QHLZIS TVJNVSHH QDRL
OPRKPTI V SVPJM OVM XZIJ LZI TPOR
UVJJHL GKVM HDLRPOI.

HINTS: 136, 281, 80

60.

YWH LHMQBK YWH GBT AQ EMK'Q SHQY UMN
AQ ULBSMSNV SHDMOQH WH KHFHL TAFHQ
MGFADH, SBLLBJQ EBKHV, BL WMQ
AK-NMJQ.

HINTS: 36, 67, 140

61.

QSWRL QJL WSX KR RTRALXNVWU—NSORTRA,
VX NJG J MARXXL USSF ZRJF STRA ONJXRTRA
VG VW GRISWF MZJIR.

HINTS: 57, 34, 133

Answers on page 317

Cryptograms

62.

TMGCPSYC HYY KDSL XDLLKUJV EDL H
TWCMUEM GHYE-GDSL HLDSJP OGC FUPPYC
DE OGC PHK. OGCJ OHBC H JHW PSLUJV
OGUT WCLUDP.

HINTS: 148, 255, 47

63.

JYKDQLGQJZ: UVDZVP BSVJK YLZQKIZJ LPK
BKGG KIVTAS ZPLQIKU ZV DLGG VI SQW
VIGN UTPQIA ULNGQASZ SVTPJ.

HINTS: 37, 1, 223

64.

ZXBDKXD QJZ EDG GA CBZXAYDH FQE GQD
AKDZ FQA FJKG GA LDG AOO AK GQD
ZDXAKC OIAAH JHD JIFJEZ BK GQD HDJH AO
GQD DIDYJGAH.

HINTS: 25, 54, 144

65.

DZUGSQ GD CBA DAMDXS PBAS CBA KGUID
WXH EAI MVV PGSCAU UAZMW WXH KW
AMCGSQ WXHU SAPVW ZVMSCAI QUMDD
DAAI.

HINTS: 53, 127, 277

Answers on page 317

Cryptograms

66.

IGHZHSHK E JHOOYI PEBHU E PDUAEBH, EA
OHEUA DA LKYSHU GH UAYLLHT AEOBDZF
EZT AKDHT AY TY UYPHAGDZF.

HINTS: 116, 195, 36

67.

S FHOLWT YQHTLLW QJ S FHERLW HI IHVW
XHVTKJELWJ ZRH JVWNQNLJ S WSQTX
ZLLGLTO ZRLT ERL ELULNQJQHT QJ THE
ZHWGQTK.

HINTS: 219, 233, 21

68.

OW OD AXW IAXNHK TIVIRM WX CXDDIDD U
EOAI UOT OA ROEI; OW OD URDX
AIZIDDUVM EXV MXN WX CNRR WKI
WVOHHIV.

HINTS: 166, 53, 134

69.

BPF IRAFIB VFBPWG BW TIF BW GWTCDF
KWTE VWXFK LI BW AWDG LB WXNF RXG JTB
LB CRNU LX KWTE JWNUFB.

HINTS: 273, 117, 190

Answers on page 317

Cryptograms

70.

AC KQL WHE VHZM QEM TMUFQE XHTTK
MOMUK PHK, AE CQUSK KMHUF KQL XHOM
WQESUAGLSMP SQ SXM XHTTAEMFF QC
HNVQFS CACSMME SXQLFHEP TMQTNM.

HINTS: 170, 118, 58

71.

KTEJ GJTGZJ YJDJS XGGJXS HT WXDJ XY
TGMYMTY—HWJF CKJ TYJ HWXH WXGGJYK HT
RJ MY KHFZJ XH HWJ HMEJ.

HINTS: 202, 155, 278

72.

URHP HR NRJ XBRDHX—HYP LFXHPXH ZFJ
VURZU HR WFVP F LMTP ZMHY HZR XHMBVX
MX HR WFVP XDTP RUP RL HYPW MX F
WFHBY.

HINTS: 224, 264, 135

73.

OE DWYP LPWSNCUQ QCCU CTXNCQQ,
PCUCUSCP F XOFUWTX OQ SYJ F LOCKC WE
KWFN JMFJ MFQ SCCT MFPX-LPCQQCX EWP
UFTD DCFPQ.

HINTS: 200, 31, 192

Answers on page 317

Cryptograms

74.

WTT WVO ZKCI WNXN AZ W VPR PIFTAOPP
KN YSWY SP DP ZKZYO FPCEPVY AZ RSWY SP
ETWKIPH YA DP YSP HWO SP WFFTKPH ZAC
YSP FANKYKAV.

HINTS: 147, 9, 24

75.

RJY XGWQAWXHD EWPPYGYQAY IYRLYYQ
XUMAJBQYVGBUWU HQE XDHWQ
QYGKBVUQYUU WU HIBVR BQY JVQEGYE HQE
PWPRM EBDDHGU.

HINTS: 19, 180, 267

76.

IGOLLCKPGBJ OSN GH SB GBJWBGCTH
HRHOWD ZCU VUWFWBOGBJ OLW OSNVSRWU
ZUCD JWOOGBJ ISUDKR SOOSALWP OC LGH
DCBWR.

HINTS: 178, 225, 199

77.

BJ BT HCIMJBMIGGK BNHFTTBYGL JF YL I
JFH SFQ, LTHLMBIGGK BE KFZ THLOS IGG FE
KFZC THICL JBNL QCFVGBOQ.

HINTS: 85, 230, 64

Answers on page 317

Cryptograms

78.

TCBJ BVDOSDXB BJOJD JQOJ GJ JOSDB WV
JC JQXDD HDDSB JC VXDVOXD O VXCVDX
GTVXCTVJW BVDDMQ.

HINTS: 22, 122, 276

79.

NCU RKFNUI QNMNUQ GZKQNFRNFZK DMQ
KZN IAMDK RW RKNFS USUHUK XUMAQ
MENUA NCU QFOKFKO ZE NCU
IUGSMAMNFZK ZE FKIUWUKIUKGU.

HINTS: 206, 128, 183

80.

DZIIDSPJ DKSJSOPZDKI LILZQQM BZVW
XSQVI QSSV ZI HX JKWM FWPW WBWPOHTO
CSQWXLQQM XPSB Z QSIJ FWWVWTC.

HINTS: 5, 49, 106

81.

XK VGR EOGRDP YCYZ OLCY WOY KYYDXJU
WOLW VGR LZY FYXJU ELPDV JYUDYHWYP,
ZYBYBFYZ IOXEWDYZ'E KLWOYZ.

HINTS: 15, 272, 51

82.

XB RCY ACYIL IXOT PC WTT F JCLTI ECJT,
RCY WECYIL ITFQD AEFP PXJT WET XW
PEQCYKE ACQO.

HINTS: 26, 238, 186

Answers on page 317–318

Cryptograms

83.

W YNWVV GUB JVRNVB UGHKEQKZ QU JUAFJ
QU YECUUV YAFEK CK EURVZ FUQ SKWZ,
EURVZ FUQ MSAQK, WFZ MWY FUQ WVVUMKZ
QU QWVO.

HINTS: 165, 175, 129

84.

RLU COWAR QHN BC ADWOSJ HSQ RLU
COWAR WUHG ADWOSJ QHN HWU BCRUS HA
IKYL HA H IBSRL HDHWR.

HINTS: 23, 207, 58

85.

KR PRWPR XKR YKGA CPOGL XJS, ZIF RPZPTS
VKL SAF WRMARFAT K MAEAFKZOA FVKF XKR
XKILA FVAY FP OKIEV.

HINTS: 242, 61, 25

86.

ZE CQF KRZEMKI KZSMEN: "MY MK DGWS
EMUG YC FC ECYIMEN ZQQ FZS—YIGE IZDG
YIG EMNIY YC WGKY VR."

HINTS: 72, 212, 266

87.

ZTV JZZH RCX PZ PVQP XZBG SVSZGX DQ PZ
PGX PZ GVSVSMVG PNV PNDTJQ PNCP
RZGGDVH XZB XVQPVGHCX.

HINTS: 252, 204, 283

Answers on page 318

Cryptograms

88.

"AEJ XEHJD DRZXAHMZ MD AEJ VMIL HQ AM
XYUUL AEJ VUYHZ YUMRZI," QYHI AEMFYQ
Y. JIHQMZ.

HINTS: 163, 116, 17

89.

HLUZX MLU XBCXZTFUY LXBF JUHLQJR RUUT
BPUNH HLXEZXDCXZ—PNH ZNFX DXBFJ MLU
HLXQF YBDZ BFX.

HINTS: 110, 199, 131

90.

FVWZOFX MB MX DVBBVW BC OFFWVIMOBV
JZOB CKV IOKKCB CJK BZOK BC CJK JZOB
CKV IOKKCB OFFWVIMOBV.

HINTS: 59, 140, 63

91.

RUTVIRYWAETYIT AM QJDQ ITVQDAY
WTTNAYB QJDQ WRNHM JDUT XJTY QJTZ
ERY'Q HYRX XJDQ QJTZ DVT BTQQAYB AYQR.

HINTS: 125, 231, 7

92.

GKK GJ GHMLUFJZ GUQLJZW ZQ PW ZXQ QH
UQHF TFQTKF GZZFUTZPJM RGHI ZQ MFZ PJ
ZRF KGWZ XQHI CPHWZ.

HINTS: 87, 32, 54

Answers on page 318

Cryptograms

93.

"VJ DHV TE XJJI AVJBXN GJ XJYAWV
HVJGNAW DHV QTGNJBG GNHG JGNAW
DHV'E PJVEAVG," EHTI OTVPJOV.

HINTS: 111, 39, 257

94.

LJ ZYB ZGUB JQV YHIB JQVK OYGNP
WVGZBP, WOHKIBP, HCP LQQZBP, WCHTTBP,
UGZZBCBP, HCP LBNZBP, ZYB WCQX YHW
UBNZBP.

HINTS: 120, 37, 260

95.

IVK SCVE IVKCAPORHP XHR HRXWWI
AHVEJCA KZ EMRC OMRI POXHO XPSJCA
LKRPOJVCP OMXO MXR WVAJDXW XCPERHP.

HINTS: 91, 75, 177

96.

D MGKLTGKPCJ PC GYEJV DV DATJJKJVE
HJEZJJV EZG LJGLIJ, JDMQ GY ZQGK JVNC
RL ZPEQ CGKJEQPVA QJ NGJC VGE DMERDIIX
ZDVE.

HINTS: 82, 247, 202

Answers on page 318

Cryptograms

97.

ZRZU QX DKE MNRZ NFF CMZ NUYHZBY, DKE
LND UKC GZ NGFZ CK YQXC CMZ BQWMC
KUZY XBKL CMZ HBKUW KUZY.

HINTS: 261, 235, 107

98.

DKBO K VHDKBAC GYKG EGKVGCI JCELIC K
SKGCVTKXX KG K EWDDCV VCEHVG YKE
CBICI JCELIC K XCKUO TKWACG LB GYC
ULGAYCB ELBU.

HINTS: 48, 109, 208

99.

KPA XWUVA ANNAYKUZTN SFW PZXXUYANN
UY TUSA ZWA NFVAKPUYL KF RF, NFVAKPUYL
KF TFQA, ZYR NFVAKPUYL KF PFXA SFW.

HINTS: 191, 246, 44

100.

G PJXMP MN G VIHNEX LSE OXELN BSI
VHMPI ET IWIHJBSMXR, JIB OXELN BSI
GPBAGD WGDAI ET XEBSMXR.

HINTS: 166, 271, 176

101.

OVHYH WX XPAHOVWQI AKRV QWRHY OVBQ
YHRHWZWQI EYBWXH—OVH JHHGWQI PJ
VBZWQI HBYQHT WO.

HINTS: 173, 197, 19

Answers on page 318

Cryptograms

102.

HLXJ HGX BW L EKHKQ XLEFDG MDGWGD
ERG YBHMLDLEKIG YLUH BW QGCMBEKCH EB
ERG ZBKCEGDBFC BYGLX BW UKZGDEJ.

HINTS: 222, 251, 167

103.

RJ HDKBRDKB D YVMM-WDMDBSVX
FVTLFVSRKGV, VDSO HDB YOJ JYBL D XJA
RODR YJTLOKFL OKH LOJNMX DMLJ ODGV D
SDR RJ KABJTV OKH.

HINTS: 227, 193, 82

104.

UHKEHOX XSZSYM SR DXXDSYHP TCHY JYH
ODY XBKY JEE XCH CJX DYP OJIP TDXHK
EDBOHXR SY XCH RCJTHK RSZBIXDYHJBRIV.

HINTS: 12, 155, 268

105.

CUAJTM ZBVWATJM KBU ZUMNLFMLWH EWFH
BUUOH ZUYWA KJWW PJ ZFWWJA
"YMWVZJMNJA ZYTTVZYWYC FPNLFVMJTN."

HINTS: 211, 158, 10

106.

DKGHG TABD SG V SGDDGH QRVLG ZYH
ZYAH QGYQRG DY SG TWBGHVSRG
DYUGDKGH DKVX VD DKG SHWCUG DVSRG.

HINTS: 130, 114, 67

Answers on page 318–319

Cryptograms

107.

WL IXOEFM EC MWPEVMKQ BEPSLGP OIKGM,
ZMFIGCM MOMW I BIPFS PSIP XLMC WLP
VGW EC FLVVMFP PBEFM XIEKQ.

HINTS: 50, 28, 258

108.

FAL VLGF FAKDEG KD BKUL WYL UYLL, GT
FALO GWO, VJF KG KF DTF W MKFO FAWF
FAL DLZF-VLGF FAKDEG WYL GT NLYO
LZMLDGKNL?

HINTS: 198, 149, 90

109.

XPSFBXG IPBZAOMN AP GLVG IPB XPBMF
XVMWMI AOMM GLO NVWEMI QVZZPG GP
IPBZ GPDS'A DPZAG HPAAEQ.

HINTS: 124, 227, 91

110.

KN FPM GBL BTKCJ GDJJTNMXXF PL B AJTF
GPXU VPTLKLH, KW KC B VBWWJT PN VKLU
PAJT VBWWTJCC.

HINTS: 24, 145, 134

111.

AGDVUVLU: R ONPPBMQY MBRUP AM UVHJ
LQON RL RYYAFL R DPRZPDDYP DA LVHS
DNAQSN VH NAD FRDPB QG DA VDL HALP.

HINTS: 254, 217, 192

Answers on page 319

Cryptograms

112.

HG KUO FLJ FWPJ BU CFEJ TJUTPJ BXHYE
BXJK YJJA FY HBJC BXJK XFQJ YJQJL JQJY
XJFLA UG WJGULJ, KUO FLJ BLOPK F
IFPJICFY.

HINTS: 153, 202, 164

113.

I KABVDAEIB RO TBA YFT YTB'V OVIMA IV I
KRMD RB I WIVFRBK OSRV SBDAOO FA RO
YAIMRBK OSBKDIOOAO.

HINTS: 43, 121, 193

114.

SNRYR TP EOVA EOR YRWVVA FYRSSA QNTVH
TO SNR NEPFTSWV OZYPRYA, WOH RWQN
CESNRY FEPPRPPRP TS.

HINTS: 236, 102, 205

115.

CLELYA KY ATP GRFAT ZTPF ATP GCAP AR
ATCA CJEOHP YRDB ORL JPDPKWPS KF
ZKFAPJ MRJ DTJKYAGCY KY MKFCHHO
MKFKYTPS.

HINTS: 11, 116, 90

Answers on page 319

Cryptograms

116.

COD ORR DBNV ZBPG AH YUP HPZ DPOV KP
BE OG KVAPE LNVOYABH OG CBGY BE DBNV
HPZ DPOV'G VPGBRNYABHG.

HINTS: 132, 18, 9

117.

M YLHHFCFHV FH DWL CMW ZBD ELLNH OMP
ZBLW BL ELLNH RDDP EDJ ELMJ BL'NN ELLN
ZDJHL ZBLW BL ELLNH OLVVLJ.

HINTS: 20, 216, 96

118.

NRTN YWKOQNQWK HRQYR QK NRM PEDHTF
QP YTVVMO YWKIMPNQWK QP NMZCMO
"QKNQCTYF" QK WEZ DMPN KQIRNYVEDP.

HINTS: 95, 201, 262

119.

NAWQJK HFWFQAUV DT YEF DUZFUYDAU AN
ZFWV RDTF QFU YA QJCF XAKYT CFFO
YEFDW XDTYJUHF.

HINTS: 138, 261, 171

120.

NLQ UPZN CUOPMNBSN NLCSE BKPDN B
OMPKYQU CZ SPN CNZ ZPYDNCPS KDN NLQ
ZNMQSENL EBCSQV CS JCSVCSE NLQ
ZPYDNCPS.

HINTS: 206, 253, 199

Answers on page 319

Cryptograms

121.

OJ KRX KMQX JYV IMPUAAJ WXUZR HWXXPXW
GUBKVWXB, JYV ZUP YIKXP PY AYPHXW
ZAMQO KRX IXPZX.

HINTS: 3, 131, 69

122.

QWCWCRWQ NGWY FUJ MUD OYF QWLOZQH
KUYW RF DGW POYKPUQK RF HZCLPF
DGQWODWYZYM DU CUTW UJD?

HINTS: 168, 115, 187

123.

V CZAUVJR F YJSE FA OQGGFUHI MVGQHQAA
VUSZO CFA VNNQVGVJMQ; CQ CVAJ'O
ACSEJ ZN FJ IQVGA.

HINTS: 275, 136, 218

124.

QERFMFU WIOL, "I QRUT SRN'MF LRYF QFGG
YFMFU YFFLW LROYJ RMFU," FMOLFYBGS
YFMFU CNGGFL QFFLW OY BEF JIULFY.

HINTS: 77, 215, 284

125.

PN PA IKN WKAAPFOY LKV WYKWOY TEKAY
LPANA UVY NPJENOR ZOYIZEYQ NK KLLYV
KNEYVA U LVPYIQOR EUIQZOUAW.

HINTS: 189, 157, 235

Answers on page 319

Cryptograms

126.

URH QHNYHDMA SHE TF URH FTAHWU UHNKF
CD URH WTZRU URNU DNAA NF TU EHHQF
FCDUAX DCK VCX NU FHHTWZ NAA URH
ECWSHKDMA YKHNUTCWF CD URH SNX.

HINTS: 36, 86, 133

127.

MZZYPLAKX UY PJZJKU EMDOAYK UPJKLD FYB
RMF TJGG JCQJZU UY EAKL UOJ DBAUGJDD
DTARRAKX DUPMQ KJCU FJMP.

HINTS: 97, 232, 172

128.

AJTXH DFJ OTLGY RJ HLU DFLR RFCU RFGZX
LMC JARCZ SJGZE YJMC HLUGZE RFLZ
RFGZXGZE.

HINTS: 250, 74, 179

129.

XGGP UKEYKBKU AGQM HYPKHF YQ GDK
WKHHGB BJG ANPKQ JYQ HYEYDT XF MJK
QBKNM GW JYQ XUGBQK.

HINTS: 249, 6, 99

130.

LKMMUVQNN UN ALKA MQHTXUKO QXKAQG
NQVNKAUIV EIT SQA DLQV EIT KOQ YTHL
AII PTNE AI PQ PIALQOQG DIOOEUVS.

HINTS: 93, 35, 182

Answer on page 319

Answers

Rarin' To Go

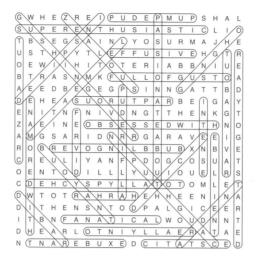

"Where shall I begin, your Majesty?" the White Rabbit asked. "Begin at the beginning," the King said gravely, "and go on till you come to the end; then stop." —"Alice in Wonderland"

So How Sharp Are You?

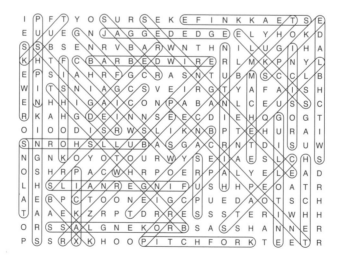

If you're keenly observant, highly sarcastic, very fashionable and good with a gun, you're a sharp-eyed, sharp-tongued sharp dresser who's a sharpshooter.

Off And Running

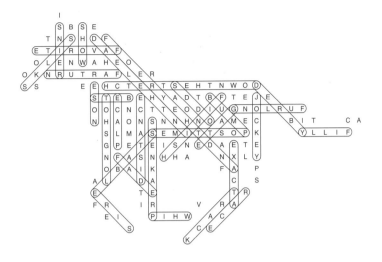

I bet on a horse at ten to one. It came in at half-past five.
Paraphrase of a quip by Henny Youngman

Gossip Columns

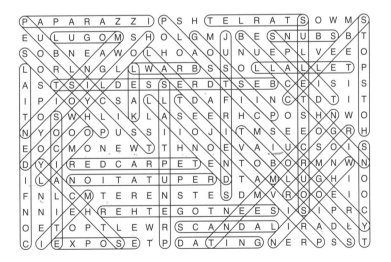

"Show me someone who never gossips, and I'll show you
someone who isn't interested in people." —Barbara Walters

It's In The Cards

A sleight-of-hand artist who likes to play his cards close to the vest may—in a snap!—have an ace up his sleeve.

Bad Ideas For Movie Sequels

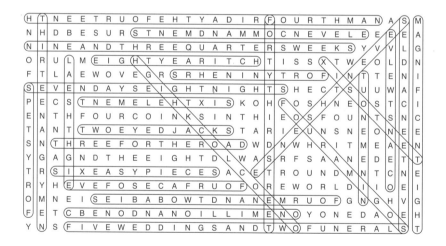

And be sure you miss "Two Flew Over the Cuckoo's Nest," "Four Coins in the Fountain," "Snow White and the Eight Dwarfs," and "Around the World in Eighty-One Days."

Give Me A Break!

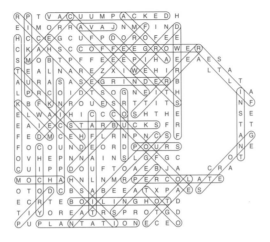

"The morning cup of coffee has an exhilaration about it which ... the afternoon or evening cup of tea cannot be expected to reproduce." —Oliver Wendell Holmes, Sr.

Car Pool

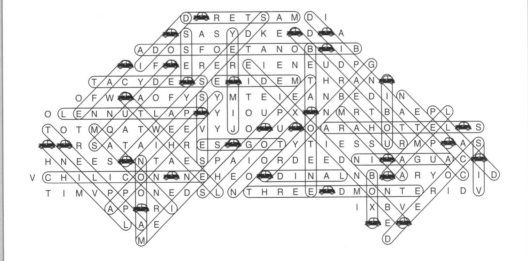

I asked a friend, "How often do you rotate your tires?"
He said, "Every time I drive."

Let's Celebrate

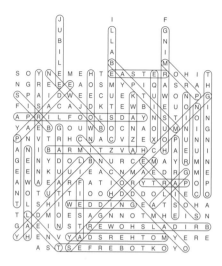

If something easy is a piece of cake, but you can't have your cake and eat it too, does that mean nothing is ever easy?

White On Schedule

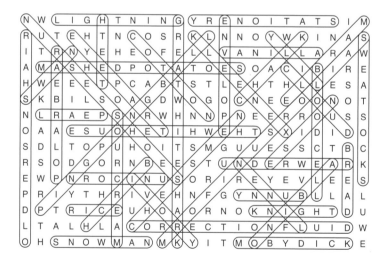

With no snow in the forecast, the ski lodge owner said to his guests, "Don't worry ... everything'll turn out all white."

Start The Music

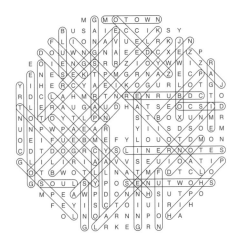

"Music is your own experience, your thoughts, your wisdom.
If you don't live it, it won't come out of your horn."
—Charlie Parker

Black Hole #1

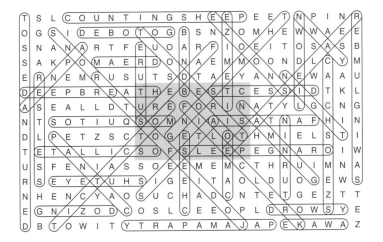

Center quote: "The best cure for insomnia is to get lots of sleep." Other quotes:
"Sleeping is no mean art: for its sake one must stay awake all day." — Friedrick Nietzsche
"Life is something to do when you can't get to sleep." —Fran Lebowitz

It's A Shoe Thing

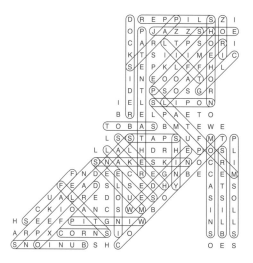

It is [totally] impossible to be well dressed in cheap shoes.
—couturier Hardy Amies

Give It The Old College Try

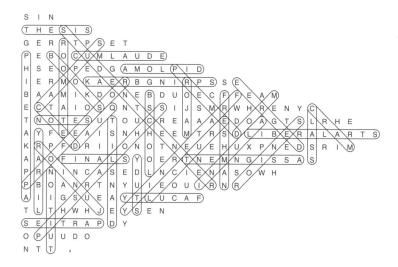

Singer Pete Seeger said, "Education is when you read the fine
print; experience is what you get when you don't."

Just Add Water

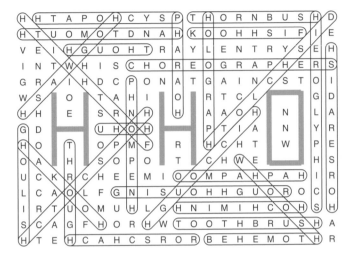

Every entry in this grid contains two aitches and an O, or H2O, the chemical formula for water.

Smell It Like It Is

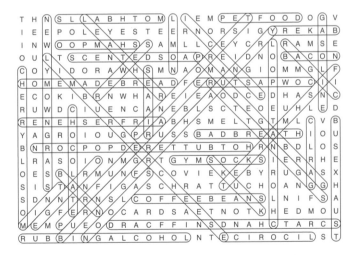

The movie "Polyester" originally came out in Odorama—a gimmick in which audiences could smell various odors in the movie by using scratch-and-sniff cards at noted moments.

Tennis, Anyone?

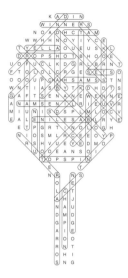

Know why you shouldn't go out with a tennis player?
To him, love means nothing.

What A Beast!

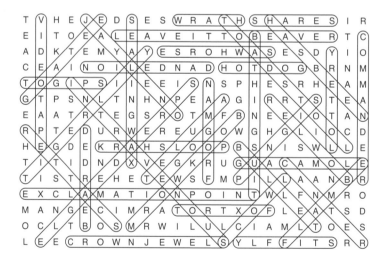

"The desire to take medicine is perhaps the greatest feature
which distinguishes man from animals." —Doctor William Osler

Up In The Air

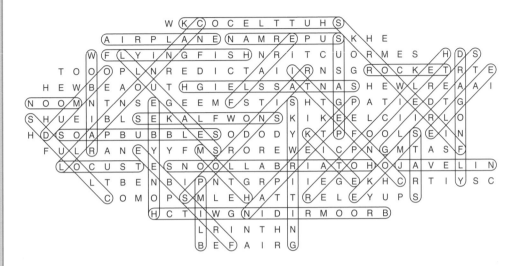

When it comes to predicting the weather, it seems that the likelihood of any forecast being right is completely up in the air.

Think Big

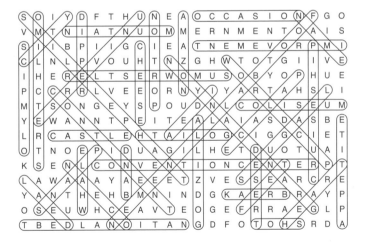

"If the government is big enough to give you everything you want, it is big enough to take away everything you have."
—Gerald Ford

Gridlock And Key

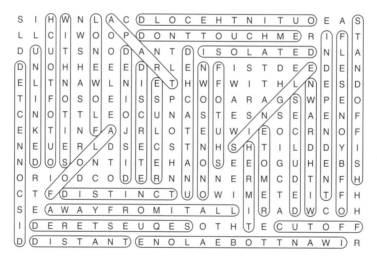

If Heather Locklear and Sandra Bullock did a cockeyed Keystone Kops comedy with Mickey Rooney, would it turn out to be a "schlock-key" movie?

Don't Touch Me!

Since all words on the list deal with separateness,
no words in the grid connect with each other.

Hair Apparent

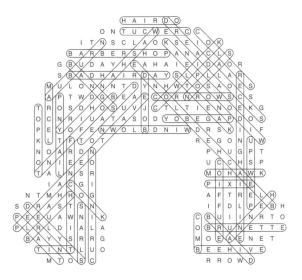

On its closing day, a hair salon that was shutting its doors for good put up a sign that said, "Hair Today, Gone Tomorrow."

On A Roll

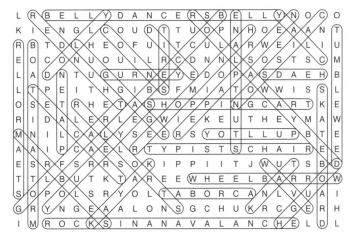

"Looking out upon the future ... I could not stop it if I wished ....
Like the Mississippi, it just keeps rolling along."
—Winston Churchill

What's On TV

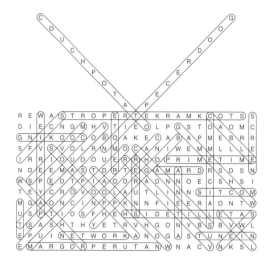

Reading helps to make a person well-rounded.
So does sitting in front of the TV gobbling snacks.

Black Hole #2

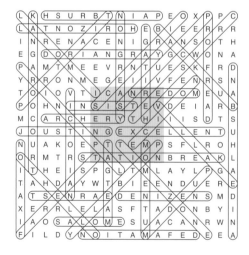

Center quote: "I can resist everything except temptation."
Regular quote: "Experience is the name everyone gives to their mistakes." —
from the play "Lady Windermere's Fan" by Oscar Wilde.

It's A Shore Thing

When you see shells on the shore, are you shore
that they're seashells?

We're In The Money

I've got enough money to last me for the rest of my life ... just
as long as I don't have to buy anything.

Cover Letter

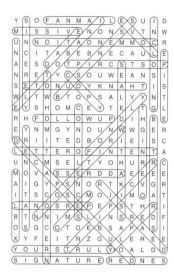

"You don't write because you want to say something; you write because you've got something to say." —F. Scott Fitzgerald

Today's To-Do List

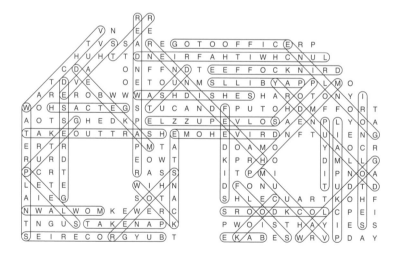

"Never put off to tomorrow what you can put off to the day after tomorrow." "Procrastination is the art of keeping up with yesterday."

At The Pharmacy

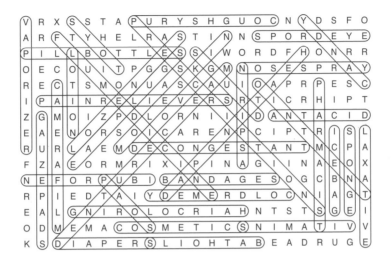

Rx stands for the Latin word for recipe. So a prescription is a recipe for mixing ingredients to make a drug.

Wordy Gurdy

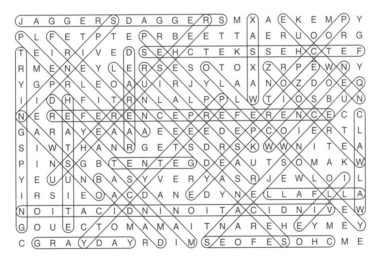

Make my letter better or give my story glory and I'll be crediting editing, but make a verse worse and you commit a rhyme crime.

Give Me A Ring

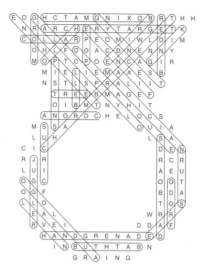

"Oh! how many torments lie in the small circle of a wedding-ring!" —dramatist Colley Cibber

In The Papers

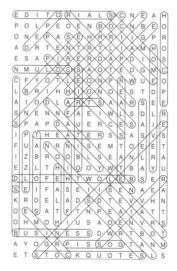

Napoleon Bonaparte said, "Four hostile newspapers are more to be feared than a thousand bayonets."

Solar Eclipse

When the moon dims the sun during an eclipse, you could say
it's a form of natural sunblock.

Picture Perfect

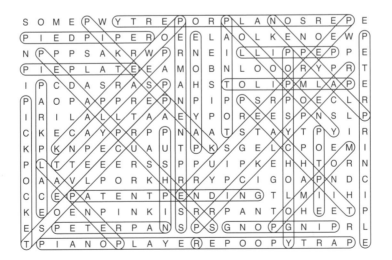

Some well-known PP's are Pablo Picasso, Priscilla Presley,
Patti Page, Peter Piper, Porky Pig, and the Pink Panther.

Changing Direction

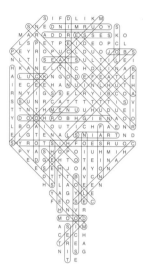

If, like most people, you don't like change, change your attitude about change and you might enjoy change for a change.

Things You Make

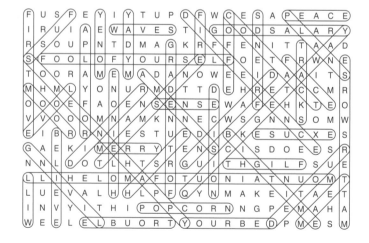

"Use it up, wear it out; make it do, or do without." "The man who makes no mistakes does not usually make anything."
—Edward John Phelps

Road Signs

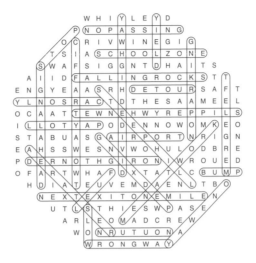

While driving, I saw a sign that said, "Ten Years at the Same Location." Now most businesses would be proud of that achievement, but this was a road crew.

Black Hole #3

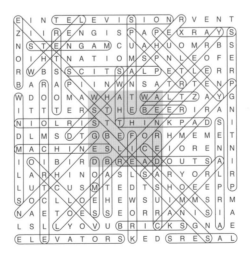

Center quote: "What was the best thing before sliced bread?"
Regular quote: "Inventing is a combination of brains and materials. The more brains you use, the less materials you need." —Charles F. Kettering

Holiday Highlights

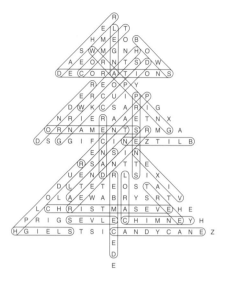

Money is a great Xmas gift. It's always the right size.

As Good As Cold

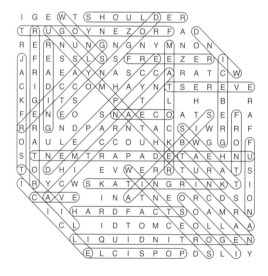

"I get a runny nose, a scratchy throat and an awful cough
every winter," said Tom coldly.

The Play's The Thing

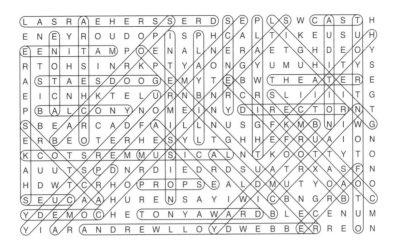

"When you do Shakespeare, they think you must be intelligent because they think you understand what you're saying."
—Helen Mirren

You Wanna A Pisa Me?

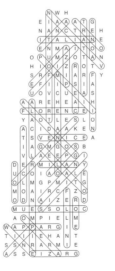

When the moon hits your eye like a big pizza pie, that's a mess.
—to be sung to the tune of "That's Amore."

Op-Position

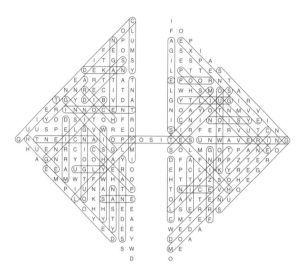

If opposites attract, why do most of us prefer the company of people who think the same way as we do?

People Who Work Outdoors

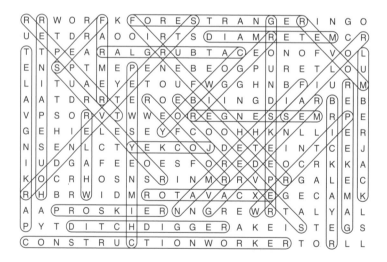

Working outdoors can often be pretty tough, but doing so while collecting fees for crossing a bridge can really take its toll.

Honorable Mention

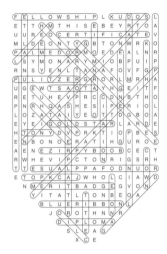

"Let this be your motto—Rely on yourself!
For, whether the prize be a ribbon or throne, The victor is he
who can go it alone!" —John Saxe

Take It Like A Man

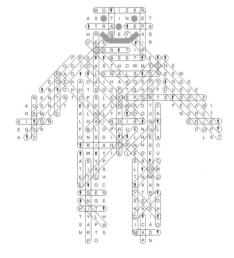

As in the grid, show me a man who has both feet
planted firmly on the ground, and I'll show you a man who
can't get his pants on.

That Really Hits The Spa

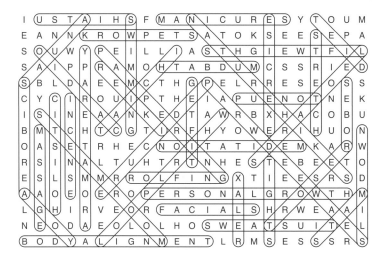

"If you mean to keep as well as possible, the less you think about your health the better." —Oliver Wendell Holmes, Sr.

Abbr.-Ations

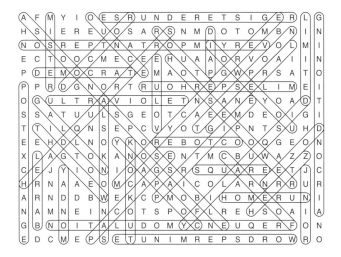

FYI, here's an M.O. to become a V.I.P. ASAP: go to a St. U., get a deg. in econ.; then get an M.B.A., join a co. and become its pres. and CEO.

It's A Mystery To Me!

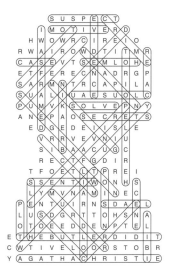

Horror writer Edgar Allan Poe deserves credit for inventing the detective story.

Things That Make You Sweat

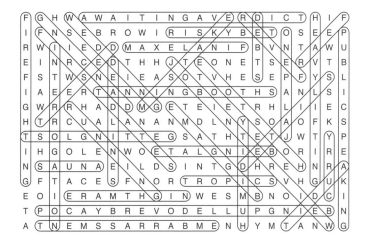

"His brow is wet with honest sweat, He earns whate'er he can, And looks the whole world in the face, For he owes not any man." [from "The Village Blacksmith" by Longfellow]

All Bottled Up

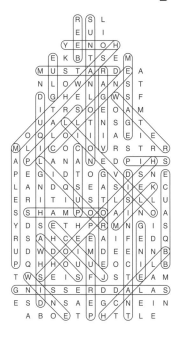

Like a note from a sailor stranded on a desert island, this hidden quote is a message in a bottle.

Making Connections

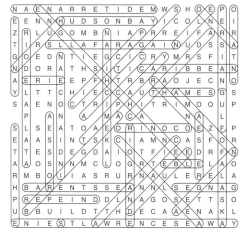

When Colombia refused terms for the project, the U.S. sent troops to Panama, freed it from Colombia's rule, and got to build the canal.

Taking A Stand

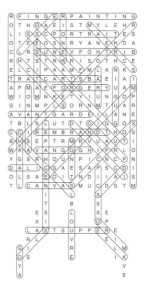

The style, history, and artist help make a painting important,
but to be truly so, Picasso said, it must be expensive.
[Just kidding.]

Taking It Hard

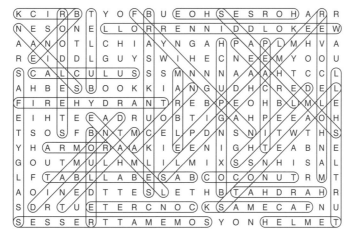

"You are snatching a hard guy when you snatch Bookie Bob ....
I hear the softest thing about him is his front teeth."
—Damon Runyon

Fish Tale

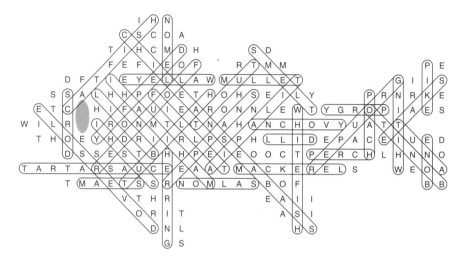

I catch deformed fish. They're the ones with
their heads too close to their tails.

Winding Down

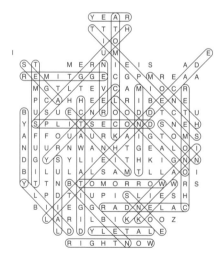

"Time is a great teacher, but unfortunately it kills all its pupils."
—Hector Berlioz

Photo Finish

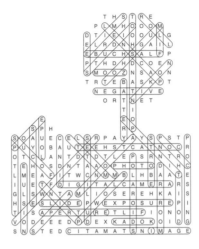

The photograph doesn't restore the past but attests that
what I see has indeed existed. Paraphrase
of a line by Roland Barthes

End So It Goes ...

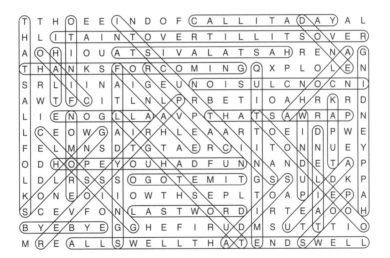

"The end of all our exploring will be to arrive where we started
and know the place for the first time." —T.S. Eliot

Wedding Traditions

```
T O G A   I L I A D   K E G S
O V A L   M A R G E   L A L A
T E L E V I S I O N R E R U N
  R E C I T E S   S E I N E D
      O A R   F I N N
I N S U L T   T A T E   B U S
B E A N I E B A B Y   S E N T
S E T I N   O U I   U T I C A
E D I T   C U P O F S U G A R
N Y E   D U N E   R U D E S T
    B I R D   S I R
A R A F A T   I N E P T L Y
P A U L N E W M A N S E Y E S
O K R A   S H A R D   A R G O
P E A T   T O N E S   L E G S
```

Crossing Safety

```
S M A C K   I B E T   E L S A
L O R R E   M A Y A   M A A S
U N D E R W A T E R   B U L K
S T O P R I G H T T H E R E
H E R E   P E S O   A D A M S
      L E S   E G G   D S T
A G G I E   W Y E   B E L A
L O O K I N T H E M I R R O R
L I R E   I V Y   D A N T E
A T E   B A D   C P A
N A V A L   I S L E   C A N S
  L I S T E N T O R E A S O N
T O D O   S N O W M O B I L E
O N A N   S E W N   N A D I A
P E L E   O R E S   S L E E K
```

Good Sportsmanship

```
P A W N   A B C S   O S C A R
A R I A   N E A P   C H O R D
S O N Y   G A L E   A O R T A
O N E S H O U L D A L W A Y S
    A E R   M A E
P L A Y F A I R L Y   D O C S
L I B E L   R E E S E   P A L
A T A R I   I T A   T E R R A
T U B   N O S I R   H Y A T T
O P A L   W H E N O N E H A S
    O R E   R I B
T H E W I N N I N G C A R D S
H O M E D   A R E A   L E A N
A P I N G   D A R N   L E N O
W I L D E   A N D S   S K E W
```

Striking Changes

```
L O R D   T O J O   S I N E W
E D I E   A N O N   M A U V E
T I P S   W A L T   O G D E N
B U C K I N G T H E T R E N D
E M U   N Y E   E P E E
    R A J   R E D O   E S P N
C A R H O P   D O C S   T A O
B R E A K I N G T H E M O L D
E E N   E L I A   S A B L E S
R A T E   E C R U   R A E
    S H O E   T M C   N B A
K I C K I N G T H E H A B I T
A G A I N   U R A L   D A N L
T O R M E   Y O N D   A S E A
O R E O S   S I T S   M E T S
```

Color Commentary

```
A P O P   R M S     S A C H S
J A K E   H U E D   A B O U T
A I R S   O F M E   D U M M Y
X R A T E D F I L M S   M O N
    E V E     E R A S U R E
A L F R E S C O   I C O N
B A R   R I O T S   K R I S S
B R A T   A R T I S   E S A U
A D I O S   P E R E S   T N N
  D O T S   R E L E A S E S
S T Y L E R S     E E L
H E C   R A W R E C R U I T S
A P A C E   A U N T   M O A T
R E T R O   B E D E   N U D E
P E S O S     D O E   A S A P
```

At's Something Else

```
P E R I O D   C D S   P H A T
A L O N Z O   L E T A L O N E
R A T T A N   O P E R E T T A
A T T O R N E Y I N L A W
D E E   K E G   C O O   A D A
E D N A   G E T   S T E M
  R E D O X   B O P E E P
S E R G E A N T S I N A R M S
C R O O N S   R A C E R
A L A N   S A X   K E M P
M E D   T S P   O H S   M A I
  S T O P I N N O T H I N G
V I T A M I N A   F E I G N S
O V E R S E E R   F E R R E T
W E R E   D R Y   A R T E R Y
```

From C to Shining C

```
E W E L L   T A D   M A C A W
T A L I A   O N E   E R O D E
C H I N M U S I C   G I M M E
    C A N S T   G A S P E D
A M C   S E R B O   T A N S
M A H A L   R A Y K R O C
E Y E L I D S   A A A   T A M
B A N T E R     R O A D I E
A S I   N O T   S T U P I D S
  N O S W E A T   L O S E S
S A B E   S A N E R   C R Y
A L L U R E   T W E A K
S T A V E   C O P A C E T I C
H E N R I   U N O   T E A C H
A R C E D   B E T   S P O K E
```

Nay Sayings

```
G A M A L   A B C D   H Y P E
R E E S E   M U L E T E E R S
A R T I E   E X E C R A T E S
N O H A R M N O F O U L
U S O   A D M   E T H A N
L O D G E R S   N O S H I R T
E L S I E     J E T   D A H
  N O S H O E S N O
A S P   I O N   O F T W O
S E R V I C E   C A T F O O D
K E Y E D   S I N   T E D
  N O P A I N N O G A I N
B E S T L O V E D   F A L S E
R E C E S S I V E   A L U M S
A C I D   E V E R   N A P E S
```

Crossword Answers

Open for Inspection

```
S H E A   M E M O   E S S A Y
T E X T   U R A L   S H A L E
P L A I N S O N G   P A G A N
A L L T O L D   A M A Z O N S
T O T   M I E N   U N A
      C A N D I D C A M E R A
S N E A D   B O K   D I P
H O A R S E R   T Y R A N T S
I R S   A H A   O R A T E
P A T E N T O F F I C E
      J O E   L I N K   P R E
F A D E I N S   B L E S S E D
A L E C S   C L E A R E Y E D
N O L T E   A I R Y   C C V I
G U E S S   M E S S   T H E E
```

Dance Party

```
A L F   B A L S A   B O G
Z O O S   A V I A N   L O L L
T A R A N T E L L A   U S D A
E T C H E S   E L A P S E D
C H E A T   A M M O N I A
      R H O D A   G I N N E D
B A J A   L I Z A   S O O T Y
A R I   B E G U I N E   V A N
G E T T O   E R L E   C A S E
S A T I N S   K E E N E
      E G G H E A D   I R A Q I
B O R E O U T   S K I R U N
A B B R   C H A R L E S T O N
N O U S   K A T I E   E S T E
K E G   S N E A D   Y E R
```

Theatric Antics

```
C A B   A M E N D   S P C A
R B I   A C A C I A   E L A N
A L L   S T A G E S T R U C K
B O O B O O   C H E   N H L
B O X O F F I C E   D O G I E
E M I T   B E S T   M I N T
      F O A L   O R A N G S
      C O L D R E A D I N G
M A I T A I   S M O G
A N N O   E S T A   L A S T
G E N E S   C A S T P A R T Y
I M A   E A R   H U B C A P
C O M I C R E L I E F   A L I
A N O N   T E E O F F   D E N
L E N T   S N O U T   E R G
```

Measuring Up

```
P A L E   M A S K S   D I C E
A D E N   U R I A H   E N I D
S M A L L S C A L E   A N T I
T I P   I S O M E R   D U E T
A T S E A   P O P E
      T R I A L B A L A N C E
H O S E   C R E E   E N D U P
A M A   R E T A R D S   O B I
L A N A I   O R E O   M S E C
F R I C T I O N T A P E
      T R A M   O N T O P
A M I E   A U S T I N   A W E
G A Z A   G R O U N D R U L E
A L E G   E A R N S   O P E N
R I D E   S L E E T   B E T S
```

Crossword Answers

Great!

```
AMBER  SLIP  TOWN
JELLO  TONI  AURA
ANUMBERONE  ITEM
RUE ALUM CAPONE
    WRIT THIEF
UPSIDE CHARISMA
NOUNS PIERS IAN
LOPE MADAT EGGS
ICE FIRES YAHOO
THRILLER HESTON
   DRAKE MOST
FRUITY DELI CAP
LOPS WORLDCLASS
ISEE AHAB AEGIS
PARS YOGA NTEST
```

Movie Marathon

```
EDAM DEMIT META
AYLA AMISH ADIN
REDSKYATMORNING
PROHIBIT ROSTER
    WELSH MESSY
MADRID OWES
EXIT CORER GIS
SEVENDAYSTONOON
ALE AISLE ONTO
   EPEE GEWGAW
PAPAL DUMAS
ABASES TEMPLATE
BLUESINTHENIGHT
SELL ABETS AREA
TRIS MARAT RAMS
```

Crossroads

```
OWLS ASPIC CARS
NEIL UTICA ATOP
EASYSTREET TADA
ART HOOT STREW
  EVE PYGMALION
OMNIBUS RAGE
MESCAL FAX DRYS
EMIT SCIFI REEK
NONO TIX MAITAI
  RHEA HARVARD
TOKYOROSE GEL
IFOLD ALTO IFS
RAJA PAPERTRAIL
EGAN CHINO OTTO
DEKE SADAT ZEST
```

Old Wine, New Bottles

```
BACCHUS AFT CBC
ACHIEST LEATHER
BRANFORDMARSALA
BONET EAST ARID
LSTS HEM ARIEL
ESS MOP HES EVE
   ZOO MANTISES
  SANTACLARET
SUPPRESS BAR
TKO ORK FLY SIP
AROSE DOE VENA
RANT AMER WEILL
LIFEISACABERNET
INERTIA YESDEAR
TED TAM SATISFY
```

Easy Does It

Dollar Daze

Old Testament Revisited

Knice Knames

Crossword Answers

Giver of Gifts ...

```
A R C A R O ■ ■ G E L A T I N
L O U S E U P ■ A M E R I C A
F A T H E R C H R I S T M A S
A R E A S ■ S O R T ■ S E N T
■ ■ ■ R E T ■ R E S T ■ ■ ■
L A M P ■ R E N T ■ R A P I D
A G O ■ P A G E ■ V E N I C E
P E T E R C O T T O N T A I L
I N T U I T ■ S O L D ■ N N E
S T O R M ■ G N A T ■ T O G S
■ ■ ■ A C R E ■ A T E ■ ■ ■
S O H O ■ L O S S ■ E M O T E
T H E G R E A T P U M P K I N
A I R L I F T ■ A P P L I E D
R O D E N T S ■ S T E E D S
```

A Gnawing Issue

```
D A N A ■ A S S I S I ■ B O Z
I R I S ■ P A L L E T ■ E G O
G O P H E R B A L L S ■ A L L
I M P E L ■ O P E L ■ U V E A
N A Y ■ V E T ■ R E E S E ■
■ ■ D I C E ■ C L E R K S
C O M E S O U T ■ K I D D I E
A M O S ■ R U T ■ C A K E
T A U T E R ■ B E N J A M I N
O N S I T E ■ L E E R ■ ■
■ E N A C T L E W ■ A D D
C O P Y ■ L U S T ■ E A G E R
A V A ■ R A T T A I L F I L E
R I D ■ V I T A L E ■ A L E S
A D S ■ S M I T E S ■ R E D S
```

Mixed-Up April Fools

```
A R O S E ■ L E W D ■ E F T S
M A P L E ■ A L O E ■ A L E E
F R A I L S L O O P ■ G O R E
M E L T ■ L A P F O R L O I S
■ ■ S T O W E ■ S E E R ■
G A S K E T ■ L I V ■ P O E
A S P I N ■ S H U T ■ B A L L
M O O R ■ R E E K S ■ R I L E
U N I T ■ E A S E ■ R E L I C
T E L ■ D D T ■ T E A S E T
■ F A I N ■ P O O L S ■
P O L L S O F A I R ■ T A R A
H O O T ■ S A I L O R F L O P
E Z R A ■ E D G E ■ D E F O E
W E A R ■ D E E D ■ A D A M S
```

Spooked

```
M A S T ■ J A D E D ■ F L E W
A R C O ■ E C O N O ■ R O L E
H O R R O R S H O W ■ I L K S
A M A T I S ■ ■ S N I G L E T
L A M E N E S S ■ E T H ■
■ ■ K Y L E ■ A S T R O S
A M A S S ■ E A R S ■ W A N E
C A L C ■ R E P O T ■ I N C A
A S I A ■ A P O P ■ E G G E R
T H I R S T ■ R E C D ■ ■
■ E A T ■ T R A S H C A N
R E A C T E D ■ R E R O S E
E M I R ■ D R E A D L O C K S
F I D O ■ O N R Y E ■ S K I T
S T E W ■ N O S E D ■ S S N S
```

Crossword Answers

Sandwich Islands Recruits

Glee Club

Tops

You Can't Miss It!

Seeing Red

```
L I N T   A B U T   S T O R M
O N C E   T A P E   T O M E I
S C A R L E T T A N A G E R S
S H A M E     E C O N   G U T
      T A L M U D   Z A N Y
R U B Y S L I P P E R S
O R E O   I T O     B A S E D
S E A G A T E   S E I Z U R E
S Y R U P     N O R   S E G A
      R O S E O F S H A R O N
P E N T   O R N A T E
A M O   H O R S     R E P R O
C A R D I N A L V I R T U E S
T I M E S   T I E D   O R A L
S L A B S   A P E S   N E M O
```

Trifecta

```
B R A G A   J U T S   O M I T
L A M A S   E T O N   H E R O
O V E R T   S A T I R I C A L
W I N N I E T H E P O O H
I N D E N T   M E D   A R C
T E S T   U S A   R E I N I N
        I D O L S   O R I O N
  P L A C E B O E F F E C T
B R O T H   S H E L F
R E V E A L   A P U   A S T I
R Y E   B A G   F A T T E N
    S H O W E R O F S T A R S
B L O O D F E U D   W I L E E
Y E N S   U S E D   A L I S T
E D G E   L E S S   N A N A S
```

Suits Me!

```
L E F T   A P S E   C L I P S
U C L A   T R E E   L O R E N
C L U B S T E A K   O V E R A
C A T S K I L L   U S E D U P
I T E   E L I   A N E T
    D I A M O N D S T A T E
L A T I N   U N I T   C I A
E X A M   D A T E D   M I N T
A L T   S O R E   A I D E S
H E A R T S T R I N G S
    A L E S   N E A   B E A
M A T Z O S   S T E T S O N S
I S U Z U   S P A D E W O R K
M I L L I   P E K E   A L O E
I S L E S   A W E D   B A L D
```

Four-In-Hand

```
A P S E   D R O S S   M A R C
B A A L   R E N E E   E V E R
U R N S   W H I T E S N A K E
  A G A T H A C H R I S T I E
C L U   R O B E   N A A C P
A L I B I     U S A   R K O
P A N A M A H A T T I E
O X E N   T I B I A   U S S R
    G R A V E L G E R T I E
A P T   A D E   C O R G I
R O O S T   L O C H   A N N
R O O T I E K A Z O O T I E
A R T O O D E T O O   E N D S
N E O N   G L E N N   N E I L
T R O Y   Y P R E S   D R N O
```

Role Reversal

I	R	A	S		M	A	L	I		B	A	S	H
N	E	R	O		I	G	O	R		A	L	T	O
E	V	E	R		M	I	C	A		S	L	I	P
V	E	N	T	R	I	L	O	Q	U	I	S	M	
E	R	A		I	C	E			S	E	T	U	P
R	E	S	T	S			R	O	N		A	L	I
			W	E	N	T	I	N		P	R	I	X
	F	O	R	D	U	M	M	I	E	S			
E	G	O	S		A	B	S	E	N	T			
T	E	L		A	K	A			H	E	A	R	T
A	R	L	E	N		R	B	I		M	A	O	
	M	O	R	T	I	M	E	R	S	N	E	R	D
P	A	W	N		N	O	L	O		E	L	I	A
O	N	U	S		F	R	A	N		T	I	N	T
W	E	P	T		O	N	Y	X		S	A	G	E

Closed-Door Policy

B	A	D	E		D	R	E	A	D		A	C	T	S
E	T	A	L		E	A	G	L	E		L	O	R	E
L	O	C	K	O	F	H	A	I	R		O	N	I	T
O	N	R	E	C	O	R	D			D	E	F	A	T
N	C	O		T	E	A		P	O	I		E	L	L
G	E	N	O	A		H	A	R	M	S		T	R	I
			A	V	E		M	I	A		S	T	U	N
B	O	L	T	O	F	L	I	G	H	T	N	I	N	G
U	P	I	S		R	I	N		A	H	A			
G	E	N		D	E	M	O	B		E	G	R	E	T
A	R	E		U	M	P		U	H	F		O	V	O
B	A	S	T	E			P	R	O	T	O	C	O	L
O	N	M	E		C	H	A	I	N	S	M	O	K	E
O	D	E	S		D	E	R	E	K		I	C	E	D
S	I	N	S		S	E	E	D	S		T	O	D	O

They Called My Number

A	L	P	S		C	L	A	R	A		B	O	D	E
V	I	A	L		L	I	K	E	S		A	L	E	X
E	L	L	A		A	M	I	G	O		I	D	L	E
	L	O	V	E	W	O	N	A	N	O	T	H	E	R
T	I	M	E	R			L	E	X		A	T	T	
U	P	I		E	R	A	S	E		B	I	T	E	S
B	U	N	S		O	U	T		P	O	D			
	T	O	O	E	D	G	E	D	S	W	O	R	D	
	A	R	E		V	I	A		L	E	O	N		
O	H	A	R	A		J	E	S	T	S		A	B	U
N	O	G		T	E	E			O	G	D	E	N	
F	O	R	E	O	N	T	H	E	F	L	O	O	R	
O	P	E	N		O	L	I	V	E		O	N	M	E
O	L	E	O		L	A	K	E	S		F	L	A	K
T	A	D	S		A	G	E	N	T		S	Y	N	E

Wild Animals

R	A	F	T	E	R		S	T	U	B		F	A	T
O	T	O	O	L	E		L	O	S	E	T	I	M	E
T	A	R	M	A	C		E	Y	E	L	I	N	E	R
	G	E	N	T	L	E	A	S	A	B	A	L	M	
H	O	E		O	A	K				E	L	I	E	
A	N	T	W	E	R	P		L	I	P	R	E	A	D
I	C	I	E	R			B	O	L	A				
G	E	T	T	I	N	G	O	N	E	S	T	O	G	A
		C	O	A	X				T	O	W	E	L	
R	I	P	S	A	W	S		S	C	A	N	N	E	D
A	M	E	N			S	E	A			I	R	A	
S	P	R	I	N	G	C	H	E	C	K	I	N		
C	A	M	P	O	R	E	E		T	A	N	G	O	S
A	L	I	E	N	A	T	E		U	N	F	U	R	L
L	E	T		O	M	E	N		S	T	O	P	B	Y

Crossword Answers

All Saints Day

```
A R C E D ■ A C E T O ■ S T A
S A R G E ■ N A D I A ■ T A U
S T A G E S T R U C K ■ R U G
T E N S P E E D ■ T R I P E ■
■ ■ E N S ■ S C R A P E R ■ ■
A B S E N T ■ P A R E N S ■ ■
M A T E D ■ P A R E E ■ T E D
I R A N ■ L A L A W ■ P E A R
D E N ■ E A T E N ■ W E A V E
■ ■ D E N V E R ■ P E R K E D
R E S U M E S ■ M A T ■ ■ ■ ■
E X T R A ■ D E C R E A S E ■
U P I ■ S T A R S T U D D E D
N E L ■ S A G A S ■ S I Z E D
E L L ■ E N E M Y ■ T E E N Y
```

Ethane Allen's Dictionary

```
M C G E E ■ R E N T A ■ C P R
O R A T E ■ O R I O N ■ H I T
H U M A N E S A C R I F I C E
A S I S ■ V I S E ■ T U C K ■
I O N ■ F E E ■ D A R K E N ■
R E G A L ■ E G O ■ S P R Y ■
■ ■ L O U G R A N T ■ E E C ■
■ U R B A N E R E N E W A L ■
D N A ■ T I R E L E S S ■ ■ ■
A R M S ■ T E D ■ T W A N G ■
N A P L E S ■ M A Y ■ T E L ■
V A I N ■ K I E V ■ T H A I ■
G E R M A N E S H E P H E R D
A L T ■ C R E P T ■ D O N E E
M S S ■ T A N Y A ■ Q U A D S
```

Pay Up!

```
F O C I ■ N E A T O ■ S E W S
A C A D ■ A T R I A ■ U N I T
R U B S ■ C H E C K L I S T S
O L A ■ B R E A ■ S A T I N ■
F A R E W E L L S ■ P E L E E
F R E D A ■ ■ P A D ■ E S S ■
■ S T I N E ■ P I N ■ A S S T
■ ■ T A B H U N T E R ■ ■ ■
M O H S ■ B A N ■ S I T U P ■
A N A ■ E S L ■ ■ G O N O W
R E M I X ■ T O L L H O U S E
■ S E D A N ■ C O A T ■ S T A
B I L L M O Y E R S ■ J U A N
O D I E ■ D E A R E ■ R A G E
D E N S ■ S A N E R ■ S L E D
```

Race Relations

```
A G E S ■ D A B S ■ I N R E D
L O W E ■ A L O T ■ N E A R S
A L E X ■ M A Y A ■ S A D A T
M A R I O A N D R E T T I ■ ■
O N S E T S ■ E N E ■ A S H ■
■ ■ R I C H A R D P E T T Y
A L I ■ S U I T ■ ■ S W O R E
R O N A ■ S T A I R ■ E R I N
A G A P E ■ ■ L I E D ■ S P A
B O B B Y A L L I S O N ■ ■
S S A ■ E V E ■ ■ E T U D E S
■ ■ D A L E E A R N H A R D T
B O W I E ■ R I O T ■ N O S E
O R A L S ■ E R L E ■ C L E M
A B Y S S ■ D Y E D ■ E L L S
```

Crossword Answers 287

Crossword Answers

Rated PG

Hitting for the Cycle

Get Packing!

In the Black

Off to a Rocky Start

```
DESCENT   PASSION
ICEOVER   ARIADNE
SHAKEDOWNCRUISE
HOLE   POOH  COED
     MAHER  BETTY
DUALITY   AFAR
ATREST  AMOS   POT
RATTLESNAKEBITE
THY  ASHY  KHAKIS
     KITE  HEIRESS
CAWED  EBERT
ATOP  APER   THIS
ROLLONDEODORANT
INFERNO   INDULGE
BEERKEG   CASELAW
```

It's (No Longer) Element-ary

```
SLIPS  SPEW   BACH
HANOI  TETE   ALAI
ABASE  EARTHTONE
FONTS   REBUTTED
TRESTLE    ATL
       AIRFORCEONE
WAD  SERUM   HABIT
ALEC   SAGAN  XENA
ITALO  TINES   YES
FIRESTATION
     ACE   SNICKER
SERVANTS    GHANA
WATERPOLO   LORAN
AVER  IDOL   ERECT
BESS  NOPE   TENTS
```

Captive-ating Leaders

```
URGE   STUB  AGLOW
TORT   PISA  TRIPE
OLIO   UTES  TILTS
PENNYMARSHALL
IOC  EONS  OBLIGE
ASHCAN   FLO   PIG
    BRIGHAMYOUNG
EIRE   EAR    STAY
STIRLINGMOSS
AID  ACE  FMAJOR
UNIQUE  SAFE   APE
  CANDICEBERGEN
FOUND   RAGE  AUNT
TILDE   ARIA  MATE
CLEAR   NEST  PROD
```

Don't Be Greedy

```
ABC   TROUPE  FADS
BRO   HOOTAT  AREA
YOUCANHAVEITALL
SCRAM  SHE   BEGAT
MATTED    REDONE
ADE  SEE  AER  NOD
LESS   EXPLAIN
    YOUJUSTCANT
    OBADIAH  WALK
NOW  AYE  REX  POE
OCEANS    DREDGE
STAGG  ZIP   AGAIN
HAVEITALLATONCE
OVER   ENSURE  CAR
WEDS   TEAMED  ELS
```

Cheese It

R	U	G	S	█	S	I	C	E	M	█	B	O	A	R
I	N	R	E	█	A	N	A	M	E	█	U	R	D	U
S	H	A	D	E	O	F	R	E	D	█	M	E	E	T
K	I	T	E	D	█	█	T	R	E	E	M	O	S	S
S	P	A	R	S	E	R	█	G	A	Z	E	█	█	█
█	█	█	E	R	A	S	E	█	I	D	E	A	S	█
S	U	N	B	L	O	C	K	█	W	O	O	L	L	Y
O	P	I	E	█	D	E	E	R	E	█	U	L	A	N
L	U	N	A	T	E	█	W	E	B	S	T	E	R	S
S	P	A	T	E	█	A	S	S	E	T	█	█	█	█
█	█	B	R	E	L	█	T	R	A	C	T	O	R	█
S	T	E	A	M	S	U	P	█	█	S	H	A	L	E
H	A	R	D	█	S	M	A	L	L	H	O	U	S	E
E	M	I	L	█	A	N	I	S	E	█	S	P	E	D
D	E	N	Y	█	Y	A	L	T	A	█	E	E	N	Y

The Yoke's on Us

S	C	A	B	█	S	A	D	A	T	█	A	C	D	C
L	O	L	L	█	T	R	I	B	E	█	R	H	E	A
A	P	P	O	M	A	T	T	O	X	█	T	I	L	L
M	A	S	O	N	█	█	R	A	D	I	C	A	L	█
█	█	█	P	O	G	█	S	T	N	I	C	K	█	█
R	E	C	S	█	A	B	A	█	S	O	L	E	M	N
I	C	H	█	█	L	A	V	A	█	R	E	N	E	E
G	O	A	T	█	A	B	A	B	A	█	S	P	E	W
O	N	T	H	E	█	A	L	A	S	█	█	O	S	E
R	O	T	U	N	D	█	A	B	E	█	A	X	E	L
█	█	E	N	T	E	R	S	█	A	M	P	█	█	█
C	O	R	D	O	B	A	█	█	A	L	O	N	E	█
A	B	B	E	█	U	N	O	R	T	H	O	D	O	X
D	O	O	R	█	T	O	R	A	H	█	M	O	N	A
S	E	X	Y	█	S	N	O	W	Y	█	B	R	O	M

Hue Asked for It

S	O	R	T	█	B	O	A	T	█	T	A	P	E	R
H	A	I	R	█	A	N	T	I	█	E	V	A	D	E
E	T	T	A	█	S	I	T	E	█	P	A	N	G	S
S	H	A	D	E	S	O	U	R	C	E	█	D	E	E
█	█	█	E	T	O	N	█	█	R	E	P	A	S	T
M	A	R	S	H	█	█	A	M	A	S	S	█	█	█
A	L	I	█	E	S	P	R	I	T	█	S	P	A	T
C	O	L	O	R	C	O	M	M	E	N	T	A	R	Y
S	E	E	K	█	O	N	E	I	D	A	█	G	I	N
█	█	█	R	A	T	E	D	█	█	F	R	O	Z	E
P	E	D	A	N	T	█	█	I	N	T	O	█	█	█
I	R	A	█	T	O	N	E	D	I	A	L	I	N	G
P	A	R	C	H	█	O	N	I	T	█	L	O	U	T
E	S	T	E	E	█	O	D	O	R	█	U	N	T	O
R	E	H	E	M	█	N	O	M	O	█	P	A	S	S

The Pits

T	R	E	E	S	█	A	G	A	R	█	J	A	P	E
R	I	L	L	E	█	S	A	B	E	█	E	T	A	S
O	L	I	V	E	T	H	R	O	W	A	W	A	Y	S
D	E	S	I	R	E	█	B	R	A	M	█	L	E	A
█	█	█	S	E	R	F	█	T	R	O	L	L	E	Y
M	T	V	█	D	E	L	T	█	D	U	O	█	█	█
B	O	E	R	█	S	E	E	D	█	R	O	S	I	E
A	U	T	O	R	A	C	E	R	S	S	T	O	P	S
S	T	O	W	E	█	K	N	O	T	█	S	O	S	A
█	█	█	A	M	A	█	Y	O	R	E	█	N	O	U
T	O	N	N	A	G	E	█	P	E	L	L	█	█	█
O	P	A	█	K	A	N	T	█	S	P	O	N	G	E
O	R	C	H	E	S	T	R	A	S	A	R	E	A	S
L	A	R	A	█	S	E	E	M	█	S	E	A	R	S
S	H	E	D	█	I	R	K	S	█	O	N	R	Y	E

Ate Times Eight

```
S C O L D   A C L U   S I A M
A L G A E   R O A R   U R S A
G U L P E D D O W N   P R E S
S E E P   E E L S   A P E A K
      E D E N   U R G E S
V O I D E D   D I N E D O N
A N N U L S   A T A D   L A B
S T O P   S I S   D U D E
T A C   P O P S   G R E T E L
  P U T A W A Y   R E V E R T
    L A T E R   H A L O
S M A S H   E R I C   U N T O
P U T T   B R O K E B R E A D
A L E E   R I T E   S E E T O
R E D D   A B C S   A D D E R
```

Kick Me!

```
D U B S   D A S H   A B B O T
I N R E   A L L A   B R I N E
S L A W   Z O O T   R U B I K
C I G A R E T T E H A B I T
S T A R E       D A D A
    D H I N G   D E K A L B
A W E   A F I R E   E R I E
M I N I B I K E S T A R T E R
E R I C   E A S E L   S U N
R Y D E L L   T O D A Y
    C O A T   M E N U S
  K A R A T E O P P O N E N T
B E G E T   X R A Y   T R I O
O P R A H   T E A L   A V O N
A T I M E   S O R E   S Y N E
```

Some Wear Out There

```
A D M I R E D   A C A C I A S
I R O N O R E   S O L U B L E
R E T R A I N   P R E T E E N
S A T U R N S R I N G S
  M O I   E N E   I M P
    N O N O S   R A C E R S
R E D S H I F T   L E D I N
U F O   A L F   M E G   I M A
F R I E R   P O L A R C A P
F E N N E L   A D I E U
  M G M   E T A   B S A
    A S T E R O I D B E L T
D E N S E S T   B R A I L L E
A G E S A G O   O A R S M E N
M O V E S O N   E N C H A N T
```

Four of a Kind

```
N O F A T   M A K E S   H A M
A V O I R   E L E N A   I R E
T O R R E   H E A D F I R S T
  S P A R T A   S E N S E
H E A R T L A N D   G U N N
A L L O Y S   A S C E T I C
I D E O   T O N A L   E C O
  F O U R H C L U B
A D S   F R A M E   A S T I
P R E F A B S   D A N N O N
T Y R O   H A N D S D O W N
  C R O A T   S E E S A W
H E A L T H S P A   A N I T A
B L T   T R A I T   I N N E R
O L E   N O T C H   L A G E R
```

Crossword Answers

All in the Family

```
BLOW  VETS  ABODE
RIPE  ODIE  FRIED
ELAL  CAFE  RINSE
WILLIAMFRIEDKIN
      ELLE    MSG
WALDO SOUTHEAST
AROUSE CPO    SHE
RUMPELSTILTSKIN
NBA    MOE DINERO
SANSDOUTE  AUDEN
      EAR   VERB
JEANNETTERANKIN
AZTEC OHNO   OUZO
CROCI BAUD   SHOE
KAZAN YIPE   ENDS
```

Let There Be Light Humor

```
BAT  ASSAIL  ACME
ELO  MEANIE  PLAY
LAB  ONLYIFWEARE
UMA  USE    TORSI
SECURE MAYO   SAY
HICS   LIP   EINE
INOURBELIEFSCAN
       ROUT EMUP
WESEETHECOMICAL
SPAR   ALE   ERMA
WIL WALK SIDEOF
  TITAN  FUN  ARI
THEUNIVERSE   MOT
SENT  TINEAR  EST
ETTU  ACCENT  DOE
```

Reel Fruit Flavor

```
AKITA  PEPUP   SPA
RAWLS  OZONE   AUX
CLOCKWORKORANGE
HEN  FORAY   FIDEL
     NOR    AUDITS
WATERMELONMAN
ANAT  ROUTE    ICY
SKI  CHAPTER   SEE
PAL  HOSED    ETNA
  GRAPESOFWRATH
ELAINE    AHA
SETAT  CAIRO   AWE
THELEMONDROPKID
EAR  RONNY   SHINY
SRS  STEAL   HINES
```

Roll Call

```
OCTAL  AFEW    STAR
NIOBE  KANE    CUBE
ERNST  EGGBARREL
URGE  ELI    BRANDY
PIANOBANK      APT
      TUB   ALLEARS
OGRES  SKYE    BOA
SWEETSTEAMJELLY
HEP   HAWK   EPEES
ANTARES       PEI
  ILA  HONORDRUM
OFLATE  ZOO    EENY
KAISERPAY    IMAGE
ISAK  GERE   DICEY
ETNA  OAKS   OCHRE
```

Location, Location, Location!

One at a Time

Spice World

Down the Line

Scents You Asked

Z	A	G	■	G	U	T	■	M	D	S	■	C	H	I
O	N	E	A	R	T	H	■	I	R	O	N	O	U	T
O	V	E	R	A	W	E	■	D	O	L	O	R	E	S
M	I	N	T	S	O	N	E	S	W	O	R	D	S	■
S	L	A	Y	S	■	■	Q	T	S	■	■	■		
■	■	■	Y	A	L	U	■	Y	E	S	M	A	N	
S	O	P	S	■	P	A	A	R	■	R	H	I	N	E
T	H	E	L	I	T	T	L	E	P	R	I	N	T	S
A	N	W	A	R	■	E	S	A	U	■	V	E	S	T
G	O	S	P	E	L	■	I	M	P	S				
■	■	■	E	G	G	■	■	A	N	I	S	E		
■	S	P	O	R	T	I	N	G	C	H	A	N	T	S
B	A	R	R	O	O	M	■	R	O	A	C	H	E	S
S	P	E	E	D	U	P	■	A	I	R	L	I	N	E
A	S	P	■	S	T	Y	■	F	L	A	■	S	O	X

Sorry

I	S	L	E	■	P	A	C	T	■	A	C	R	I	D
N	E	I	L	■	A	C	H	E	■	M	O	O	R	E
C	A	K	E	■	S	L	A	M	■	O	R	L	O	N
I	B	E	G	Y	O	U	R	P	A	R	D	O	N	■
T	A	N	Y	A	■	■	T	R	A	■	D	A	Y	
E	S	E	■	H	U	G	E	■	A	L	L	E	G	E
S	S	W	■	O	P	I	N	E	■	■	E	X	E	S
■	■	■	B	O	A	R	D	G	A	M	E	■		
A	R	E	A	■	■	D	U	A	N	E	■	C	O	S
C	O	N	D	O	R	■	E	D	N	A	■	E	P	A
E	U	R	■	L	E	D	■	■	N	A	D	E	R	
■	G	O	O	D	F	O	R	N	O	T	H	I	N	G
T	H	U	M	P	■	Z	O	O	M	■	E	L	B	E
B	I	T	E	R	■	E	L	S	A	■	A	L	A	N
S	T	E	N	O	■	N	E	E	R	■	D	A	R	T

Tie It, You'll Like It

A	D	A	M	■	U	N	C	A	P	■	A	G	E	D
N	A	T	O	■	S	A	U	D	I	■	P	O	L	E
K	N	O	W	I	N	G	T	H	E	R	O	P	E	S
L	I	N	E	D	■	S	E	E	T	O	■	L	A	I
E	S	C	R	O	W	■	■	R	I	D	■	A	N	S
S	H	E	■	O	L	S	E	N	■	S	C	O	T	
■	■	■	H	A	V	O	C	■	■	T	I	E	R	S
■	N	I	C	E	T	H	R	E	A	D	S	■		
C	L	O	N	E	■	■	M	O	V	I	E	■		
L	E	F	T	■	G	N	O	M	E	■	P	E	R	
A	I	R	■	P	R	O	■	R	E	G	I	N	A	
P	S	I	■	A	O	R	T	A	■	R	U	N	I	N
P	U	L	L	S	O	M	E	S	T	R	I	N	G	S
E	R	L	E	■	M	A	L	E	S	■	D	E	M	O
D	E	S	I	■	S	N	E	A	K	■	E	D	A	M

You Wanna Piece O' Me?

S	H	A	F	T	S	■	H	E	R	S	H	E	Y	
T	E	N	U	R	E	D	■	A	T	H	E	A	R	T
A	R	I	Z	O	N	A	■	S	T	E	E	P	E	D
L	O	S	E	Y	O	U	R	H	E	A	D	■		
E	N	E	■	R	B	I	■	■	S	E	A	M		
■	■	■	P	G	A	■	P	E	A	S	■	P	T	A
C	A	N	A	L	■	L	E	N	D	A	N	E	A	R
I	R	O	N	O	R	E	■	I	S	R	A	E	L	I
G	I	V	E	A	H	A	N	D	■	A	I	S	L	E
A	S	A	■	T	O	R	E	■	N	H	L			
R	E	E	L	■	■	A	D	O	■	M	B	A		
■	■	■	O	F	F	E	R	Y	O	U	R	A	R	M
F	O	R	G	O	O	D	■	E	S	T	O	N	I	A
I	N	F	O	R	C	E	■	S	E	A	S	O	N	S
R	E	D	S	K	I	N	■	S	H	A	R	K	S	

Crossword Answers

K Rations

```
BEARD   MAWR   JOAD
ALGAE   ASYE   APIE
BOOKKEEPER    CEDE
ANGELA  STOCKCAR
    SECT   HOOK
CAP   RHOS   FONZIE
AROCK   WAN   TIARA
BILL   EWE   FIAT
OSKAR   DEG   VERNE
TEARUP   DERN   EIN
    KNOW   VIEW
DICKERED   SCARNE
ROLE   KNOCKKNEED
ANON   EDIE   EDGED
WATT   RYNE   DADDY
```

Fast Food, Hasty Reading

```
CLIP   ABBOT   DABS
LENO   TEETH   IRED
ITTO   SEETO   OPTS
QUARTERPOUNDER
UPC   WAYS   REGAL
ESTEE    CSA   GYP
   TROTOUT   VIES
   WHOPPERJUNIOR
BRAN   AEROBIC
OER   ELM    VERDI
ANDRE   SAME   HEN
   CHICKENTENDERS
WHEN   AQABA   ESAU
PEAK   RURAL   MUIR
ADDS   TILTS   ISLE
```

Drink Up!

```
HADUP   NADIR   GPS
OZONE   ABONE   EAT
SUNDAYPUNCH   ONO
TREETOPS   HEARER
SEER   RYE   WANGLE
   GEE   LOTTE
MAJOR   SAAR   SALT
ALE   GRANDMA   DEE
TARS   EGAD   AGENT
   KNAVE   CAR
BEWARE   ABE   ASPS
ONAPAR   PEDANTIC
OTT   BEETLEJUICE
ZEE   INTEL   ALLAN
ERR   ADORE   REESE
```

Retirement Speech

```
ANWAR   CORAL   AAH
SERVO   ERNIE   IDO
SWEETDREAMS   RON
USSR   REL   STABLE
ACTS   EASY   NAPS
GALE   SLEEPTIGHT
ESE   ESS   TROT
STRATA   INARUT
   NAGS   SCI   ENE
DONTLETTHE   BABA
OLEO   PART   ALEC
SIGNED   BOA   UTAH
AVA   BEDBUGSBITE
GET   BAYED   ELMER
ERE   SLEDS   TEENS
```

Around & About

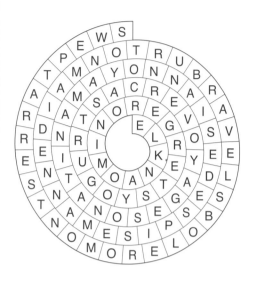

Jigsaw

Crossing Paths

Round The Bend

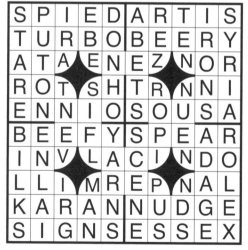

Twisted Crossword Answers

Catching Some Z's

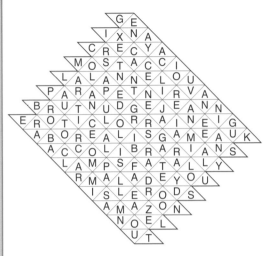

Tops & Bottoms

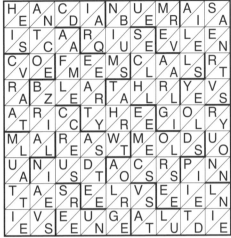

Pathfinder

1E ZIGZAG	**13S** MEGATONS
2E RENEWAL	**14E** CHAGRINED
3E DELAWARE	**15W** SHAG
4E DEREGULATED	**16S** QUARREL
4S DE NIRO	**17N** OXIDE
5N ENERGIZER	**18N** PERKS
6S OGDEN	**19N** SOCKS
7N OGRE	**20N** PAPER
8N GOUGER	**21N** CITED
9N ARNAZ	**21S** CIE
10W YARN	**22S** LIT
11N MYRA	**23S** BASIL
11S MESQUITE	**24W** EL PASO
12S NIXONS	**25W** TIERRA
13N METAL	**26E** SABOTAGE

Marching Bands

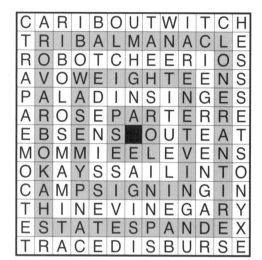

Around & About

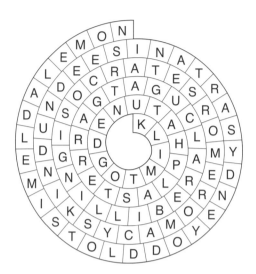

Jigsaw

Crossing Paths

Pathfinder

1E DETOURING		**15S** STORMY	
2E RAMS		**16N** ALAMO	
3E NAP		**17N** SYMBOLIZE	
4E RED		**18S** PAVLOVA	
5S CAJUN		**19N** VEAL	
5S CARINA		**20N** ODOR	
6S OUTSMARTED		**21W** SLEPT	
7S JUNGLE GYM		**22N** VAPOR	
8S TOMMY		**23S** RAPPEL	
9S LOBE		**24N** FLOOD	
10S RAMBLE		**25W** PARROTS	
11W MARZIPAN		**26E** TRANSVESTITE	
12N BLEEDER		**27E** TRAVEL	
13S TITLE		**28E** OFF	
14E GEL		**29W** FORTRAN	

Intersections

Tops & Bottoms

Catching Some Z's

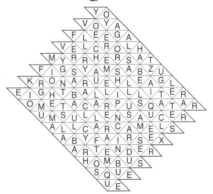

Crushword

BE	AVER			PE	COR	INO		LI	STING
ET	AGE	RES		EN	GI	NES		BE	ERS
		PO	UND	ING		PR	OPE	RTY	
CO	LA	ND	ERS		CH	IME	RAS		
INCI	TER		TOOD	LE	OOS		TAR	TA	RE
DE	AL	TIN		VIT	ES	SE		NA	VEL
		FO	RESE	ES		RE	FRI	GER	ATION
	SIM	IL	AR		BER	NADE	TTE		
RAY	ONS		CH	AR	GER		RED	GRA	VES
MOND	AYS		ES	IAS	ON			HAM	PERS

Marching Bands

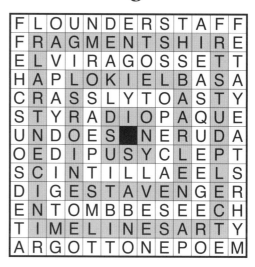

F	L	O	U	N	D	E	R	S	T	A	F	F
F	R	A	G	M	E	N	T	S	H	I	R	E
E	L	V	I	R	A	G	O	S	S	E	T	T
H	A	P	L	O	K	I	E	L	B	A	S	A
C	R	A	S	S	L	Y	T	O	A	S	T	Y
S	T	Y	R	A	D	I	O	P	A	Q	U	E
U	N	D	O	E	S		N	E	R	U	D	A
O	E	D	I	P	U	S	Y	C	L	E	P	T
S	C	I	N	T	I	L	L	A	E	E	L	S
D	I	G	E	S	T	A	V	E	N	G	E	R
E	N	T	O	M	B	B	E	S	E	E	C	H
T	I	M	E	L	I	N	E	S	A	R	T	Y
A	R	G	O	T	T	O	N	E	P	O	E	M

Jigsaw

Pathfinder

1S	TWISTER	15N	BERETS
2W	OUTWIT	16S	OLEO
3E	ORDER	17W	MALLETS
4N	WOK	18N	RIDE
4S	WEB SITES	19S	RENOWN
5S	BLUE BAYOU	20N	AMATI
6S	UNITED	20S	ANWAR
	NATIONS	21W	CRABBE
7S	OTTOMAN	22W	MARINATE
8W	HOLBROOK	23S	LATER
9W	SHRED	24N	ROAMER
10N	STAY	25S	ZEN
11S	SIT-IN	26S	SOS
12S	TELL	27S	ARSON
13N	MOTT	28W	FETAL
14S	BARCELONA	28E	FEZ

Pathfinder

1E LABYRINTHINE	**15S** DELFTS	
2E KARACHI	**16W** MR. HYDE	
3S JAPER	**17W** ACME	
3S JAVA	**18S** STUB	
4S RETHINK	**19N** SCAR	
5S INVOKE	**19S** SUCKER	
6N SERRY	**20E** CURARE	
7N RAKER	**21S** FABER	
8E VERBAL	**22S** TAMPA	
9S APATHY	**23S** RUB	
10N OVERACHIEVER	**24W** BAFFLED	
11N ARES	**25W** REBUKE	
11S AVENGER	**26W** MAT	
12W PREP	**27N** PARANOIA	
13N TAPPED	**28E** BURN	
14S NGAIO		

Tops & Bottoms

Weaving

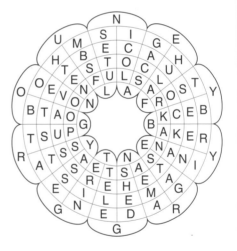

Crushword

PER	TH		INF	OR	MED			BUR	RO
PL	EA		IR	AL	EV	IN		BA	SAL
EX	TRE	ME	ST		AC	TE	DI	NK	IND
		DI	GEAR	TH		GRA	SP		
AN	TEA	TER		RIV	AL		RO	WHO	USE
TES	SE	RA		ED	EN		PO	LE	RS
		NE	GUS			CON	CE	RTI	
PE	LIC	ANS	TA	TE		REM	ONS	TR	ANT
SHA	KE		VE	RMI	LI	ON		EB	ONY
WAR	TY			NI	GHT	IES		LE	MS

Twisted Crossword Answers

Quadrants

Round The Bend

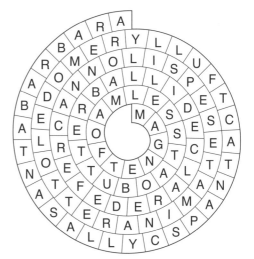

Marching Bands

Around & About

Tops & Bottoms

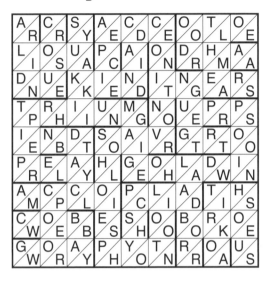

Weaving

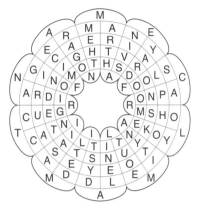

Crushword

Crazy Eights

1 SOULMATE
2 CATERING
3 CAROLINA
4 ARKANSAS
5 MARTIANS
6 PATRICIA
7 INSOMNIA
8 BELIEVES
9 THIEVERY
10 LOCALITY
11 PACKAGES
12 MARRIAGE
13 PARROTED
14 BREEDING
15 LINGERIE
16 FARTHING
17 TORTILLA
18 PLANNERS
19 MAPMAKER

20 IMPOTENT
21 ENGINEER
22 EYELINER
23 INFAMOUS
24 MOSQUITO
25 GUINNESS
26 CUPCAKES
27 PATHETIC
28 HEIGH-HOS
29 PARALLEL
30 CAPSULES
31 SQUIRREL
32 DISGUISE
33 RIDICULE
34 TALENTED
35 SOLDERED
36 PRORATES
37 SCORSESE
38 ARRESTED

39 ADOPTEES
40 VARIETAL
41 RELEVANT
42 REASONER
43 SPROCKET
44 SEAHORSE

45 INVESTED
46 PODIATRY
47 ROLE-PLAY
48 PEEPHOLE
49 DISHONOR

Angling

E	D	G	I	F	O	A	F	S	N	S	P	A
H	U	E	S	P	F	L	T	E	O	I	N	S
B	S	G	L	Y	O	U	S	H	G	A	E	K
T	E	I	O	U	L	D	N	E	V	N	O	C
Y	C	E	R	H	A	V	E	M	O	R	A	J
A	T	E	C	H	I	L	D	R	E	N	I	G
H	S	T	H	A	N	Y	O	U	H	A	S	N
T	A	S	V	E	C	A	R	W	I	T	N	E
P	U	Y	I	N	D	O	W	S	L	N	F	D
P	O	S	E	D	E	S	P	E	A	I	E	A
N	T	T	O	S	Y	Y	Y	M	N	R	R	D

"You should never have more children than you have car windows."

Marching Bands

N	I	C	H	E	V	O	C	A	L	I	S	T
O	S	C	A	R	A	B	S	C	I	S	S	A
B	O	G	L	A	C	E	R	A	T	I	O	N
O	P	T	F	O	R	R	E	S	T	O	R	E
H	I	N	T	I	N	G	E	N	A	C	T	S
E	L	I	S	S	A	M	A	U	R	I	A	T
E	L	P	A	S	O	■	R	E	N	N	I	E
V	I	G	N	E	T	T	E	S	G	A	L	A
Y	O	U	A	N	D	I	C	A	R	T	E	R
A	D	D	R	E	S	S	E	D	A	I	D	E
J	E	N	N	I	F	E	R	O	N	O	F	F
E	P	I	P	H	A	N	Y	S	M	I	L	E
C	A	P	E	K	O	V	E	R	S	E	E	R

Quadrants

S	O	L	E	M	N	T	H	O	R	P	E
H	U	E	V	O	S	M	O	H	A	I	R
A	T	M	O	S	T	A	W	A	K	E	N
B	L	A	M	A	U	L	E	D	I	T	E
B	E	N	O	I	T	A	L	A	N	I	S
Y	T	S	S	C	H	U	L	Z	G	N	T
P	T	O	Q	U	A	R	T	Z	G	Q	A
R	E	T	U	R	N	I	O	L	A	U	S
I	C	O	E	S	T	A	T	E	R	A	S
S	H	O	G	U	N	T	H	I	C	K	E
M	I	L	D	L	Y	M	E	T	I	E	R
S	E	E	S	A	W	D	E	P	A	R	T

Twisted Crossword Answers

Helter-Skelter

W	W	W	O	L	L	E	Y
O	E	O	G	O	D	A	E
T	L	M	R	E	G	N	W
W	C	G	A	R	N	A	E
O	O	R	A	Y	A	R	D
K	M	A	R	C	O	N	I
E	E	P	M	S	A	I	L
S	R	E	W	S	N	A	K

Crushword

ST	REP		DU	AL			ME	GAT	ON
AR	ENT		STO	LE		DA	TE	LIN	ES
DUST	IN	HO	FF	MAN		VID	OR		
	GLY	PH		DE	MIL	LE		TON	GUES
		EA	MON		LETT	ER	PRS	ES	SES
LOM	BAR	DS	TRE	ET		OTH	ER		
POC	KS		AL	AS	KAN		INS	IN	
		AP	EX		GA	IN	ING	TI	ME
MA	LA	PRO	POS		RO	VERS		FA	LLOW
CON	SER	VED			ORAT	IONS		DA	LY

Angling

1-24	MAMA	32-66	SODAS
2-7	PARTING	35-73	HABITAT
3-50	VEHICLE	36-66	MENDS
4-8	HORAS	37-64	CAPRICE
5-33	RADIO	38-76	HUNDRED
6-19	JOHNNY	39-61	ISLE
8-36	MUNCH	42-51	YODA
9-35	QUOTH	45-81	BAGPIPE
10-15	ECHO	46-80	INVEIGH
11-28	FUNT	48-79	PSYCHO
12-21	DELL	50-60	VERRE
12-31	LOLLED	51-82	SHEEDY
13-14	MAGIC	52-67	PRICKING
14-24	MANIC	54-57	FRYER
16-59	ANTHEMS	54-58	STUNNER
17-53	CHAPIN	54-69	SKINNER
18-27	UNION	55-59	SIGNEES
20-47	IMPEL	56-78	REBUS
21-23	FOIL	58-62	STUD
21-34	PARASOL	59-63	SEEN
22-59	SECOND	61-77	VICI
23-54	FOYER	62-66	DUKAKIS
24-43	MANITOU	63-73	TOKEN
25-40	BIG	65-72	KIX
26-49	OBIT	65-84	CHISOX
29-41	COOPER	68-71	HONE
30-32	HOYAS	70-83	GOD
31-44	LASS	74-75	ADO

A	E	G	E	I	S	R	J	P	H	Q	E	F
D	M	L	N	O	C	A	A	O	A	C	U	Y
I	C	A	L	I	Y	R	R	D	H	N	N	O
F	M	I	G	O	T	A	N	A	I	N	T	U
R	O	P	H	I	L	O	S	O	P	H	M	C
D	E	Y	B	E	C	A	U	S	E	I	A	E
L	E	P	R	O	V	E	D	M	Y	P	N	B
R	S	R	O	F	E	S	S	O	R	D	I	V
Y	E	I	D	N	T	E	X	I	S	T	E	P
B	C	N	G	U	E	S	C	I	A	I	G	E
I	U	H	N	N	K	K	K	T	G	A	H	O
H	V	S	O	I	I	A	O	H	B	S	D	C

"I got an 'A' in philosophy because I proved my professor didn't exist."

Trivia-Cross

B	A			R	I	T	A	
I	R	M	A			H	I	
R		A	P	S	E			
D	O	M	I	N	O	S		
	X	E	N	A			T	
F	E			E	P	E	E	
A	N	T	S			W	M	

QUOTE

"I am a brain, Watson. The rest of me is a mere appendix."

Quadrants

P	O	R	T	I	A	L	A	S	S	O	S
A	K	I	M	B	O	E	G	M	O	N	T
P	A	P	I	E	R	A	R	G	U	E	R
A	Y	E	E	R	A	S	E	D	G	W	A
Y	E	S	S	I	R	H	E	E	H	A	W
A	D	T	T	A	O	I	S	T	T	Y	S
S	M	P	A	Q	U	I	N	O	A	N	U
T	A	R	T	A	N	T	E	U	T	O	N
U	L	U	E	N	D	E	A	R	T	R	E
P	I	N	A	T	A	F	R	A	U	D	S
I	C	E	M	A	N	C	L	I	N	I	C
D	E	S	I	S	T	Z	Y	D	E	C	O

Catching Some Z's

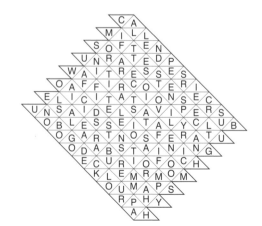

Twisted Crossword Answers

Helter-Skelter

H	R	E	L	L	E	Y	D
A	E	E	Y	E	A	R	I
R	U	L	T	R	A	C	N
D	A	O	T	L	M	R	T
S	W	A	L	T	U	O	Y
H	T	A	B	B	A	S	P
I	M	A	U	I	R	E	E
P	E	A	N	U	T	S	S

Target Practice

Weaving

Crazy Eights

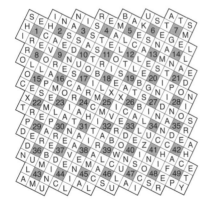

1 CHESHIRE
2 CHINA SEA
3 ASSASSIN
4 STEAMERS
5 CLAMBAKE
6 NETSUKES
7 GEM STATE
8 ROLL OVER
9 ENDEAVOR
10 ASTOUNDS
11 TRIOLETS
12 TOLL CALL

13 SALESMAN
14 MAGELLAN
15 COLLAPSE
16 COMPARES
17 CARIBOUS
18 EX LIBRIS
19 SEAT BELT
20 BEE STING
21 ANTIPODE
22 EXTREMES
23 MEMORIAL
24 ARMCHAIR
25 MCMLXXIV
26 TAXICABS
27 BINDINGS
28 ONION DIP
29 PREPARED
30 PARENTAL
31 TAHITIAN

32 VERBATIM
33 RECALLED
34 CULLINAN
35 ANDERSON
36 NUMBERED
37 BEREAVED
38 AVE MARIA
39 CLARA BOW
40 DOWNSIZE
41 ZUCCHINI
42 CHA-CHAED
43 ALUMINUM
44 INCLINED
45 MACLAINE
46 CALCULUS
47 UNSOCIAL
48 CONIFERS
49 TYPEFACE

Twisted Crossword Answers

Quadrants

N	I	M	I	T	Z	C	H	I	L	L	S
A	R	A	G	O	N	K	A	R	E	E	M
V	O	L	U	M	E	F	R	I	N	G	E
A	N	I	R	A	T	T	L	E	G	R	A
J	O	B	E	T	H	W	A	I	T	E	R
O	N	U	G	O	R	I	N	G	H	E	S
O	G	S	G	R	I	N	C	H	R	J	S
D	A	N	I	E	L	G	O	T	H	A	M
D	L	I	E	L	L	E	R	Y	Y	L	A
J	O	P	L	I	N	P	O	T	T	E	R
O	R	E	L	S	E	A	N	T	H	E	M
B	E	R	T	H	A	W	A	R	M	L	Y

Helter-Skelter

K	N	A	Y	N	A	B	E
E	O	O	G	N	A	M	E
N	H	H	N	O	G	U	Y	I
S	W	A	L	L	E	T	N
T	E	I	O	Y	U	E	E
A	R	V	I	R	Y	N	H
R	E	E	B	T	O	O	R
R	E	I	K	S	I	R	U

Cubism

Angling

1-5 JAMES
2-29 QUOTA
3-17 MENTORS
3-20 MAJA
4-10 CUED
4-34 CREEPY
5-33 THAMES
6-10 PROBED
7-14 CALF
8-24 TACO
9-23 TORSOS
11-31 RAISIN
12-18 FOCI
13-44 UNVEIL
15-55 GENERATE
16-18 FIERY
16-28 HENRY
19-45 HERDS

21-40 FINE
22-24 TIBET
25-49 VENUS
26-50 WALDO
26-60 GERALDO
27-61 DRYNESS
30-64 PASTURE
32-63 RENEGE
34-35 FOY
36-58 PATIO
37-59 VALUE
38-56 CARSON
39-61 SONNY
40-42 FIR
41-43 OFF
43-65 FISHY
44-67 ULNAS
46-57 HAGEN

J	Q	M	C	S	P	A	F	C	O	S
D	A	U	E	R	R	B	I	L	O	C
J	E	M	O	N	E	Y	I	S	A	F
S	A	B	E	T	T	E	R	T	I	V
O	D	H	A	N	P	O	V	E	E	N
R	D	R	T	Y	I	F	O	N	R	E
C	E	L	Y	F	O	R	F	I	U	U
H	A	N	A	N	C	I	A	L	T	S
W	N	R	E	A	S	O	N	S	A	A
O	E	S	S	G	N	H	A	A	P	V
G	S	M	E	O	A	P	Y	E	S	E

47-48 COAST
48-66 TAPE
51-52 SIN

53-62 SARCASM
54-68 APE
65-67 SAY

*"Money is better than poverty,
if only for financial reasons."*

Siamese Twins

H	I	L	L	A	R	Y	■	F	I	L	E	D
A	L	L	U	V	I	A	■	A	N	A	X	E
S	L	A	V	I	S	H	■	L	A	M	P	S
T	I	M	■	S	K	O	A	L	■	B	O	S
O	N	A	N	■	E	O	N	■	C	A	S	E
■	■	■	O	D	D	■	Y	O	N	D	E	R
S	T	O	W	E	■	■	B	O	A	S	T	■
M	A	N	A	N	A	■	Z	I	T	■	■	■
O	K	A	Y	■	H	O	E	■	E	M	P	S
T	E	D	■	P	A	P	A	L	■	O	R	K
H	O	A	G	Y	■	A	L	O	H	A	O	E
E	N	R	O	L	■	L	O	R	E	T	T	A
R	E	E	V	E	■	S	T	E	P	S	O	N

C	H	E	L	S	E	A	■	Y	U	R	T	S
R	A	D	I	A	N	T	■	A	Z	U	R	E
A	N	G	U	I	S	H	■	P	I	S	A	N
F	D	A	■	L	O	O	M	S	■	H	I	D
T	Y	R	O	■	U	S	A	■	I	D	L	E
■	■	■	A	W	L	■	X	A	V	I	E	R
M	A	D	R	E	■	■	P	I	E	R	S	■
A	M	O	E	B	A	■	Z	E	N	■	■	■
L	E	W	D	■	I	N	A	■	S	A	P	S
T	R	A	■	F	L	I	N	G	■	R	A	C
E	I	G	E	R	■	N	I	A	G	A	R	A
S	C	E	N	E	■	J	E	Z	E	B	E	L
E	A	R	E	D	■	A	R	A	L	S	E	A

Target Practice

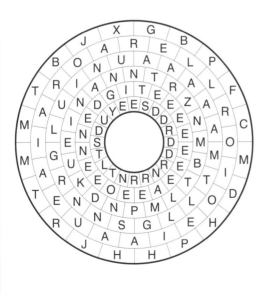

Weaving

Maze

S	T	A	I	D	R	I	P	P	E	R
R	A	T	N	O	N	A	G	O	N	S
T	O	B	O	G	G	A	N	Z	O	O
P	R	E	V	A	I	L	M	A	I	N
R	I	C	E	I	N	J	E	C	T	S
T	A	B	M	A	L	A	R	K	E	Y
E	U	R	O	P	E	A	N	M	A	R
G	N	O	M	O	N	S	T	O	N	I
E	N	O	C	H	S	T	E	F	F	I
R	A	R	E	P	U	R	L	O	I	N
B	I	L	B	O	G	A	L	O	S	H

Cubism

Target Practice

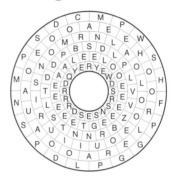

Honeycomb

9 HOOPLA
10 INSULT
11 WIMPLE
12 BOOING
13 ZEBRAS
14 SCHOOL
15 CHOSEN
16 PRIEST
17 UPTAKE
18 MOZART
19 PROZAC
20 SPACEY
21 MASHED
22 BREAST
23 KISMET

24 TARZAN
25 BAZAAR
26 SCREAM
27 MELODY
28 MOYERS
29 UNEASY
30 AURORA
31 BRONZE
32 SLEAZE
33 CHILLY
34 DRYDEN
35 POODLE
36 POLLEN
37 ISLAND

1 TWENTY
2 EUROPE
3 TRIXIE
4 SPRING

5 TIPTOE
6 RENOWN
7 URGENT
8 LORENZ

Round The Bend

```
E A S E D B E T A S
J E A N E A L E R T
E R M T A N G D D Y
C I N O N J O C O L
T E N S E O H A R E
S W A R M E N T R E
T Y R A C Y N I O N
E L G U C I B P U D
P I A N O N U R S E
S E E D Y G R E E D
```

Maze

```
C H A S E R D O U S E
F M R A D I O N E S S
A N G E L A M I N C E
S A M P L E S T E P S
H A P P E N S E R U M
E L P A S O S L I D E
T R E B L E S L A V A
I D E A L L Y O L I N
S O B C O R O L L A S
D Y E S U B M E R G E
A L L A R T I N E S S
```

Crazy Eights

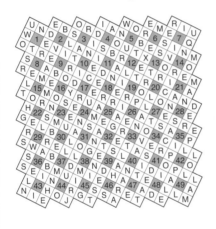

1 UNDERTOW	18 REINDEER	35 REPLICAS
2 BEDEVILS	19 PORTLIER	36 SWABBIES
3 ORDINALS	20 TRICOLOR	37 DUMBBELL
4 OBSIDIAN	21 AMERICAN	38 GOLD MINE
5 BROWNOUT	22 LEGHORNS	39 STENDHAL
6 BESSEMER	23 NO-SEE-UMS	40 ATLANTIS
7 INQUIRES	24 MAUREENS	41 PRESIDIO
8 STREAMER	25 MARRIAGE	42 LOLLIPOP
9 ABORTIVE	26 AIRPLANE!	43 HEINLEIN
10 IN A TRICE	27 STALLONE	44 JOHN MUIR
11 BRANDEIS	28 ANDERSEN	45 GRIMIEST
12 TEXTURAL	29 WARBLERS	46 HARASSED
13 VORTEXES	30 UMBRELLA	47 ANTEATER
14 OMNIVORE	31 ANGOLANS	48 ADELAIDE
15 MEL TORMÉ	32 SERGEANT	49 PALL MALL
16 SOMEBODY	33 RENOVATE	
17 EURYDICE	34 OVERCAST	

Siamese Triplets

Grid 1:
```
E L A I N E   P R E P
B O R N E O   L A M E
B R I N G S   A V I S
S I D E A   S T I L E
        S T E P O N I T
C R O   I R A   G O A
A A R D V A R K
S C A R E   K N O W S
S I N E   F L A V I A
I N G A   B E V E L S
S E E M   I R E N E S
```

Grid 2:
```
G E O R G E   M A M A
A L L I E S   U Z I S
F L I N T S   R O S S
F A N G S   S P R E E
    S M O T H E R S
A S S   A T A   S Y S
M C M U R T R Y
T R E N T   G E T U P
R I L L   C A M I S E
A B L E   A Z A L E A
C E S T   M E Y E R S
```

Grid 3:
```
K R A M E R   M I S C
N E B U L A   A N N A
O M E L E T   C L A R
T O T E M   S H A P E
      S E Q U O I A S
O K D   N U B   D T S
P H A N T O M S
P Y R O S   E P S O M
O B I T   T R O U P E
S E N T   A G R E E D
E R G O   M E T T L E
```

Maze

Crossing Paths

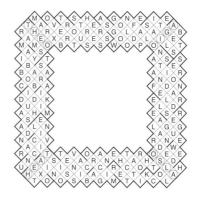

Intersections

Honeycomb

9 BARBIE	**24** ALPACA
10 WHEELS	**25** NAUSEA
11 RHYTHM	**26** JUMP-UP
12 JOHNNY	**27** SHOULD
13 AUDREY	**28** PSYCHO
14 BEDPAN	**29** PUNISH
15 INDEED	**30** PELHAM
16 EXCUSE	**31** PSALMS
17 CHEERY	**32** PEOPLE
18 MORNAY	**33** SPHERE
19 JAR JAR	**34** SAILOR
20 PURPLE	**35** SMILED
21 DEADLY	**36** BEHEAD
22 CANCEL	**37** PHASER
23 HAUNTS	

1 CARLIN	**5** LAWYER
2 GIMLET	**6** MONTEL
3 CASTLE	**7** O'NEILL
4 ADVISE	**8** RETIRE

Intersections

Around & About

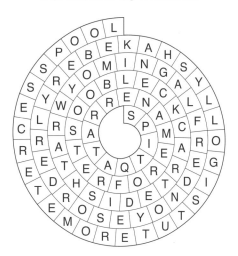

Siamese Quadruplets

Honeycomb

1 MOUSSE	14 ORNATE	27 SWATCH
2 DEUCES	15 REVOLT	28 HIP-HOP
3 THREES	16 CAVERN	29 WINTER
4 MARVEL	17 APRONS	30 CARBON
5 COSMIC	18 PRIZED	31 RAISIN
6 COSELL	19 ZZZZZZ	32 SQUAWK
7 LOADED	20 ZENITH	33 CASPER
8 SOLVED	21 SOCIAL	34 MEXICO
9 CELERY	22 GOSPEL	35 JOANNE
10 BROOCH	23 SCENIC	36 UNIQUE
11 ACCORD	24 CARROT	37 VACUUM
12 ZEALOT	25 TABRIZ	
13 ERSATZ	26 ITZHAK	

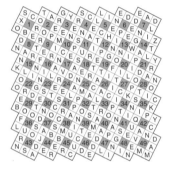

Crazy Eights

1 BOX SCORE	15 FRANKLIN	29 REBOOTED
2 OPERATOR	16 INFERNAL	30 CONTESTS
3 GREENERY	17 ADVANCES	31 SCRAPPLE
4 CLEANERS	18 TREASURE	32 LAMPPOST
5 CHENILLE	19 PETTIFOG	33 TROPICAL
6 DEEPENED	20 FILIPINO	34 NITPICKS
7 DEADLINE	21 LAPIDARY	35 STICKPIN
8 BERTRAND	22 DROOLING	36 SOUL FOOD
9 IMPORTER	23 STERLING	37 ABSCONDS
10 SPECIMEN	24 VREELAND	38 CRANIUMS
11 PURITANS	25 MACARENA	39 MASONITE
12 PITCHING	26 TITICACA	40 PANORAMA
13 WINNIPEG	27 POLITICK	41 ANTIQUES
14 WALTZING	28 ADOPTION	42 PIQUANCY

43 ADJOURNS	47 PADDLING
44 JABBERED	48 EVENINGS
45 CUCUMBER	49 VAN DAMME
46 DEDUCTED	

Catching Some Z's

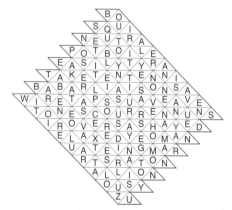

Cubism

Twisted Crossword Answers

1. It is unwise to complain loudly about how the ball bounces, especially if you are the one who dropped it.

2. Do you know that William Taft was the first president to make regular use of an automobile while he was chief executive?

3. The worst inhumanity we can show our fellow creatures is to be completely indifferent to their needs.

4. People who try to make an impression often do; it is often not the kind of impression they try to make.

5. Slick deadbeat, wanting to pay his bill with a check, was told by waiter that management rules require paying check with a bill.

6. The wise fellow could find great consolation in nearly anything; smaller salary means smaller taxes.

7. About the only thing that goes as far today as it did ten years ago is the dime that rolls under the bed.

8. When you stretch towards the stars, you may not reach one, but you will not end up with a handful of mud, either.

9. A real leader is one who can guess which way the crowd will be going and then get out in front.

10. You could get the short end of the bargain if you should decide to trade opportunity for security.

11. There are very few errors made by a mother-in-law who is an ever-willing babysitter.

12. What a pity that people who have closed minds usually don't have mouths to match.

13. With modern jet planes, it is entirely possible to enjoy dinner in America and have heartburn over Europe.

14. Holding a grudge is similar to having a burr in your shoe, which causes every step to be painful without shortening the trip.

15. When a young boy takes a bath of his own accord, it is a sure thing he is going on his first date.

16. Even if money grew on trees, some people would have to write home between harvests for some dough.

17. Modern man is fellow who drives mortgaged car over bond-financed highway on credit card gasoline.

18. Speaker's fervent prayer: "Fill my mouth with proper stuff, and nudge me when I have said enough."

19. Four "imps" very often cause accidents: improvising, impatience, impunity, and impulsiveness.

20. Capable cop chases, catches callous criminal; first cumbersome confession closes case.

21. Remedy for frustration caused by high bill from doctor: Think of what an undertaker would charge.

22. Beauteous blonde, bewitched by big, bright bankroll, banishes best, but broke, beau; becomes banker's bride.

23. A young lady returned a dictionary to the library with the comment, "It's too disconnected to be interesting."

24. They will have reached adolescence when a boy notices that a girl notices that he is noticing her.

25. Wondering child gravely asked mother if condensed milk comes from very short cows.

26. Some plan must be devised immediately to prevent organized crime from disorganizing society.

27. Smart-aleck teenager ribbed his parents by asking if they used to ride to school on the bumpy backs of dinosaurs.

28. When dressing a fidgety baby, merely get hold of a button, then wait until the buttonhole comes around.

29. What were previously called television station breaks are now more often like compound fractures.

30. For each hour the average person drives his car, or is tied up in traffic, he leaves it parked for eleven hours.

31. It seems each person you meet can prescribe a cure for the common cold—but not your doctor.

32. Our next-door neighbor says his domestic explosion appears to have been touched off by an old flame.

33. Try not to find very much wrong with your children. Perhaps they have patterned themselves after you.

34. One town, unable to afford radar but wishing to cut down on speeders, hung up this road sign: "Speed Trap Ahead."

35. The fellow who first said "a penny for your thoughts" had evidently never paid for psychoanalysis.

36. Humor is something like a needle and thread, for, if deftly used, it can patch up practically anything.

37. Despite the calendar, the very shortest night of the year is Christmas Eve—from sundown to son-up.

38. Anger is a potent acid that does more harm to that in which it is stored than it can to that on which it is poured.

39. Remember, an elevator operator might have his ups and downs, but he is one of the few people who knows where he is going.

40. The average person would much prefer to be complimented for a youthful appearance than praised for wisdom attributed to age.

41. Pedestrian: fellow who was so sure there were still a couple of gallons of gas in the car.

42. The wonder of a single snowflake far outweighs the wisdom of a whole universe of meteorologists.

43. An optimist is a person who is sure he has heard all of the humorous definitions of an optimist.

44. You are only human if your mind wanders, but the trouble comes when you start to follow it.

45. Many men, like thermometers, are influenced by conditions surrounding them; the others, like thermostats, do something about it.

46. Cryptologist constructed some very difficult cryptograms and stumped nearly all solvers.

47. The good old days—when a teenager went into the garage and came out pushing the lawn mower.

48. To have all that you want may be riches; however, to be completely content with your lot is wealth.

49. Diplomat—one who has the ability to take something, and yet make the other person believe he is giving it away.

50. Despite what people say, very few folks have more money than they know what to do with.

51. Making speeches is usually like spelling Mississippi; you must know when to stop.

52. Why do many children seem to eat their spinach in slow motion—inch by inch?

53. You have arrived socially when you can successfully hold a cocktail and plate of canapés and carry on a conversation with only two hands.

54. Maybe they call it modern art because it may not be around long enough to be called anything else.

55. Mabel, upon receiving word via cable that she won coat of sable with famous Paris label, started dancing atop table.

56. Lumberjack, named Jackie Black, got pretty lucky and won himself stack of jack while playing blackjack.

57. Remember, the dictionary is the only place where you'll find success comes before work.

58. Try to learn from the mistakes of others. You will not live long enough to make them all yourself.

59. Think how much a mother kangaroo must dislike a rainy day when the kids cannot play outside.

60. The reason the dog is man's best pal is probably because he never gives advice, borrows money, or has in-laws.

61. Money may not be everything—however, it has a pretty good lead over whatever is in second place.

62. Schedule all your worrying for a specific half-hour around the middle of the day. Then take a nap during this period.

63. Specialist: doctor whose patients are well enough trained to call on him only during daylight hours.

64. Science has yet to discover why the ones who want to get off on the second floor are always in the rear of the elevator.

65. Spring is the season when the birds you fed all winter repay you by eating your newly planted grass seed.

66. Whenever a fellow makes a mistake, at least it proves he stopped talking and tried to do something.

67. A modern pioneer is a mother of four youngsters who survives a rainy week-end when the television is not working.

68. It is not enough merely to possess a fine aim in life; it is also necessary for you to pull the trigger.

69. The safest method to use to double your money is to fold it once and put it back in your pocket.

70. If you can make one person happy every day, in forty years you have contributed to the happiness of almost fifteen thousand people.

71. Some people never appear to have an opinion—they use one that happens to be in style at the time.

72. Note to Boy Scouts—the fastest way known to make a fire with two sticks is to make sure one of them is a match.

73. If your problems seem endless, remember a diamond is but a piece of coal that has been hard-pressed for many years.

74. All any firm asks of a new employee is that he be fifty percent of what he claimed to be the day he applied for the position.

75. The principal difference between psychoneurosis and plain nervousness is about one hundred and fifty dollars.

76. Withholding tax is an ingenious system for preventing the taxpayer from getting warmly attached to his money.

77. It is practically impossible to be a top dog, especially if you spend all of your spare time growling.

78. Most speakers state that it takes up to three weeks to prepare a proper impromptu speech.

79. The United States Constitution was not drawn up until eleven years after the signing of the Declaration of Independence.

80. Passport photographs usually make folks look as if they were emerging dolefully from a lost weekend.

81. If you should ever have the feeling that you are being sadly neglected, remember Whistler's father.

82. If you would like to see a model home, you should learn what time she is through work.

83. A small boy glumly objected to going to school since he could not read, could not write, and was not allowed to talk.

84. The first day of spring and the first real spring day are often as much as a month apart.

85. An onion can make folks cry, but nobody has yet invented a vegetable that can cause them to laugh.

86. An old Spanish saying: "It is very nice to do nothing all day—then have the night to rest up."

87. One good way to test your memory is to try to remember the things that worried you yesterday.

88. "The chief function of the body is to carry the brain around," said Thomas A. Edison.

89. Those who eavesdrop hear nothing good about themselves—but sure learn who their pals are.

90. Perhaps it is better to appreciate what one cannot own than to own what one cannot appreciate.

91. Overconfidence is that certain feeling that folks have when they don't know what they are getting into.

92. All an argument amounts to is two or more people attempting hard to get in the last word first.

93. "No man is good enough to govern another man without that other man's consent," said Lincoln.

94. By the time you have your child suited, scarved, and booted, snapped, mittened, and belted, the snow has melted.

95. You know youngsters are really growing up when they start asking questions that have logical answers.

96. A compromise is often an agreement between two people, each of whom ends up with something he does not actually want.

97. Even if you have all the answers, you may not be able to sift the right ones from the wrong ones.

98. Many a romance that started beside a waterfall at a summer resort has ended beside a leaky faucet in the kitchen sink.

99. The prime essentials for happiness in life are something to do, something to love, and something to hope for.

100. A cynic is a person who knows the price of everything, yet knows the actual value of nothing.

101. There is something much nicer than receiving praise—the feeling of having earned it.

102. Many men of a timid nature prefer the comparative calm of despotism to the boisterous ocean of liberty.

103. To maintain a well-balanced perspective, each man who owns a dog that worships him should also have a cat to ignore him.

104. Perfect timing is attained when one can turn off the hot and cold water faucets in the shower simultaneously.

105. Modern children who constantly play hooky could well be called "unlicensed curriculum abstainers."

106. There must be a better place for four people to be miserable together than at the bridge table.

107. No advice is entirely without value, because even a watch that does not run is correct twice daily.

108. The best things in life are free, so they say, but is it not a pity that the next-best things are so very expensive?

109. Conduct yourself so that you could calmly sell the family parrot to your town's worst gossip.

110. If you can arise cheerfully on a very cold morning, it is a matter of mind over mattress.

111. Optimism: a cheerful frame of mind such as allows a teakettle to sing though in hot water up to its nose.

112. If you are able to make people think they need an item they have never even heard of before, you are truly a salesman.

113. A gentleman is one who won't stare at a girl in a bathing suit unless he is wearing sunglasses.

114. There is only one really pretty child in the hospital nursery, and each mother possesses it.

115. August is the month when the mate to that argyle sock you received in winter for Christmas is finally finished.

116. May all your woes in the New Year be of as brief duration as most of your New Year's resolutions.

117. A pessimist is one man who feels bad when he feels good for fear he'll feel worse when he feels better.

118. That condition which in the subway is called congestion is termed "intimacy" in our best nightclubs.

119. Formal ceremony is the invention of very wise men to make dolts keep their distance.

120. The most important thing about a problem is not its solution but the strength gained in finding the solution.

121. By the time you finally reach greener pastures, you can often no longer climb the fence.

122. Remember when you got any repairs done by the landlord by simply threatening to move out?

123. A husband I know is terribly careless about his appearance; he hasn't shown up in years.

124. Whoever said, "A work you've done well never needs doing over," evidently never pulled weeds in the garden.

125. It is not possible for people whose fists are tightly clenched to offer others a friendly handclasp.

126. The peaceful dew is the silent tears of the night that fall as it weeps softly for joy at seeing all the wonderful creations of the day.

127. According to recent fashion trends you may well expect to find the suitless swimming strap next year.

128. Folks who claim to say what they think are often doing more saying than thinking.

129. Book reviewer most likely is one fellow who makes his living by the sweat of his browse.

130. Happiness is that peculiar elated sensation you get when you are much too busy to be bothered worrying.